wanderlust

wanderlust

WRITERS ON TRAVEL AND SEX

edited by Daniel O'Connor

thunder's mouth press • new york

WANDERLUST: WRITERS ON TRAVEL AND SEX

Compilation © 2003 by Daniel O'Connor

Published by
Thunder's Mouth Press
An Imprint of Avalon Publishing Group Incorporated
161 William Street, 16th Floor
New York, NY 10038

Library of Congress Cataloging-In-Publication Data is available.

ISBN 1-56025-431-9

9 8 7 6 5 4 3 2 1

Designed by Pauline Neuwirth, Neuwirth & Associates
Printed in the United States of America
Distributed by Publishers Group West

contents

wanderlust

passable

A. J. Liebling

FROM *BETWEEN MEALS*

F OLLOWING THE PUBLICATION of some of the foregoing papers I had an avalanche of letters—perhaps a half dozen—asking scornfully whether, in my student days in Paris, I did nothing but eat. I tried conscientiously to think of what I had between meals in the years 1926–7, when I was twenty-two–three, and it seems to have been quite a lot. For one thing, in those days young men liked women. We did not fear emasculation. We had never heard of it. This would today be considered a subliterary approach, but there it was. Havelock Ellis was the sage who made authority in the dormitories. Freud had not yet seeped down to the undergraduate level. Molly Bloom was the pin-up girl of the *nouvelle vague*, and we all burned to beat out Blazes Boylan.

Women offered so much fun from the beginning that further possibilities appeared worth investigating. For this we considered acquaintance, or even marriage, with an undergraduate of the opposite sex insufficient. We assumed, perhaps overoptimistically, that the possibilities of the subject were limitless. They may not be, but no finite man will ever be able to brag that he has exhausted them.

For the beginning student of all essential subjects, the Latin Quarter was an ideal school. The Restaurant des Beaux-Art, as I have indicated, was a great place to learn to eat because the items on the menu were good but simple. The cafés on the Boulevard Saint-Michel offered self-instruction of another kind, but similarly within the grasp of the beginner. You could find any feature of a beauty queen in our cafés, but they were all on different girls. A girl who was beautiful all over would pick a better neighborhood. So, just as at the restaurant, you had to choose a modest but satisfying agenda. In doing that you learned your own tastes.

It was trickier than that because a woman, unlike a *navarin de mouton*, has a mind. A man may say, when he begins to recognize his tastes, "Legs, on a woman, are more important to me than eyes." But he has to think again when he must choose between a witty woman with good eyes and a dull one with trim legs. Give the witty woman a bad temper and the dull one constant good humor and you add to the difficulty of the choice. To multiply the complexity the woman, unlike the *navarin*, reacts to you. She may be what you want, but you may not be what she wants. In such a case she will turn out to be not what you wanted at all.

The unimaginative monogamist has none of these perplexities, but I doubt that he has fun either. I attribute the gloom of many young novelists to an adolescent mistake made at a church. Afterward belated curiosity clashes with entrenched ignorance and produces that *timor mundi* which is the *mal de siècle*. "Ain't It Awful, Mabel?" is their strange device, instead of "Up in Mabel's Room."

The girls would arrive at their customary tables soon after lunch, in late afternoon, and establish themselves with a permanent *consommation*, something inexpensive and not tempting, for they would make it last until somebody treated them to something better. This might be a long time, and they had a skill in husbanding the drink that would have stood them in good stead if they had been airmen downed in the Sahara.

When treated, they exhibited another desert talent, the opportunism of the camel. They drank enough to last them to the next oasis.

They spent the afternoon writing on the house stationery. If the waiter caught them doodling or doing ticktacktoes he would cut off their supply. With the hour of the *apéritif* came animation and hope. After the dinner hour, if they had not been invited to eat, there remained animation. It could always happen that, if they kept up their spirits, some late customer would offer them a sandwich. The girls were like country artisans; they took money for their services, but only when they felt like working. On occasion they would accept payment in kind—a dinner or a pair of stockings—but then, as often as not, they would ask you to lend them their current week's room rent.

I suppose some of them had sweet men, but these must have been *dilettanti* too. No protector worthy of the name would have tolerated such irregularity. He would have said the girls of the Boulevard Saint-Michel were not serious. And he would have starved on a percentage of their earnings, like a literary agent who depended on poets. All the girls were young. It was easy to comprehend that this was a phase without a future; there was no chance to accumulate. Where they went after they disappeared from the Quarter I do not know. They were brisk rather than chic, and they made up without exaggeration. My memory is not tenacious in matters of dress, but I am sure the girls wore short skirts—I remember the legs. One girl helped me select a hat for a woman in America, and this would not have been possible except in a period when all hats were essentially alike. It was the age of the face *sous cloche.*

The *cloche* was an enlarged skull cap, jammed down on the head like an ice-cream scoop on a ball of vanilla. For the rest, their clothes were not elaborate, with the short skirt, a short blouse and short jacket, and underneath a *soutien-gorge* and *pantalon.* Having the *points de repère* once well in mind, one saw at a glance what was what.

Sometimes a girl would enter *en menage* with a student, usually a Romanian or an Asiatic. If it was one of the latter, with an allowance from home, the girl would disappear from her customary café for a while or appear there only with him. If it was a Romanian, she would be on the job more regularly than before. Often a girl would make such an arrangement to gain the status of a kept woman, which would protect her from the jurisdiction of the *police des moeurs.*

Once the cops of this unsavory group picked up a girl without visible means of support they would force her to register. Then they would give her a card that subjected her to a set of rules.

"Once a girl has the card she is bound to infract the rules," the girls said. "We are all so lazy. She misses a couple of visits; she is subject to heavy penalties. Then comes blackmail. The police put her to work for chaps who give them a cut. *Hop,* then, no more chattering with student friends who have no money.

"It's the pavement for her, and turn over the receipts to the mackerel at five o'clock in the morning. The police have opened another account."

I was glad to know how things were. It made me feel like an insider, and it helped me understand cops, who run to form everywhere.

Our girls were not intellectuals. None was a geisha primed with poems, nor were there hetaerae who could have disputed on equal terms with Plato, or even with Max Lerner. But all served as advisers on courses of study. They knew the snaps and the tough ones in all faculties, which professors were susceptible to apple polishing and which the most resolutely *vache.* Above all, they had anticipated a theory that was to be imparted to me later as a great original discovery by T. S. Matthews, an editor of *Time,* who told me that the content of communication was unimportant. What did count, Matthews said, was somebody on one end of a wire shouting, "My God, I'm alive!" and somebody on the other end shouting, "My God, I'm alive too!"

It was a poor prescription for journalism, but a good program for conversation between the sexes. (The girls did not keep us at the end of a wire.)

To one I owe a debt the size of a small Latin American republic's in analysts' fees saved and sorrows unsuffered during the next thirty-odd years. Her name was Angèle. She said: *"Tu n'es pas beau, mais t'es passable."* ("You're not handsome, but you're passable.")

I do not remember the specific occasion on which Angèle gave me the good word, but it came during a critical year. I am lucky that she never said, *"T'es merveilleux."* The last is a line a man should be old enough to evaluate.

My brain reeled under the munificence of her compliment. If she had said I was handsome I wouldn't have believed her. If she had called me loathsome I wouldn't have liked it. *Passable* was what I hoped for. *Passable* is the best thing for a man to be.

A handsome man is so generally said by other men to be a fool that in many cases he must himself begin to believe it. The superstition that handsome men are dull is like the prejudice that gray horses quit. Both arose because their subjects were easy to follow with the eye. The career of the late Elmer Davis, a handsome but intelligent man, was made more difficult by his good looks. Favored with a less prepossessing appearance, he would have won earlier acceptance. There are homely fools too, and quitters of all colors.

Women who are both randy and cautious, and therefore of the most profitable acquaintance, avoid handsome lovers because they are conspicuous. He who is *passable* escapes attention. To be *passable* is like a decent suit. It gets you anywhere. *Passable* and *possible* are allied by free association. A young man wants desperately to be considered at least a possibility. But it is the only game in which there is no public form, and he can't present a testimonial from his last employer. He is like a new player in a baseball league where there are no published batting averages. To be *passable* gets him in the ball park without arousing inflated expectations. The ugly man is the object of a special cult among women, but it is relatively small. He runs well only in limited areas, like a Mormon candidate in Utah.

A heartening fact, if you are *passable*, is that there are more *passable* women than any other kind, and that a *passable* man establishes a better rapport with them. Very pretty girls are preferable, of course, but there are never enough to go around. Angèle was *passable* plus—a woman who looks pretty at her best and *passable* at her worst. Her legs, though well-tapered, were a trifle short and her round head a trifle large for good proportion with her torso, in which there was no room for improvement. It was solid Renoir. Her neck was also a bit short and thick—a good point in a prizefighter but not in a swan. She had a clear skin and a sweet breath, and she was well-joined—the kind of girl you could rough up without fear of damage. Angèle had a snub nose, broad at the base, like a seckel pear tilted on its axis.

It was a period when the snub nose enjoyed high popular esteem. The fashions of the day called for a gamine, and a gamine cannot have a classic profile. A retroussé nose, for example, looked better under a cloche. The cloche made a girl with an aquiline nose look like the familiar portrait of Savonarola in his hood. It gave her the profile of that bigot or a spigot.

I had an early belief that I could get along with any woman whose nose turned up. This proved in later life to have been a mistake based on a brief series of coincidences, but when I knew Angèle it still influenced me. Among snub-nosed idols in the United States we had Mary Pickford, Marion Davies, Mae Murray, and Ann Pennington, to name a few I remember. The last two were dancers, and when they kicked, the tips of their noses and their toes were in a straight line. In France they had Madge Lhoty and a girl named Lulu Hegoboru.

Here memory, furtive and irrelevant, interpolates a vision of La Hegoboru taking a refrain of "Tea for Two" in English, in the Paris production of *No, No, Nanette:* "I will back a sugar cack—" as she jumped right, kicked left.

We have no such artists today. The profession of ingenue exists no longer. There was a girl in *Little Mary Sunshine* who had the gist of it, but she will have no chance to develop. In her next job she may have to play an agoraphobic Lesbian in love with her claustrophobic brother. The tragic siblings will be compelled to tryst in a revolving door. It is the kind of play people like to write now, because it can be done in one set, in this case the door.

Angèle had large eyes with sable pupils on a pale-blue field, and a wide mouth, and a face wide at the cheekbones. Her hair was a black soup-bowl bob, as if she had put a cloche on and let a girl friend cut around it. (Girls in the United States went to barber shops for their haircuts.) The corners of her mouth were almost always turned up because Angèle was of a steady, rough good humor. Angèle was a Belgian; half the girls in Paris were Belgians then, and all of them said their parents had been shot by the Germans in World War I.

I met Angèle at Gypsy's Bar on the Rue Cujas, a late place outside the circle of tranquil cafés in which I usually killed my evenings. Most of the time I tried to live like a Frenchman, or, rather, like my idealized notion, formed at home, of how a Frenchman lived. The notion included moderation: I would drink only wine and its distillates, cognac, Armagnac, and marc. I did not class French beer among alcoholic drinks. In the United States I had been accustomed to drink needle beer, reinforced with alcohol; a six-ounce glass for twenty-five cents hit as hard as a shot of whiskey for half a dollar.

I did not get drunk as long as I followed what I imagined was the French custom. I thought a sedentary binge effeminate. Now and then, though, I would suffer from a recurrent American urge to stand up and tie the one on. It was like the *trouvère*'s longing to hear the birds of his own province:

> *The little birds of my country,*
> *They sing to me in Brittany;*
> *The shrill-voiced seagulls' cries among*

Mine ears have heard their evensong,
And sweet, it was of thee.

When this yearning struck during the solvent week of my month—the first after receiving my allowance—I would go to Gypsy's and drink Scotch. The bar was in the Quarter but not used by students. It was too dear. There were even gigolos there—what student would tip a gigolo? I shall not try at this distance in time to guess the nature of Gypsy's sustaining clientele. There may have been a *spécialité de maison*, but I never learned what. I would stand at the bar and think my own thoughts, clear and increasingly grandiose as the level dropped in the bottle. People whose youth did not coincide with the twenties never had our reverence for strong drink. Older men knew liquor before it became the symbol of a sacred cause. Kids who began drinking after 1933 take it as a matter of course.

For us it was a self-righteous pleasure, like killing rabbits with clubs to provide an American Legion party for poor white children. Drinking, we proved to ourselves our freedom as individuals and flouted Congress. We conformed to a popular type of dissent—dissent from a minority. It was the only period during which a fellow could be smug and slopped concurrently.

Angèle impinged on my consciousness toward the end of one of these reveries. She said that I needed somebody to see me home. In Tours the previous summer, a girl making a similar offer had steered me into the hands of two incompetent muggers. Angèle was of a more honorable character. She came home with me. In the morning, when we had more opportunity to talk, we found that we were almost neighbors. She had a room in the Hôtel des Facultés, where the Rue Racine and the Rue de l'Ecole de Médecine form a point they insert in the Boulevard Saint-Michel. My room, one of the pleasantest of my life, was in the fifth (by French count) floor, front, of the Hôtel Saint-Pierre, 4 Rue de l'Ecole de Médecine, next door to a Chinese restaurant that had dancing. At night, while I read, the music from the dancing would rise to my window and a part of my brain would supply the words to the tune as I tried to maintain interest in the *Manual of Provençal Documents* of Monsieur Maurice Prou. One that recurred often was *"Oh, les fraises et les framboises, le bon vin qu'nous avons bu,"* from *Trois Jeunes Filles Nues,* one of Mirande's great hits.

It was an atmosphere not conducive to the serious study of medieval history, which was my avowed purpose in the Quarter.

Angèle not only lived by day on the same street, but frequented by night the same cafés I did—the Taverne Soufflet, La Source, the Café d'Harcourt, all strung along the Boulevard Saint-Michel. She made her headquarters in the d'Harcourt, where it was the merest chance that she had not remarked me, she said. She had so many friends, she explained, there was always somebody engaging her attention.

I said that in any case I spent most of my time in the Soufflet, where the boss was a pal of my landlord. But after that I would go to the d'Harcourt whenever I wanted to see her. It had a favorable effect on her standing if I bought her a drink there, and none on mine if I took her to the Soufflet. If she was not at her post, her waiter would take her messages. He would also tell her to dress warmly in winter and not get her feet wet, to take sufficient nourishment to keep up her strength, and not to be beguiled by clients who had to his experienced eye the aspect of musclemen recruiting for a brothel. It was a relationship already familiar to me from New York, where a waiter was the nearest thing to a mother lots of girls had.

When we had established the similarity of our *frequentations,* Angèle and I marveled that we had to go all the way to Gypsy's, a good fifty meters from the Boulevard, to find each other. We sounded like the traditional New Yorkers who inhabit the same apartment house but meet for the first time in Majorca.

After that I was with her often. I do not know if she had a heart of gold, but she had what I learned long years later to call a therapeutic personality. She made you feel good.

When I took her out in the evening we sometimes strayed

from the Quarter. This was like taking a Manhattan child to the Bronx Zoo. Girls did not shift about in Paris. Clienteles were localized, and so were usages. Montparnasse, although not a long walk away from the Quarter, had all the attributes of a foreign country, including, to a degree, the language.

In Montparnasse the types in the cafés spoke English, American, and German. The girls there had to be at least bilingual. In the Quarter, the languages, besides French, were Vietnamese, Spanish, Czech, Polish and Romanian. But the specimens of all these nationalities spoke French at least passably. The girls consequently could remain resolutely monolingual. The clients were students, or simulated students, at the University. Those were the days of the Little Entente, and France set the cultural and military pattern for the East Europe that is behind the Curtain now. Romanian students came to French universities as freely as if they had done their secondary work in France.

The pre-eminence of the University of Paris was acknowledged as it had been in the Middle Ages. All the tribes rescued from the Austro-Hungarian and Turkish Empires flocked there—Serbs and Croats, Egyptians, Greeks, Armenians, along with Haitians and Koreans, Venezuelans and Argentines. There were also, of course, the North Africans. It would have been a great place to form friendships that would serve in the convulsive years to come. But I thought, if I thought about it at all, that regional convulsions were as out-of-date as *écriture onciale* or horse armor.

Our foreignness made each more confident of his speech than he would have been among the French. From my first appearance in the Quarter, my French was no worse than that of a White Russian or a Czech, and I rose rapidly and successively through the grades of being mistaken for a Hungarian, German Swiss, Alsatian, and Belgian from the Flemish-speaking provinces. Beyond that point I have not since progressed, except in Algeria, where I am mistaken for an old lag of the Foreign Legion who has all kinds of accents so inextricably mixed that it is hopeless to attempt to disassociate them.

Angèle did not like Montparnasse. Neither did I. I had come to France for the same reason that at home I would go out to a beach and swim out just beyond the breakers. There I could loaf. Lying on my back, I would paddle just enough to keep out of the pull, and draw my knees up to my chin and feel good. The Americans in Montparnasse, sitting at their tables in front of Le Sélect and talking at each other, reminded me of monkeys on a raft. They were not in the water at all. One reason I didn't think I liked them was that they had all decided they were writers, or painters, or sculptors, and I didn't know what I was. During my residence in the Hôtel Saint-Pierre I never heard of Gertrude Stein, and although I read *Ulysses*, I would as soon have thought of looking the author up as of calling on the President of the Republic.

Angèle disliked Montparnasse because the people looked at the same time too prosperous and too bizarre. The American women, she said, did not look like Frenchwomen and the Frenchwomen did not look like other Frenchwomen. There were no serious bookstores stacked with doctoral dissertations and tributes to deceased savants. (She herself was not a reader, but she liked academic surroundings.) The types appeared smug and possibly addicted to narcotics. The waiters in the cafés were insolent and Italian, and the *consommations* were overpriced. There were too many fairies and they gave her *drôles* of looks. Let them not fear, she was not in competition. We wound up our tour at the Closerie des Lilas, the border post, at the corner of the Boulevard Montparnasse and our own Boulevard Saint-Michel. The Montparnassiens occupied the post—its tariff was too high for the Quarter. I offered her a whiskey there, but she said it smelled of bedbugs. Now all the French drink Scotch.

Angèle could not get back to the d'Harcourt with sufficient celerity, but once there, it pleased her to have voyaged. She talked as if she were home from a world cruise. But when we went to Montmartre, she was in her glory. She had talked all her life about the *nuits blanches* of Montmartre but had never been there. I took her to Zelli's and we drank several bottles of champagne. She was a solid drinker. All her appetites were robust. In bed she was a kind of utility infielder. She made me buy half a dozen flashlight photographs of us and the bottles, like sportsmen and sailfish, to serve as documentation when she recounted our adventure. Her room, in the prow of a ship-shaped building, was barely wide enough for a single bed. I was there only once, in September of 1927, when she was ill. Half of the mirror was covered with photographs of us at Zelli's.

Aside from her concession that I was passable, which is wrapped around my ego like a bulletproof vest riveted with diamonds, I retain little Angèle said. The one other exception is a report so vivid that I sometimes confuse it with a visual memory.

Angèle told me one morning that she and a number of her colleagues had been playing cards in her room. There were a couple of girls sitting on her bed, a couple more on the bureau, one on the only chair and another on her trunk, when one took off her shoes.

A second girl said, after a moment, "It smells of feet in here!" The shoeless girl said, "Say that once more and you will say *Bon jour* to the concierge."

"You get it?" said Angèle. "The concierge is on the ground floor, we are on the sixth. She will throw her down the stairs. The other comrade who commenced says again, 'It smells of feet.'

"So the other hooks on and drags her out on the landing, and they roll down the stairs together, interscratching with all claws. On the fifth, two law students, interrupted in their studies, pull them apart from each other. The girls couldn't work for three nights afterward.

"One student took up for the girl he had pulled upon, and the other took up for the adversary. Now the students have quarreled, and the girl whose feet smelled has moved in with one of them at the Facultés, while the other student has moved in with the girl whose nose was delicate. It is romance in flower."

Life in the Quarter was a romance that smelled of feet.

I am afraid that I do not succeed in making Angèle's quality come clear. To attempt a full description of a woman on the basis of a few fragmentary memories is like trying to reconstruct a small, endearing animal from a few bits of bone. Even some of the bits are not much help. My arms try to remember her weight—I should say 118, give or take two pounds.

It makes me wince, now, to recall that she used to butt me in the pit of the belly, quite hard, and that we both thought it chummy. My point of view has changed with the tone of my muscles.

Yet she existed. The proof is that my old landlord, Perès, remembers her well. I sometimes meet Perès at a brasserie called l'Alsace à Paris. The proprietor there is M. Perès' old friend, the former owner of the Taverne Soufflet, which failed in 1931 because he had a wife who did not keep her mind on the business. (It is too much to expect the *patron* of a café to keep his mind on the business himself.) Now M. Robert, whose last name I have not learned in thirty-six years of greeting him, has an excellent wife who does not have to keep her mind on the business. It goes as if on rollers.

M. Perès, who retired from the management of the Hôtel Saint-Pierre shortly after World War II, continues to live in the Quarter because, he says, it keeps him young. He has recently been made an Officer of the Legion of Honor. He was a Chevalier, *à titre militaire*, as I have said before, when I first came to live under this roof in 1926, having distinguished himself by courage in World War I. I always suspected him of trying to give the impression, however, that he had won the ribbon for some discovery in Aramaic intransitive verbs or the functioning of the gall bladder. This would have been more chic in his neighborhood. During World War II he served as a captain of infantry, at fifty-one, and distinguished himself again.

"I was a bit put out," he said to me when I congratulated him on his new rosette, "because my promotion was slow in arriving. A man of seventy in the vicinity of the University who has only the ribbon has the air of a demifailure. But the delay was occasioned by the nature of my business. The Chancellery of the Legion is cautious in awarding the higher grades to hotelkeepers, because the hotel may be a *maison de passe*. Once I announced my retirement, the rosette was not long on the way."

M. Perès, in thirty years at the Saint-Pierre, lodged an infinity of students. It makes him think of himself as a housemaster. "One of our fellows is raising the question of confidence in the Chamber today," he may say when you meet him, meaning a Deputy who used to live at the Saint-Pierre as a student. "He has gone farther than I would have predicted." Or, "One of our fellows is now the leading internist in Port-au-Prince—I had a card last week." Or, "One of our chaps who is the professor of medieval history at the University of Jerusalem has, it appears, achieved a remarkable monograph on secular law in the Latin kingdom of Acre. He had your room about ten years after you left. He, at least, worked from one time to another." It is M. Perès' contention that I was a *farceur*, a do-nothing, because we sneaked out so often for a drink at the Soufflet when his wife was in bad humor.

The Anciens de l'Hôtel Saint-Pierre is the sole alumni association of which I would willingly attend a reunion; unhappily it does not exist. If it did, it would include the ladies' auxiliary, *bien entendu*; the girl who lived with the Korean on the floor below me, the mistress of the Dane upstairs, Angèle and subsequent and preceding Angèles of all promotions, and the two little maids from Dax, Lucienne and Antoine, who led the way to the bathroom, which was on the third floor, when the client had ordered a bath. They then allowed themselves to be trapped long enough for an invigorating tussle.

M. Perès remembers Angèle almost as well as if she had made a name for herself as a comparative zoologist in Peru.

She died in the winter of 1927–28, not of a broken heart, but flu. I was no longer in Paris, but in Providence, Rhode Island, where I had returned to a job on the Providence *Journal* and *Evening Bulletin*, and Perès included word of her death, along with other neighborhood news, in a letter that he sent me.

"She had a felicity of expression," he said of her one day thirty years later. "Once she said to me, 'Head of a ruin, how much do you extort for your cubicles?' There wasn't a sou's worth of harm in her. What a pity that she had to die. How well she was built!" he said in final benison.

"She was *passable*," I said.

I could see that M. Perès thought me a trifle callous, but he did not know all that *passable* meant to me.

tammy

Clarence Major

FROM ALL-NIGHT VISITORS

We are the kind of short-
term visitors who
each engage the heart
of each
others lives, one
anothers bodies;
sometimes forever yet
so brief the
sad distance
of
our all-night transit
leaves us
numb: to love

HAVE COME IN from the street. A few moments ago I was frustrated, almost unhappy, but Tammy is on the bed. Her name isn't really important. All I want her for is to fuck her. She is hardly worth anything else. She has a kind of savage ability to fuck well—we screwed a lot last night, and probably didn't sleep until three o'clock. For some reason I suddenly feel very insecure. Her pussy hasn't helped. I had been at it as though it might in some way give me protection.

Everything will be all right, I tell myself. I know everything will be all right, and yet I am not quite sure of what I mean by "everything." I look down at the girl. In a way she is very sad . . .

I found her three weeks ago sitting outside, outside the door, on the stoop. She had no place to go. She got the address of the woman who has the apartment next to mine; she got it from the Diggers' Free Store. The message she had was: "Can you put this girl up until she gets on her feet?" Apparently, the woman next to me, who is really not bad-looking, kind of fat, a redhead, certainly no more than thirty but kind of mean-looking, had left word at the Diggers that she would be willing to let people sleep on her floor. This kind of thing is being done a lot in the East Village.

But I came up the steps and said, "Hello" and that was it. She was more than friendly, more than willing, she accepted every invitation I made.

Inside my place, she ran her mouth, a Midwestern cracker accent, a mile a minute. She was telling me about how she hitchhiked from some little dinky town in Illinois, got arrested in Ohio, got out of jail when they checked back by phone with somebody there at the reform school where she practically grew up, and discovered that she *was really* twenty years old like she had been telling them all along, from the moment they picked her up.

She wasn't pretty to me and she doesn't even begin to "shape up" now, though I feel sympathy for her. I mean the sometimes-warmth I feel for her doesn't make her look better, but she knows how to fuck. She is a master at it, and works her ass off.

I realize that I am simply evading so many things by lying around all day like this, letting her play with my dick, sit on my lap, suck it, get down on her knees, upside down, backwards, any way you can think of. I can do nothing else right now. My dick is my life, it has to be. Cathy certainly won't ever come back. I've stopped thinking about the possibility. Eunice has of course gone away to Harvard, and I'm taking it in my stride. My black ramrod *is* me, any man's rod is himself.

This thing that I am, this body—it is me. *I* am it. I am not a concept in your mind, whoever you are! I am *here,* right here, myself, MYSELF, fucking or being driven to the ends of my ability to contain myself in the ecstasy her little red mouth inspires as it works at the knobby head of my weapon, or if I am eating this goat's cheese, the pumpernickel, drinking the beer I have just bought, or whatever I happen to be doing, I am not *your idea* of anything.

YES, THIS *IS* distraction. I sit down now on the side of the bed, I am about to wake her, *because* I am depressed, frustrated. Her round, innocent-looking face is hard, deep in the pillow. Her pink cheeks are red, her hands are folded beneath her face, and there is a frown between her eyebrows. I know she is really a very fucked-up, unhappy girl, but somehow basically strong, rebellious; I touch the wet edge of her scalp, like black women. Jokingly I said, "Damn, baby, I think you been lying to me! You *really* a secret nigger!—" She is nude beneath the sheet, I know. I pull it all the way down, and stroke her little girl-size body. Each tit is no bigger than half an orange: I turn her little white wrists over and look at them. They are healing, where she cut them with the coke bottle that first night here, after getting drunk from wine I offered her. Now I have beer here, this is the first booze I've had in the apartment since the end of the wine three days ago. I want to fuck her, like she's a *thing.* I don't want to see her eyes when I screw her, because sometimes they are *too* sad. The overpowering rapture of just grinding gently with her, without compassion, because I know there is no future for us, no real reason why we should protect each other's feelings. I feel I can almost see a pig looking at me from her eyes, at times. I touch her pussy now, the dry hair. My sperm dry on it. Little streaks of dry *cum.*

She rolls over automatically without waking up, and it is easy to spread her legs. I am sitting in a very uncomfortable position like this. I want her to wake up and suck me, but it must be done in a very subtle way. I must convince her that I am really passionately intent on making love to her, that I want to turn her ass every way but loose! This is a ritual. I'm sure. She knows I'm lazy. That I will make a big showing, maybe for a few seconds, with great ambition, in a kind of hungry struggle to rip her open since she likes it rough, then I'll stretch out on my back, on this tiny cot we have here, and take a deep breath. And she is asking, "You like my pussy?" And I am saying, "Yes, yes, it's good." She is adjusting herself over me, so that she's sitting astraddle my hips, with the mouth of her pussy just at the tip of my meat. The female smell of her these three days hasn't been unpleasant at all, though she's had only one bath. Strange that she doesn't smell sour. But there is something about a twenty-year-old girl that simply doesn't get too odious. Maybe I shouldn't say that because it probably isn't always or even generally true. This morning I do not even want to go through the ritual of pretending I am going to be very manly and supervise her, so to speak, sexually. I want her to wake up right now and get to this proposition; I am beginning to feel a streak of evilness creeping in me. I want to *force* her, I can almost see my hands lifting her, opening her mouth, as though she were some kind of doll, and choking her with the splatter of my dick.

The dried sperm on her hair turns me off. I don't want to bother with getting that stuff on me. It's old, dry, and the stuff inside her, this morning, from last night, is thick by now, like some kind of cheese, so it is understandable, or should be, that I now want the relatively clean receptacle of her mouth. I know that she won't want to, but I can't put my clean ecstatic dick into her, not right now. Not while I'm depressed. Sometimes I can do it, no matter how sloppy the snug, sumptuous hole is. I am stroking the insides of her thighs, and unbuttoning my shirt.

I stop fooling around, stand up and strip down to my birthday suit, my butterscotch body, my half of the feast of life!

Suddenly I am straddling her, my knees on either side of her head, I feel playful *and* evil, I am holding my supernatural enravisher, and just thinking about her tongue, the pressure of the walls of her mouth—how they could work together to get it all out of me (flowing, endlessly flowing, waves and waves of enchantment, voluptuousness, and it seeming so scrumptious all the while *to her*, and she never gags) and the tickling sensations of rubbing the tip of it against her half-opened mouth, is causing it to swell, the veins in it standing up, the bulbous head, purple and spongy against the sleep-dry small lips; I'm watching all this. And her eyes are coming open, but she is not fully aware.

She is yawning now, turning away from my playful dick. She's rejecting it, and I feel only more frustrated. Well, I'll fuck her, just to wake her. She's always willing to fuck, even while sleeping. She'll fuck in her sleep anytime, keeping the rhythm, everything going, just as though she were conscious . . .

I suck the hard, small red nipple of the left tit, it tastes of sweat, but not really nasty sour sweat; just as I am beginning on the other tit, I can feel her eyelids blinking against my arm, which is somewhere up there against her face. I have one hand gently moving over her bush.

Then, I feel the gentle pressure of her small delicate expert hand beginning to stroke Mr. Ill-Bred. He begins to get vulgar with his uppity big head swelling bigger, ready for an engagement. But he has a definite nobility, and she respects it. I feel her tight, firm stomach, beneath me, move up deliberately against mine. She is trying to be physically closer. It is enticingly pleasant.

It is genial; I feel a healthy henry miller kind of vitality toward it all; her hands—she's now using both of them. The pleasure of it almost equals the early stages of a good, drawn-out blow job. She has a kind of rhythm, but the position I am in is complicated, and a strain . . .

I take my hand from her cunt, knowing instinctively that this will increase her focus on what *she is doing* to me, not on what I am doing to her. The attraction of my hand, my fingers at her clitoris, only distracts from her skill on my dibbler. I slowly lie down beside her; she's moving a little to make room for me, the cot is so small. Lying down, the odor of her alluring body is stronger, but I do not want to hassle with it, only to let it seep into my psyche, to stretch out in the huge comfort of this luxury . . .

She hasn't noticed the beer sitting on the sink yet, I am leery, if she sees it she'll surely want to get drunk. She's so easily distracted. And even beer will make her drunk. Or so she says. No reason not to believe her. Meanwhile, she sits astride me, easing her honeypot down around the throbbing upstanding round rod. She watches my eyes in their rapture—I know I must have this kind of look. The muscles in her cave of life suck with real strength at the prepuce.

The wet sound, I listen to it, I am enjoying the exiguity of her doing her thing. It surprisingly does not worry me that the hole is not clean, not much anyway, and even the little worry that is here, around the hairs of things, is leaving. This is agreeable. Life seems so large and natural, like it should be. The way I feel, the navigation of her hips. The SLAP, slap, *pop* slap, SLAP, slap, *pop* slap! the luxuriance of her walls around my bluejacket, the scudding hammer looking straight up, its one eye, up into Life, the Beginning, raceless beginning, of everything deeper than anything social. And her words come back to me: "Do you hate me because I'm white?" "I don't hate you—What makes you think I hate you?" "I don't know . . . this colored boy I used to go with in Chicago used to make me get down on my knees and blow him, he said I was a no-good white trampy bitch and the only place for me was on my knees sucking him. *Boy!* did he hate white people! I just thought maybe all colored guys were that way." This conversation took place yesterday. The edge of it comes back because I am thinking of asking her to float my *coc* in her skilled slimy wet pink cave; but

I know my reason isn't the same as that other black dude's. I would dig it just as much from a "sister," morals aside; as a matter of fact the best head I've had came from the knowledge box of a beautiful, down, black chick, long-standing; but I now pop the question in the middle of all this intense gratification, "Some head, baby?" "But isn't *this* good?" I'm lying here on my back, and she's working with the faucet like a champ, sure it's great, but I want the extra punch of those magic heights—her tongue, teeth, walls, lips, the mobility of the whole thing, the sucking, biting, pumping, that performance itself! The slick walls, the hair, my twin wrinkled and frolicsome balls being carefully caressed all the while, and the other hand busy gently gliding over the babyhairs up and down my stomach. "Yeah, it's good—you know you're good, but—" "*But* you want me to give you a blow job! I think you just like the idea of having a *white* girl give you a blow job!" There is this sideways half-assed grin on her face, it's a jest and not unkind, saying tacitly, Huh? . . .

"I really think you're sick with all this racism, baby, every minute you're into *that* bag . . ." I hear myself saying, also fearing that I'm blowing my chances. "I bet that's why you woke me," she says, ignoring my statement against her mind. She's now simply sitting there dumbly on my *kok*, with a dreamy expression, looking down into my face, but not seeing me, probably seeing something, somebody, some sad scheme in downstate Illinois. She knows that I'm "from" Chicago, which impresses her, but I have refused to talk about Chi with her because we obviously don't have notes to exchange. She came through the city, but was in the hippy intrigue, driven and pestered by cops on the near North Side; I know the area, but in a different time element, I'm seven, eight years older than she.

I really begin to give up, thinking surely I've blown it, the dicker will simply have to settle for the appetizing second-choice of warmed-over stale pussy with old *cum* still in it; gooey valley with *so* much profusion, when she surprises me by lifting all the way up, the draft of warm air striking the wet milky nakedness of my *dik*, which begins now to become flaccid, and I'm not ashamed of its sudden enfeebled face at a moment like this as I used to be, say, at sixteen, because unlike then, now, I understand MY MIND, and trust its relationship with this experienced *cokke* of mine; and not even a broad can *runmedown*, you know, like this hippy here once or twice jokingly has tried to do with something like, "You're so ole you can't fuck no more." It doesn't get to me, this kinda thing. I just want her to understand *her function*, that this isn't *romance* for me either, she sometimes seems to forget *that*, though she ain't fooled about her *own* position . . .

I'm about to give up when it happens: the caress, the hand, its strength embraces my reclining soldier, I can now close my eyes, no need to fill the insipid psychological space between us because this womanish "treat" will revive my gun to its frisky textured life, I trust. With the stunning firmness of my big toe I wiggle her clitoris. It is a small man-in-a-boat, she obviously hasn't masturbated a lot; I remember now, that first night, during her wild, frantic, endless monologue, slowly it became clear that she has been humped, been working the hardness out of roosters since she was ten or eleven years old . . . The wrap. Her lips wrap around it, the wet usage. The "root" feeling, deep down feeling, the pressure—up. She is beginning slowly, these gateways into simple beauty, these slabs of life, these tissues wrapping around each other, the texture of this plant, growing bigger in the spit—slick walls of mother nature. Growing john is growing so mighty he does not need the shims of her hands, the gentle strength of those fingers, the weight of it. The pulling goodness, tugging at the nerves beneath the skin, the root, at the base of my nuts, the tickle in my ass, running up my spine, the weightless rivers running all through me, into the ends of my scalp, my back, flat, though still, deliberately not tense—though I am tempted to tighten up—seem to ripple. My stomach ripples.

Her mouth cascades, the tight grip lifts, drops again, lifts higher this time, almost pulling up to the tip—almost losing the meat, air felt moving around its wetness. My eyes are closed. Why is this as beautiful to me as writing a poem? As *important* as philosophy, or anthropology, or music? BECAUSE IT IS. Her fingers—of both hands—tickle, caress, flutter it, add to the total flourishing of the act! She is percolating me, and I can lie here in the extravagance of it. No, it doesn't matter *who* or what she is now, I do not love her, I do not hate her, her skin is not white, is not black, is not skin, necessarily. Drenching me with the sweet tidal rides of her mouth! I *deliberately* fight the tendency to *stiffen* from the excitement of it. I am fighting it so hard, the soft membranes slapping, *slush slush*, she tightens up, then, *slush slush* again; the plush washing tides of it, into me, into the waterfalls of my mind, my psyche, my fingertips, my deep canals, the silent nerve dark blood riverbeds of my human self responding to the gesture, the wave of her velvet tongue, the "chewing," gentle chewing, permeating action. I am coming, coming slowly, just very very slowly, a draining, that she nurses carefully, licks at, rolls around on her tongue, teases, washes down, her tongue stabs one or two times playfully at Mr. Perpendicular. He does not react with fluid, he is so stunned in the paradox of being *relaxed* under the command of my body, this black castle, its intelligence, and logically wanting to, needing to *explode in orgasm* a steady "serum" of overflowing, sopping-life—the spurt of life! but cannot gush forth, its need for a climax, to *keep* existence itself, the deepest definition of its agony, to keep it going, *going*.

My mind begins to wander when she bogs. I am so content, arrogantly almost, that I need not be alert. I even allow Mr. Ill-Bred to get soft in her so she'll have to wonder about her skill, doubt herself, feel threatened, do better, work harder at the dibble of him. I know her neck is very tired by now, she complained about it last night, and the day before. The position is very uncomfortable, but so is anything of value that is in the—

Ahhhh, in gentle appreciation I lazily reach down and stroke her hair. It is moist. Suddenly, like a character out of

Batman Comics being sprung out of captivity, her head shoots up, her mouth, a wet radius, closes; she catches her breath, I see the Adam's apple move almost imperceptibly, like the neck of a tense lizard filtered through the brilliant electric technological media of Walt Disney, and she asks: "Say—by the way, were you in Chicago last Christmas, during that grand hoax, when everybody thought God was coming down from the clouds to save us poor sinners?" I am completely thrown into a state of emotional and mental chaos and deep lassitude by this untimely question. I simply whisper, "Yeah, yeah—but come, please, don't stop *now!*" And I force her head down. She begins again . . . I know she will soon stop, though she knows that *I* want her to continue until I complete the circle. The "aching sweetness," a phrase commonly used, does not describe it precisely. She has made the dome by now spit-slick and it is sliding easily.

The softness, she begins to work at it, for the hardness. Dead tired, I know. I feel some anxiety, pity, fear. But please don't stop, not yet, I say silently. This can go on for over an hour "if" she is strong enough. With my toe I examine her split, and discover that it is very marshy (*she* has been coming all this time, enjoying it?), the gooey stuff drips down around my toe, between the cracks (I am able to work at her vagina like this because my knees are bent, and my feet are together meeting directly beneath her bottom), it is watery-fresh, so definitely not from last night's making. The head is throbbing and jumping in her thrifty enclosure, when she suddenly disconnects, lifts her face, red as a tomato, her eyelids droopy with tiredness; she's holding herself on one arm, still sitting on her knees, she brushes her hair back from her face. "Fuck! Ain't you never gonna come?" This increases my anxiety—my frustration. I hardly know what to say, but I say, "I'm coming, now, baby—I was almost *there* when you stopped." Like on the edge of wisdom, but I was always there, at the point and *that* was the dark rich joy of it, being stunned in a pivot . . .

She starts this time, *really* working for a quick explosion from me. I'm holding back as much as possible. I relax, fighting the excitement she is pumping into my limbs, throughout the channels of myself! Her pink grip is tighter, the pumping is automation! It washes me! Giant waves shock my skull, to my fingertips, my lips dry up, my throat dries up, I feel my head lift and fall in hydraulic waves, I can hardly keep still. Everything in me is pushed to the point of a silent—stillness, on the edge of a massive flesh*kok* human storm—on the edge now, as she pumps it (and I still fight her!)—she means to finish, to shrink me! Mr. Rooster slides madly in the pink walls, her fingers dancing everywhere from nuts to staff, helping the mouth at its work, the serpent is stern in her depths though, holding back, expressing its sweet happiness by emitting a superficial little stream of false sperm into her hardworking membraney cave, as though to pacify her, give her hope, make her think she is getting somewhere. And she is! ! She really is! ! I can't *hold* on much longer, the emission is pushing against the many bevels of the dammed-up walls of myself. *Oh shit*, I think, *oh shit*, this is *too* much! I really begin to submerge, sink down into levels of self as I feel it lift—I am dying, flowing down as the *splash!* enters the first stages of its real career issuing out of the gun, it is coming—now—out—of—the—firearm *valve*, its ordeal beats me back into ancient depths of myself, back down to some lost meaning of the male, or deep struggling germ, the cell of the meaning of Man, I almost pass into unconsciousness the rapture is so overpowering, its huge, springing, washing infiltration into Her, an eternal-like act, a Rain, I am helpless, completely at her mercy, wet in her hands, empty, aching, my ass throbbing with the drained quality of my responsive death . . .

And she stays at it gently, knowingly, not irritating it unnecessarily, but just long enough to glide it to security discreetly, to empty it of every drop that might leave it otherwise pouting, to suck, suck, suck, suck, pull the very last crystal drop of *cokke* lotion out of me, into this specific cycle of herself, beautiful! beautiful! to the last drop, and I'm in a deep sleep again.

IT IS THREE hours later. She is not here. I have been sleeping, I feel fine, very good, like I felt this morning, on the street, going to the bank, thinking of the city's pollution, happy with being— just being, watching Catholic kids going to school, the hippies, passing the vegetable stands—I feel now happy like that, again. What she said, just before she left, it is vague in my mind, but it comes back. Something about going to the Diggers to see if she could find a kitten. I know that I must not get attached to her, so I must get rid of her soon. She is a whore, admits she is a whore, there is nothing wrong with it, but I cannot get attached to a whore. It is no good for me to be involved too long with a whore. It can become a sick thing . . . So she must go soon and remain only a reference, a good sexual shadow.

florangel

Rachel Kushner

A RIVER DIVIDES THE island of Hispaniola into the Dominican Republic and Jamaica, and Jane had read that people standing on its banks are occasionally heaved up by spirits and tossed to the opposite shore, the crucial matter of where life is lived thus resolved. Jane loved the idea, as she interpreted it, that a person could be flung over if his or her desire to be on the other side were strong enough. She was in the Dominican Republic, in a town on the border with Haiti that was mostly dust and miniature bottles of Barbancourt rum. She stood on the riverbank, imagining herself floating up on her toes, then disconnecting with the earth; but nothing happened, except that an officer with a semi-automatic weapon over his shoulder told her she was in a high-security area, and to keep moving.

JANE EMERGED FROM the Santo Domingo bus station, back in the capital after two weeks of traveling around the island. The sun was sinking into the bands of pollution over the city's cluttered skyline, fanning out into an unnatural pinkish brown that appealed to her after so many small coastal towns and their mercilessly perfect sunsets. Pressing the numbers on a grimy pay phone, she noticed a sticker on the side of the phone kiosk, an illustration of a woman with a large, plum-colored hibiscus behind her ear; underneath it, *Florangel*, and a telephone number.

She waited for her taxi in the stagnant heat, waking up to the chaotic emanations of the city after seven hours on a frigid, air-conditioned bus, the no-choice entertainment of Spanish-dubbed *Incredible Hulk* reruns on the corner-mounted TV, turned to maximum volume. She watched a girl and a boy, both about eight or nine years old, weaving in and out of rush hour traffic with cakes on cardboard platters balanced on their heads like oversized Easter bonnets. Occasionally one would stop, cut a crumbly, delicate wedge and hand it through a dri-ver's side window in exchange for a few coins. The boy, walk-ing along the gutter next to diesel trucks and noisy mopeds idling in the gridlock, picked up a tree branch from a pile of prunings below a red-leafed flamboyant and began lightly whipping the girl on the backs of the legs. She, too, selected a branch from the gutter and tried to hit him back but kept miss-ing. Jane was amazed at how expertly the girl balanced her cake with one hand and wielded her switch with the other, all the while trying to duck the boy's floggings. But as the boy kept swinging, what at first seemed like a game digressed into some-thing more serious. The girl was crying, wet rivulets on her small, dust-streaked face, as she held her cake, iced in yellow and red and blue, dutifully balanced overhead.

JANE WAS WANDERING the air-conditioned aisles of the super-market near her hotel when she encountered Al. It was the hottest time of the day, when locals wisely retreated to dark-ened interiors and slept. She had a room at an inexpensive place in the old colonial zone, but there had been a continual power outage since she arrived the day before, and thus no working fan in her room. There was also no water, because her room was upstairs where the water had to be pumped. And if that weren't enough, her siesta had been interrupted by the sound of the man in the next room vomiting loudly.

Jane was looking for a shrink-wrapped dessert called *dulce de leche*, which had been taunting her sweet tooth since she first arrived in the D.R.: slabs of a caramel-colored substance, plain or studded with walnuts or chunks of marshmallow, or striated with regal bands of caramel and chocolate. Some of the wrappers featured roses or the Dominican flag, or a picture of a woman with a flower behind her hair that reminded Jane of Florangel, the female icon she'd seen on the pay phone outside the bus station, her gaze cool, distant and imperial—somehow not at all what the phone number under the image implied.

As she picked up a smallish piece of *dulce de leche* to try and discern what the ingredients were, Jane heard a voice in English—not just English, but English with the unmistakable inflections of an old New York Jew: "Hey, don't eat that! It'll make you fat!" A man in his mid-sixties, bald and in bifocals, with a faint Rodney Dangerfield sort of air was standing in the aisle holding a half-gallon of orange juice. He smiled and said, "No but, seriously, I was just kidding. Jesus, look at you, you can eat whatever you want I bet, right? So, Christ, tell me, what brings *you* here?"

He was the first American Jane had encountered in her two weeks of traveling; everyone foreign seemed to be European, and to not speak English. Jane spoke a little Spanish, but not enough for actual conversations. It was strangely relieving to be having any sort of interaction at all, even with an old guy selecting juice from the refrigerated section of the supermarket. She told him a bit about her traveling, how she had seen most of the island by *guagua*, the local transportation system of minivans with cracked windshields and loose battery connections that carried people—and chickens, pygmy goats, and occasionally, as Jane had witnessed at a stop in Puerto Plata, a six-foot pine box with a bouquet of plastic flowers laid over it—from village to village for nominal fare.

Al beamed at her when she'd finished describing the places she'd been. "Jesus, you got a lot of guts, traveling all alone like that. You didn't feel unsafe?"

Jane had been wondering why she'd come on such a difficult vacation, to this poor and frenetic country, but Al's impressed reaction made her feel proud of her recent travels. "No, I didn't feel unsafe. But I have to admit, I thought there'd be more, you know, fellow travelers, but there really weren't."

"Well, sweetheart, it's all Europeans here is why, and they go to those big fancy resorts, you know, plush package deals, they don't cram in a *guagua*, for Christ's sake. Gals in sandals, vagabonding around, you just don't see that stuff here." He laughed and shook his head. "You are just a wacko little thing, you know that? You remind me of my daughter. How old are you, twenty-six?"

That was her age. Jane felt comfortable around this man, and the mention of his daughter seemed to dispel the likelihood of lecherous intentions. He was a retired New York City court clerk, and had been coming to Santo Domingo for thirty years. When he got his pension, he bought himself an apartment in the colonial zone, where he lived nine months of the year. During the summer, he escaped back to the Lower East Side of New York.

"A guy can live very well over here on a fixed income. I'm a bachelor—divorced, you know, and the girls here, Jesus! Have you ever seen such beautiful girls?"

Jane agreed—they were maybe the most incredible looking women she'd ever seen, with full mouths, almond eyes and tiny waists, sauntering along El Conde, the main shopping street, with Hormel-chili-can-sized rollers in their hair, their faces smooth and richly colored and round. But one day, watching women in a rainy fishing village walking on a muddy, unpaved road in high-heeled shoes and tight miniskirts, Jane had felt frustration, not only for the women dressed in such impractical gear, but for herself. As though the Dominican women were a testament to what was expected of all women, that those in more comfortable shoes, looser clothing, were somehow less truly feminine.

"So, Jane, I gotta finish this shopping thing here, but listen, some friends and I are going to dinner tonight, a real authentic joint; they don't even have a sign outside—it's like high-class Dominican style. You know, no pressure, but if you want people, you got Al and his crazy buddies."

He wrote on the back of a business card, *Alfredo!* with his phone number, and then *Paco's! Nine o'clock!*

Jane went back to her room, wrote a couple of postcards and lay down. For once the electricity was working, and she trained the fan on herself and listened to the incessant high-toned whine of two-stroke mopeds circling the roundabout outside her open window. She had spent a week on the beach in Las Terrenas, on the Samaná Peninsula, reading day and night until she'd finished every last book she'd brought with her. One day she'd gone from Las Terrenas to Limón, an eleven-mile distance, to see a particular waterfall. She had wanted to take in everything along the way, see every sight by the side of the road, smell every smell. It seemed too easy to hop in a *guagua*, roar down a bumpy road with wind blowing in her face and simply be there, so she walked, in 95-degree heat, along a gravel and dirt road. She saw people living in corrugated tin shacks cooking outdoors on open fires, men cutting coconuts down with long machetes, and a boy seated in a chair on the poured-concrete foundation of an unbuilt house, draped to the neck in a barber's smock, having his hair cut. Garbage burned in little piles along the road, flames flickering lurid red and then invisible in the intense sunlight. Over that eleven miles, she passed no one else walking. People said *hola* or waved, and Jane smiled and waved back. But seeing every outlying cluster of shacks, every bend in the road between two towns, had only made her feel more separate from the place. And not only was she an outsider, her thoughts were cloaked in a hazy scrim, the result of walking unshaded in such ferocious heat.

Originally, Jane was supposed to vacation with a man who'd once been her boyfriend, but was no longer. They had broken up a year earlier when he'd left New York and moved to Seattle, but he and Jane had been talking on the phone, and things had evolved, gotten taken up again. Despite the impracticality of dating someone on the West Coast, and the unrealistic notion that this particular guy was going to give her what she really wanted, Jane had her heart set on things working out. They decided to meet someplace, neither's home turf, and Jane chose the Dominican Republic. But one day she called him and a woman answered. When he got on the phone, debilitating static crept into the line (as if he'd willed it there, like willing oneself flung over a river), thwarting her from even asking him who was in his apartment with him, and she'd had to simply hang up. The next day, she called and called until he finally answered. He was involved with someone, and he wasn't coming on a vacation with her. At the end of a lengthy and circular conversation, he offered to pay for her trip, and she accepted, terribly unhappy, but ready to take any reparation over nothing at all.

By the time she left for the D.R. three months later, Jane was beginning to get over him, and looking forward to a vacation alone. After the mess with the ex-boyfriend, a solo excursion to a tropical island sounded purifying, a way for her to sort out her thoughts and forget her busy New York life. She had a job as an art assistant for an aging Minimalist sculptor who would sometimes pay her a full day's wage just to sit with him for a couple of hours and drink coffee, absorb his chatter about how his ex-wife wouldn't let him see his own son, how different Soho was from the old days, how much he hated the art world. It should have been easy money, but somehow it wasn't.

Now that she was here, she craved companionship; traveling alone was beginning to seem more pointless than purifying. Every town she visited, she would go to the restaurant recommended in her guidebook and end up feeling a sense of sadness and loss that the people who wrote the book and described the restaurant had been there once but were gone now, leaving her to eat by herself.

With a faint click, the electricity in Jane's room went out. The fan blades slowed to a languorous twirl and then stopped. It was dusk, and there was just enough light for her to see her way around the room. She decided to get dressed and take a walk, and told herself that if she felt like meeting up with that character Al from the supermarket, then she would. It would be an adventure, and it wouldn't kill her to have a bit of company.

AT PACO'S, A twenty-four-hour open-air restaurant on the end of El Conde, Al introduced Jane to his friends Phillipe and Henry. Phillipe was a Polish Jew who ran a cigar factory and was barely five feet tall, with a crooked spine and giant hands that gaped from his shirtsleeves. He had spent his childhood in concentration camps. (As Al later blurted to Jane, "His growth got stunted by malnutrition.")

Phillipe said in his Yiddish accent, "I have cigars if you want for souvenir, young lady."

Al kept beaming at her and saying, "I'm telling you guys, this girl is just like my daughter Harriet!"

Henry was from Argentina, younger than Phillipe; but emanated botched attempts to appear younger than he was. His skin was curiously taut, his hair stiff looking and an inky black—an obvious dye job. Henry ran a wholesale vitamin business. Al introduced him as a "health nut," but Jane thought he didn't look so healthy.

As they all sat talking, a girl walked by and Al indiscreetly went, "Pssssst." It was a sound Jane had been hearing all over the island, and although she knew it was the Dominican way to get someone's attention, she found it obtrusive. Men did it to her constantly—*Hey rubia, Mommy, pssssst;* she could not go anywhere without hearing it, and if she ignored it and kept walking they would do it louder and louder. And here was Al, retired New York Jew, co-opting Dominican street style. Jane figured she could speak her mind to him, that he was the sort who liked spunkiness and opinions, and she came right out and said, "That is disgusting. You do that?"

He shrugged, half-smiling, "What?"

"You know, that pssst. I hate that."

"What, this?" And then he leaned forward as another young woman passed, and issued a sensationally awkward, saliva-flecked "Pssssssssssst." Whether it was to be perverse, or to demonstrate what he thought was his élan in handling the ritual, Jane wasn't sure. Al said, "Jane, sweetie, it's part of Dominican culture. You think that girl is bothered by it? Let me show you something." He pointed out yet another girl walking past, pretty and dressed professionally, a bank teller, or salesclerk, and then he called her over. The girl walked toward them. She was trim and shapely, with dark plum-jelly eyes and a pink-frosted mouth. She stood before them, smiling submissively, as Al sized her up behind his thick glasses. If that weren't bad enough, he asked her to do a spin by twirling his finger, and she did as he asked, turning slowly before his eyes. Al said, "Como se llama, sweetheart?" And shook his head in reverence, staring at her legs, which were smooth and brown and bare up to the line of a short skirt.

She answered shyly, "Maria."

"Maria, show Jane here your *bolsa*. I'm gonna teach you something, Jane. Look at this." When she heard the word *bolsa* Maria turned to show them the purse hanging from her shoulder, a burgundy leatherette handbag with a pink scarf tied on its handle. Al grabbed onto an edge of the scarf and said "Soltara, si?"

Maria smiled and nodded, "Si."

"Y, aqui?" Al motioned to the back of her head, to the base of her ponytail, "Aqui, casada, si?"

She smiled and nodded again, "Si." Al turned to Jane. "Isn't that something? They got a system here. She's single, see? They got that scarf on their pocketbook, and they're letting everybody know. If she was married, she'd be wearing it around her ponytail. I'm telling you Jane it's a nutty, wonderful place, this country." Then Al abruptly waved the young woman away, saying, "OK, gracias, adios, muchacha." He nudged Jane and said, "You see, she wasn't offended. That's their culture. These girls, they come when you call them."

Al and his friends were dirty old men, and Jane understood that sitting at Paco's, checking out girls was their routine. They seemed pathetic, but their world was something she knew nothing about: a set of cryptic rules, an engagement in something that had to do with women, and how men think about women, and Jane wanted to understand more.

Henry, the "health nut," piped in, "Not only do they do like you tell 'em, but they're the sexiest girls in the world. No offense, I mean, you seem like a nice person and all, but a lot of American women, they don't even *act* like women. Dominican girls, they're feminine. And they know how to make a man feel like a man. That's why we're all down here—the girls!"

Al cut in, "*Some* of us are here for the girls, and *some* of us are here because we can't exactly go home, right Henry? Jane, don't listen to anything these guys tell you. Neither one of these bastards has what you could call an open invitation to go back where they came from." And they all laughed, but Jane was sure that it was not a joke.

Henry said, "Yeah and Al, he lives here cause he's—" And Henry slapped one hand against the backside of his forearm, near the elbow.

"What does that mean?" Jane asked.

Al said, "It means I'm cheap, but you can ask any of the girls on El Conde, Alfredo here is *muy generoso*. They always come back to my house, and they come to my house after they been at Henry's house, complaining how stingy he is."

Phillipe, the old Holocaust survivor, leaned forward at this point, shaking his head with emphatic, theatrical emotion. He put a thick hand over Jane's and in his heavy accent said, "Young lady, don't listen to zees fools. Ze girls here, it is terrible, zey are second-class citizen. Zey start having sex at eight, nine years old. And you see all ze time teenage girl with old man, and zey do whatever zey are told, and for so little money. It is tragedy."

Henry snorted, "Yeah, what a tragedy Phillipe. Didn't I see you with that Carlotta yesterday? She's like seventeen right, and you're, what, pushing a hundred and twenty?"

Phillipe turned to Jane and shrugged, both enormous, wrinkled palms turned skyward. "I can't find girl my age here, is why. Zat is *another* tragedy! It's ze life expectancy, zey don't live so long as Polish Jew!" He shook his head and sighed heavily. Suddenly remembering that he'd been insulted, he pointed at Henry and said sharply, "I am only sixty-nine years old, by the way, Henry. Just because I don't go under ze knife, dye my hair and make bargains with ze devil like you and your crazy vitamins, doesn't mean I am so old!"

HENRY DROVE THEM to dinner. He crept along at fifteen miles an hour in traffic that was going fifty. Cars honked and swerved dangerously around them. But whenever they were approaching a red light, he would mash down on the gas and lurch violently ahead, and then slam on the breaks at the last minute, to avoid rear-ending someone. Jane was biting her lip, waiting for the car to plow into a pair of glowing orange taillights, preparing for her inevitable flight through the windshield's safety glass, wondering if this had all been a mistake.

They stopped at a casino to pick up Henry's date, who was supposed to meet him in front. They all got out of the car, and Al, who suddenly seemed drunk, tugged on Jane's arm and slurred, "Come on, I want to show you something, American gal." Across the street from the casino were three Dominican girls leaning like bright, tropical flowers against a stretch of chain-link fence.

"Hola, muchachas!" Al waved to them as he and Jane approached, and the girls sprang to life at his greeting. They stepped forward and smiled widely, a trio of *holas*. Not one of them could have been more than twelve or thirteen years old—junior high school age, Jane figured. The one that looked the youngest was also the prettiest and the most confident (but perhaps she was the oldest, and simply the most petite—or the youngest but the first to get that initial and troublesome hormone surge). She stepped toward Al and Jane in her skimpy halter-top. The two top buttons of her faded jeans were undone, her taught belly button smiling up at them.

Al introduced himself and then, after learning the girls' names, introduced each of them to Jane. Feeling slightly ridiculous, Jane nodded hello to each girl. It was awkward, humiliating even, to be introduced by a potential john to the prostitutes he was ogling. But on this evening, Jane was going with the flow, the lack of options for company somehow making people and situations softer, more palatable than they would have been under different circumstances.

Henry's date was a cute and slightly chubby college student named Miranda who looked to be less than half his age. She and Jane shared the front passenger seat in the car, with Jane squeezed in the middle and balanced precariously over the emergency brake, and they laughed together at Henry's crazy driving. Miranda was immediately friendly, and the presence of another woman made Jane feel less frightened about the likelihood of a disaster with Henry behind the wheel of the car. At dinner, Jane and Miranda exchanged knowing looks as Henry, Phillipe, and Al each proceeded to cause some sort of scene, complaining about the wait service, asking stupid questions about the menu, and shouting in English at reserved Dominican waiters in crisp, white dinner jackets who didn't understand a word they said. Although Henry was allegedly from Argentina and spoke English with a Spanish accent, his Spanish didn't quite sound like Spanish; his words all ran together with the vowels sheared off, and he seemed to be having trouble communicating with Miranda and the waiters. Jane suspected that perhaps it was just a combination of booze and whatever pills he kept popping. Miranda and Jane giggled together in the car on the way back to the colonial zone, but when everyone got dropped off and Miranda remained, Jane remembered that despite her complicity in rolling her eyes at these men's buffoonery, Miranda was on a date with one of them—with Henry, vitamin salesman, likely fugitive, terrible driver with rubbery skin—and she was driving away with him now.

The next day, Jane was in her room sweating in cotton underwear. There was another power outage, and hence no fan. She dressed and walked down to the Malecon, the boardwalk along the water, where it was cooler. There was a strong breeze blowing off the Atlantic that rustled the tall palms lining the street. She passed fruit carts, hamburgesa carts, carts full of coconuts on beds of ice, holes drilled in their tops for inserting a straw. Military officers in faded lavender uniforms stood around eating mangoes, leaning forward as they sucked flesh off the large, almond-shaped seeds, careful not to drip juice on their uniforms. They all smiled at her, but thankfully no one gave her the *pssst.*

She passed a movie theater and decided to go in, thinking the air conditioning would do her good. The *Selena* story was playing. She had needed to pee for several blocks, and as she paid, she asked the usher where the bathroom was. He left his post and led her down a hallway, opened a door, and motioned her to follow. She was suddenly in a darkened theater, and an X-rated movie was in full swing, bodies splayed, gruesome as open-heart surgery. Jane didn't quite know what to do, but she was about to pee in her pants, so she walked down the side aisle to a door marked *baño.* She relieved herself in a grimy unisex bathroom to the muffled sounds of faked orgasm, and then walked quickly back to the lobby, not turning to acknowledge the men in the theater, who were undoubtedly staring at her. The screen where *Selena* was showing was upstairs. On her way up, she noticed that there were bathrooms at the top of the stairs, marked men and women.

The theater was not exactly air-conditioned, but it was a little cooler than the air outside. The sound, however, was so warbled that Jane had to resort to reading the Spanish subtitles with her poor comprehension. The teenage girls sitting next to her sang along with Selena in sweet and husky voices. They knew all the words, even to the lyrics in English. When Selena was killed, the girls sitting next to Jane cried, and Jane cried a little bit too.

Al had mentioned to Jane that he often drank an evening beer in the cafeteria below her hotel. On her way back from the movie she peered through the window and saw him sitting at a table by himself, a 24-ounce bottle of beer parked in front of him, with a short glass. Part of her wanted to pretend she hadn't seen him, and just move on upstairs, but she went in.

Al broke into a smile when he saw her. "Hey! Look at that! See, what'd I tell you? This is my spot, right under the flop-house where you're staying! Here, have a seat, tell me what you been up to. You want a beer or a soda or something?"

When she told him she had gone to the movies hoping for a bit of air conditioning he laughed and slapped the table, and said, "Jane, this ain't New York City!" And he was right; she hadn't any idea there'd be no air conditioning in the theater. Jane felt glad, rather than regretful, that she'd stopped in to say hello rather than sneaking up to her room. She appreciated that Al had a local's insights, and he seemed to understand that this was what entertained her about him.

The electricity was still out, and the cafeteria was lit only with candles (the colonial zone had constant blackouts, and Jane had heard the government bought used generators that were always malfunctioning. The electricity in Gazcue, the district where the president's mansion was, apparently never went out). There were four girls working behind the cafeteria counter, scooping food from large pans with Sternos lit beneath them. They looked like sisters, probably in their teens. Al motioned to one of them, a petite girl with long hennaed red hair and large gold earrings. She approached the table, and he put his arm around her and said, "This is my darling Eeliizaaa," and stared at her body as he uttered an elongated version of her name. He tried to pull Eliza onto his lap, but she demurred and leaned away from him, smiling. When she retreated to the counter, Al said, "My, my. Isn't she something?"

Jane said, "Yeah, she's cute, Al." It occurred to her that at twenty-six, she was too old for Al's taste, as every girl he'd openly admired was a teenager. Jane felt essentially safe, but more conflicted than comforted. She would not have welcomed Al's advances, but she didn't like the feeling that she was over the hill, that this old guy should have the power to legislate which women were, and were not, appealing.

"I'm gonna tell you something, Jane. See all those girls back there behind the counter?"

"I see them, Al." A girl with her hair pinned up neatly was carrying a rack of bread loaves out from the kitchen, putting them in a glass case with charred oven mitts on her hands.

"They're for sale."

Each girl had a small rosary around her neck, and they were dressed in identical parochial school uniforms; one had on wire-rimmed glasses. Jane assumed this was an after-school job for them—a family business, perhaps, and she was surprised by what Al said. She interjected, "But Al—"

"In fact, any girl over here can be bought. Secretaries, postal workers, waitresses . . . these girls, you think they make enough at this job to get by? They have to supplement their income, and bring money back to the family. That's the way it is in this country."

"But they look like students."

"They *are* students. But this is the Dominican Republic, and there's no money here, Jane. People have to make ends meet."

Jane watched Eliza serving portions of meat and rice and fried plantains to customers who sat at the counter and pointed to what they wanted. She thought of the image of Florangel, her remote, airbrushed face, and it occurred to her that if you called the number underneath, girls like these probably answered the phone. She felt foolish for not having had any idea that the girls behind the counter weren't just sweet things fending off Al's advances. They were involved in something more complicated that Jane knew nothing about.

Al said, "It's not considered shameful, it's just part of life here. A lot of very respectable women, married women even, they do it on the side. These girls, they got pride, and they're clean, too, let me tell you, I mean like in a female way they're clean, if you know what I'm saying."

"Al, don't be disgusting."

"Jane, I'm trying to teach you something, kiddo. Now you watch." He yelled over to the counter "Eliza! Venga, venga aquí." Eliza, who had been working the cash register, came over, smiling. Al handed her some money, "Por la cuenta." Then he asked her, in his crude Spanish, if she wanted her tip then, or later, at his casa.

"Más tarde. A tu casa," she said, and then winked at him before walking away.

Two days later, early on Saturday morning, Al took Jane to a Haitian flea market, *la pulga.* Jane loved flea markets and when Al had mentioned it, her curiosity had been piqued. It was a local's thing, not in the guidebook, and she would have had no idea how to get there on her own, so she'd asked Al to take her. When they met on El Conde, he pulled a baseball hat out of his backpack and handed it to her. "Here. I brought you something for your bean, you need a hat when you're going to the pulga, or you'll get sunstroke out there." There was a letter J on the bill. "How 'bout that, huh? J! It's your hat, kiddo!"

The bus they took to the pulga wound through the barrio, and became so crowded that passengers were climbing in and out of the windows. They passed makeshift shanties where people lived with no electricity and no running water. Children filled buckets from a gurgling pipe in the sidewalk. Al said, "That water is treacherous. One night I left a glass of it next to my bed. The next morning there were guys—they looked like toy soldiers on parachutes—spiraling down in my water glass!"

The market was vast and dusty, with piles and piles of

clothing on blue tarps, Haitian women with their hair tied up in rags drinking baggies of water and digging change out of their aprons. There was no shade, and Jane was glad to have the "J" hat on. Al knew how to negotiate, certainly better than Jane did, and he helped her buy a sundress and some old postcards from the Trujillo era. On their way home, he said, "When did you say you're splitting out of here, day after tomorrow?"

She nodded.

"I'll tell you what. On account that you're leaving, and I'm gonna miss you, Alfredo here is treating you to a Chinese dinner tonight."

Calle Duarte was a chaotic strip of cheap hotels with soiled awnings, discount jewelry stores and household goods. In the daytime, the street was clogged with shoppers and traffic, but at night it was deserted, and littered with the tailings of the day's commerce: chewed mango pits and cracked coconut shells emptied of their milk and piled high along the sidewalk like furry brown skulls. As they walked, Al leading her to what he said was "a real nice joint," the sour smell of rotting juice-orange remnants wafted up from the curb, and an effluvium the color of antifreeze flowed along the gutters.

The restaurant was up a flight of stairs, and nicer than Jane had expected, with red flocked wallpaper embossed with a golden dragon. Al devoured his plate of chow mein and then started in on Jane's Buddha's delight, wilted greens and soggy eggplant that glistened with oil. There was something faded and old about Al, but at the same time he looked strong, with dense, broad arms and calf muscles the size of grapefruits. He ate heartily, with the appetite of a much younger man, shoveling food in with the fork he had asked for in place of chopsticks. He complained how Eliza had not called him that day they had been in the cafeteria, like she had promised. He said, "But then again, I passed out from drinking; maybe she called and I didn't hear the phone."

Jane asked him if he'd ever had a Dominican girlfriend, or just girls who came over and visited him to pick up their "tip."

He said there was a girl he had been fond of, that they'd had an arrangement where she cooked and cleaned for him, and he supported her. "This girl was amazing, I'm telling you. I go over there, to her family's place, and she's preparing this elaborate meal—on charcoal briquettes! That's barrio-style cooking, without the convenience of electricity. So anyway, we sit down to eat, me and her whole entire family, and this girl serves meat to everyone at the table except herself, her mother, and her sister. And I spear mine with a fork and say, 'Here, take Alfredo's meat, I don't need it, really,' and one of her brothers, he pushes my hand back towards the plate, and get this—he tells me the women, they don't *need* to eat meat because they don't work. And this girl is cleaning, and doing for me all the time, and I know she's bringing in more money than anyone else in that household because I'm giving it to her! Her brothers, there were like six of them, not one of 'em had a job." Al was shaking his head.

"So what happened to her?"

"One summer I went away; she was taking care of my place, and when I get back I hear she married some European guy. I saw them on the street together one time, and he looks like a greasy Italian. I didn't want to embarrass her, you know, so I laid low."

Al told Jane he would have liked to meet another girl, maybe have some sort of arrangement like he'd had before, but that he never could stand to see any of the girls more than once or twice. He said, "I don't know, it's weird, I don't mean to get personal, but as soon as I sleep with 'em, if it seems like they're starting to get to understand old Alfredo, I can't like 'em anymore. I guess I'm funny that way."

Jane wasn't surprised to hear him say this, but she wasn't sure what it really meant. Did Al have the upper hand with these women, or not? He seemed weak to her for his inability to be known, but then again, *he* was turning the women away. When she asked him about his ex-wife, why they got divorced, he shrugged. "I figured I'd be a lot happier eating ketchup and rice than putting up with all the bullshit."

Jane didn't volunteer anything about her own love life, and Al didn't ask. From the beginning their acquaintance had been about him telling her his stories, and this is what they stuck to. Al's acknowledgement of Jane, the connection with his daughter and the frankness with which he discussed his own romantic travails, all seemed to preclude the recognition of her as a female with a love life of her own. And what was there to say, really? That she'd had her heart broken, which was why she was here? To introduce such a confession into his realm, where women were simply key holders to lust, would have seemed absurd.

ON JANE'S LAST day in Santo Domingo, she ran into Al at his spot at the cafeteria below her hotel. He said, "Listen, I want to show you my place before you scram. Why don't you come over this afternoon?"

In front of Al's apartment, they ran into a man he knew named Patrick. He seemed different than Al's other buddies, Phillipe and Henry, less clownish. He was a handsome, middle-aged American, polite and soft-spoken. Al said, "Hey Patrick, Jane here would love to see your place, I bet; could you give her a little tour? Jane, this guy is restoring a sixteenth-century villa, just down the block. It was a complete dump, and Patrick here is turning it into a palace. You really should see it. Jane's a smarty-pants, she reads books and stuff like you, Patrick. Jane, Patrick here is a big shot architect back East. Me, I'm a Jew with no brains." Jane was suddenly embarrassed to be with Al, and she wondered how well Patrick knew him, what he thought of Al's "bachelor" lifestyle.

Patrick agreed to show her his place. Al called after them, "You can see my place when you're through—just shout up to old Alfredo! I ain't going anywhere."

Patrick walked Jane down to his villa, which, as it turned out, was quite impressive. He was re-creating the original façade of the building, and he explained to Jane the process of finding the appropriate replacement stones for the foundation, locating moldings and lintels at salvage sites, getting ironwork done on the elaborate gates. His project—restoration, seemed a lot more honorable than Al's project—Dominican girls. Patrick was there studying the country's architectural history, bringing something back from a state of decay. Jane admired that; it appealed to her own romantic notions of being in Santo Domingo, the oldest city in the New World. As they spoke, Jane was wishing she would have met him, and people like him, earlier in her trip, rather than getting mixed up with Al and his sordid preoccupations.

In the open atrium of Patrick's villa, mango trees stretched taller than the building's three stories, speckling the clay patio tiles in leaf-shaped blobs of shade and sunlight. At a table in the center of the patio a beautiful black woman with long, cornrowed hair sat drinking espresso from a tiny cup, reading a Haitian newspaper. Patrick said, "This is my wife, Delphine."

The woman nodded and said, "Hola." The three of them sat for a bit, Jane drinking the ice water Patrick brought her. She tried to strike up a conversation with Delphine, but as it turned out, she spoke both French and Spanish, but no English.

After Jane's tour of the villa, she thanked Patrick and went back to Al's. As they drudged up the stairs to his third-floor apartment, Jane commented that she wondered how Patrick and his wife communicated, that his Spanish sounded pretty rough, and she seemed to speak no English.

"His *wife*, did I hear you say?"

"Yeah. Delphine."

"Jane, sweetheart, that is not his wife." Al was laughing.

"But, he said, *This is my wife, Delphine.*"

"Well, I'll tell you something, his so-called wife was at my place less than a week ago. Delphine, she gets around. I used to see her years ago selling bras and panties out on Calle Duarte—that sewer stretch where we ate Chinese."

Al's apartment was a lot more disheveled, simultaneously bare and messy, than Jane had expected. The sink was full of dirty dishes. In the living room there was one chair and a television, and many cardboard boxes full of empty beer bottles. Al pointed out all his minor renovations. He'd cut a hole in the wall that looked out onto the building's draftway, and he'd put another hole through the wall that divided the kitchen and living room, so that air would flow through. He said, "When the girls come over, I tell 'em Alfredo's place is like Swiss cheese." He seemed drunker than Jane had seen him before, talking loudly and knocking things over in the kitchen. He grabbed a liter bottle of gin off the kitchen counter, unscrewed the cap, turned it upside down and took a hefty swig.

The phone rang, and the machine picked it up on the first ring. Al's voice boomed out of the microphone, speaking Spanish like a true New Yorker. *Alfredo no en casa.*

It was Eliza, from the cafeteria, and Al ran to the phone and picked it up, "Eliza! Sweetie, venga a casa de Alfredo? Bueno! Mas tarde? OK, OK, bueno!" Al was elated when he hung up the phone. "That Eliza, boy oh boy."

"You've known her long?"

"No, no, she's new over there. That's the whole thing, I ain't slept with her yet. I told you, right?"

Jane asked to use the bathroom. She had to walk through his bedroom to get to the bathroom, and she tried not to look as she passed through. She didn't want to see Al's bedroom. She wanted to pee and then get out of his place; there was something about being there that felt like time thrown away, and not just wasted, but time she would regret. She'd seen enough. In the bathroom, she noticed that his medicine cabinet was locked with a tiny padlock. When she returned to the living room, Al said, "You see how I got it all locked up in there? It's always new girls I got coming over here, is why. And some of them are honest, but some of them steal, and you'd never believe it if I didn't tell you, but you know what they take? Deodorant, bars of soap, that sort of thing. They're crazy for that stuff. I got it all girl-proofed around here."

Jane said, "Al, I should be going. Thanks for showing me your place."

He protested, "Hey, what's the hurry, you're at casa Alfredo! At least have a beer, or let me finish giving you the tour."

"Al, I really need to pack and do some things, so I am gonna go—"

Al put his hand on her shoulder and said, "Come on, have a cold one on Alfredo. You're my guest!"

Jane said, "Al thanks for everything, and take care," and she resolutely turned to go, but Al tightened his grip on her arm.

"Let me show you one more thing. See this?" He tugged her over toward the wall and pointed above the light switch, where he had mounted a convex mirror the size of a tea saucer, the sort of thing they put in the corner of New York elevators. He said, "Now, when a girl wants to use the john, I got to be careful, because I keep my cash in the bedroom. But this way—" He leaned his back flat up against the side of the refrigerator, his head snug to the wall and turned to the side, as if demonstrating stealth, his eye on the mirror's reflection of the bedroom. "When I'm in the kitchen, I can keep an eye on things, see? They think they're so goddamn clever." Then his hand tightened around Jane's upper arm, a firm, constricting grip. "No one's fucking with old Alfredo. Not one of these stupid whores."

He was drunk and slurring his words, and she could smell the gin-fermented air wafting off of him. Breathing heavily, he asked, "Do you understand?" He pushed her hard up against the wall with both hands and asked again. "Do you? Huh?"

something nice

Mary Gaitskill

FROM BAD BEHAVIOR

"WHAT'S YOUR NAME, sir?" The freckled woman wore green stretch pants, and had her red hair tucked under a neat pink scarf. "Fred?" She was making her naturally coarse voice go soft and moist as warm mayonnaise. "I'd like you to meet my girlfriends, Fred." The four girls stared at him. Two sat up and smiled, holding their purses with tight fingers, their legs pinched together at the knees. A beautiful black-haired girl, with jutting cheekbones and a lush, full mouth, lolled in an orange bean-bag chair, her long legs sprawled rudely on the floor, half open and tenting her tight silk dress so you could almost see between her legs. She gawked at him with open disgust.

"Sit up, Jasmine," snapped the stretch-pants woman through her smile. She held out her freckled hands toward the last girl, who sat with one leg tucked underneath her, looking out the window. "And this is Lisette." The girl wore a short red-and-black-checked dress, white ankle socks and black pumps. Her bobbed brown hair was curly. When she turned to face him, her expression was mildly friendly and normal; she could've been looking at anybody or anything.

The strangeness of it all delighted and fascinated him: the falsely gentle voice, the helpless contempt, the choosing of a bored, unknown girl sitting on her ankle, looking out the window.

"Do you see a lady who you'd like to visit with?"

"I'll see Lisette."

The girl stood up and walked toward him as if he were a dentist, except she was smiling.

The room was pale green. The air in it was bloated with sweat and canned air freshener. There was a bed table set with a plastic container sprouting damp Handi-Wipes, a radio, an ashtray, a Kleenex box and a slimy bottle of oil. The bed was covered by a designer sheet patterned with beige, brown and tan lions lazing happily on the branches of trees or swatting each other. There was an aluminum chair. There was a glass-covered poster for an art exhibit. There was a fish tank with a Day-Glo orange fish castle in it. He lay on the bed naked, waiting for her to join him. He turned on the radio. It was tuned to one of those awful disco stations. *"I specialize in love,"* sang a woman's voice. *"I'll make you feel like new. I specialize in love—let me work on you."*

He smiled as he listened to the music. It evoked the swirling lights of dance floors he'd never been on, the tossing hair and sweat-drenched underwear of girls who danced and drank all night, girls he never saw except in commercials for jeans. He anticipated Lisette as he imagined her, the grip of her blunt-fingered hands, her curly head on his shoulder. Did she dance in places like that, in her white socks and pumps?

She came in with a white sheet under her arm. She clipped across the floor, sharp heels clacking. She turned off the radio. The silence was as disorienting as a sudden roomful of fluorescent light. "I hate that shit," she said. "I hope you don't mind. I have to put this sheet down." She snapped the sheet open and floated it down over him. He scrambled out from under it, banging into the wastebasket as he stepped to the floor.

"Here," he said. He took a corner of the sheet and awkwardly stretched it over the bed.

"No, it's okay, that's good enough." She sat on the bed and stared at him, her small face gone suddenly grave. Her eyes were round and dark. Her muddy black makeup looked as if it had been finger-painted on. He sat down next to her and put his hand on her thigh. She ignored it. He felt as though he was bothering a girl sitting next to him on a bus. His hand sweated on her leg and he took it away. What was wrong? Why wasn't she pulling her dress off over her head, the way they usually did?

"Do you come to places like this often?" she asked.

"Not too much. Every month or so. I'm married, so it's hard to get away."

She looked worried. She reached out with nervous quickness and picked up his hand. "What do people do now, mostly?" she asked.

"What do you mean?"

"I mean I'm new here. You're only my second customer and I don't know what I should do. Well, I know what to *do*, basically, but there's all these little things, like when to take off the dress."

He felt a foolish smile running over his face. Her second customer! "But you've worked before."

"You mean done this before? No, I haven't."

He looked at her, beaming greedily.

"What do you do for a living?" she asked.

"I'm an attorney," he said. "Corporate law." He was lying. He felt cut loose from himself, unmarried, un-old, because of the lie.

"How old are you?"

"How old do you think I am?"

She smiled, and her black eye paint coiled like a snake in the corners of her eyes. "Fifty?"

"You're exactly right." He was fifty-nine. "How about you?"

"Twenty-two."

She looked as though she could be that age, but he had a strong feeling that she was lying too.

"Why do you come to places like this?" She lay across the bed, her head on her hand, her legs folded restfully. "Do you not get along with your wife?"

He leaned against the headboard, his naked legs open. "Oh, I love my wife. It's a very successful marriage. And we have sex, good sex. But it's not everything I want. She's willing to experiment, a little, but she's really not all that interested. It can make you feel foolish to be doing something when you know your partner isn't an equal participant. Besides, this is an adventure for me. Something nice."

"Is it something nice?"

"With you it's going to be very nice."

"How do you know?"

"What a strange question."

She crossed the bed to adjust her body against his, to put her head on his shoulder. She stroked his chest hair. "It's not so strange."

"Well, I just know, that's all."

They kissed. She had a harsh, stubborn kiss.

She took off her checked dress, button by button, very neatly. Her body was extremely pretty: white, curvy and plump. When she took off her high heels he saw that her legs were a little too short and her ankles a bit thick, but he liked them anyway. She folded her dress over the aluminum chair and turned to him with an uptilted chin, looking as if she might break into a trot, like a pony. She was proud of her body.

Her pride was pitiful in the stupid room. It made him feel superior and tender. He gushed a smile and held out his arms. She met him with a surprisingly strong hug, the pouncing grab of a playful animal.

"Goodness, you're healthy."

She grinned and squeezed him. "What do you want to do?"

"We'll play it by ear. Don't be nervous. It's going to be lovely."

The way she touched became unsure. She talked to him as they touched, and her crude, frank words were like pungent flowers against the gray of her shyness. When he touched her hips, he thought he could feel her innermost life on the sensitive surface of her body.

"IT WAS LIKE a honeymoon," he said to her afterward. "Just like I knew it would be."

"Oh, it was not." Her face was in the mirror; she was swiping her mouth with lipstick. "Don't be silly."

"Have you ever been married?"

"Uh-uh."

"Then you don't know what a honeymoon is like." She was right though. It wasn't like a honeymoon at all.

SHE WALKED HIM to the door and he kissed her in front of the other girls. The stretch-pants woman smiled. "Good night, Fred," she said.

When he got on the highway to Westchester, he used his push-button device to roll down the windows and drove too fast. When he arrived home he walked through the entire first floor of his house, turning on all the lights. His wife really was out of town, and he didn't like to be alone in a dimly lit house. The refrigerator was clean and neatly stacked with food his wife had prepared for him. He got into his pajamas and slippers and made himself a sandwich of cold cuts and mayonnaise. He stood at the kitchen counter and ate the sandwich from a paper plate with a smiling cat face on it. He thought of Lisette lying across the bed like an arrangement of fruit, her shoulder snuggled against her cheek, watching him clean himself in the bathroom with a cheap pink loofah. She had a curious, sober look on her round face. She's an intelligent girl, he thought. You can see it in her eyes. Why hadn't he told her that he was a veterinarian? He had never lied to a prostitute before.

He made himself a piña colada, with lots of crushed ice and a tiny straw—his wife had left a Dixie cup of red-and-white straws next to the blender—and went to bed.

THE NEXT NIGHT, he drove into Manhattan to see her again.

"Boy, I'm glad to see you tonight," she said as she clacked into the room with the sheet.

"Are you? Why?" He stood to let her crack the sheet above the bed.

"Oh, it's been sort of a bad night. I couldn't stand to deal with another idiot."

"I'm sure you get some pretty undesirable people in here."

"You said it."

"Nobody violent or anything, I hope?"

"No, just stupid." She floated the sheet down and turned to curl against him.

Later, they lay folded together, listening to the sad gurgle of the fish tank. "Look at those poor, dumb things swimming around in there," she said. "They haven't got any idea of the filth going on in here."

"What did you mean about the men who come here? When you said they're . . . just stupid." He'd said "stupid" too loud.

"I don't really mean they're stupid. A lot of them are businessmen. They must have some kind of brain to do that. But they're dumb about women and they're dumb about sex." She rocked him over on his back and lay on him, her fingers perched on his shoulders, her face right against his. "They actually think they can buy you for a hundred and fifty dollars. Like you're going to become sexually excited because they give you money. I mean they can pay you to do certain things. But they can't buy anyone for a hundred and fifty dollars." She rolled off him and flopped on her back. "It's so retarded. They don't have any idea of what good sex is, so they wouldn't know you can't buy it." She turned her head to him. "I hope I'm not insulting you. I'm not talking about you."

He stuck his body up on one elbow so he could look at her.

"No. No, I think it's very interesting. I'm flattered that you choose to tell me these things." Her stomach was sticking out like a little bread loaf. He tickled it lightly.

She scratched her stomach. "Why did you come back so soon?"

"Don't you remember last night? I find our, uh, sex highly erotic. Not because I pay for it, but because it just is." He paused to let her react. She stared at him and blinked. "Besides, I like you. I think there's something between us. I think that if I were a few years younger and we met under slightly different circumstances, we might even have what's now called a relationship."

She smiled and looked at the happy lions snoozing on the designer sheets. He put his hand on hers. "The first night I came here, you were uncertain, kind of shy. You came out and admitted it, you asked me questions. You trusted me. Tonight when you were mad, you didn't put on a phony smile. You let off steam, told me how you felt. You didn't treat me like a customer. That's nice. There's hardly anybody that'll be real with you like that anymore. Sometimes even my wife isn't honest with me."

She looked up from the smiling lions. "You shouldn't come to prostitutes looking for honesty."

"You're not a prostitute. Don't say that about yourself."

"What do you think I am?"

"You just happen to be a pretty, sexy girl who uh—"

"I have sex for money."

"Well, all right." He slapped her thigh nervously. "You're right. You're a prostitute." It sounded so horrible. "But you're still a wonderful girl." He grabbed her and snuggled her.

"You don't know me."

"You're wonderful." He squeezed her like he wanted to break her ribs. She shoved her pelvis against him, threw her arms and one leg around him and squeezed with all her slippery might. She smiled with half-closed eyes, and bit her grinning lip. He squeezed harder. She jammed her elbows into his sides and he made a meek "whoof" noise.

He dropped his arms, panting. "God, you're strong. How did such a small person get so strong?"

She grinned like a wolf. "I dunno." She let go and rolled off, and padded into the bathroom.

He followed her. "Are you a gymnast? A dancer?"

"No. I used to work out with weights in school." She dabbed between her legs with a nubbly white washcloth.

"University?"

"Yeah." She grabbed a fat economy-size jar of mentholated mouthwash, threw her head back and dumped a big splash into her mouth. Her cheeks worked vigorously as she sloshed it to and fro.

"Do you show your strength in the way you deal with people? I mean, outside of this place?"

She spat a green burst of mouthwash into the sink and looked at him. "Yeah. I do."

"How do you make them aware of it?"

She leaned against the sink, facing him with her arms behind her, her face thoughtful and soft. "I just . . . don't let people sway my thinking. I don't mold myself to fit what other people think I am." She came forward and put her arms around him. "It's interesting that you find strength in women attractive."

"Why?"

"Don't most older men like passive, dependent women?"

"Oh, that's an awful stereotype. Don't believe it."

"Is your wife a strong woman?"

"Yes, she is."

"Is she a lawyer too?"

"No. She's an antiquarian. She's got a small rare-book business."

"Did you meet her in college?"

"Yes. She studied art history and Latin. I was very impressed by that."

"Was she the first person you had sex with?"

"Almost."

"I bet that's why you see prostitutes." She let go of him and hurried to get dressed. The outermost flesh of her backside jiggled as she balanced on one spike heel and stuck the other through a leg of her underpants.

"What do you mean?"

"You had so little chance to screw around when you were young. You're trying to get it now." Her fingers were flying over the tiny buttons of her checked dress.

"You know, I think you're writing a book. That's what you're doing here. You're one of those journalists doing undercover work on prostitution."

She smiled miserably. "No."

"What do you do, besides work here? I think you do something. Am I right?"

"Of course I do something." She said "do" very sarcastically. She trotted to the mirror and got out her shiny silver lipstick case.

"What? What do you do?" He came toward her.

"I don't like to talk about it here." She opened her black leather bag to replace the lipstick. He glimpsed a roll of money and a packet of condoms in sky-blue tinfoil.

"Why don't you like to talk about it?"

"It makes me unhappy."

The telephone by the bed rasped, indicating the end of their hour.

HE SAW HER again the following night, and the night after that. He relished the way she laughed and playfully squeezed him around the stomach with her hefty thighs, or impatiently squiggled out from under him so they could change position. Her nonchalant reaction to his efforts to impress her sexually made him believe that her excitement, when it did occur, was real, that she wanted him. But if he so much as put a hand where she didn't want it, she'd fiercely slap it away and snap, "I don't like that."

"That's why I like you so much," he said. "You don't let me get away with anything. You're straightforward. Like my wife."

During that time, she told him that her real name was Jane. She still wouldn't talk to him about her life outside the pale green room. Instead, she asked him questions about himself. He was too embarrassed by now to tell her that he'd lied about his job. The lie turned out to be a mistake. Not only was she unimpressed by his false attorneyhood, she was an animal lover. The longest conversation they ever had on a single subject was about a cat that she'd had for fifteen years, until the fat, asthmatic thing finally keeled over. "He had all black fur except for his paws and his throat patch. He looked like he was wearing a tuxedo with a white cravat and gloves, and he was more of a gentleman than any human being I've ever known. I saw him protect a female cat from a dog once."

The cute stories he could've told about all the kittens and puppies that came into his office, clinging to the shirts of their owners, the birds with broken wings in white-spattered boxes!

THE FIFTH NIGHT he came to see her, she wasn't sitting in the waiting room with the other girls. "Where's Jane?" he asked the stretch-pants woman nervously.

"Jane? You must mean *Lisette*. She's busy right now," she answered in her placid, salad-oily voice. "Would you like to see another lady?"

A very young girl with burgundy hair smiled brightly at him. She was clutching a red patent-leather purse in purple-nailed hands.

"I'll wait for Lisette."

The stretch-pants woman widened her naked-lashed eyes in approval. "All right Fred, just sit down and make yourself comfortable. Would you like something to drink?"

She brought him a horribly flat, watered-down Scotch in a plastic cup. He held it, smiling and sweating.

The burgundy-headed girl curled her legs up on the couch and turned back to her Monopoly game with the contemptuous black-haired girl, who lay across the couch like an eel on a market stand. The stretch-pants woman tried to talk to him.

"Do you work around here, Fred?"

"No."

"What kind of business are you in?"

"Nothing. I mean, I'm retired." The patches of shirt under his arms were glued with sweaty hair-lace. Jane was being mauled by a fat oaf who didn't care that you could feel her innermost life on her skin.

The stretch-pants woman asked him to step into the kitchen. This house advertised its discretion and made sure men did not meet each other. He saw only the man's dismal black-suited shape through the slats of the swinging kitchen door as he stood there holding his drink, the ice cubes melting into a depressing fizz. He heard the black shape's blurred rumble and Jane's indifferent voice. She sounded much nicer when she said good-bye to him. The pale-eyed hostess opened the swinging door and gave him a flat smile. "Okay, sir, would you like to step out?"

Jane stood smiling in her checked dress, her hands behind her back, one white-socked ankle crossing the other, her chin tilted up. He remembered how he had seen her first, how she could've been any girl, any bland, half-friendly face behind any counter. He felt a funny-bone twinge as he realized how her body, her voice, her every fussy gesture had become part of a Jane network, a world of smells, sounds and touches that found its most acute focus when she had her legs around his back.

THE MINUTE SHE came into the room, he went to her and put his arms around her hips. "Hello, Jane."

"Hi."

"It was strange not seeing you out there waiting for me."

She looked puzzled.

"I guess I somehow got used to thinking of you as my own little girl. I didn't like the idea that you were with some other guy. Silly, huh?"

"Yes." She broke away and snapped the sheet out over the

bed. "Do you say things like that because you think I like to hear them?"

"Maybe. Some of the girls do, you know."

He could feel the sarcasm of her silence.

He watched her pull her dress off over her head and drop it on the aluminum chair. "I guess it's only natural that you've begun to get jaded."

She snorted. "I wouldn't call it that."

"What would you call it?"

She didn't answer. She sat on the bed and bent to take off her heels, leaving her socks on. When she looked at him again she said, "Do you really think it's a good idea for you to come to see me every night? It's awfully expensive. I know lawyers make a lot of money, but still. Won't your wife wonder where it's going?"

He sat next to her and put his hand on her shoulder. "Don't you see how special you are? No other girl I've seen like this would ever have thought to say something like that. All they can think of is how to get more money out of me and here you are worrying about how much I'm spending. I'm not trying to flatter you, you *are* different."

"Aren't you worried about getting AIDS?"

"From a girl like you? C'mon, don't put yourself down."

She smiled, sad and strained, but sort of affectionate, and put her hands on his shoulders. She felt to him like one of his puppy patients embracing him as he carried it across the room for a shot.

"I'm sorry I'm being so shitty," she said. "I just hate this job and this place."

"Here," he said. "I'm going to buy two hours, so we can just relax and unwind. You just lie down and get snuggled up in the sheet." He got up and turned off the light. He found a romantic jazz station on the radio. He undressed and got under the sheet with her, wrapping them both in a ball. He held her neck and felt her forehead against his shoulder. Her limbs were nestled and docile, as if all her stiff, pony-trot energy had vanished. The dim light of the gurgling fish tank cast an orangy glow over the room. "This is so nice and glamorous," he said.

"When is your wife coming back?" asked a voice from the nuzzling bundle on his arm.

"In three days." He sighed and stared at the stupid, lovely slivers of fish darting around their ugly castle.

OF COURSE HE knew that concern for his financial situation wasn't the only reason she'd suggested that he shouldn't see her so often. She was probably sick of him. He remembered dating well enough to know that women didn't like to be pursued too closely. It could seem sappy, he supposed, to come grinning in there after her every single night. The next night he would stay home, and read or watch television.

He enjoyed making dinner for himself. There were still a lot of good things left in the refrigerator—herring, a chunk of potato salad that was only slightly rancid, cream cheese, a jar of artichoke hearts, egg bread. It was too messy to eat in the kitchen—the counter was covered with encrusted plates and pans filled with silverware and water.

He arranged the slices and oily slabs on two different plates and carried the stuff into the living room to put on the coffee table. He clicked on the TV with his remote-control device, flicked the channels around a few times and then ignored it. He ate with his fingers and a plastic fork, mentally feeling over the events of the day, like a blind person groping through a drawer of personal effects. There had been the usual parade of cats and dogs, and one exotic bird with a mysterious illness. He had no idea what to do with the crested, vividly plumed thing, which was apparently worth a lot of money. He had pretended that he did, though, and the bird was sitting in his kennel now, gaping fiercely at the cats with its hooked beak.

Then there was the dog that he had had to put to sleep, a toothless, blind, smelly old monster with toenails like a dinosaur's. He thought the dog was probably grateful for the injection, and he said so, but that didn't console the homely adolescent girl who insisted on holding it right up until the end, tears running from under her glasses and down her pink, porous face. Poor lonely girl, he thought. He had wanted to say, "Don't worry dear, you're going to grow up to be a beauty. You're going to get married and have lots of wonderful children." Except it probably wasn't true.

He picked up his remote-control device and switched channels thoughtfully. What would Jane think when he didn't show up? Would she think he'd gotten bored with her, that he was never coming back? Would she go home wondering what had happened? He tried to picture her in her apartment. She had told him it was very small, only one room with a tiny bathroom. She said the bathroom had big windows and a skylight, and that she had so many plants in there that you couldn't use the toilet without arranging yourself around the plants. She said she didn't have a chair or a couch, that she sat on the floor to eat. When she came home from work she often ordered Chinese food and ate it straight from the cardboard boxes set out on the floor between her spread legs.

"What do you have for breakfast?" he asked.

"Ice cream, sometimes. If it's warm."

"What do you find to do in that little room?"

"I read a lot."

"What do you like to read?"

She named a few writers, one that he'd been forced to read in college and others he'd never heard of.

He picked up a tiny bit of herring and mashed it with the edges of his front teeth. Maybe he could start seeing Jane in her apartment. It would be more money for her certainly. He would like to spend time in that funny little place. He could buy her a chair. Maybe even a table.

He wouldn't be able to see Jane much at all once Sylvia got back. He thought of his wife getting on the plane in her green-and-white dress, the handle of her wicker suitcase in hand, her gray hair wound into an elegant bun that displayed her graceful neck and gently erect shoulders. Her smile was beautiful when she turned to wave good-bye.

He pictured Sylvia sitting in her favorite armchair across from him. She would be relaxed but sitting up straight on the tautly stuffed, salmon-colored cushions. Her legs would be crossed at the ankle. She would have her pale beige glasses on her nose, she would be in a trance over her latest book catalogues. If he stood up and put his hand on her shoulder, he would feel how slender and strong she still was, how well defined her small bones were.

He thought of her collection of rare books, arranged and locked in the glass cabinet in a sunny corner of her study. They were beautiful to look at and extremely expensive; other book dealers had offered her thousands of dollars for some of them. Every time he looked at them, he felt depressed.

One Christmas, he bought Sylvia a book entitled *Beautiful Sex*. It made him unhappy to remember that night when, with *Beautiful Sex* lying open on their bed to reveal a series of glossy pink-and-white photos, she cooperatively arranged herself into one of the more conventional positions illustrated, sighing as she did so. "Now honey," she said, "tell the truth. Don't you feel foolish doing this?"

He clicked off the TV and left the room, making a mental note to put the plates in the dishwasher before he went to bed.

THE NEXT DAY he drove to Manhattan right after work, without stopping at home for a shower. Perhaps Jane would notice the vague animal smell on him. She might ask him about it and he could tell her the truth about what he did.

It was already dark when he reached the city. He drove slowly through Times Square, fascinated by the night's ugliness. He stopped for a red light and looked up at a movie marquee towering on the corner, its dead white face advertising *The Spanking of Cindy*. There was a short man in a black leather jacket standing by the box office, hunching his cadaverous shoulders in the wind. "Now there's a queer," thought Fred.

"Wonder what he's doing in front of that movie house?" He looked at the marquee again, and noticed that the billboard next to it was painted with a girl in jeans thrusting her bottom out, her blond hair swirling across her back, her mouth open in laughter. It was an ad for jeans, but it suited the movie; he vaguely wondered if it had been arranged that way. He turned his head to look at the other side of the street and saw a broken old woman lying unconscious in the middle of the sidewalk with her face against the concrete, her ragged dress spattered across her ugly thighs. He was disgusted to see a young man pissing against the wall not two feet away from her. People were stepping over her as if she were an object, vicious people, it seemed to him, swinging their arms and legs in every direction, working their mouths, yelling at each other, eating hot dogs or Italian ices. What would it be like to be among them? He watched a couple of hookers in miniskirts and leather boots kick their way through a pile of garbage, screaming with laughter.

As soon as he got to a different neighborhood, he stopped at a Chinese flower store and bought Jane a single long-stemmed rose.

"Just so you wouldn't think I'd forgotten you," he said when he handed it to her.

"Thanks." She laid it on the night table, between the bottle of baby oil and the flowered Kleenex box. "Were you sick?"

"No. I just had some . . . things to do. Did you miss me?"

"Yeah." She began undoing her buttons.

"Listen, Jane. Tomorrow night will be the last night I can see you for a while. I was thinking maybe we could do something special."

"Like what?"

"Like you could call in sick and we could meet somewhere for dinner."

She put her hands in her lap and stared at him with something like alarm in her wide, smudged eyes.

"We could have dinner, go to a movie or a concert—whatever you'd like. Then we could go to a hotel—or maybe your apartment—and spend the night together."

She looked at her nails and picked them.

"Of course I realize that I can't ask you to take a night off work without making it worth your while. You'd do all right."

"How much?"

"Five hundred."

She didn't say anything.

"It could be very nice. We'd have time to really act like people in a relationship. What do you say?"

"I don't know."

"What are your reservations?"

"I don't think people in these circumstances can act like people having a relationship."

"Well, maybe you're right about that. But still it might be fun. I'd love to talk to you about a movie we'd seen or . . ."

"I think you'd be surprised if you found out what I'm like outside of here."

"I can't believe I wouldn't like you."

"You'd think I was weird."

"I'm not as closed-minded as you think."

"It's just that we might not have anything to talk about."

She didn't notice the animal smell.

HE WAITED FOR half an hour at their appointed meeting place. He wasn't surprised when she stood him up. He was somewhat surprised when he called the escort service to make an appointment and they told him she'd quit. She'd often told him she hated it and that she was going to quit soon, but girls talked like that all the time and stayed for months, even years.

Sylvia returned the next day, smiling and suntanned, happy to wash the dishes on the kitchen counter and pick up the damp, scrunched-up towels that were wadded up on every rack in the bathroom. She told him nice stories about the Arizona desert and the book fair she'd gone to there. He made love to her in a quiet, respectful way. She put her slender arms around his shoulders and held him tight. But when he tried to show her some of the things he'd done with Jane, he could feel her body become docile and patient.

HE DROVE INTO Manhattan about once a month to pay for girls. He went to different establishments each time, hoping to find Jane. Every time he saw a new girl he suffered from nostalgia and the irritating nag of unfavorable comparison.

When he thought of her he didn't feel love or anything like it. He felt a sort of painful fondness. He remembered having a similar feeling when he ran into a girl he'd been crazy about in college and saw that she'd gotten fat and was buying a box of Pampers. It was strange to be having that feeling now for someone he met in a brothel.

It was almost a year later when he went into Manhattan one afternoon to do Christmas shopping. The city had a different quality during the day. When he thought of daytime Manhattan, the first thing he imagined was a pretty young woman with dark, wavy hair and an unnatural burst of red on both cheeks, walking down the wide, crowded sidewalks more quickly and sharply than anyone had to, her worn, brightly colored shoes marching in close, narrow steps, her cheap, fashionable jacket open to show her belted waist, her handbag held tightly under her arm, her head turned away from anyone who might look at her, turned so she could skim the window displays as she clipped by, one hand jammed into a pocket of her jacket, nothing swinging loose. And then he thought of a lumbering, middle-aged man in a suit, his glasses on the tip of his nose, a lace of greasy crumbs on his lapels, his briefcase clutched at his side, rolling down the street as fast as his plump body would go, jacket flapping open, his bored eyes skimming quickly over the girl and every other girl like her as he rushed to the office.

There was something sad and poignant about this image, but that didn't prevent him from spending as much time staring at girls as he spent shopping. At the end of the day he'd found only two gifts—a sweater-guard made of twin silver bunnies for a teenaged niece and, for Sylvia, an elegant old-fashioned wristwatch from a Village watch shop.

By the time he had found these gifts it was late afternoon and he was hungry. The watch shop was close to a particular café he liked because the food was good and because he enjoyed looking at the strangely dressed young people who often went there.

The hostess, a tall girl with a high, perspiring forehead and pleasantly freckled cheeks, smiled as she ran toward him with a long plastic menu, and immediately raced him to a corner table that had yellow flowers in a green bottle on it. "Enjoy," she panted, and ran off. He shook off his heavy coat and looked over the crowd with relish. He picked up the menu and glanced at the table on his left. From then on the rest of the people in the room became a herd of anonymous colored shapes that could've been eating their fingers for all he cared. Jane was sitting next to him. She was with a boy. She glanced at him too quickly for him to see her expression. She immediately put her elbow on the table and her hand to her face.

He looked away. He squeezed the laminated menu between his fingers. He read the description of cold pasta three times. He turned his head and stared at her. She'd grown her hair out and was wearing it up in a ponytail that looked like a ball of brown wool. Even with her hand blocking her face, he could see that she wore almost no makeup, that her skin looked fresh and rosy in daylight. She was wearing an old cream-colored sweater with pink and blue tulips woven into it.

He stared at the boy who sat across the table from her. He was a homely kid in his early twenties with a thick thatch of badly cut sandy hair that roared up over his forehead in a hideous bush. His crooked tortoiseshell glasses had one arm held on by a piece of grayish masking tape, and he wore a brown sweater thick enough to be a coat. His complexion was ruddy and coarse, his expression horribly cheerful.

On a cruel impulse, he leaned forward and leered at the

kid. The boy glanced at him affably and buried his spoon in the bowl of stew he had before him.

"Yeah," he said. "Simone's been experiencing a lot of rejection from her old friends."

"I'm not really rejecting her," said Jane. "I just want to put some distance between us emotionally. Enough so that she doesn't feel compelled to call me every time her psychotic girlfriend starts slapping her around."

She was going to sit there and continue her conversation.

"How many times has it been now?" asked the ugly kid through a mouthful of stew.

"Five, counting the last girlfriend, three times at six in the morning. I mean, my God, where does she find these women? I didn't think lesbians were into beating each other up."

A waitress in a short black leather skirt and leopard-skin tights charged his table. "Are you ready to order?"

"No, no, not yet." She smiled and roared off. He lowered his head to the plastic menu. He was not sure why this experience was such an unpleasant one.

"I mean, her life is her life," said Jane. "But the last time she called she actually got me over there to mediate between her and this crazed, muscle-bound black belt in God knows what, and they're screaming at each other and Simone is threatening to cut her wrist, and oh, it was a mess."

"It sounds very theatrical."

"It's like not only is she going to be a masochistic asshole, she wants an audience. I know I'm being cruel."

"I don't think you're cruel. Most people wouldn't have put up with it as long as you did."

"It's so tragic, though. She's such a great person. And I know at least two really attractive, charming girls who're dying to get into her pants, but she's not interested. She likes bitches."

"Look, Simone sets herself up for disaster. She always has. Then she tries to drag anyone within range into it."

They gnawed their food righteously. Jane still had her elbow up and her hand blocking her face.

"How's the job search going?" she asked.

"It looks good so far. Like I said, I think I did all right at Ardis films. And I know somebody who used to work there. The only thing about that place is that the people are so pretentious. Everybody there is a 'close personal friend' of Herzog or Beth B. or somebody. Everybody has this certain pompous accent, especially when they say 'film.'"

"That's professional New York," said Jane. "People who work in the arts are always that way."

"Maybe I'll just come work in the museum with you."

"If we're not on strike. And it looks like we're going to be."

"Could you survive on free-lance work if that happened?"

"Maybe." She dropped the hand at her chin, exposing her face to him. "I don't know."

He got up from the table, looking straight ahead, and slowly gathered his coat around his shoulders. He could sense no movement of her head turning to look at him as he left the restaurant. He wouldn't realize that he'd left the bag containing the bunny sweater-guard and Sylvia's watch under the table until he arrived home in Westchester.

FROM **the sheltering sky**
Paul Bowles

H E WALKED THROUGH the streets, unthinkingly seeking the darker ones, glad to be alone and to feel the night air against his face. The streets were crowded. People pushed against him as they passed, stared from doorways and windows, made comments openly to each other about him—whether with sympathy or not he was unable to tell from their faces—and they sometimes ceased to walk merely in order to watch him.

"How friendly are they? Their faces are masks. They all look a thousand years old. What little energy they have is only the blind, mass desire to live, since no one of them eats enough to give him his own personal force. But what do they think of me? Probably nothing. Would one of them help me if I were to have an accident? Or would I lie here in the street until the police found me? What motive could any one of them *have* for helping me? They have no religion left. Are they Moslems or Christians? They don't know. They know money, and when they get it, all they want is to eat. But what's wrong with that? Why do I feel this way about them? Guilt at being well fed and healthy among them? But suffering is equally divided among all men; each has the same amount to undergo. . . ." Emotionally he felt that this last idea was untrue, but at the moment it was a necessary belief: it is not always easy to support the stares of hungry people. Thinking that way he could walk on through the streets. It was as if either he or they did not exist. Both suppositions were possible. The Spanish maid at the hotel had said to him that noon: *"La vida es pena."* "Of course," he had replied, feeling false even as he spoke, asking himself if any American can truthfully accept a definition of life which makes it synonymous with suffering. But at the moment he had approved her sentiment because she was old, withered, so clearly of the people. For years it had been one of his superstitions that reality and true perception were to be found in the conversation of the laboring classes. Even though now he saw clearly that their formulas of thought and speech are as strict and as patterned, and thus as far removed from any profound expression of truth as those of any other class, often he found himself still in the act of waiting, with the unreasoning belief that gems of wisdom might yet issue from their mouths. As he walked along, his nervousness was made manifest to him by the sudden consciousness that he was repeatedly tracing rapid figure-eights with his right index finger. He sighed and made himself stop doing it.

His spirits rose a bit as he came out onto a square that was relatively brightly lighted. The cafés on all four sides of the little plaza had put tables and chairs not only across the sidewalks, but in the street as well, so that it would have been impossible for a vehicle to pass through without upsetting them. In the center of the square was a tiny park adorned by four plane trees that had been trimmed to look like open parasols. Underneath the trees there were at least a dozen dogs of various sizes, milling about in a close huddle, and all barking frantically. He made his way slowly across the square, trying to avoid the dogs. As he moved along cautiously under the trees he became aware that at each step he was crushing something beneath his feet. The ground was covered with large insects; their hard shells broke with little explosions that were quite audible to him even amidst the noise the dogs were making. He was aware that ordinarily he would have experienced a thrill of disgust on contact with such a phenomenon, but unreasonably tonight he felt instead a childish triumph. "I'm in a bad way and so what?" The few scattered people sitting at the tables were for the most part silent, but when they spoke, he heard all three of the town's tongues: Arabic, Spanish, and French.

Slowly the street began to descend; this surprised him because he imagined that the entire town was built on the slope facing the harbor, and he had consciously chosen to walk inland rather than toward the waterfront. The odors in the air grew ever stronger. They were varied, but they all represented filth of one sort or another. This proximity with, as it were, a forbidden element, served to elate him. He abandoned himself to the perverse pleasure he found in continuing mechanically to put one foot in front of the other, even though he was quite clearly aware of his fatigue. "Suddenly I'll find myself turning around and going back," he thought. But not until then, because he would not make the decision to do it. The impulse to retrace his steps delayed itself from moment to moment. Finally he ceased being surprised: a faint vision began to haunt his mind. It was Kit, seated by the open window, filing her nails and looking out over the town. And as he found his fancy returning more often, as the minutes went by, to that scene, unconsciously he felt himself the protagonist, Kit the spectator. The validity of his existence at that moment was predicated on the assumption that she had not moved, but was still sitting there. It was as if she could still see him from the window, tiny and far away as he was, walking rhythmically uphill and down, through light and shadow; it was as if only she knew when he would turn around and walk the other way.

The street lights were very far apart now, and the streets had left off being paved. Still there were children in the gutters, playing with the garbage and screeching. A small stone suddenly hit him in the back. He wheeled about, but it was too dark to see where it had come from. A few seconds later another stone, coming from in front of him, landed against his knee. In the dim light, he saw a group of small children scattering before him. More stones came from the other direction, this time without hitting him. When he got beyond, to a point where there was a light, he stopped and tried to watch the two groups in battle, but they all ran off into the dark, and so he started up again, his gait as mechanical and rhythmical as before. A wind that was dry and warm, coming up the street out of the blackness before him, met him head on. He sniffed at the fragments of mystery in it, and again he felt an unaccustomed exaltation.

Even though the street became constantly less urban, it seemed reluctant to give up; huts continued to line it on both sides. Beyond a certain point there were no more lights, and the dwellings themselves lay in darkness. The wind, straight from the south, blew across the barren mountains that were invisible ahead of him, over the vast flat sebkha to the edges of the town, raising curtains of dust that climbed to the crest of the hill and lost themselves in the air above the harbor. He stood still. The last possible suburb had been strung on the street's thread. Beyond the final hut the garbage and rubble floor of the road sloped abruptly downward in three directions. In the dimness below were shallow, crooked canyon-like formations. Port raised his eyes to the sky: the powdery course of the Milky Way was like a giant rift across the heavens that let the faint white light through. In the distance he heard a motorcycle. When its sound was finally gone, there was nothing to hear but an occasional cockcrow, like the highest part of a repeated melody whose other notes were inaudible.

He started down the bank to the right, sliding among the fish skeletons and dust. Once below, he felt out a rock that seemed clean and sat down on it. The stench was overpowering. He lit a match, saw the ground thick with chicken feathers and decayed melon rinds. As he rose to his feet he heard steps above him at the end of the street. A figure stood at the top of the embankment. It did not speak, yet Port was certain that it had seen him, had followed him, and knew he was sitting down there. It lit a cigarette, and for a moment he saw an Arab wearing a chechia on his head. The match, thrown into the air, made a fading parabola, the face disappeared, and only the red point of the cigarette remained. The cock crowed several times. Finally the man cried out.

"*Qu'est-ce ti cherches là?*"

"Here's where the trouble begins," thought Port. He did not move.

The Arab waited a bit. He walked to the very edge of the slope. A dislodged tin can rolled noisily down toward the rock where Port sat.

"*Hé! M'sieu! Qu'est-ce ti vo?*"

He decided to answer. His French was good.

"Who? Me? Nothing."

The Arab bounded down the bank and stood in front of him. With the characteristic impatient, almost indignant gestures he pursued his inquisition. What are you doing here all alone? Where do you come from? What do you want here? Are you looking for something? To which Port answered wearily: Nothing. That way. Nothing. No.

For a moment the Arab was silent, trying to decide what direction to give the dialogue. He drew violently on his cigarette several times until it glowed very bright, then he flicked it away and exhaled the smoke.

"Do you want to take a walk?" he said.

"What? A walk? Where?"

"Out there." His arm waved toward the mountains.

"What's out there?"

"Nothing."

There was another silence between them.

"I'll pay you a drink," said the Arab. And immediately on that: "What's your name?"

"Jean," said Port.

The Arab repeated the name twice, as if considering its merits. "Me," tapping his chest, "Smaïl. So, do we go and drink?"

"No."

"Why not?"

"I don't feel like it."

"You don't feel like it. What do you feel like doing?"

"Nothing."

All at once the conversation began again from the beginning. Only the now truly outraged inflection of the Arab's voice marked any difference: *"Qu'est-ce ti fi là? Qu'est-ce ti cherches?"* Port rose and started to climb up the slope, but it was difficult going. He kept sliding back down. At once the Arab was beside him, tugging at his arm. "Where are you going, Jean?" Without answering Port made a great effort and gained the top. *"Au revoir,"* he called, walking quickly up the middle of the street. He heard a desperate scrambling behind him; a moment later the man was at his side.

"You didn't wait for me," he said in an aggrieved tone.

"No. I said good-bye."

"I'll go with you."

Port did not answer. They walked a good distance in silence. When they came to the first street light, the Arab reached into his pocket and pulled out a worn wallet. Port glanced at it and continued to walk.

"Look!" cried the Arab, waving it in his face. Port did not look. "What is it?" he said flatly.

"I was in the Fifth Battalion of Sharpshooters. Look at the paper! Look! You'll see!"

Port walked faster. Soon there began to be people in the street. No one stared at them. One would have said that the presence of the Arab beside him made him invisible. But now he was no longer sure of the way. It would never do to let this be seen. He continued to walk straight ahead as if there were no doubt in his mind. "Over the crest of the hill and down," he said to himself, "and I can't miss it."

Everything looked unfamiliar: the houses, the streets, the cafés, even the formation of the town with regard to the hill. Instead of finding a summit from which to begin the downward walk, he discovered that here the streets all led perceptibly upward; no matter which way he turned; to descend he would have had to go back. The Arab walked solemnly along with him, now beside him, now slipping behind when there was not enough room to walk two abreast. He no longer made attempts at conversation; Port noticed with relish that he was a little out of breath.

"I can keep this up all night if I have to," he thought, "but how the hell will I get to the hotel?"

All at once they were in a street which was no more than a passageway. Above their heads the opposite walls jutted out to within a few inches of each other. For an instant Port hesitated: this was not the kind of street he wanted to walk in, and besides, it so obviously did not lead to the hotel. In that short moment the Arab took charge. He said: "You don't know this street? It's called Rue de la Mer Rouge. You know it? Come on. There are *cafés arabes* up this way. Just a little way. Come on."

Port considered. He wanted at all costs to keep up the pretense of being familiar with the town.

"Je ne sais pas si je veux y aller ce soir," he reflected, aloud.

The Arab began to pull Port's sleeve in his excitement. *"Si, si!"* he cried. *"Viens!* I'll pay you a drink."

"I don't drink. It's very late."

Two cats nearby screamed at each other. The Arab made a hissing noise and stamped his feet; they ran off in opposite directions.

"We'll have tea, then," he pursued.

Port sighed. *"Bien,"* he said.

The café had a complicated entrance. They went through a low arched door, down a dim hall into a small garden. The air reeked of lilies, and it was also tinged with the sour smell of drains. In the dark they crossed the garden and climbed a long flight of stone steps. The staccato sound of a hand drum came from above, tapping indolent patterns above a sea of voices.

"Do we sit outside or in?" the Arab asked.

"Outside," said Port. He sniffed the invigorating smell of hashish smoke, and unconsciously smoothed his hair as they arrived at the top of the stairs. The Arab noticed even that small gesture. "No ladies here, you know."

"Oh, I know."

Through a doorway he caught a glimpse of the long succession of tiny, brightly-lit rooms, and the men seated everywhere on the reed matting that covered the floors. They all wore either white turbans or red chechias on their heads, a detail which lent the scene such a strong aspect of homogeneity that Port exclaimed: "Ah!" as they passed by the door. When they were on the terrace in the starlight, with an oud being plucked idly in the dark nearby, he said to his companion: "But I didn't know there was anything like this left in this city." The Arab did not understand. "Like this?" he echoed. "How?"

"With nothing but Arabs. Like the inside here. I thought all the cafés were like the ones in the street, all mixed up; Jews, French, Spanish, Arabs together. I thought the war had changed everything."

The Arab laughed. "The war was bad. A lot of people died. There was nothing to eat. That's all. How would that change the cafés? Oh no, my friend. It's the same as always." A moment later he said: "So you haven't been here since the war! But you were here before the war?"

"Yes," said Port. This was true; he had once spent an afternoon in the town when his boat had made a brief call there.

The tea arrived; they chatted and drank it. Slowly the image of Kit sitting in the window began to take shape again in Port's mind. At first, when he became conscious of it, he felt a pang of guilt. Then his fantasy took a hand, and he saw her face, tight-lipped with fury as she undressed and flung her flimsy pieces of clothing across the furniture. By now she had surely given up waiting and gone to bed. He shrugged his shoulders and grew pensive, rinsing what was left of his tea around and around in the bottom of the glass, and following with his eyes the circular motion he was making.

"You're sad," said Smaïl.

"No, no." He looked up and smiled wistfully, then resumed watching the glass.

"You live only a short time. *Il faut rigoler.*"

Port was impatient; he was not in the mood for café philosophizing.

"Yes, I know," he said shortly, and he sighed. Smaïl pinched his arm. His eyes were shining.

"When we leave here, I'll take you to see a friend of mine."

"I don't want to meet him," said Port, adding: "Thank you anyway."

"Ah, you're really sad," laughed Smaïl. "It's a girl. Beautiful as the moon."

Port's heart missed a beat. "A girl," he repeated automatically, without taking his eyes from the glass. He was perturbed to witness his own interior excitement. He looked at Smaïl.

"A girl?" he said. "You mean a whore."

Smaïl was mildly indignant. "A whore? Ah, my friend, you don't know me. I wouldn't introduce you to that. *C'est de la saloperie, ça!* This is a friend of mine, very elegant, very nice. When you meet her, you'll see."

The musician stopped playing the oud. Inside the café they were calling out numbers for the lotto game: *"Ouahad aou tletine! Arbaine!"*

Port said: "How old is she?"

Smaïl hesitated. "About sixteen. Sixteen or seventeen."

"Or twenty or twenty-five," suggested Port, with a leer.

Again Smaïl was indignant. "What do you mean, twenty-five? I tell you she's sixteen or seventeen. You don't believe me? Listen. You meet her. If you don't like her, you just pay for the tea and we'll go out again. Is that all right?"

"And if I do like her?"

"Well, you'll do whatever you want."

"But I'll pay her?"

"But of course you'll pay her."

Port laughed. "And you say she's not a whore."

Smaïl leaned over the table towards him and said with a great show of patience: "Listen, Jean. She's a dancer. She only arrived from her bled in the desert a few weeks ago. How can she be a whore if she's not registered and doesn't live in the quartier? Eh? Tell me! You pay her because you take up her time. She dances in the quartier, but she has no room, no bed there. She's not a whore. So now, shall we go?"

Port thought a long time, looked up at the sky, down into the garden, and all around the terrace before answering: "Yes. Let's go. Now."

WHEN THEY LEFT the café it seemed to him that they were going more or less in the same direction from which they had just come. There were fewer people in the streets and the air was cooler. They walked for a good distance through the Casbah, making a sudden exit through a tall gateway onto a high, open space outside the walls. Here it was silent, and the stars were very much in evidence. The pleasure he felt at the unexpected freshness of the air and the relief at being in the open once more, out from under the overhanging houses, served to delay Port in asking the question that was in his mind: "Where are we going?" But as they continued along what seemed a parapet at the edge of a deep, dry moat, he finally gave voice to it. Smaïl replied vaguely that the girl lived with some friends at the edge of town.

"But we're already in the country," objected Port.

"Yes, it's the country," said Smaïl.

It was perfectly clear that he was being evasive now; his character seemed to have changed again. The beginning of intimacy was gone. To Port he was once more the anonymous dark figure that had stood above him in the garbage at the end of the street, smoking a bright cigarette. *You can still break it up. Stop walking. Now.* But the combined even rhythm of their feet on the stones was too powerful. The parapet made a wide curve and the ground below dropped steeply away into a deeper darkness. The moat had ended some hundred feet back. They were now high above the upper end of an open valley.

"The Turkish fortress," remarked Smaïl, pounding on the stones with his heel.

"Listen to me," began Port angrily; "where are we going?" He looked at the rim of uneven black mountains ahead of them on the horizon.

"Down there." Smaïl pointed to the valley. A moment later he stopped walking. "Here are the stairs." They leaned over the edge. A narrow iron staircase was fastened to the side of the wall. It had no railing and led straight downward at a steep angle.

"It's a long way," said Port.

"Ah, yes, it's the Turkish fortress. You see that light down there?" He indicated a faint red glimmer that came and went, almost directly beneath them. "That's the tent where she lives."

"The tent!"

"There are no houses down here. Only tents. There are a lot of them. *On descend?*"

Smaïl went first, keeping close to the wall. "Touch the stones," he said.

As they approached the bottom, he saw that the feeble glow of light was a dying bonfire built in an open space between two large nomad tents. Smaïl suddenly stopped to listen. There was an indistinguishable murmur of male voices. *"Allons-y,"* he muttered; his voice sounded satisfied.

They reached the end of the staircase. There was hard ground beneath their feet. To his left Port saw the black silhouette of a huge agave plant in flower.

"Wait here," whispered Smaïl. Port was about to light a cigarette; Smaïl hit his arm angrily. "No!" he whispered. "But what is it?" began Port, highly annoyed at the show of secrecy. Smaïl disappeared.

Leaning against the cold rock wall, Port waited to hear a

break in the monotonous, low-pitched conversation, an exchange of greetings, but nothing happened. The voices went on exactly as before, an uninterrupted flow of expressionless sounds. "He must have gone into the other tent," he thought. One side of the farther tent flickered pink in the light of the bonfire; beyond was darkness. He edged a few steps along the wall, trying to see the entrance of the tent, but it faced in the other direction. Then he listened for the sound of voices there, but none came. For no reason at all he suddenly heard Kit's parting remark as he had left her room: "After all, it's much more your business than it is mine." Even now the words meant nothing in particular to him, but he remembered the tone in which she had said it: she had sounded hurt and rebellious. And it was all about Tunner. He stood up straight. "He's been after her," he whispered aloud. Abruptly he turned and went to the staircase, started up it. After six steps he stopped and looked around. "What can I do tonight?" he thought. "I'm using this as an excuse to get out of here, because I'm afraid. What the hell, he'll never get her."

A figure darted out from between the two tents and ran lightly to the foot of the stairs. "Jean!" it whispered. Port stood still.

"*Ah! Ti es là!* What are you doing up there? Come on!"

Port walked slowly back down. Smaïl stepped out of his way, took his arm.

"Why can't we talk?" whispered Port. Smaïl squeezed his arm. "Shh!" he said into his ear. They skirted the nearer tent, brushing past a clump of high thistles, and made their way over the stones to the entrance of the other.

"Take off your shoes," commanded Smaïl, slipping off his sandals.

"Not a good idea," thought Port. "No," he said aloud.

"Shh!" Smaïl pushed him inside, shoes still on.

The central part of the tent was high enough to stand up in. A short candle stuck on top of a chest near the entrance provided the light, so that the nether parts of the tent were in almost complete darkness. Lengths of straw matting had been spread on the ground at senseless angles; objects were scattered everywhere in utter disorder. There was no one in the tent waiting for them.

"Sit down," said Smaïl, acting the host. He cleared the largest piece of matting of an alarm clock, a sardine can, and an ancient, incredibly greasy pair of overalls. Port sat down and put his elbows on his knees. On the mat next to him lay a chipped enamel bedpan, half filled with a darkish liquid. There were bits of stale bread everywhere. He lit a cigarette without offering one to Smaïl, who returned to stand near the entrance, looking out.

And suddenly she stepped inside—a slim, wild-looking girl with great dark eyes. She was dressed in spotless white, with a white turbanlike headdress that pulled her hair tightly backward, accentuating the indigo designs tattooed on her forehead. Once inside the tent, she stood quite still, looking at Port with something of the expression, he thought, the young bull often wears as he takes the first few steps into the glare of the arena. There was bewilderment, fear, and a passive expectancy in her face as she stared quietly at him.

"Ah, here she is!" said Smaïl, still in a hushed voice. "Her name is Marhnia." He waited a bit. Port rose and stepped forward to take her hand. "She doesn't speak French," Smaïl explained. Without smiling, she touched Port's hand lightly with her own and raised her fingers to her lips. Bowing, she said, in what amounted almost to a whisper: *"Ya sidi, la bess álik? Eglès, baraka 'laou'fik."* With gracious dignity and a peculiar modesty of movement, she unstuck the lighted candle from the chest, and walked across to the back of the tent, where a blanket stretched from the ceiling formed a partial alcove. Before disappearing behind the blanket, she turned her head to them, and said, gesturing: *"Agi! Agi menah!"* The two men followed her into the alcove, where an old mattress had been laid on some low boxes in an attempt to make a salon. There was a tiny tea table beside the improvised divan, and a pile of small, lumpy cushions lay on the mat by the table. The girl set the candle down on the bare earth and began to arrange the cushions along the mattress.

"*Essmah!*" she said to Port, and to Smaïl: "*Tsekellem bellatsi.*" Then she went out. He laughed and called after her in a low voice: "*Fhemtek!*" Port was intrigued by the girl, but the language barrier annoyed him, and he was even more irritated by the fact that Smaïl and she could converse together in his presence. "She's gone to get fire," said Smaïl. "Yes, yes," said Port, "but why do we have to whisper?" Smaïl rolled his eyes toward the tent's entrance. "The men in the other tent," he said.

Presently she returned, carrying an earthen pot of bright coals. While she was boiling the water and preparing the tea, Smaïl chatted with her. Her replies were always grave, her voice hushed but pleasantly modulated. It seemed to Port that she was much more like a young nun than a café dancer. At the same time he did not in the least trust her, being content to sit and marvel at the delicate movements of her nimble, henna-stained fingers as she tore the stalks of mint apart and stuffed them into the little teapot.

When she had sampled the tea several times and eventually had found it to her liking, she handed them each a glass, and with a solemn air sat back on her haunches and began to drink hers. "Sit here," said Port, patting the couch beside him. She indicated that she was quite happy where she was, and thanked him politely. Turning her attention to Smaïl, she proceeded to engage him in a lengthy conversation during which Port sipped his tea and tried to relax. He had an oppressive sensation that daybreak was near at hand—surely not more than an hour or so away, and he felt that all this time was being wasted. He looked anxiously at his watch; it had stopped at five minutes of two. But it was still going. Surely it must be later than that. Marhnia addressed a question to Smaïl which seemed to include Port. "She wants to know if you have heard the story about Outka, Mimouna, and Aïcha," said Smaïl. "No," said Port. "*Goul lou, goul lou,*" said Marhnia to Smaïl, urging him.

"There are three girls from the mountains, from a place near Marhnia's bled, and they are called Outka, Mimouna, and Aïcha." Marhnia was nodding her head slowly in affirmation, her large soft eyes fixed on Port. "They go to seek their fortune in the M'Zab. Most girls from the mountains go to Alger, Tunis, here, to earn money, but these girls want one thing more than everything else. They want to drink tea in the Sahara." Marhnia continued to nod her head; she was keeping up with the story solely by means of the place-names as Smaïl pronounced them.

"I see," said Port, who had no idea whether the story was a humorous one or a tragic one; he was determined to be careful, so that he could pretend to savor it as much as she clearly hoped he would. He only wished it might be short.

"In the M'Zab the men are all ugly. The girls dance in the cafés of Ghardaia, but they are always sad; they still want to have tea in the Sahara." Port glanced again at Marhnia. Her expression was completely serious. He nodded his head again. "So, many months pass, and they are still in the M'Zab, and they are very, very sad, because the men are all so ugly. They are very ugly there, like pigs. And they don't pay enough money to the poor girls so they can go and have tea in the Sahara." Each time he said "Sahara," which he pronounced in the Arabic fashion, with a vehement accent on the first syllable, he stopped for a moment. "One day a Targui comes, he is tall and handsome, on a beautiful mehari; he talks to Outka, Mimouna, and Aïcha, he tells them about the desert, down there where he lives, his bled, and they listen, and their eyes are big. Then he says: 'Dance for me,' and they dance. Then he makes love with all three, he gives a silver piece to Outka, a silver piece to Mimouna, and a silver piece to Aïcha. At daybreak he gets on his mehari and goes away to the south. After that they are very sad, and the M'Zabi look uglier than ever to them, and they only are thinking of the tall Targui who lives in the Sahara." Port lit a cigarette; then he noticed Marhnia looking expectantly at him, and he passed her the pack. She took one, and with a crude pair of tongs elegantly lifted a live coal to the end of it. It ignited immediately, whereupon she passed it to Port, taking his in exchange. He smiled at her. She bowed almost imperceptibly.

"Many months go by, and still they can't earn enough money to go to the Sahara. They have kept the silver pieces, because all three are in love with the Targui. And they are always sad. One day they say: 'We are going to finish like this—always sad, without ever having tea in the Sahara—so now we must go anyway, even without money.' And they put all their money together, even the three silver pieces, and they buy a teapot and a tray and three glasses, and they buy bus tickets to El Goléa. And there they have only a little money left, and they give it all to a bachhamar who is taking his caravan south to the Sahara. So he lets them ride with his caravan. And one night, when the sun is going to go down, they come to the great dunes of sand, and they think: 'Ah, now we are in the Sahara; we are going to make tea.' The moon comes up, all the men are asleep except the guard. He is sitting with the camels play-ing his flute." Smaïl wriggled his fingers in front of his mouth. "Outka, Mimouna, and Aïcha go away from the caravan quietly with their tray and their teapot and their glasses. They are going to look for the highest dune so they can see all the Sahara. Then they are going to make tea. They walk a long time. Outka says: 'I see a high dune,' and they go to it and climb up to the top. Then Mimouna says: 'I see a dune over there. It's much higher and we can see all the way to In Salah from it.' So they go to it, and it is much higher. But when they get to the top, Aïcha says: 'Look! There's the highest dune of all. We can see to Tamanrasset. That's where the Targui lives.' The sun came up and they kept walking. At noon they were very hot. But they came to the dune and they climbed and climbed. When they got to the top they were very tired and they said: 'We'll rest a little and then make tea.' But first they set out the tray and the teapot and the glasses. Then they lay down and slept. And then"—Smaïl paused and looked at

Port—"Many days later another caravan was passing and a man saw something on top of the highest dune there. And when they went up to see, they found Outka, Mimouna, and Aïcha; they were still there, lying the same way as when they had gone to sleep. And all three of the glasses," he held up his own little tea glass, "were full of sand. That was how they had their tea in the Sahara."

There was a long silence. It was obviously the end of the story. Port looked at Marhnia; she was still nodding her head, her eyes fixed on him. He decided to hazard a remark. "It's very sad," he said. She immediately inquired of Smaïl what he had said. *"Gallik merhmoum bzef,"* translated Smaïl. She shut her eyes slowly and continued to nod her head. *"Ei oua!"* she said, opening them again. Port turned quickly to Smaïl. "Listen, it's very late. I want to arrange a price with her. How much should I give her?"

Smaïl looked scandalized. "You can't do that as if you were dealing with a whore! *Ci pas une putain, je t'ai dit!"*

"But I'll pay her if I stay with her?"

"Of course."

"Then I want to arrange it now."

"I can't do that for you, my friend."

Port shrugged his shoulders and stood up. "I've got to go. It's late."

Marhnia looked quickly from one man to the other. Then she said a word or two in a very soft voice to Smaïl, who frowned but stalked out of the tent yawning.

They lay on the couch together. She was very beautiful, very docile, very understanding, and still he did not trust her. She declined to disrobe completely, but in her delicate gestures of refusal he discerned an ultimate yielding, to bring about which it would require only time. With time he could have had her confidence; tonight he could only have that which had been taken for granted from the beginning. He reflected on this as he lay, looking into her untroubled face, remembered that he was leaving for the south in a day or two, inwardly swore at his luck, and said to himself: "Better half a loaf." Marhnia leaned over and snuffed the candle between her fingers. For a second there was utter silence, utter blackness. Then he felt her soft arms slowly encircle his neck, and her lips on his forehead.

Almost immediately a dog began to howl in the distance. For a while he did not hear it; when he did, it troubled him. It was the wrong music for the moment. Soon he found himself imagining that Kit was a silent onlooker. The fantasy stimulated him—the lugubrious howling no longer bothered him.

Not more than a quarter of an hour later, he got up and peered around the blanket, to the flap of the tent: it was still dark. He was seized with an abrupt desire to be out of the place. He sat down on the couch and began to arrange his clothing. The two arms stole up again, locked themselves about his neck. Firmly he pulled them away, gave them a few playful pats. Only one came up this time; the other slipped inside his jacket and he felt his chest being caressed. Some indefinable false movement there made him reach inside to put his hand on hers. His wallet was already between her fingers. He yanked it away from her and pushed her back down on the mattress. "Ah!" she cried, very loud. He rose and stumbled noisily through the welter of objects that lay between him and the exit. This time she screamed, briefly. The voices in the other tent became audible. With his wallet still in his hand he rushed out, turned sharply to the left, and began to run toward the wall. He fell twice, once against a rock and once because the ground sloped unexpectedly down. As he rose the second time, he saw a man coming from one side to cut him off from the staircase. He was limping, but he was nearly there. He did get there. All the way up the stairs it seemed to him that someone immediately behind him would have hold of one of his legs during the next second. His lungs were an enormous pod of pain, would burst instantly. His mouth was open, drawn down at the sides, his teeth clenched, and the air whistled between them as he drew breath. At the top he turned, and seizing a boulder he could not lift, he did lift it, and hurled it down the staircase. Then he breathed deeply and began to run along the parapet. The sky was palpably lighter, an immaculate gray clarity spreading upward from behind the low hills in the east. He could not run very far. His heart was beating in his head and neck. He knew he never could reach the town. On the side of the road away from the valley there was a wall, too high to be climbed. But a few hundred feet farther on, it had been broken down for a short distance, and a talus of stones and dirt made a perfect stile. He cut back inside the wall in the direction from which he had just come, and hurried panting up a gradual side hill studded with the flat stone beds which are Moslem tombstones. Finally he sat down for a minute, his head in his hands, and was conscious of several things at once: the pain of his head and chest, the fact that he no longer held his wallet, and the loud sound of his own heart, which, however, did not keep him from thinking he heard the excited voices of his pursuers below in the road a moment later. He rose and staggered on upward over the graves. Eventually the hill sloped downward in the other direction. He felt a little safer. But each minute the light of day was nearer; it would be easy to spot his solitary figure from a distance, wandering over the hill. He began to run again, downhill, always in the same direction, staggering now and then, never looking up for fear he should fall; this went on for a long time; the graveyard was left behind. Finally he reached a high spot covered with bushes and cactus, but from which he could dominate the entire immediate countryside. He sat down among the bushes. It was perfectly quiet. The sky was white. Occasionally he stood up carefully and peered out. And so it was that when the sun came up he looked between two oleanders and saw it reflected red across the miles of glittering salt sebkha that lay between him and the mountains.

glory hole
Alfred Chester

M Y NAZARENE," SAYS Dris, "is only twenty-five and he's got flesh on him. And he's an American."

"Your Nazarene is forty if he's a day," says Abdlkadr. "Mine is thirty-two and was made a Duke by Queen Victoria. And he's ten times as rich as yours. Just look at my clothes."

"Your Nazarene is sixty or seventy, you lying snake, and all you ever wear are his old faggot pants. Mine has bought me a yacht and a Cadillac."

"I've never seen your yacht or your Cadillac. Where are they?"

"None of your business. You think I'll tell you and then you'll go steal them from me?"

"OH, IT ISN'T so bad now with the skies still blue and the weather mild," says the middle-aged Nazarene. "But when the rains come and the cold! There's really nothing to do in Tangier, is there? I throw on my djellaba and run down to the Spanish café and sit there drinking wine and looking out at the rain. Year after year after year I've been doing that, and what for?

For that ungrateful boy who goes off God-knows-where at nine in the morning and never comes home until long after midnight. I sit at the café every day with the rain falling, and I say to myself: you must be mad, you really must be mad."

"FOR ME," SAYS the youngish Nazarene with his cheek twitching and despair in his eyes, "Morocco has been the great sexual liberation."

Tanjah. Tingis. Tanger. Tangier.

Who is immune to the magic of the name? Nazarenes—the term is applied by Moslems to all those whose allegiance is neither to Islam nor to Israel—who've been here a decade or more will tell you that the very sight or sound of the name still throws enchantment over the mind. One hears the solitary flute, drums from beyond the sand hills. One smells the moonlight. One smells figs bursting in moonlight. One sees Bagdad and hooded figures under tall palms. One longs for the taste of sweet water.

Tangier is actually a bunch of small unlovely towns in which a hundred and fifty thousand people appear to be living in exile. No one looks quite at home here. The city itself can look unanchored. Built as it is on a series of rises, when seen from a distance, it seems to be slightly up in the air, hovering just above the ground like a magic carpet—or, better, a crazy quilt—that can neither land nor gain altitude. You can almost hear it buzzing and groaning in its effort to rise or descend. Or perhaps the sounds aren't of effort at all, but of confusion, indecision. Should it finally land in Morocco or head across the Straits for Europe?

THE NAZARENE WAKES in the dark. Through the door opposite his bed he can see waves of candlelight in the living room.

"Ahmed," he calls. "What are you doing?"

"Nothing. Go to sleep. No, no, don't come in here. Don't come in here or it will be bad for you."

The Nazarene goes into the room and finds the naked

Moslem sitting crosslegged on the floor. On a straw mat in front of him is a candle, an ashtray, a bit of newspaper with incense on it, a handkerchief, a pencil, and a small red leather money-box. One hand is behind his back.

"What are you doing? What are you hiding?" asks the Nazarene. The scene is so exotic, so unexpected of the familiar Ahmed who loves blue jeans and jazz, that the Nazarene is embarrassed. He feels he has stumbled into someone else's house.

"Go to sleep. Leave me alone. It will be terrible for you."

"What are you hiding?"

The Moslem springs to his feet, and a chase begins. Since the Moslem runs backward to keep his hand hidden, the Nazarene soon corners him.

"Stop, stop, you'll make me break it," cries the Moslem. "All right, I'll show it to you."

He holds out an egg, and the Nazarene grabs it from him. The shell is covered with Arabic letters, sexual symbols, lines, circles, numerals.

"I know what that is," says the Nazarene, horrified. "I've heard about that. It's black magic, isn't it—*seuheur!* You're trying to cast a spell. You're trying to get power over me."

"No, it isn't for you. I swear it isn't for you. Mustapha paid me to do it because his Nazarene is getting tired of him."

The Nazarene does not believe in witchcraft, yet he believes it is himself over whom the Moslem wants to get control. He is angry, slightly afraid, but most of all fascinated. "I want to see you do it," he says.

"No."

"I'll break the egg."

The Moslem squats on the floor again, picks up the pencil and continues making marks across the eggshell. He is counting under his breath. Suddenly his head snaps back, his eyes roll, then shut, his body stiffens, his breathing stops, his legs twitch. The Nazarene slaps him ferociously; it is unbearable to be alone in the house with this strange Moor, without Ahmed whom he trusts. But the slap seems to land on stone. It is a moment before the Moslem recovers and continues writing as though nothing had happened.

The egg is ready now. He puts it in the money-box, puts the money-box in a sling made of the handkerchief. In the ashtray, he builds an incense fire, fueled by candle drippings, and then holds the handkerchief over the flame. He mutters and mumbles and whines and groans. After a quarter of an hour, he puts out the fire, hands the sling to the Nazarene.

"Here, take the egg."

The Nazarene opens the box. It is empty. "This isn't possible. I don't believe you."

"No? Haven't you seen magicians do the same thing in circuses?"

"Yes, but that's all done with the hands or with trick boxes."

"That's what you think," says the Moslem.

"I don't believe this," insists the Nazarene and breaks the box into pieces. "Where is it, for God's sake. Where is it?"

The Moslem nods. "Under the pillow of Mustapha's Nazarene." Presently he says: "Are you afraid?"

"Yes," admits the Nazarene.

"I am more afraid than you are."

"IF I DIDN'T think he'd die without me after all these years," says John, "I'd leave Morocco tomorrow. He knows I'd leave him money, quite a lot of money. But I'm afraid he'd die if I went. You don't really know what these people are like, Henry. When they finally trust you and love you—"

"*Love?* These savages can't love; they can only exploit."

"You don't know them, Henry. You've been here a thousand years and you don't know them. They give up Islam for you. They leave their own world and come into yours, and then you become everything for them."

"You're an ass. How can you go on being sentimental when he's robbed you and betrayed you the whole time? If you had any sense you'd be doing what wise old Henry does—bang, bang, a few hundred francs, and out-you-go!"

. . .

"THEY'RE SICK," SAYS the Moslem. "The Nazarenes are sick with a plague that is taking away all their strength. They are getting weak and old. The men are like women and the women are like men. They come here to buy our strength and our youth. Without us, they would wither and die. We renew them. We make them healthy again, young and pink and fat."

YOU FREEZE IN the shade and you boil in the sun. The winds fly in from all directions, sometimes hot and violent skimming off the desert, sometimes cool as grass. Driven mad by the Atlantic, the Straits of Gibraltar, and the Mediterranean, the air comes on like Ophelia or Lucia; it sings and it rings and it tosses flowers around; it is a berserk coloratura that tastes like stained glass. Your blood goes lunatic. Not even Greece has this wild drunken sky and this sunlight falling like diamonds. Not even Greece has the blue of Morocco, nor the white. Here, these colors hypnotize. They stun you, catch you, hold you, refuse to let you go. Time disappears in the air and the light.

The youths and unveiled girls are dramatically beautiful, relentlessly their bodies, dangerously guiltless, sinless, innocent. They are not Semites, but Hamites, Berbers, brought to Islam by the sword. Come close to one of their faces and with a sudden drop you leave the known world. A kiss is terrifying. You sail into uncharted hills and deserts. There are no maps, no guidebooks, no how-to-do-it manuals for newlyweds. You can't even be sure the world isn't, after all, flat and that you aren't sailing at the very edges.

The hills of Spain are there like civilized laughter across the narrow water; two ferries a day, or six, or ten—who can remember anymore? Spain is on the other, the inaccessible side of Styx. There is a terminal feeling here for the Nazarene; it feels like destiny. It feels as if you've been summoned here. When you're smoking kif, you imagine that the friend who told you to come here was the devil's advocate. You imagine he went all the way back to New York for no other purpose than to bring you here. Like the saints and the black magicians, he spat in the palm of your hand and thereby passed on his good or his evil. Under kif, everyone becomes part of the network. Friends, lovers, all of them are agents of another power. Only you are in the dark. They are all surgeons and Morocco is the table over which your helpless soul is spread.

THE EUROPEAN SECTIONS are hideous, blocks of icy concrete dumped out of those frozen wastes—the minds of northern architects. Functional? Everything functions except beauty and the imagination. Not that the Medina is any more exciting; it has some enclaves of charm, but mostly at night after the kids and the flies go to sleep. Romance and mystery? Not really. It is too much like daily life, dark and dank; one worries about the plumbing and rheumatism. The Casbah is very cute, of course, especially where the Nazarenes have bought and rebuilt the Arab houses, turning them into a miracle of confectioners sugar and milk fat: whipped cream on the outside, frozen custard on the inside. Yummy as all get out. With maraschino-colored drapes and walnut window bars. Like a bunch of tiny movie theaters named the Alhambra or the Alcazar.

Downhill from the Casbah is Barbarahuttonville, some twenty or thirty houses turned into a low rambling ranch-style palace that appears—from the terrace of Abdlkadr's café, whence my only view of what some of those nickels and dimes have added up to—to have a wedgwood roof. Surely not, but it looks that way. And once, like catching a glimpse of the gods, I saw laundry hanging out to dry on that lovely blue and white roof.

There is in Tangier a hill with a great many villas and mansions on it. It is called The Mountain by the Nazarenes and The Big Mountain, Jbil Kbir, by the Moslems. The Sultan of Morocco and one or two of his relatives have palaces up there, but most of the other great houses do not belong to natives.

Lots of rich Nazarenes, some of whom have been here for decades. I went to dinner there one night; it's the first party I've been to since the age of nine that had place cards on the table. Noteworthy aside from the gardens, the pools, the gracious walks, the Louis Quelquechose furniture, la-simple-mais-excellente cuisine, and the distinguished company is the fact that I heard one gentleman say on three different occasions to three different people: "I don't know why I live in Tangier. Nothing but the same people at the same parties and always saying the same things to each other."

One longed to get down to the scullery where one belonged.

THE CRUSADERS HAVE arrived, and they lie fallen on the shores of Islam, stripped of all but their bikinis. The soft white beaches are littered with bodies going pink to mottled red, grey to bronze. The Moslem armies cavort and frolic, playing leapfrog and soccer, obliviously watching to see who is watching.

"Vous like me?" asks a teen-age Moslem.

"Yes, I do. Mmmm *hmmm*. Yes, I do," says the fatherly Nazarene, huffing and puffing himself into a sitting position. "Do you like me?"

"Oh, yes. I me like vous bery much. Vous wants go me house, sir?"

Before the Nazarene can reply, a Moslem in his early twenties approaches, puts his hand on the boy's shoulder. His face is very dark, his bluish lips set hard together. "Don't go with him. Don't go with that used-up Nazarene for his lousy five hundred francs. Don't go with that pig."

"Why, does he belong to you?" asks the boy.

"I'd never have anything to do with them, any of them. You come with me and I'll give you two thousand."

SHE IS EIGHTY and was born here, a huge Spanish woman with the face of a big painted marshmallow. In her black satin dress, she spreads across the room like oil, servants with mops at the edges. "They are all donkeys, all of them. I can call them donkeys to their faces and get away with it, can you?"

"DON'T THINK YOU'RE going to get rid of me that easily," says the Moslem. "I've worked for you for more than three months. The strength is drained out of me. You'd better pay me ten billion francs."

"Get out," says the Nazarene.

"I'm only nineteen years old. You know what the law says."

"I don't give a damn about your law, and neither do you. Get out. Besides you're twenty-one."

"Who do you think you're talking to? I'm bigger and stronger than you are even if you have taken most of my strength. And I can be dangerous. I stabbed a man once—five men, maybe ten. You know what I've got in my pocket now?"

"Yes, my money. Get out."

"Remember those three Americans who were arrested? You remember what they were arrested for?"

"Smoking kif."

"What's that on the table there?"

"It's the kif you bought for me, and I had to pay twice as much as I would if I'd bought it myself. You're not scaring me. I'm sure the police would like to know who stole that ten thousand francs from the female impersonator. You'd better shut up and get out because the more you say now the harder it's going to be for you tomorrow when you try to make up."

"I'll never make up with you. Never. Never. I don't want anything from you. I've got five hundred francs in my pocket and you can have them all. Where I'm going, nobody needs money. I don't want to live if I can't live with you."

"Oh, God, tears again. Here, take my handkerchief."

"No, I want nothing of yours. I'm going now, far away, forever."

"No you're not. Let's stop all this. Come back, please come here."

"No, I'm going."

"Oh, please, oh, please, don't leave me."

THE NAZARENE IS always either hetero, homo or bi; the Moslem is merely sexual. The mind may insist upon the difference between the sexes, but the body will not. The flesh *wants* even before it wants an object, and before it wants a particular object, it wants what is alive and warm and, best of all, available.

The Moslem's society is kinder to the flesh than is the Nazarene's. The Moslem, like the Nazarene, would sooner die than go to bed with what is socially incorrect. It is always correct to go to bed with one's inferiors. When the Moslem and the Nazarene go to bed together, each is under the impression that the other is the inferior. Probably they are both right.

Luckily for the Nazarene, what he considers an ugly face can be attractive to the Moslem. The Moslem knows perfectly well that Brigitte Bardot is prettier than, say, the middle-aged man in his arms, but the one fact doesn't, as it does for the Nazarene, cancel out the other. Curiously enough, what feels good is very important to the Moslem. What or who is there is more important than what isn't there. Laughter is attractive and liveliness. Youth is very important as are meat, cleanliness, and good smells. Weddings have been cancelled because of bad breath. What is most important to the Nazarene is to find someone who looks like a statue from Classical Greece and to drag him through the mud.

It is traditional in Morocco to pay for sex. There are nicer, but not truer, ways of putting it. The lover gives a gift to the beloved: food, clothing, cash. The older pays the younger. The man pays the woman. The active partner pays the passive partner. The husband buys then feeds and clothes his wife. The wanter pays the wanted—which could mean, after all, that money need never change hands.

The benighted Nazarene almost invariably pays, for who could admit to wanting him? Certainly no self-respecting

Moslem, unless he goes and lives with the Nazarene. If the Nazarene looks young enough and rosy enough, he can get away for nothing without too much of a struggle. In a rare, rare case he might even get paid. To the Nazarene, the Moslem's price is nominal. To the Moslem it can be enough to live on— and when it is, there is no escaping the fact that, however gilded it is by tradition, prostitution is taking place. What makes it adorable to the people at either end of the banknote is that, though the Moslem is an employee, he really and truly loves his work.

IN THE WORLD of the Nazarene, nothing is happening *now*. Everything is always tomorrow. Today is a moment in history. The Nazarenes have lived too long. There is too much past to see the present as anything but a moment collapsing into memory, into history, onto paper, into filing cabinets and note-books. The Nazarenes believe they are masters of their fates, creators of their own destinies. They believe tomorrow is some-thing they can manufacture with their own hands.

For the Moslem, there is only now. *Redda insha'allah.* Tomor-row is the will of God. The Moslem is at the mercy of fate and fortune; if an outcome can be altered, it is only through mag-ical intervention. The Moslem is a fabulist; he can never tell the "truth" like a Nazarene. He cannot describe events as they "actually" happened. Because what matters is Now, to whom the story is being told, to what purpose.

THE SOCCO CHICO looks like a stage set. Three cafés crowded around a tiny square. Lots of whores. Lots of queens. Lots of secret police. Lots of foreigners. Everyone looks like an extra. It is the great melting pot of Tangier, but it never comes to a boil. The chunks of tin, lead, iron, and gold clink and clank, stir up, but never come to a boil.

The beatniks sit in small groups like people walled inside a bubble. They seem untouched by Morocco, as they seemed untouched by Mexico, by France, by the world. They are like the old British colonialists; they don't like to mix with the natives; they have a horror of assimilation. The faces are young and sweet, often pretty, the eyes somewhat dazed, rather stupid-looking. There is something provincial, old-fashioned about their beards, their long hair, their clothes. What was that rebellion all about? It was, ah, yes, it was . . . Who can remember? One longs to take a pin to the bubble, stroke the beards gently and say: Christendom is a dream. This is Islam, here and now. What can there be to rebel against?

"WE, WESTERN CIVILIZATION, do present our warlike credentials to you, King Islam!" says the Nazarene.

"What? What are you talking about?" asks the Moslem.

"Here on this battlefield stained with the blood of our sons and brothers and ourself, we ask another engagement to the death. We are two kings meeting on this sheet like continents. We are not men but civilizations."

"What's the matter with you? Are you going crazy with kif or something? Stop it. You're scaring me."

"We engage you in this war, for it is your duty to destroy us."

"Aie, *habibi!*" The Moslem understands and, exalted, nuzzles his head against the Nazarene's shoulder. "And who always wins? Who wins day after day? Oh, my soul's beloved! Thank you for letting me kill you. Thank you for letting me win."

"So long as you win, Oh Islam, we cannot lose."

"I GOT A thousand francs off my Nazarene to go to the soccer game," says Mohammed. "And then I made another five hundred by telling him I paid three thousand for the sheep's skin. He'll buy anything if I convince him every Arab owns one. How much money do you have?"

"Not a bean," says Larbi. "Mine counted all the change in his pockets before we went to bed last night."

"Well, let's go get ourselves a couple of tourists. That'll be two thousand more if we're lucky. We can dump them in twenty minutes and then go and get drunk at the whore house."

"That sounds nice," says Larbi wistfully. "But mine will have a fit if I come home drunk again."

"Come on. You'll give him two kisses and it'll all be all right. You know how they are—they're just like children."

"I MUST GET away from this place," says the young Nazarene. "What am I doing here? If I had the money, I'd leave tomorrow. Oh, what a lie that is, as if I don't have the three dollars for Gibraltar. I don't want another pipe of kif ever, nor another one of those greedy boys. I want love. It's such an embarrassing thing to admit in this country. Nobody comes here for love. We come here to kill ourselves. I want to go away where people understand each other. I want to write a book. I'm afraid to stay here any longer. I'm terrified."

THE OLD NAZARENE with the red fleshy face closes his eyes in agony. "What more could he have wanted? Six years he's been with me, and I've given him everything. He's lived in my house and never had to do a thing all day. I changed my will and left him sole heir. When I went to Europe last year for a month, he sold the refrigerator, the television set, the gas stove, and both radios, and practically turned the house into a brothel. But I forgave him. And now he's gone away to Belgium to work for almost no money in some filthy factory or some airless coal mine. It will wreck him. He's not as young as he used to be, you know—probably twenty-two or three now. I simply can't understand these people, can you?"

IT IS SHOCKING. It is stunning. You walk out of your life and into that world of banks and grocers, butchers, hardware shops, wars, government offices, newspapers. The streets and cafés are crowded. Automobiles everywhere. Moroccan schoolgirls in middy blouses and blue skirts, talking French to each other and flirting with boys. The veiled women are disappearing. The boys are in blue jeans. Trance music and trance cults are being wrapped up in packages marked: Folklore, hold for tourism. Kif is illegal. Liquor, in spite of Allah and his Prophet, is chic. Western dress and western inhibitions are becoming signs of progress rather than the customs of another tribe, and a tribe moreover that has forsaken all truths but the apparent ones, the ones that work, the ones that bring home the forbidden bacon. There's one more great day coming, halleluyah!

It is unbearable and you run home to Islam which will not free you until the conversion of your bodily cells, until the metamorphosis of your soul. You cannot remember good and evil, those provincial, arbitrary judgments. You repeal the antiquated laws of your flesh and forget about legislation altogether. Your spirit, your mind, your body are no longer the familiar baggage you disembarked with. You open, you open, like a hand, like a cocoon, like a volcano. You start going mad. At last you are not afraid of giving yourself up to your madness. You are afraid of nothing now, not of the smiler with the knife in your bed, not of bronze Prometheus spraying fire across your life. You are afraid of nothing but the loss of Islam.

THE OLD TESTAMENT in Hebrew begins with the word B'raysheet which means "at first." The initial letter is Bet, which is of course the second letter in the alphabet. It is said that the Bible begins with Bet because what is really at first man cannot know. The Aleph does not appear, is not apprehensible. Human wisdom begins after at first and ends before at last. Alpha is off with Omega in Ultimate Reality, in God.

When the Nazarene smokes kif, he makes the mistake of imagining he can see through the veil of illusion, through the intermediate letters, out to Alpha and Omega. The reason for this is that kif lets you see things as they are; it is like the penultimate chapter of a mystery novel. All the clues are suddenly revealed as clues. You begin to see what you have overlooked or hidden from yourself. You see illusions as illusions, delusions as delusions. But the mind of the Nazarene, that restless searching mind, is built to go further. He thinks if he spots all the illusions and the self-deceptions, they will total up to a reality. It is like imagining that zero plus zero equals one. The Nazarene likes to draw conclusions, write last chapters, find out who the murderer is. He makes an order and a logic out of his clues and picks a guilty party. Because he can see that all the letters from Beta to Upsilon are frauds, he imagines he is on the edge of Alpha-Omega.

With kif, the Nazarene feels he is on the verge of a new understanding, a new consciousness. It is as if a fresh card were being slipped into the mind's filing cabinet. If he could just read it, he would know the truth at last.

But the card is blank. It is the Nazarene mind tricking itself back into illusion. It is not the new card that tells the truth; it is all the old cards, so clearly legible, so inescapably shabby and tattered that tell the truth. One after another; one before another. They fill you with horror and hilarity. Between Beta and Upsilon all letters are equal, all one's urgent acts are vanities. But the mind must stop there, must sleep now.

With kif you do not pay attention to what is being said. You pay attention to who is saying what to whom.

As, for example, I am saying this to you.

"YOU KNOW WHAT I'm waiting for?" says the Nazarene. "I'm waiting for him to get married. I passed the word along through his friends that if he got married I would give him my house and my shop for a wedding present and leave Morocco. He'll be married in a month, you watch and see. He's my third one in twelve years; I know them like I know the palm of my hand. And when he gets married, I'll give him nothing, nothing at all. He'll be back to a torn djellaba and shoeless feet, just the way I found him. And he'll have a wife he despises and a new shoeless baby every year. And then I'll never touch another Moor as long as I live. I'll have my revenge. I'll get even with Morocco."

NIGHT FALLS QUICKLY now, and the evenings are cold. The Nazarene, suffering his mysterious Nazarene anguish, is standing on a corner looking at feet. They scurry past like mice. They scramble nestward like poultry. It is difficult remembering why he is standing there. Oh, yes. He wants to go home. But home is not here in Tangier; it is fifty miles to the south, a small Moroccan town. He can go by cab or by bus; he can share a cab with four others or a bus with forty others. Before he can reach a decision, he knows he will never get home. Death is imminent. It is about to happen. His terror is sudden and acute. He runs from the corner, along the avenue, down the street where the taxis are.

The dark here is the dark of a light blown out, blinding. A hooded figure walks toward him slowly, hand outstretched. It is Death. The Nazarene stands petrified as Death approaches with its white hand and its black open mouth.

"No no no no no no," pleads the Nazarene, and he goes on pleading even after he sees that Death is only a toothless beggar boy.

The Nazarene flees out to the bright crowded square and to the bus terminal. He buys a ticket, but as he passes his money across the counter, he realizes that he has been duped. Death is actually waiting for him on the bus. Leaving the money and the ticket, he runs from the terminal, back to the taxi stand. One of the drivers recognizes him.

"Are you going home?"

"Yes," says the Nazarene, and before he can change his mind, the door opens and he is in the taxi with four men in djellabas, their hoods up.

The car starts, drives along the beach, then west and out of Tangier. The Nazarene sits in horror, waiting for the strike. The Moslems are silent, appearing not to notice him, their faces hidden in their hoods. There is a moon now and the sands are bluish gold, being quietly eaten by moonlight. Through the Nazarene's horror comes a slow feeling of peace. His heart grows tranquil like the moon and the sand. This is the night, and he sighs with relief. At last, this is the night.

．　．　．

"I LOVE YOU," cries the Moslem ecstatically. "I really do."

"Do you?" asks the Nazarene wearily. "What is it you want me to buy you now?"

"Nothing, nothing. You always think I want something when I love you. But I only want you. Oh, don't fall asleep!"

"I must. I'm not as young as you are, and I'm worn out. No, stop that, are you out of your mind? Not again, dear God, not again!"

"I love you. I love you," cries the Moslem.

Is it possible, wonders the Nazarene.

FROM the orton diaries
Joe Orton

EDITED BY John Lahr

Sunday 7 May

WE GOT UP early; a grey morning, drizzle. We'd done most of the packing last night. We had only to pack shaving materials and clothesbrushes. We had one medium-sized suitcase each, and I carried a canvas bag, originally intended for fishermen. At London Airport terminal I bought a Mickey Spillane detective novel from the Smith's bookstand, Kenneth bought the paperback edition of *A Case of Human Bondage* by Beverley Nichols. We neither of us read them on the plane.

We had an uneventful journey. We saw Bill Fox, an acquaintance from last year, on the plane and chatted to him. He had a woman with him. 'She's some silly whore I picked up at the customs,' he said. 'You didn't think I was a convert, did you?' 'I wondered,' I said. 'Good God no!' he said, 'I shall be taking it up the arse as usual during the next fortnight.' We talked a little more and he went back to his seat. We waved goodbye at the airport at Tangier.

We were driven into town to the flat which is actually half a villa in an alley way called the Rue Pizzarro.[1] The actual owner—a gentle French homme-femme—showed us around the place. It is furnished in a most 'luxurious' manner—antique furniture and mirrors, gilded chandeliers—awful shit, but comfortable. The kind of taste I abhor, but as I am staying in Tangier for two months I want privacy, comfort, and quiet. If I have to have a flat decorated by a gentle French queer it's a small price to have to pay. The main advantage the flat has is a terrace overlooking an enclosed garden and so when the hellish Tangier wind blows—as it is sure to do—we have a sheltered spot out of the way. We have to lock the place securely when we go out, including pulling shutters over the windows because 'the Moroccans get in.'

After changing we went down to The Windmill, a beach place run by an Englishman (Bill Dent) and an Irishman (Mike). The Windmill is right along the beach and so it is very quiet. Bill D. gave us a long talk about his health—he has shaking fits, he looks thinner than last year. Kenneth Halliwell says, with some truth, that what most of the Tangier regulars suffer from is drink. 'He's got cirrhosis of the liver, I bet,' K.H. said darkly. Mochtzar—who I had briefly last year—is now a sort of waiter at The Windmill. 'He's going into the army in June,' Bill Dent said. 'I'll have to have him quick then,' I said. We had tea and went out on the terrace, which is by the railway line. As I was sitting half-asleep, a small voice said 'Hallo.' It was a little boy. I had a little conversation. He asked my name. 'Joe,' I said. He nodded. 'Joo,' he said, 'yes.' 'Are you going home now,' he said. 'No,' I said, lying, 'I'm staying with friends.' He spoke then of how he was at school and was learning English. After

---

[1]The flat—No. 2 Rue Pizzaro—is where Tennessee Williams wrote *Suddenly Last Summer* which dealt, in part, with cannibalism and the barbarity of sexual promiscuity, of which Orton got a glimmering on this Tangier visit. One of Williams's last plays, *The Blonde Europeans*, is dedicated to Orton. "Tennessee Williams has been to see it twice," Orton wrote to Halliwell in October 1965, about the Broadway previews of *Entertaining Mr Sloane*. "And, so I'm told, is wild over it. Says it's the funniest play he's ever seen."

more conversation, during a lull, he said, wistfully, 'Do you like boys?' 'Sometimes,' I said. He nodded. 'You fuck him?' he said, nodding at Kenneth. I shook my head and he said, conspiratorially, 'He is asleep.' And then, 'You will be here many days?' 'Yes,' I said. 'Good-bye,' he said, with a smile and stopped. 'I am Hassan,' he said. After he had gone, K. said, 'You can't have him—he is about ten.' 'It'll have to be a cabin job,' I said. 'They won't allow him in the cabins,' he said. 'Along the beach then,' I said.

We came home and Kenneth said, 'You go for some tea, bread, sugar, etc. They think you are poor and are nicer to you.' So I went to the corner shop and a fat, very friendly boy served me with provisions. When I got back, I had a cup of tea and two of Kenneth's librium tablets. They are excellent and make me feel wonderfully relaxed and confident. We had dinner at a small French restaurant. We had a pleasant stroll along the boulevard and down to the Petit Socco. We bought two coffees and spoke to a youth. He seemed a nice bit of rough—though he had clearly been on the Kif. 'I'm much too tired for anything tonight,' I said to Kenneth. We said goodbye, drank our coffee and strolled past the Hotel Mamora which, from being a semi-brothel two years ago, is now a 'tours' hotel with fat women and children sitting eating and drinking under pink lighting. When we were at the steps leading from the casbah, three very beautiful boys approached. 'You English?' 'Yes.' 'You like to come for a ride in a taxi?' the prettiest one said. We were too wise to be caught in that trap and we said 'no.' 'I'll take a single one back sometime,' I said to Ken. 'But not three and not in a taxi.' 'The taxi driver is probably in the act,' Ken said. We walked on and met a couple of Moroccans we knew from previous years. The effect of the librium was wonderful, so calming. We were able to carry on perfectly warm, friendly conversation in a most un-English way. 'The funny thing is,' Kenneth said, 'they're so surprised by the complete lack of nervousness on our parts that they don't try to pester us at all.' When one of them suggested that we come and smoke Kif

I was able to say 'no' in a firm, yet friendly way. I was really tired, and went to sleep having no sex, no inclination for any.

Monday 8 May

KENNETH WORRIED ABOUT changing money. The £50 allowance simply won't take us to the end of June. We must find someone who will cash sterling and travellers' cheques of which we have £400 worth. We went to Kents (the Moroccan Woolworth) and bought shaving cream. The morning was cloudy. No sign of the sun, but it was pleasant and relaxing to stroll in the warm air. We saw Bill Fox sitting and drinking coffee at a café. He said, as we sat down, that he's had a little chicken who'd sucked his cock. 'He said he loved it,' he laughed. 'I thought of you immediately Joe, though he's too small to fuck, I'm sure.' I asked him his name. 'Hassan,' he said. 'That's the one I spoke to at the Windmill,' I said. 'I must have him, only I can't take him back to our place. Not after last year, and we are staying the summer.' 'You can have him at my flat,' Bill said. 'I'll fix it up for you.' He then took us to a woman who changed all Kenneth's cheques on the black market, and so that problem was settled. We all went to The Windmill for lunch. Met a nice ex-Merchant Navy man called Alan. Seems a good, decent type. 'I like doing anything,' he said. 'I've tried women and I have come to the conclusion that two men in bed together can enjoy themselves ten times more than with a bird.' We're meeting him tonight for a meal. We've locked the main salon of the flat, which is enormous and gives an impression of millionaire elegance. We'll just pretend that the flat consists of the kitchen bathroom and two bedrooms. Kenneth worried. 'It's so dangerous,' he says. 'Look,' I've said perhaps rashly, 'if there's a real nastiness we can just sling him out. We're never having more than one in at a time, our money is locked away, and, up to date, I've *never* had any trouble with a boy.' 'There's always a first time,' Ken said darkly, with which I can't argue.

We had dinner at a restaurant called Nino's. A notorious Italian runs it. When we asked what had become of Abdul-Kador, the waiter he employed last year, he pursed his lips in disapproval and said simply, 'A prostitute.' Kenneth gave me four librium tablets and then gave Bill Fox two, and the ex-navy man called Alan two also. They seemed to have an alarming effect on Bill, who was drinking wine with his meal. 'I simply *must* take it up the arse tonight,' he said, 'or there will be no doing anything with me tomorrow.' He said he had been a miner when he was fourteen. 'I was first fucked down a mine,' he announced to Nino. 'Yes?' Nino said, not understanding. 'Among the coal,' Bill said, trying to explain. 'A miner did me.' Nino shook his head. 'Another prostitute, yes?' 'She thinks I did it for a bucket of coal,' Bill said.

Tuesday 9 May

WE WENT DOWN to the beach early today. It had cleared up. Clouds passing over the sun, but enough heat to be pleasant. We were hailed with 'Hallo' from a very beautiful sixteen-year-old boy whom I knew (but had never had) from last year. Kenneth wanted him. We talked for about five minues and finally I said, 'Come to our apartment for tea this afternoon.' He was very eager. We arranged that he should meet us at The Windmill beach place. As we left the boy, Kenneth said, 'Wasn't I good at arranging the thing?' This astounded me. 'I arranged it,' I said. 'You would have been standing there talking about the weather for ever.' K. didn't reply.

I borrowed the keys of Bill Fox's flat—(because I thought I must test the boy out in less grand surroundings than the flat we've taken) and went over to the boy. He was standing under a tree in the rain. He smiled, I nodded in the direction of the waste ground opposite the beach. He took my hand and we ran across the wasteland in the rain. We reached the flat and I had difficulty in finding how to open it. Fortunately nobody came up. I was dressed poorly myself in a pair of ordinary trousers and a polo-necked jumper—now wet with rain. I got the door open and we went inside—I pissed. The boy stood in the centre of the room. I tried to explain that this apartment belonged to a friend. He seemed to understand neither French, English, or Spanish. I took him to the bed. Kissed him. He was shy and didn't open his mouth. He got very excited when I undressed him. I undressed myself and we lay caressing each other for about ten minutes. He had a heavy loutish body, large cock, but not so large as to make me envious or shy. I turned him over. He wouldn't let me get in so I fucked along the line of his buttocks which was very exciting. He'd wiped his spit on his bum. When I'd come a great patch on Bill Fox's coverlet, I went and fetched a towel—then we kissed some more, neck, cheeks, eyes—he still wouldn't open his mouth—strange for an Arab boy—he must be about fifteen, surely he'd have learned (I later was told that he had only recently come up from the country). He then turned me over and came along the line of my buttocks in the same way. Suddenly he stopped and said, 'How much you give me?' 'Five dirham,' I said. 'No, please, fifteen.' 'No,' I said, 'five.' He grinned. 'OK,' he said and went on. He took a very long time to come. We lay together for an hour afterwards while the rain poured down outside and the thunder roared. His name is Mohammed.

We then took a shower together. I then gave him five dirhams, slipped it into his pocket. He said, 'Please, one more.' Because he was sweet, and even on a matter of one dirham, they like to gain a victory, I gave him an extra. He kissed my cheek, I hugged him and said I'd see him again. He left the flat first. I wiped up the floor in the bathroom, which was swimming, and left. Alan, who had had a most unsatisfactory experience with a drunken English sailor the night before, said, 'Well I don't really mind,' and laughed. He went off with a very attractive but very young boy later, after inviting Bill Fox, Kenneth, and I up to his flat for a glass of wine before dinner. Bill

Fox told me that the Baron Favier (from whom we rent our flat) likes to dress young men up in military uniform. 'One night,' Bill said, 'he picked up a sailor in uniform, he took him back, made him take off his naval uniform and put on a military uniform before he could have him.' Bill went off with a waiter, a nice Moroccan in his twenties. Not pretty but a good, friendly man. 'Lovely sex, dear,' Bill said. 'He's promised to make me some hashish cakes.' These are cakes made with hash—they look the same as ordinary confectionery but are greatly superior to anything sold at Fullers . . .

Wednesday 10 May

WEATHER VERY BAD. Cloudy. Pleasant to walk around. We met Bill sitting on the boulevard. He looked very happy, having had another sailor. Kenneth and I went down to The Windmill and I was going to have Mohammed again only Kenneth said, 'Larbi is coming at four for tea—I shall not want him, so you can have him.' So, I gave Mohammed a couple of dirhams, though I would much have preferred to have had him. Then we met the two thirteen-year-olds from last year, Mustapha and Absolem. But it really is too dangerous to go with the little ones so I said 'no'. We went back to the flat. We had tea and Ken and Larbi went into the bedroom. I'd had a couple of librium tablets and switched all the lights out in the salon and lay on the leopard-skin couch and dozed off. When Ken came back, they had had sex. 'I've arranged for you to have him tomorrow,' Kenneth said in a confidential tone when the boy was out of the room. 'But I've already arranged to have Mohammed tomorrow,' I said. 'I really wish you wouldn't play the procuress quite so much. I'm quite capable of managing my own sex!' Kenneth then went into the bedroom to put his tie on and I sat next to Larbi and kissed him. We then lay on the couch. I put my hand between his legs and felt his arse, to which he had no objection. 'We make *l'amour* tomorrow?' he said. I nodded, excited by the prospect, yet wondering how to put the other one off.

Thursday 11 May

WEATHER A LITTLE better, the sun came out and was very hot. Got slightly burnt across the shoulders. I arranged to go with Mohammed tomorrow, and in the early afternoon Ken and I went home to the flat. I took three valium tablets which had the most odd effect of making me take hours to come. I fucked Larbi a bit up the bum, with him making grunts and then, the valium, I suppose, I lost the hard. I went to the loo and had a piss, came back, tried to turn him over again. He shook his head and said, 'No, please.' 'You don't want me to fuck you?' I said. 'No,' he said. We made love a lot longer and I came on his belly. Then he made me toss him off with my come. We lay for about half an hour after this, stroking each other, and then took a shower. Later Ken and I went out to dinner. We've seen no sign of Bill Fox all day.

Friday 12 May

WEATHER STILL CLOUDY. We went to The Windmill. I wanted to see Bill Fox. There was no sign of him. I couldn't explain to Mohammed about the flat and Kenneth says I am not to bring him back until I know him better. In the end Mohammed had an idea. He gave a loud whistle and a younger boy came running. He could speak a little English, so I explained how it wasn't possible for me to take him to my friend's flat. He looked puzzled and said, 'Malabota? Yes,' and pointed into the country. I agreed to go into the country with him at three. It turned cold at about eleven, so I went into The Windmill and said to Kenneth that I was going back to the flat for my woolly. I walked along the rue d'Espagne and met Abdullah, who I always called Paddington, because he said he had once worked in Paddington. He had a friend with him and they said they'd like to buy me a mint tea. So we went into a café, drank mint tea, and I was given two pipes of Kif to smoke. They said would I like hashish. I said, 'Yes.' They tried to sell me a piece for 50 dirham which is ridiculous. Then they said, 'How much you give for this?' 'Ten,' I said, and immediately realised that even ten was ridiculously expensive. Anyway I bought it. 'Crumble it up in a little soup,' Paddington said.

I went back and faced Kenneth in such a rage at The Windmill. 'Where've you been? You have been gone an hour and a half. I was nearly out of my mind with worry.' With that, on the terrace of The Windmill, he burst into tears, to my own embarrassment. 'My nerves can't stand you going off without my knowing where you are.'

After a great scene, he said that Mohammed el Khomsi with the gold tooth, a boy of about eighteen, had been looking for me. 'I've arranged for him to come to the flat tomorrow,' he said. I was rather choked by this as it ties me down. 'Well you said you wanted to fuck him,' Kenneth said peevishly, 'and he's going to Gibraltar in a fortnight to work as a page-boy in a hotel.' He then began complaining about my liking Mohammed (the first one) and how he was a nasty bit of work. 'And you're mad to go along the beach with him. Absolutely mad.' He then began saying I would get into trouble. 'That boy of yours looks a nutter to me.' In the end, fed up to the back teeth with nagging, I said, 'Every boy in town is no good except the marvellous one you attach yourself to.' K. calmed down later. I had lunch. Chicken soup and I crumbled some hash into it. Then I went with Mohammed into the country, walking down dirt-tracks among the monkey shit. We walked for a mile or more and then he stopped at a village shop, try tumbled-down, and went inside. He came out again with a half loaf and two oranges. The half loaf had fish in it. He ate this himself. He gave me the two oranges to eat. We walked on and lay in the grass. Found it was possible to be seen by the odd person from the road, the railway line, and even from houses and bridge across a stream. 'No good,' Mohammed said and suggested the German baths. It was much too late by now to go into the casbah to the baths—especially as I had told Kenneth that I would be back by four and I couldn't risk a repeat of this morning. So we walked back. I stopped at The Windmill and asked Mike if I could take the boy into the beach cabin. 'Oh no,' he said. 'I have to be so careful you see.' Stupid cow! What had he to be careful over? I told Mohammed it was too late. Gave him a couple of dirham and came home. By now the hash I had taken earlier had begun to work—I felt very confident, very lovely, had tea. Larbi had also taken hash and so had K. by this time, and so we had a rather hysterical time. Then I lay on the leopard-skin couch and had a siesta.

Saturday 13 May

FELT VERY GOOD today. Very relaxed after hash. The sun shone out of a clear blue sky all day. Got very sunburnt today. Mohammed Khomsi arrived at The Windmill. He's full of the fact that he's starting life as a page-boy at a hotel in Gibraltar. He's the perfect fantasy page-boy. He's small, happy-looking and nineteen. He has a good body, not over-developed, not under-developed. I don't know, though, it doesn't seem to work with me. He's a sweet boy, though, and so I invited him back to the flat for tea. Larbi came later, bringing three sticks of hashish at 50 francs a piece. He had already eaten two sticks so was in a very giggly mood. I went to bed with Mohammed Khomsi. We had a long love session. 'Please, I must fuck you,' he said, 'I've had no *l'amour* for many weeks.' I let him. He didn't get right in though. He came. We went on with the session. Stroking each other's bodies. Kissing necks, tits, running the finger over every part. I found something wrong, I've always been unexcited by Mohammed Khomsi. After a long while he fucked me again. Right in this time. I went for a piss and he tossed me off, shrieking with maniacal laughter as I came over the top of his head. Why can't I fuck him though? He's quite young and pretty. What chemical is missing that makes him, for me, totally unexciting? We lay for a while longer and got up and took a shower. Kenneth later said that Larbi had been half asleep with the hash. When Mohammed had gone, Larbi had a cup of tea and then had to run to the lavatory to be sick. He looked very shattered. 'Too much hashish.' He went. I told Kenneth how Mohammed had wanted to have a threesome with a girl. 'You, me and girls,' he said. 'But where?' I said, not going to go in for that kind of thing in the apartment. 'Along the beach,' he said. I said 'perhaps.' We saw Bill with a very dreary American. Bill said he'd be at the Oriental Palace tomorrow afternoon and I could have the key to his flat if I wished, and so I shall take Mohammed (I) to Bill's flat if possible.

Sunday 14 May

RIDICULOUS DAY. MOHAMMED (I) outside beach bar from eleven to two. I'd arranged to meet him at three. Found Bill. Got key to flat. Bill said, 'When you've finished bring the key to me at the restaurant across the road.' I went back to The Windmill. No sign by now of the boy. No sign at 3:15. Decided to scrub the idea. Went in search of Bill to give him the key back. The restaurant was closed, it being Sunday. Couldn't find Bill. Walked up and down the street. Met Kenneth coming home, who said my life was one long round of ridiculous complication. Then we saw Bill and a good looking American called Gerry. I handed Bill back the key. The American came back to the flat with Kenneth and I. I had promised to give him a stick of hashish candy. I gave him half a stick, then Larbi arrived. We all drank tea. The American said that Bill had a youth from Meknès coming at five and why didn't I come over and have a threesome. I said 'OK,' Kenneth being occupied with Larbi. We walked along the rue d'Espagne and met Mohammed (I). It was now 4:30. I'd arranged to meet him at three. The American suggested we take him to Bill's. I said, 'But he won't want the flat full of Moroccans,' so we parted from Mohammed (I). We got to the flat. I waited till 6:30. No boy turned up. Several little boys of about ten rang at the doorbell, but I'm not interested in them and Bill turned them away. Finally I came home. Kenneth had arranged for us to go to the Mauretania Cinema tonight where we were supposed to be seeing Moroccan dancing—the original dancing boys, etc. It turned out to be the Senegal National Dance Company. I left at the interval finding it very boring.

Kenneth has now arrived home with the Moroccan boy, Larbi. I don't mind him but when one considers the restriction placed on my own freedom, the nagging, the rows, the constant complaints, I feel like pissing off and spending the night in some Arab doss house. Later Kenneth and Larbi made such a racket, talking and laughing, which could be clearly heard through the communicating doors of the two bedrooms, that I picked up a blanket and pillow and went into the main living-room, locking the door behind me, and spent the night on the couch in quiet.

Monday 15 May

MOHAMMED (1) TURNED up at The Windmill at twelve and suggested we go to the baths. So I followed him into the casbah. On the way we met Nasser, the waiter from the Hotel Cleleh, who is going to make me some hashish cake. Kenneth says it won't be as good as valium or librium with a glass of wine. He looked at Mohammed (1) and said, 'This your friend?' 'Yes,' I said. 'Good,' he said in a very appreciative way. 'A good boy.' I arranged to give him five dirham for the ingredients and then he'd take them to Bill Fox's flat. We walked a little way and then Nasser left us. Mohammed (1) pinched a lot of monkey nuts from a cart which was going by loaded with them, and gave me a handful. We went through miles of twisting evil-smelling alleys and finally got to the Spanish Baths. There were small cubicles and a heated room. The Moroccan attendant smiled and said something to the boy, who nodded. We went into the room, undressed, and lay on the heated, tiled floor.

I found it less exciting than I had at first imagined. The boy was as beautiful and as willing, though I found the heat unbearable. I tossed him off. He came only a small amount. They're pulling their cocks twenty-four hours a day I suppose . . . We went into the other cubicle, where I realised that he'd forgotten to bring in a towel. I opened the door and the attendant appeared. He immediately looked down in the direction of my prick, which, since it was still semihard, was impressive enough. 'Towel,' I said. He disappeared and went for a towel. We dried ourselves and went outside. The attendant asked for five dirham each from me and the boy. Daylight robbery, but they know that the bath hadn't been used for bathing. Mohammed (1) said 'Too much money,' when we were away from the baths. 'You English they want too much money.' I gave Mohammed (1) five—he asked for two more. I gave him one more. He smiled, shook hands and we parted.

Later, after sunning myself for the rest of the morning, we talked to a very beautiful German girl called Vipsil. She is one of the most beautiful people I have ever met. Larbi, who fancies himself as a lady-killer, was trying to interest her in him. But, like most Arabs, his technique with women left a lot to be desired. It consists of flashing eyes, the grin, and a barrage of more or less direct questions. When she tried to read her book, he suddenly said, 'Hey, you. Why you not speak?' The girl got more and more irritated until I said in a quiet voice, 'They're rather boring when they are trying to impress, aren't they?' She immediately smiled and said, 'They are, yes.' When we left, Larbi said, 'Girl she likes me, yes?' Ken and I laughed. Larbi, whose sense of his own sexual attractiveness borders on the insane said, 'Tomorrow I speak then I fuck her.' I said, 'I'll fuck her before you do. If you get your hand anywhere near her cunt I'll give you 50 d.' '50 dirhams if I fuck her?' he said. 'OK.' We all laughed, especially as I learned later that the girl couldn't stand these boys. We got home, Larbi disappeared into the corner shop and came back with spaghetti. He insisted on making a meal, he said, for himself, Kenneth and I. Also Mohammed Khomsi, who had just arrived. Kenneth and I had had a meal earlier. Larbi said, 'I make eats for Joe, Kenef and you perhaps?' In the end Mohammed and Larbi ate the spaghetti, which, in fact, was extremely well cooked. I had some myself and Larbi is a good cook (judging by his spag). I went into the bedroom with Mohammed later. I wasn't really feeling very much like sex after the baths this morning, but I took two valium tablets which seemed to work. Mohammed did the full love-play bit, kissing all over, lips, eyes, belly, the stroking and the exotic positions. Then he fucked me and afterwards a lot more love, and he slowly tossed me off.

We went back into the salon after a shower and sat talking. 'I like you very much,' he said. 'You very nice.' Then we spoke of his forthcoming job as a lift-boy in a Gibraltar hotel. He told me how he had worked for a time for a bank manager. 'Another boy work also. One day I come back with my patron and find boy fucking Moroccan boy in house. My patron say, "Off out of my house, I no want boys to fuck in this house." ' He said how his patron, who was employing him in the Gibraltar Hotel, had interviewed him. 'Does he like boys?' I said. 'No,' Mohammed said. 'He likes big boys, gentlemen with a big cock.' He nodded saying, 'When I grow bigger I fuck him too perhaps.' We talked in this fashion for two hours until Mohammed said of Kenneth and Larbi, 'What they do in the bedroom, eh?' I had been wondering this for a long time and I went to the bathroom door and opened it. Kenneth was standing just inside looking worried. 'You'd better go and get rid of Larbi,' he said. I went into the bedroom and Larbi was lying on the bed naked, playing with his cock which was completely limp. 'He hasn't been able to get a hard on!' Kenneth said in tones of the utmost disapproval. 'A fifteen-year-old boy and he can't get a stand on. It's absolutely shameful.' I felt very excited by Larbi's complete passivity, brought on by the hashish and whiskey. However, I thought it was much too late, seven o'clock and two orgasms too late, to turn him over, so I picked him up and carried him to the shower. When I poured cold water on him he shrieked and giggled hysterically. 'He likes being manhandled,' Kenneth said bitterly. 'Larbi said that when he'd left here early this morning he'd gone into the lavatory of his house and wanked himself off, like any English schoolboy,' Kenneth said, though Mohammed said he'd been with tourists. 'I fuck him,' said Mohammed, 'sure I fuck him.' But Mohammed isn't always to be trusted.

Friday 19 May

FINE BRILLIANT WEATHER. We had a walk to the Boulevard Pasteur in the morning to find vaseline. I went into a chemist's where, two or three days ago, I had asked for benzyl benzoate. (I'd a couple of spots round my cock and, though I'm sure now it's nothing serious, I thought I'd better be perfectly sure.) I'd explained what I wanted, when he hadn't understood benzyl by scratching my cock. The French bourgeois shopkeeper had given a horrified, 'Non!' and practically shoved me from his shop. When I went in for 'le tube de vaseline,' he looked on in disapproval as I bought two tubes.

Went to The Windmill and, because the beautiful German (or Danish) Vipsil wished to buy some souvenirs, I walked her into the casbah. How slow women walk. She talked all the way of how in Islam women were 'treated so bad you know'. How she couldn't walk down the street without 'the bad things being said to me, you know'. And I thought, what a beautiful cow, and how right the Arabs were about women. I enjoyed the looks of envy as I walked along with her. In a shop a shopkeeper lifted a silver chain and offered it to her. 'Where does it go?' she said. He was just about to put it round her waist when I took it from him and put it round her waist. He completely accepted the reason for my taking the waistband from him, accepting also that she, whilst in my company, was my possession. And so, in fact, for a morning's walk around the town, I possessed the most beautiful and desirable girl in Tangier. I was curiously excited by this fact.

I showed her the flat. She seemed very impressed. Then I took her back to the beach, having bought nothing. 'It is all so bad,' she said. 'What rubbish,' I said. On a great Moroccan plate was stamped 'Made in Belgium.' Stayed sun-bathing until 2:30 when I went down to The Pergola—the beach place where the uglier queers in Tangier gather to stare at each other across professional beach boys. Larbi's father is the cabin attendant. I was hailed by the proprietor, Peter Pollock. Very blond, almost certainly dyed, a sort of demi-queen, more queen by desire than nature. He has a shy, winning smile. He asked me to have a drink. 'I don't drink,' I said, 'but I'll have a Coca-Cola.' It was nice to think that before *Loot* and the £100,000, I wouldn't have been such a desirable personage. The Pergola had always slightly frightened me. A large bank balance in a gathering of queers is as popular as a large prick.

I drank my Coke and went for a drink with Larbi and a friend. We swam. I dived from the top board, something I'd done only once before—a day or two ago—to impress Vipsil— why I should want to impress her is impossible to imagine. Ken and I were supposed to be having a Dutchman, resident for fifteen years in Paris, to tea. But he didn't show up at The Windmill by 3:30, so we went home. We found that the Fatima had done all the weekly work and left all the clothes in water and bleaching solution, in the bath. Also that the stove wouldn't work. Larbi arrived and, when we told him that the stove didn't work, he grinned and said, 'I make it work, I fuck it good, yes?' He showed his cock. Laughed. Went into the kitchen and found that the Fatima, for some reason not able to be explained, had turned the gas off at the mains. So I got on to Agipgas and cancelled the order. Kenneth and Larbi went into the bedroom. I said to Mohammed, 'I shall give you a *petit cadeau.*' He immediately looked interested. 'These,' I said, indicating the trousers I was wearing. He looked put out because, as it turned out, he wanted the other, more expensive pair which I'd no intention of giving him. 'No *l'amour* today,' I said. 'Pourquoi?' I suddenly remembered it's always 'Why? Why?' with Mohammed. 'I don't feel well, I have a cold,' I said, and then desperately, 'I have syphilis.' 'Show me your cock,' he said, becoming most professional. I did. He examined the spots and said, 'This isn't syphilis. You can have *l'amour* today.' 'Non,' I said, 'today no *l'amour.*' I gave him the trousers, refused to give him the belt. He went and knocked on the door of Kenneth's room, had a long emotional scene in which he said I was behaving badly and didn't like him. 'For Christ's sake, give him five dirham!' Kenneth shouted. 'That'll make him shut up.'

So I took Mohammed back into the bedroom, explained that though I didn't want *l'amour* I would still give him the money. 'I know that,' he said, indignant. 'You give me money, yes—but me want *l'amour*. Me like you. Me want *l'amour*.' So we had sex, or at least I lay and allowed him to fuck me, and thought as his prick shot in and he kissed my neck, back, and shoulders, that it was a most unappetising position for a world-famous artist to be in.

Kenneth and I went to dinner at a restaurant called Grillon. An American woman runs it. She looks as if she's Eve Arden's stand-in's stand-in. She makes witty wise-cracks throughout the meal. She's not a bad type and her food is good. We saw George Greeves again on the boulevard as we strolled along. George was with a rather stuffy man with gingery hair, nearly bald, who he introduced as Somebody St. John. The man chatted—when he finally got up I said, 'Who is he?'

'Oh,' George said, 'she's a silly queen who's lived out here for years. She's doing some typing for me.' 'He looks rather tight-arsed,' I said. 'Don't you believe it, laddie, she's had camels up her ring-piece. I don't mean their pricks,' he said, as an afterthought, 'I mean their heads.' A little later the Dutchman, Stalk, sat with us. He looks like a fucking stork. Very tall and blond. Looks as if he ought to be singing songs in praise of beer in some dreadful German shitty musical. He behaved like a pest.

Two boys went by, one of whom was Absolem, whom I had had last year, but found him too lethargic, like something off a Rubens canvas. I didn't want the whore sitting next to me, but Stalk spoke to them and, before we knew where we were, the great beauty rose was parked next to me and asked 'Why no *l'amour* for me?' Frank, the little old man of seventy-six with the white moustache who'd lost his voice the previous night, having found it again, sat with us. Absolem said to me, 'Frank very good friend of mine for two years—why he no speak to me now?' 'I don't know,' I said. 'He's probably found someone with a bigger prick than yours.' He was most put out. 'I go and speak with him.' He went and sat next to Frank, who was rather annoyed and tetchy. He's frightened of these boys I think. I heard Kenneth saying, 'Oh Frank, we're too middle-class to deal with them. Joe can deal with them. He comes from the gutter like they do.'

Absolem's friend then said to me, 'Hey, you had six today?' 'Six?' I said. 'No only one.' 'Six,' he said. 'Fuck?' 'Yes,' I said. 'You like to be fucked or fuck?' he said. 'I like to fuck, wherever possible,' I said. He leaned across and said in a confidential tone, 'I take it.' 'Do you?' I said. 'Yes,' he said, 'up to the last hair.' 'You speak very good English,' I said. 'Where did you learn?' 'In school,' he said. It crossed my mind to ask who had taught him a sentence like the one he'd just used. 'Where you go tomorrow?' he said. 'Malabata,' I said. 'We could fuck at Malabata if we took enough towels,' he said, 'and the vase-line.' I was quite bowled over by his command of the English, and said again how excellent his command of my native tongue was. 'No doubt the command he had over his own tongue was even greater,' said Nigel, who'd just joined us. 'I have very good English,' said the boy, whose name was inevitably Mohammed, and he produced a battered book, *Colloquial English for the Beginner.* I leafed through it but found hardly a reference to Vaseline and none to taking it up to the last hair. 'We must make a date,' the boy said. 'I'll see you sometime,' I said, refusing to make any more dates. My life beginning to run to a timetable no member of the royal family would tolerate.

Wednesday 24 May

KENNETH DECIDED TO stop at home today. I went down to The Windmill. Frank, who arrived at 11:30, an hour after me, had a tale to tell of how he was making a papier-mâché mask of Kevin's boy 'because I collect beautiful boys' faces you know.' 'What about their cocks,' I said. 'Well they can't stay hard long enough for the plaster of Paris mould to set,' he said, bitterly. 'I've tried, you know, to discover whether there isn't a quick-drying plaster.' 'You mean some quick-drying emulsion for preserving the pricks of the contemporary male?' I said. 'Something like that,' Frank said.

Went home. Kenneth's boils are a bit better. Larbi arrived at five with no Mohammed Swinnerton. 'Boy crazy, he go off to eat with English tourists.' So no boy. 'I got another boy for you. He's outside. Please look.' So I looked outside, and there was a not bad boy—nothing to give your cock the shrinkings, but nothing to start the balls rolling. I looked back. 'Not today,' I said. Larbi nodded. 'OK. I tell boy,' he said. He leaned round the door and shouted something in Arabic. It sounded like some phrase like, 'You won't be needed tonight.' The boy pissed off. Larbi and Kenneth and I sat talking, and then Larbi and K. went into the bedroom to have sex, and I sat writing this diary. I have just taken two valium tablets to see what effect they have. (Later . . .) The tablets worked to the extent of sending me into a semi-trance for the rest of the evening. Larbi relaxing and perfectly pleasant.

We went to Nino's. It was almost empty except for a party of English women who were busy wondering whether it was *oeuf* or *boeuf* which meant 'beef.' 'Because if it's beef, I've been warned,' one of them said. Later, as we strolled towards the Boulevard Pasteur, a quite nice boy of about seventeen approached me. 'Hallo,' he said. I didn't think I'd ever seen him before but I said, 'Hallo,' and we shook hands. 'You like love with me?' he said. 'No,' I said. 'I do the *soixant-neuf*,' he said and added with a beam, 'I suck you.' This is something I'd never heard a Moroccan offer before. 'Someday,' I said. 'Now,' he said. 'He'll do the 69!' Kenneth said in a loud hiss. 'I'm not keen on that sort of thing,' I said. Kenneth turned to the boy and shrugged at his shoulders. 'He crazy,' he said. The boy laughed too and shook hands. 'Sometime, eh?' I nodded, dazed by the whole episode which I'd only dimly grasped. 'He wasn't trade,' Kenneth said. 'He genuinely fancied you.' 'He was trade,' I said.

We sat at the boulevard and drank Coca-Cola. We were joined by Frank and Kevin (the man everyone calls a millionaire). Very boring conversation, but a succession of very pretty boys to look at passing at intervals. And all available!

Thursday 25 May

KENNETH DECIDED NOT to go to the beach. His boils slightly better, but still painful. 'Imagine how Job felt,' I said, 'and you'll forget your troubles.' 'Piss off,' he said, 'and get down to The Windmill.' Arrived at beach at about eleven. Weather perfect though a cold wind by the shoreline. On the way to The Windmill I met the boy I'd had at Bill Fox's and at the baths. I had already warned Kenneth that I intended bringing him back if I met him. 'Hallo,' he said. 'Hallo,' I said. '*L'amour* today?' I said. 'Today,' he nodded slowly. 'What time?' 'Come to The Windmill at two o'clock.' He nodded and went away.

I lay in the sun till twelve. Went for a swim. Talked to Frank. 'My mask of that young Moroccan,' he said, 'came out rather well. I'm engaged on doing the eyes. I colour them the best I can.' 'What colour do you use for the face?' I said. 'Oh I try and get it as exact as I can,' he said, 'though I'm afraid my efforts could hardly compare with the works of the divine Madame Tussaud.' At one o'clock Ken rang. 'Your waiter's just turned up,' he said. 'But I told him Friday at one.' 'He must have lost his appointment diary then,' Ken said. 'I said you were at the *plage*.' A few minutes later Nasser hovered on to the scene. He hadn't understood the day. 'Come tomorrow at one for *l'amour*,' I said, 'to the apartment at one.' He smiled, tossed a few remarks about how 'wapu' I was, and how he liked *l'amour* with me, didn't 'go with tourists.' All of which may or may not be true.

After he'd gone, the boy Larbi brought round last night appeared. I returned his greetings and approached him. He was an English schoolboy too, but the tall blond type who looks fetching in tennis flannels. I was pretty vague with him. I then saw Mohammed (the one that was coming at two—he wore a yellow jersey and, to distinguish him from the rest of his kind, I'll call him Mohammed Yellow-jersey). So I had a couple of poached eggs and a coffee, and nodded for Mohammed Yellow-jersey to follow.

I went onto the Avenue d'Espagne and Mohammed Yellow-jersey was still following. I let him in and he sat on my bed smiling. Kenneth came out of the bathroom. I went in for a shit. When I came back Kenneth was sitting in a dressing gown. 'Do you want tea?' I said to Yellow-jersey. 'Yes, please,' he said. I made a pot. He had condensed milk in it and three spoonfuls of sugar. Kenneth and I talked. He had a piece of hash cake. I wasn't going to risk it fucking up the sex. I took a couple of valium though. I usually find a mild muscular relaxant helpful. I took the boy (who is about fifteen) into the room. We took off our clothes and lay together. I stroked him, kissed his nipples. When I'd got a spanking good hard-on, I turned the lad over and, using a little grease mixed with my spit, I put my prick up his arse. I found he wouldn't take the cock up the arse. He cried out as it went in. But he allowed me to have the prick between the buttocks which, as I fucked, he agitated in a most alarming way. At this point I, my hand well-greased, put my hand under him and took his medium-to-large tool in my hand. While I fucked him, I pressed his prick between my clenched fist and had a truly satisfactory orgasm.

We dozed for fifteen minutes or so and then he had a *douche*. We smiled a lot and I gave him six dirham and he asked for another, so I gave him seven. We displayed more affection and then he went and drenched himself with a cheap kind of eau-de-cologne which Kenneth had bought for midge bites. I made a pot of tea, had a largish slice of hashish cake and came into the living room. 'Very good,' I said to Kenneth. 'Just my type.' 'You must let Nasser fuck you occasionally,' Kenneth said, 'or otherwise we shall not be able to get the hashish.'

When Larbi arrived at five, I went to the boulevard to get some tablets for Kenneth. I bought them and sat on the Place de France drinking mint tea. Nearby was a quartet of English tourists and one woman was saying 'Well, the best holiday we ever had was in Plymouth, but we didn't have the weather unfortunately.' As I walked back a Moroccan approached me. 'You English?' 'Yes,' I said. He looked at me. 'You want girls?' he said. 'No,' I said. He paused and coughed a bit and said in a tentative tone, 'You like boys?' 'No,' I said. 'OK. Goodbye,' he said.

I had a very pleasant stroll back, the hash and valium working well. Met Ian Horrible. 'How are you?' I said. 'Alive, I regret to say,' he said. 'Has anything exciting been happening?' he said, and I told him of my Yellow-jersey episode. 'Yes,' he said, 'he's quite a nice kid.' 'A very valuable addition to my collection,' I said. He chortled to himself and gave a spin into a café, leaving me relieved by his departure. I found Ken and Larbi still in the bedroom when I returned. After a while Larbi came out quite naked parading up and down in front of the long mirror in the hall admiring himself. I gave Kenneth the tablets. He took two and said they gave him the most odd feeling on top of the hashish.

We sat talking of how happy we both felt and of how it couldn't, surely, last. We'd have to pay for it. Or we'd be struck down from afar by disaster because we were, perhaps, too happy. To be young, good-looking, healthy, famous, comparatively rich *and* happy is surely going against nature, and when to the above list one adds that daily I have the company of beautiful fifteen-year-old boys who find (for a small fee) fucking with me a delightful sensation, no man can want for more. '*Crimes of Passion* will be a disaster,' Kenneth said. 'That will be the scapegoat. We must sacrifice *Crimes of Passion* in order that we may be spared disaster more intolerable.'

We went to the Alhambra for dinner. I had a glass of wine because it works well with hash. Kenneth already with hash and valium inside him decided *not* to risk vino as well. We went for a stroll. Sat on the boulevard at the Café de Paris and, at ten, rose to go, only to meet Nigel, Frank, and Kevin who persuaded us to stay a little longer. In the re-allotment of places, I sat next to a rather stuffy American tourist and his disapproving wife. They listened to our conversation and I, realising this, began to exaggerate the content. 'He took me right up the arse,' I said, 'and afterwards he thanked me for giving him such a good fucking. They're most polite people.' The American and his wife hardly moved a muscle. 'We've got a leopard-skin rug in the flat and he wanted me to fuck him on that,' I said in an undertone which was perfectly audible to the next table. 'Only I'm afraid of the spunk you see, it might adversely affect the spots of the leopard.' Nigel said quietly, 'Those tourists can hear what you're saying.' He looked alarmed. 'I mean them to hear,' I said. 'They have no right to be occupying chairs reserved for decent sex perverts.' And then with excitement I said, 'He might bite a hole in the rug. It's the writhing he does, you see, when my prick is up him that might grievously damage the rug, and I can't ask him to control his excitement. It wouldn't be natural when you're six inches up the bum, would it?'

The American couple frigidly paid for their coffee and moved away. 'You shouldn't drive people like that away,' Nigel said. 'The town needs tourists.' 'Not that kind, it doesn't,' I said. 'This is *our* country, *our* town, *our* civilisation. I want nothing to do with the civilisation they made. Fuck them! They'll sit and listen to buggers' talk from me and drink their coffee and piss off.' 'It seems rather a strange joke,' Frank said with an old school-teacher's smile. 'It isn't a joke,' I said, 'there's no such thing as a joke.'

Nigel, who was drinking some strange brandy, got very excited by a girl who passed. She looked like a boy. She was German. We discussed women for a bit and I wrote them off as a mistake. 'Who wants a girl to look like a boy?' I said. 'Or a boy to look like a girl? It's not natural.' 'I really think, Joe,' Nigel said, 'that you shouldn't bring nature into your conversation quite so often, you who have done more than anyone I know to outrage her.' 'I've never outraged nature,' I said. 'I've always listened to her advice and followed it to wherever it went.' We left at eleven. I feel so content.

I slept all night soundly and woke up at seven feeling as though the whole of creation was conspiring to make me happy. I hope no doom strikes.

FROM rital and raton

Pier Paolo Pasolini

FROM *ROMAN NIGHTS AND OTHER STORIES*
TRANSLATED BY John Shepley

E SAID: *"J'AI FA'."*

In a country voice—rather shrill: for an Arab, to learn French means to repeat a rustic condition—with thoughts of the city in a house crumbling in the sun, the fetid sheep, the hens on the roost, the neighbors dressed in rags, their shrewd old ideas, the dreamlike gestures at the end of the cultivated horizon, the destiny that combines sex and death: and since the peasant universe is petit-bourgeois, an Arab's French has that shrill sound, high in tone and weak, plaintive, bad, like a postal clerk in a bad mood due to bad digestion or wounded pride, dry, sterile, immature, like certain little shoots of tender winter saplings. The emission of this little vocal shoot comes from the head. Oddly enough, it doesn't pass through the male glands. Sensuality appears bitter and sharp—as in a barnyard animal—treacherous and aggressive. That vocal emission, light, feeble, scourging—the voice of the mother—conceals a sensuality that attacks like a snake, first coiling, then straight, then coiling again on its desert road.

Brahin is like a Sicilian boy, but without that soft fecundating will that goes back more to the mother than to the father. Tallish, with narrow shoulders, broad hips, the magical gaze of a girl: the two eyes set close above the slightly hooked nose, the thumbprint of beauty of another race, which appears alien, with a faintly repellent aura. As though the presence of other destinies were a threat to our own. Or rendered them vain by suggesting other ways of being in the sun, amid the houses, along the dry rivers, between the walls, etc.

The water of a river that you see after showing your passport. To sip that water as an unnatural act of baptism, to accept its taste like a nonexistent beast that at its contact comes into existence and cries, screaming for everything it has lost by watering at other springs.

The fact that Brahin is walking through the heart of Paris is thus the beginning of a story.

I'll go further and say: the fact that Brahin is walking through Pigalle.

I said his eyes are those of a girl, or a still immature boy, all lucid flesh: with his shrill voice that strikes the upper part of the palate like a current of cool and unhealthy air. Almost as though a throttle were located at the top of the lungs, similar to the constriction of a sore throat, but due to sun rather than snow, to malnutrition rather than wind. Above the eyes is a big circle, a big black circle—irregular and quivering. Really and truly a big circle, looking as though it had been traced at that moment, or woven with the wings of southern birds.

Next to that big, black, shining circle is a thin white line and a small undeveloped circle, most surely trimmed by Parisian scissors as it emerged, reluctant and inarticulate, above the ear, so as to leave as much space as possible for the big, indeed enormous, circle that starts from the thin white line and lunges like a beating wing over the hairline, over the forehead, over the eyebrows, until, like a frayed but living silk beret, it skims and almost covers the starry eyes, etc.

· · ·

THE JOURNEY FROM Batna ("On what mountain chain, or plain, or coast of Algeria?" I, that fatuous author of a few years ago, would have wondered) to Lyons, the *banlieue*, crammed with wogs and wops exchanging illusions of nationality. And the journey from Lyons to Paris, with his blond friend. That blond friend who has no racial prejudices—like two pigeons flying together.

Let the blond friend—in the gratuitousness of the unwritten story—also have a big blond wheel over his eye. But a dirty one—and dry, not greasy, bristling, not soft, heavy, not quivering, dull, not light, ruffled, not shining or smooth. Underneath, the little blue eyes.

And further underneath, the ugly mouth—the wog's mouth is pretty ugly, too—like a sort of fat rodent's, etc., etc.

That night a Corsican was murdered by some of his compatriots: he went into a bar, had a drink, asked for the telephone book, went over to the phone, the two killers, his fellow countrymen, came in and shot him, they punctured his hands, which he had put up to shield his face, punctured his head, and left him bleeding on the red floor of the bar, with the customers crowded at the tables in the back room coming out to watch like crows. The dead man lay on his stomach, *and he seemed to be sleeping with his forehead on his arm, this slumber making him once again as defenseless as a child.* Brahin was among those watching.

MAYBE BRAHIN HASN'T enough breath to finish the word: *Fa'*. But it's the lack of breath of kids who grow up in cities of gangsterism. More than a lack of breath, it's an aspiration, a silent *h*, or a sigh due to sensitivity—or maybe, as the case may be, to a calculated excess of patience; or to the wish to disappear, expiring in the painful reverence he has for himself; or else to the need to discredit in the presence of third parties the legend of his own wickedness. Or maybe it's some unrecognizable symptom of shyness, after all.

. . .

As for Brahin, he's now at the foot of Pigalle, near a big round public square. His sidekick and "blond counterpart" has disappeared.

Brahin is now alone, and so his staring gaze is infinitely more significant. He is alone with his gaze, which is now the only vital thing about him (his body, in its solitude, appears crushed; his trousers hang limply over that mortal flesh that he too can be said to share with us; his shoulders are narrower). He stares at the people inside the plate-glass window of a café—like a lot of fish motionless inside a fish bowl, etc., and their immobility makes them seem more luminous—almost as though they were on a small stage lit by reflectors in a performance by the Living Theatre. The leading character in their midst is "the blonde." I say *the* because she is a character denoted and connoted in Brahin's life. My *the* is almost one of definition.

About her, whom I know only visually, through Brahin's gaze from afar, a long shot to that little stage at the end of one of the countless squares of Paris, with its open-air oyster stands that seem sculpted in wrought iron, deeply democratic and art nouveau, with a grandiose anonymity inconceivable anywhere else but Paris—I can still allow myself to say many things. For a writer's gaze has its rights, especially if that writer isn't afraid of being infected by literature, like a Hindu by poor human beings of another caste, if he does not have the altogether bourgeois terror of seeming and being what the bourgeoisie wants and imagines him to be, or as the Communist Party wants and imagines him to be, if he's not continually obsessed by the thought of not being what he's expected to be, whether as vulgar as he is, or as nowadays it's no longer permitted to be, etc. So, arbitrarily, as an impure writer, I can write the following notes about the blonde whom I've merely seen. First of all, obviously, she had split herself by the fact of being one of the girls of Pigalle. Merchandising herself had not been without its consequences. She had lost any conceivable idea of what sexual life was, since sexual life was something she experienced as merchandise and not as herself. As for pure and simple physical pleasure, at first she had been unable to feel it because, as a virgin, she could not allow herself to yield to such weaknesses, attributed entirely to men; later, as a whore, these pleasurable weaknesses were a question of money, and not for a moment could she allow herself to yield for any other reason but money. In the presence of the sexual act, therefore, she placed herself in a state of mind in which, not having to show pleasure, she was prevented from feeling it.

True, her professional deformation presented life to her in the guise of a male member emerging from and going back into its nest inside the dark trousers of taxi drivers, porters at Les Halles, provincial students, foreign immigrant workers in Paris, and so on, but this constant, nagging appearance and disappearance of the member, which in itself had left its mark on her whole existence, reducing it to a sluggish theater of such monotonous, hot, guilty, and often painful performances, had imprinted on her face a changeless expression of nonexistence, sometimes melancholy, sometimes fierce. But Brahin saw nothing of all this. Or—who knows?—maybe he liked it. Maybe he liked the seeming death of that body.

BRAHIN GOES WITH the blonde along a street so Parisian as to seem a dream, one small hotel after another, under red neon signs that glow in patient defeat. Until they come to the one they were looking for. The old hag takes their documents at the desk in the clean little lobby—with its overhanging staircase that, precipitously beckoning, rises upward without even giving you time to catch your breath—behind a glass door as in a post office. Unlike Europeans, Brahin is not modest about his member. Ever since he was a little boy—as we will see—an erection has been taken for granted as one of his public rights, it has had the approval of onlookers, an approval not even based on the triumph of virility as a norm, as health, etc., but directly on his feeling of sweet and confused adolescent desire (among non-Western peoples it is difficult for a man to emerge entirely from adolescence; his ideal age is the moment when he becomes a man: a man determined to renounce all the responsibilities of men in exchange for the sweet right to pursue, with his great mop of hair and beautiful lips, the course of his erection).

BRAHIN IN THE hotel room with the blonde. There would be a bed with a red cover, an ugly wooden wardrobe, light and polished, a washstand behind a cheap cloth curtain with a pattern of small flowers, a window beyond the foot of the bed. The blonde, as far as the sexual act she is about to perform is concerned, an act for which Brahin is quite ready, is nothing but an object. An object that takes off its clothes as though doing a duty. Any judgment of Brahin, on her part, has been suspended. She doesn't have to have seen him, or see him. The rules of the game keep her from having any curiosity about him. He could be a blond Belgian with a potbelly, his member cold and all skin and hair inside his brown trousers. There's no reason why he should be Brahin, an Arab grown pale in the weak sunlight of the *banlieue,* with the black trousers of the underworld and the erection of a boy without father and mother, who goes forth into the world with nothing to boast but his mop of hair as in his dusty native village.

But what's eating Brahin?

As far as the little act of coitus is concerned, which she's about to perform, in a few minutes and for a few minutes, on that dry bed of dust, the blonde, I repeat, is an object. But when it comes to that "other thing" that's in Brahin, in Brahin as customer and acquaintance, with his intentions, his character, his relations to the same world in which they both live—the blonde exists, thinks, has a life of her own, possesses eyes. What's eating Brahin, who seems always to turn away, so that he is seen foreshortened, the eye sidelong, the pupil sharp and distraught at the white corner of the eyeball, over the cheekbone with its equivocal tenderness? He takes off his shoes, unbuttons his pants, goes from the bed to the washstand and from the washstand to the bed, as though performing other gestures. There's a kind of uncertainty in everything he does, like a shivering due to some illness—or rather a curious air of distraction that draws his attention elsewhere, toward an action the way to which he's unable to find. He's as restless as a caged animal. His eyes have become curdled in an expression somewhere between grief and rage. One might call it anxiety at committing the act on the part of a nice village boy the right of whose ardor has always been unchallenged—if on the other hand every one of his gestures were not as though secretly slackened and diverted by abrupt and smothered pretexts that tend to make him do some "other thing," or at least to take his time, to proceed with calm—as though awaiting the moment when he will feel ready to do that "other thing" that will make the blonde, this dead and unjudging object, alive and judging.

"J'AI FA' " ARE the only words we've heard uttered in French direct discourse by Brahin (a hunger assuaged standing against the white walls of a small brasserie opposite some shooting galleries). The Jew with the adult face knows that, in Brahin's speech, the Arabs are called *ratons*, "wogs," by French racists. And the Italians for the same reasons are called *ritals*, "wops" (a reminder?). But, of course! Let Brahin's tough, mysterious friend be an Italian! Let him be Palmiro, that Prenestino boy of Calabrian origin, with his mop of blond hair—not a barbarian: it's the brutality of emigration that will turn him into a barbarian. For the moment neither Brahin nor Palmiro speak French. But they will speak it, and once they do they'll be completely Frenchified. Then, within the sphere of Frenchification, they can be expected to take up slang.

BRAHIN HAS SCARCELY mounted the blonde—with the baleful air of one who isn't doing it because he's paying for it, but out of violence—when, in some twenty angry and punitive thrusts of the loins, it's all over. What's eating Brahin? What's he waiting for now?

This uncertainty, I repeat, brings the blonde to life; otherwise she'd be dead. She pretends to be in a hurry, but without the blind fury typical of such circumstances. One would say she's worried. And that to conceal her worry she pretends to more naturalness and calm than what is called for in fastening her snaps or putting on her stockings. She's almost nice, good-natured. What is Brahin doing behind her back? He looks like a millipede a row of whose feet has been crushed, and which continues to move as though it had lost its sense of direction, turning round on itself, innocently incapable of going on its way. Brahin seems to want to stretch himself, or take a breath of air at the window, but he would have to force himself to do it. Meanwhile he is seen more foreshortened still, with the high cheek-bone, and above it the black pupil of the eye, more curdled than ever with grief and rage. Brahin no longer holds back. He looks at the blonde in dismay, furious as a bandit about to kill a traveler from another social class, upright, uncommunicative as a serpent. He says he's sick, that he's crazy. That he can do as he likes, because he doesn't care if he ends up in prison, and anyway he's already been in prison, it's not so bad there, and in prison he met other Arabs, three or four non-Algerian Arabs, with whom he became friends. Who cares if in prison there are no women, it's all the same. Why does he say all this? As he speaks, he gazes steadily, his face averted, at the window—then he gazes at the blonde—and then again at the window—as though to set up a bond between them. His anxious cheekbone is seen fore-shortened, and the wave of his full mop of hair, now of a point-less beauty.

The blonde is very busy putting on her clothes.

Brahin takes a few steps directly toward the window, stopping in front of the washstand.

Gazing at the blonde, he begins saying once more that he's *like* a madman, a lone gypsy who goes about the world, and already there'd been times when he was about to jump out the window, and now too he'd like to jump—or would she like to jump? And meanwhile he approaches the window, and touches it, as out of an old passion, which subsides a bit at the touch—or prepares to explode with more violence. The window, cracked and pitiful, with its shutters closed on the Rue du Loup Blanc, lets itself be touched.

Brahin is in the middle of the room, at the foot of the bed. Something has curdled in his eyes that does not dissolve. If it's a question of grief, it's nevertheless replaced by that special feeling by which we blame our grief on someone else, and we provoke this someone else into insisting on being to blame, so that the grief will have good reason to be transformed into rage.

And so Brahin seems to be prodding the blonde to make her insist on taking the blame for his grief, leaving him free to let himself go—through slow phases, increasing in an almost voluptuous way—in a state of blind and turgid rage.

Since the blonde, as though chilled, keeps putting on her clothes, turning her back on him, he, with swift and continuous glances toward the window—like an old man who as he speaks feels a cold draught from a crack, and automatically looks around at the window behind him to see where it's coming from—starts confessing something, his words put together as though for a popular song, or a faint and broken melody.

One by one, his words can be "seen."

He says: when he was a child, in Algiers, he was walking by himself one night through the streets of a remote suburb, which smelled of dynamite that had just exploded, amid twisted store shutters and rubble strewn like garbage—I was ten years old, and five or six youths and boys, in European clothes and carrying a machine gun, called me over to them, they grabbed me with their Muslim hands, which smelled of saffron, they put me up against the demolished wall of a French store as though they were going to shoot me, and there they all took advantage of the fact that I was a child.

Of course, Brahin's speech, as an auditory fact, cannot be reproduced: true, like an exercise in penmanship it is all frontal and linear, but in the tremor between one word and another there are holes, and when you look into those holes your head starts to spin, because they give on endless depths illuminated by a sun, the sun of Algiers and of another life: they are pure abysses of previous existence, unthought, unconceived in French.

He says that from that night on he got in the habit of doing the same thing himself, with the dead (but does he say it? or does he let it be imagined? what grammatical connection does he use to carry on such a discourse, a discourse that cannot be heard?). It was a time when there were many of them, dead youths in the streets of Algiers.

They lay stretched out, half an hour, an hour after the last bursts of machine-gun fire had faded away, as though to ponder, or to breathe the lingering odor of saffron: perhaps to remember it forever, on the new journey they had undertaken by the will of Allah: they lay face down, in their military shirts and warriors' trousers, as though better to concentrate, youths in appearance, children in strength. I took advantage of the silence of the curfew, and went looking for those dead bodies that awaited me defenseless.

He was completely excluding them from himself, obviously with the single-mindedness felt by children when they play. He had been so intent on performing his act—like hunting or fishing—an act that gave an exclusive and experimental pleasure to him alone—that he was unaware of them. They had gone away, and the odor of saffron had stayed behind in the world.

As for myself, I limit myself to placing the reader in the presence of a different vital experience. Try to imagine it, if you can, and not be carried away by your moralism.

One day I saw my little brother (saying this, even if he's about to commit a murder or whatever, he quickly makes the graceful gesture of someone calmly sleeping, with his forehead resting on his arm): and then I did it, you know, as with a dead body, I held him tight, taking advantage of the fact that he had a child's turban wound around his head and was wearing a long Arab shirt, on which only the faintest traces of red and green embroidery were left.

Even this voluptuous speech of Brahin's, poured forth on

the girl to goad her into taking on herself the blame for his grief, has no voice: perhaps it is translated quite literally from a dialect in which there is no need for ties, and words can be aligned like so many things, in the tearful confusion of unknown tragedies. The Arabs I met in jail, in Lyons, were like those dead men, brought back to life exactly the same, with their partisans' trousers: they were going through France like murderers, together with Italians and Spaniards.

His voice cracked and trembling, a lump at the back of his throat, Brahin moves toward the ashtray on the night table, touches it, lets go of it, picks it up again, but as though that hand, a schoolboy's large hand, were very far from his body, in another world full of dust. The ashtray was a plastic one, light as cardboard . . .

OUTSIDE, PARIS WAS filled with a profound odor, which was not only that of the rain. It was the odor of the time, of the authority and inconceivable and brutal grandeur of reality— it was the odor of power. A power all the more harsh the more truly it was based on freedom, which had become intoxication and habit. And yet you could feel that the world had need of change, of great changes.

for the relief of
unbearable urges

Nathan Englander

FROM *FOR THE RELIEF OF
UNBEARABLE URGES*

THE BEDS WERE to be separated on nights forbidden to physical intimacy, but Chava Bayla hadn't pushed them together for many months. She flatly refused to sleep anywhere except on her menstrual bed and was, from the start, impervious to her husband's pleading.

"You are pure," Dov Binyamin said to the back of his wife, who—heightening his frustration—slept facing the wall.

"I am impure."

"This is not true, Chava Bayla. It's an impossibility. And I know myself the last time you went to the ritual bath. A woman does not have her thing—"

"Her thing?" Chava said. She laughed, as if she had caught him in a lie, and turned to face the room.

"A woman doesn't menstruate for so long without even a single week of clean days. And a wife does not for so long ignore her husband. It is Shabbos, a double mitzvah tonight—an obligation to make love."

Chava Bayla turned back again to face her wall. She tightened her arms around herself as if in an embrace.

"You are my wife!" Dov Binyamin said.

"That was God's choice, not mine. I might also have been put on this earth as a bar of soap or a kugel. Better," she said, "better it should have been one of those."

THAT NIGHT DOV Binyamin slept curled up on the edge of his bed—as close as he could get to his wife.

After Shabbos, Chava avoided coming into the bedroom for as long as possible. When she finally did enter and found Dov dozing in a chair by the balcony, she went to sleep fully clothed, her sheitel still on top of her head.

As he nodded forward in the chair, Dov's hat fell to the floor. He woke up, saw his wife, picked up his hat, and, brushing away the dust with his elbow, placed it on the nightstand. How beautiful she looked all curled up in her dress. Like a princess enchanted, he thought. Dov pulled the sheet off the top of his bed. He wanted to cover her, to tuck Chava in. Instead he flung the sheet into a corner. He shut off the light, untied his shoes—but did not remove them—and went to sleep on the tile floor beside his wife's bed. Using his arm for a pillow, Dov Binyamin dreamed of a lemon ice his uncle had bought him as a child and of the sound of the airplanes flying overhead at the start of the Yom Kippur War.

DOV BINYAMIN DIDN'T go to work on Sunday. Folding up his tallis after prayers and fingering the embroidery of the tallis bag, he recalled the day Chava had presented it to him as a wedding gift—the same gift his father had received from his mother, and his father's father before. Dov had marveled at the workmanship, wondered how many hours she had spent with a needle in hand. Now he wondered if she would ever find him worthy of such attentions again. Zipping the prayer shawl inside, Dov Binyamin put the bag under his arm. He carried it with him out of the shul, though he had his own cubby in which to store it.

The morning was oppressively hot; a hamsin was settling over

Jerusalem. Dov Binyamin was wearing his lightest caftan, but in the heat wave it felt as if it were made of the heaviest wool.

Passing a bank of phones, he considered calling work, making some excuse, or even telling the truth. "Shai," he would say, "I am a ghost in my home and wonder who will mend my tallis bag when it is worn." His phone card was in his wallet, which he had forgotten on the dresser, and what did he want to explain to Shai for, who had just come from a Shabbos with his spicy wife and a house full of children.

Dov followed Jaffa Street down to the Old City. Roaming the alleyways always helped to calm him. There was comfort in the Jerusalem stone and the walls within walls and the permanence of everything around him. He felt a kinship with history's Jerusalemites, in whose struggles he searched for answers to his own. Lately he felt closer to his biblical heroes than to the people with whom he spent his days. King David's desires were far more alive to Dov than the empty problems of Shai and the other men at the furniture store.

Weaving through the Jewish Quarter, he had intended to end up at the Wall, to say Tehillim, and, in his desperate state, to scribble a note and stuff it into a crack just like the tourists in their cardboard yarmulkes. Instead, he found himself caught up in the crush inside the Damascus Gate. An old Arab woman was crouched down behind a wooden box of cactus fruit. She peeled a sabra with a kitchen knife, allowing a small boy a sample of her product. The child ran off with his mouth open, a stray thorn stuck in his tongue.

Dov Binyamin tightened his hold on the tallis bag and pushed his way through the crowd. He walked back to Mea Shearim along the streets of East Jerusalem. Let them throw stones, he thought. Though no one did. No one even took notice of him except to step out of his way as he rushed to his rebbe's house for some advice.

MEIR THE BEADLE was in the front room, sitting on a plastic chair at a plastic table.

"Don't you have work today?" Meir said, without looking up from the papers that he was shifting from pile to pile.

Dov Binyamin ignored the question. "Is the Rebbe in?"

"He's very busy."

Dov Binyamin went over to the kettle, poured himself a mug of hot water, and stirred in a spoonful of Nescafé. "How about you don't give me a hard time today?"

"Who's giving a hard time?" Meir said, putting down the papers and getting up from the chair. "I'm just telling you Sunday is busy after a day and a half without work." He knocked at the Rebbe's door and went in. Dov Binyamin made a blessing over his coffee, took a sip, and, being careful not to spill, lowered himself into one of the plastic chairs. The coffee cut the edge off the heat that, like Dov, sat heavy in the room.

THE REBBE LEANED forward on his shtender and rocked back and forth as if he were about to topple.

"No, this is no good. Very bad. Not good at all." He pulled back on the lectern and held it in that position. The motion reminded Dov of his dream, of the rumbling of engines and a vase—there had been a blue glass vase—set to rocking on a shelf. "And you don't want a divorce?"

"I love her, Rebbe. She is my wife."

"And Chava Bayla?"

"She, thank God, has not even raised the subject of separation. She asks nothing of me but to be left alone. And this is where the serpent begins to swallow its tail. The more she rejects me, the more I want to be with her. And the more I want to be with her, the more intent she becomes that I stay away."

"She is testing you."

"Yes. In some way, Rebbe, Chava Bayla is giving to me a test."

Pulling at his beard, the Rebbe again put his full weight on the lectern so that the wood creaked. He spoke in a Talmudic singsong.

"Then you must find the strength to ignore Chava Bayla, until Chava Bayla should come to find you—and you must be strict with yourself. For she will not consider your virtues until she is calm in the knowledge that her choices are her own."

"But I don't have the strength. She is my wife. I miss her. And I am human, too. With human habits. It will be impossible for me not to try and touch her, to try and convince her. Rebbe, forgive me, but God created the world with a certain order to it. I suffer greatly under the urges with which I have been blessed."

"I see," said the Rebbe. "The urges have become great."

"Unbearable. And to be around someone that I feel so strongly for, to look and be unable to touch—it is like floating through heaven in a bubble of hell."

The Rebbe pulled a chair over to the bookcases that lined his walls. Climbing onto the chair, he steadied himself, then removed a volume from the top shelf. "We must relieve the pressure."

"It is a fine notion. But I fear that it's impossible."

"I'm giving you a heter," the Rebbe said. "A special dispensation." He went over to his desk and flipped through the book. He began to scribble on a pad of onionskin paper.

"For what?"

"To see a prostitute."

"Excuse me, Rebbe?"

"Your marriage is at stake, is it not?"

Dov bit at his thumbnail and then rushed the hand, as if it were something shameful, into the pocket of his caftan.

"Yes," he said, a shake entering his voice. "My marriage is a withered limb at my side."

The Rebbe aimed his pencil at Dov.

"One may go to great lengths in the name of achieving peace in the home."

"But a prostitute?" Dov Binyamin asked.

"For the relief of unbearable urges," the Rebbe said. And he tore, like a doctor, the sheet of paper from the pad.

* * *

DOV BINYAMIN DROVE to Tel Aviv, the city of sin. There he was convinced he would find plenty of prostitutes. He parked his Fiat on a side street off Dizengoff and walked around town.

Though he was familiar with the city, its social aspects were foreign to him. It was the first leisurely walk he had taken in Tel Aviv and, fancying himself an anthropologist in a foreign land, he found it all quite interesting. He was usually the one under scrutiny. Busloads of American tourists scamper through Mea Shearim daily. They buy up the stores and pull tiny cameras from their hip packs, snapping pictures of real live Hasidim, like the ones from the stories their grandparents told. Next time he would say "Boo!" He laughed at the thought of it. Already he was feeling lighter. Passing a kiosk, he stopped and bought a bag of pizza-flavored Bissli. When he reached the fountain, he sat down on a bench among the aged new immigrants. They clustered together as if huddled against a biting cold wind that had followed them from their native lands. He stayed there until dark, until the crowd of new immigrants, like the bud of a flower, began to spread out, to open up, as the old folks filed down the fountain's ramps onto the city streets. They were replaced by young couples and groups of boys and girls who talked to each other from a distance but did not mix. So much like religious children, he thought. In a way we are all the same. Dov Binyamin suddenly felt overwhelmed. He was startled to find himself in Tel Aviv, already involved in the act of searching out a harlot, instead of home in his chair by the balcony, worrying over whether to take the Rebbe's advice at all.

He walked back toward his car. A lone cabdriver leaned up against the front door of his Mercedes, smoking. Dov Binyamin approached him, the heat of his feet inside his shoes becoming more oppressive with every step.

"Forgive me," Dov Binyamin said.

The cabdriver, his chest hair sticking out of the collar of his T-shirt in tufts, ground out the cigarette and opened the passenger door. "Need a ride, Rabbi?"

"I'm not a rabbi."

"And you don't need a ride?"

Dov Binyamin adjusted his hat. "No. Actually no."

The cabdriver lit another cigarette, flourishing his Zippo impressively. Dov took notice, though he was not especially impressed.

"I'm looking for a prostitute."

The cabdriver coughed and clasped a hand to his chest.

"Do I look like a prostitute?"

"No, you misunderstand." Dov Binyamin wondered if he should turn and run away. "A female prostitute."

"What's her name?"

"No name. Any name. You are a taxi driver. You must know where are such women." The taxi driver slapped the hood of his car and said, "Ha," which Dov took to be laughter. Another cab pulled up on Dov's other side.

"What's happening?" the second driver called.

"Nothing. The rabbi here wants to know where to find a friend. Thinks it's a cabdriver's responsibility to direct him."

"Do we work for the Ministry of Tourism?" the second driver asked.

"I just thought," Dov Binyamin said. His voice was high and cracking. It seemed to elicit pity in the second driver.

"There's a cash machine back on Dizengoff."

"Prostitutes at the bank?" Dov Binyamin said.

"No, not at the bank. But the service isn't free." Dov blushed under his beard. "Up by the train station in Ramat Gan—at the row of bus stops."

"All those pretty ladies aren't waiting for the bus to Haifa." This from the first driver, who again slapped the hood of his car and said, "Ha!"

THE FIRST TIME past, he did not stop, driving by the women at high speed and taking the curves around the cement island so that his wheels screeched and he could smell the burning rubber. Dov Binyamin slowed down, trying to maintain control of himself and the car, afraid that he had already drawn too much attention his way. The steering wheel began to vibrate in Dov's shaking hands. The Rebbe had given him permission, had instructed him. Was not the Rebbe's heter valid? This is what Dov Binyamin told his hands, but they continued to tremble in protest.

On his second time past, a woman approached the passenger door. She wore a matching shirt and pants. The outfit clung tightly, and Dov could see the full form of her body. Such immodesty! She tapped at the window. Dov Binyamin reached over to roll it down. Flustered, he knocked the gearshift, and the car lurched forward. Applying the parking brake, he opened the window the rest of the way.

"Close your lights," she instructed him. "We don't need to be onstage out here."

"Sorry," he said, shutting off the lights. He was comforted by the error, not wanting the woman to think he was the kind of man who employed prostitutes on a regular basis.

"You interested in some action?"

"Me?"

"A shy one," she said. She leaned through the window, and Dov Binyamin looked away from her large breasts. "Is this your first time? Don't worry. I'll be gentle. I know how to treat a black hat."

Dov Binyamin felt the full weight of what he was doing. He was giving a bad name to all Hasidim. It was a sin against God's name. The urge to drive off, to race back to Jerusalem and the silence of his wife, came over Dov Binyamin. He concentrated on his dispensation.

"What would you know from black hats?" he said.

"Plenty," she said. And then, leaning in farther, "Actually, you look familiar." Dov Binyamin seized up, only to begin shaking twice as hard. He shifted into first and gave the car some gas. The prostitute barely got clear of the window.

When it seemed as if he wouldn't find a suitable match, a strong-looking young woman stepped out of the darkness.

"Good evening," he said.

She did not answer or ask any questions or smile. She opened the passenger door and sat down.

"What do you think you're doing?"

"Saving you the trouble of driving around until the sun comes up." She was American. He could hear it. But she spoke beautiful Hebrew, sweet and strong as her step. Dov Binyamin turned on his headlights and again bumped the gearshift so that the car jumped.

"Settle down there, Tiger," she said. "The hard part's over. All the rest of the work is mine."

THE ROOM WAS in an unlicensed hostel. It had its own entrance. There was no furniture other than a double bed and three singles. The only lamp stood next to the door.

The prostitute sat on the big bed with her legs curled underneath her. She said her name was Devorah.

"Like the prophetess," Dov Binyamin said.

"Exactly," Devorah said. "But I can only see into the immediate future."

"Still, it is a rare gift with which to have been endowed." Dov shifted his weight from foot to foot. He stood next to the large bed unable to bring himself to bend his knees.

"Not really," she said. "All my clients already know what's in store."

She was fiery, this one. And their conversation served to warm up the parts of Dov the heat wave had not touched. The desire that had been building in Dov over the many months so filled his body that he was surprised his skin did not burst from the pressure. He tossed his hat onto the opposite single, hoping to appear at ease, as sure of himself as the hairy-chested cabdriver with his cigarettes. The hat landed brim side down. Dov's muscles twitched reflexively, though he did not flip it onto its crown.

"Wouldn't you rather make your living as a prophetess?" he asked.

"Of course. Prophesying's a piece of cake. You don't have to primp all day for it. And it's much easier on the back, no wear and tear. Better for *you*, too. At least you'd leave with something in the morning." She took out one of her earrings, then, as an afterthought, put it back in. "Doesn't matter anyway. No money in it. They pay me to do everything *except* look into the future."

"I'll be the first then," he said, starting to feel almost comfortable. "Tell me what you see."

She closed her eyes and tilted her head so that her lips began to part, this in the style of those who peer into other realms. "I predict that this is the first time you've done such a thing."

"That is not a prophecy. It's a guess." Dov Binyamin cleared his throat and wiggled his toes against the tops of his shoes. "What else do you predict?"

She massaged her temples and held back a naughty grin.

"That you will, for once, get properly laid."

But this was too much for Dov Binyamin. Boiling in the heat and his shame, he motioned toward his hat.

Devorah took his hand.

"Forgive me," she said, "I didn't mean to be crude."

Her fingers were tan and thin, more delicate than Chava's. How strange it was to see strange fingers against the whiteness of his own.

"Excluding the affections of my mother, blessed be her memory, this is the first time I have been touched by a woman that is not my wife."

She released her grasp and, before he had time to step away, reached out for him again, this time more firmly, as if shaking on a deal. Devorah raised herself up and straightened a leg, displayed it for a moment, and then let it dangle over the side of the bed. Dov admired the leg, and the fingers resting against his palm.

"Why are we here together?" she asked—she was not mocking him. Devorah pulled at the hand and he sat at her side.

"To relieve my unbearable urges. So that my wife will be able to love me again."

Devorah raised her eyebrows and pursed her lips.

"You come to me for your wife's sake?"

"Yes."

"You are a very dedicated husband."

She gave him a smile that said, You won't go through with it. The smile lingered, and then he saw that it said something completely different, something irresistible. And he wondered, as a shiver ran from the trunk of his body out to the hand she held, if what they say about American women is true.

Dov walked toward the door, not to leave, but to shut off the lamp.

"One minute," Devorah said, reaching back and removing a condom from a tiny pocket—no more than a slit in the smooth black fabric of her pants. Dov Binyamin knew what it was and waved it away.

"Am I really your second?" she asked.

Dov heard more in the question than was intended. He heard a flirtation; he heard a woman who treated the act of being second as if it were special. He was sad for her—wondering if she had ever been anyone's first. He did not answer out loud, but instead nodded, affirming.

Devorah pouted as she decided, the prophylactic held between two fingers like a quarter poised at the mouth of a jukebox. Dov switched off the light and took a half step toward the bed. He stroked at the darkness, moving forward until he found her hair, soft, alive, without any of the worked-over stiffness of Chava's wigs.

"My God," he said, snatching back his hand as if he had been stung. It was too late, though. That he already knew. The hunger had flooded his whole self. His heart was swollen with it, pumping so loudly and with such strength that it overpowered whatever sense he might have had. For whom then, he wondered, was he putting on, in darkness, such a bashful show? He reached out again and stroked her hair, shaking but sure of his intent. With his other arm, the weaker arm, to which he bound every morning his tefillin, the arm closer to the violent force of his heart, he searched for her hand.

Dov found it and took hold of it, first roughly, as if desperate. Then he held it lightly, delicately, as if it were made of blown glass—a goblet from which, with ceremony, he wished to drink. Bringing it toward his mouth, he began to speak.

"It is a sin to spill seed in vain," he said, and Devorah let the condom fall at the sound of his words.

DOV BINYAMIN WAS at work on Monday and he was home as usual on Monday night. There was no desire to slip out of the apartment during the long hours when he could not sleep, no temptation, when making a delivery in Ramot, to turn the car in the direction of Tel Aviv. Dov Binyamin felt, along with a guilt that he could not shake, a sense of relief. He knew that he could never be with another woman again. And if it were possible to heap on himself all the sexual urges of the past months, if he could undo the single night with the prostitute to restore his unadulterated fidelity, he would have them tenfold. From that night of indulgence he found the strength to wait a lifetime for Chava's attentions—if that need be.

When Chava Bayla entered the dining room. Dov Binyamin would move into the kitchen. When she entered the bedroom, he would close his eyes and feign sleep. He would lie in the dark and silently love his wife. And, never coming to a conclusion, he would rethink the wisdom of the Rebbe's advice. He would picture the hairy arm of the cabdriver as he slapped the hood of his taxi. And he would chide himself. Never, never would he accuse his wife of faking impurity, for was it not the greater sin for him to pretend to be pure?

It was only a number of days from that Sunday night that Chava Bayla began to talk to her husband with affection. Soon after, she touched him on the shoulder while handing him a platter of kasha varnishkes. He placed it on the table and ate in silence. As she served dessert, levelesh, his favorite. Dov's guilt took on a physical form. What else could it be? What else but guilt would strike a man so obviously?

It began as a concentrated smoldering that flushed the

whole of his body. Quickly intensifying, it left him almost feverish. He would excuse himself from meals and sneak out of bed. At work, frightened and in ever-increasing pain, he ran from customers to examine himself in the bathroom. Dov Binyamin knew he was suffering from something more than shame.

But maybe it was a trial, a test of which the Rebbe had not warned him. For as his discomfort increased, so did Chava's attentions. On her way out of the shower, she let her towel drop in front of him, stepping away from it as if she hadn't noticed, like some Victorian woman waiting for a gentleman to return her hankie with a bow. She dressed slowly, self-consciously, omitting her undergarments and looking to Dov to remind her. He ignored it all, feeling the weight of his heart—no longer pumping as if to burst, but just as large—the blood stagnant and heavy. Chava began to linger in doorways so that he would be forced to brush against her as he passed. Her passion was torturous to Dov, forced to keep his own hidden inside. Once, without any of the protocol with which they tempered their lives, she came at the subject head-on. "Are you such a small man," she said, "that you must for eternity exact revenge?" He made no answer. It was she who walked away, only to return sweeter and bolder. She became so daring, so desperate, that he wondered if he had ever known the true nature of his wife at all. But he refused, even after repeated advances, to respond to Chava Bayla in bed.

SHE CALLED TO him from the darkness.

"Dovey, please, come out of there. Come lie by me and we'll talk. Just talk. Come Doveleh, join me in bed."

Dov Binyamin stood in the dark in the bathroom. There was some light from the street, enough to make out the toilet and the sink. He heard every word his wife said, and each one tore at him.

He stood before the toilet, holding his penis lightly, mindful of halacha and the laws concerning proper conduct in the lavatory. Trying to relieve himself, to pass water, he suffered to no end.

When he began to urinate, the burning worsened. He looked down in the half darkness and imagined he saw flames flickering from his penis.

He recalled the words of the prostitute. For his wife's sake, he thought, as the tears welled in his eyes. This couldn't possibly be the solution the Rebbe intended. Dov was supposed to be in his wife's embrace, enjoying her caresses, and instead he would get an examination table and a doctor's probing hands.

Dov Binyamin dropped to his knees. He rested his head against the coolness of the bowl. Whatever the trial, he couldn't bear it much longer. He had by now earned, he was sure, Chava Bayla's love.

There was a noise; it startled him; it was Chava at the door trying to open it. Dov had locked himself in. The handle turned again, and then Chava spoke to him through the door's frosted-glass window.

"Tell me," she said. "Tell me: When did I lose my husband for good?"

Every word a plague.

Dov pressed the lever of the toilet, drowning out Chava Bayla's voice. He let the tears run down his face and took his penis full in his hand.

For Dov Binyamin was on fire inside.

And yet he would not be consumed.

good night, my dear

(fiction)

Jonathan Ames

FROM MY LESS THAN SECRET LIFE

WENT TO A famous, old European city. I read in my guide-book that transvestite prostitutes could be encountered in the woods at the edge of the city. This wasn't mentioned as a recommendation, but, rather, as a warning about an area that could be dangerous at night, and for most readers of the guide-book it would be a warning, but for me it was very helpful, a point of interest.

It was around ten pm when I left my hotel. It was early March, so it was cool out, but not freezing. I took the metro and found the woods and felt accomplished as a tourist. There was a long road that bisected the woods and led the way out of the city to the suburbs. A few cars drove by, quick and small with their jaundiced European headlights. Some cars were parked on the road and it was quite dark—there were no streetlights.

Along the edge of the road was a muddy path. I walked along this path and there was one man up ahead of me at some distance. There were only two transvestites standing in the road, and I was disappointed. I thought there would be more.

I walked past them—they weren't pretty. The man ahead of me had somehow mysteriously disappeared. I kept walking. Then there was this path that led into the woods. There was moonlight and starlight, enough to see by. I walked in about ten yards. Men were hovering about, moving through the trees, walking down dirt paths as if they had somewhere to go.

Some men stood motionless, hiding by trees in the darkness, but because of the silvery light from the sky, I could see them, their bulk, their shape. The men were playing this tedious game of waiting and looking. I've seen it in woods and parks all over the world. Patience is needed—a man waits by a tree for another man to approach. There are those who wait and those who keep moving, and everyone is furtive and malevolent, unwelcoming, really. Afraid of not being wanted, I guess. And I've never seen anything happen; have never seen a man kneeling in front of another man or standing behind another man. But something must happen; woods like this are always filled—the men wouldn't come if *something* didn't happen.

So I walked around a bit, testing my courage, going deeper into the woods, wanting for once to catch a glimpse of sex, but I saw no coupling. Men sallied forth on their missions, their hunt in these woods, and I thought maybe I would let something happen to me, but I'm never quite sure how to play this game—I'd love to ask someone how it works but no one talks in these woods and I guess it's the kind of thing that you just know how to do. So I'm frightened by this game I don't fully understand, and that night in the woods, my courage failing, I walked back out to the road.

The two transvestites were gone. They were either in the woods or men in cars had stopped for them. The transvestites had been large, with bulky, unfeminine bodies. They had no beauty, no illusion of beauty, but now that they were gone I despaired that I had missed out, that I had come to the woods and would have no solace.

I kept walking on the muddy path. Maybe farther up I would find something. The road was very long. I walked for several minutes. I wished I could go back to my hotel, but I wouldn't let myself. Once a night like this starts, it's very rare that I can turn back. I have to see it through. I *have* to have an adventure. I *have* to hurt myself.

Then my perseverance was rewarded. I saw a light go on and off in a thicket of trees a few yards from the path. I walked towards the light. It was exciting how it went on and off, that someone was there, calling to me, signaling. I kept walking towards the light and then the light went off one last time and I was right next to the person. It was a woman. Not a transvestite. She was in a small fur because of the chilly March air. She had on a blonde wig. I liked her face. She smiled sweetly. She looked to be in her early forties and she was large-breasted. She wore a white skirt, fishnet stockings, and high red boots, good for the mud.

We talked. I knew the language. Her price was very fair: I did the math: only thirty American dollars, and yet a cup of coffee in the ancient city cost nearly four dollars. I've never understood the market place. The guide-book should have listed the woods as a spot where a tourist could get a bargain. I took out the necessary currency. She put the flashlight and my money in her purse. I admired her ingenuity, using the light to let men know where she was. She opened my pants and squatted in front of me, balancing nicely in her boots. She put a condom on me and she went about things happily, peacefully, not in a rush. She gave me a few sucks to wet the condom and to arouse me. Two men approached from within the woods to watch; they stood just a few feet away. She took her mouth off me and cursed at them violently and they retreated back into the darkness.

Then she stood up and grabbed hold of a thin white tree, a young tree. She bent over a little and reached behind herself, lifting up her skirt. No panties. Looking over her shoulder, she took hold of me and guided me in. It was lovely, it's always lovely to be in a woman, and she smiled at me, a kind smile, an older woman smiling at a young man who is inside her. Then she turned and faced the tree.

I pushed it in some more. I was pleased not to come right away. I moved it back and forth slowly. I kept one hand on her hip and with the other I stroked her blonde wig, like it was real hair. She pushed back to take me deeper. Then I reached around with both hands, got them under the short fur coat, and squeezed her large, heavy breasts. I liked having them in my hands.

I lay my chest against her back. I held her to me and we fucked. She took quick little breaths, either from the exertion or she may have actually liked it, there's always that chance, that hope, but it was probably the exertion, but at least she wasn't moaning with exaggeration, like most prostitutes. She held on to that tree and kept pushing back for more and I felt almost happy.

We were doing it for a good ten minutes, sometimes I'd just lie against her back and feel good about being in a dark woods and being inside this woman, and I'd kiss her neck beneath the stiff hair of the wig. But I do always like to please the woman I'm with and I knew that what pleases a prostitute is for it to be over sooner rather than later, even though I felt like she was actually enjoying it or at least not finding it horrible, but, still, I thought it would be better to end it, that she would appreciate this, so I came, pushing into her deeply one last time. Then I rested on her back, holding her.

She waited a few seconds, then let go of the tree and I pulled myself out. She took a tissue from her purse and cleaned me up gently. I closed my pants and she said next time we should go to her apartment. Then with both her hands, she held my face, and she looked at me and she laughed happily, her soul wasn't heavy, at least not in that moment, and how can I explain her mirth? Was it because I was young? Then her hands slid off my face, caressing me, and she said, "Good night, my dear."

Her English was beautiful and unexpected. She walked out of the woods and onto the muddy path. I followed her and then went the opposite way, not looking back, remembering that somebody once told me that you jinx things with women if you look back.

I RETURNED THE next night to see her. I had been fantasizing all that day about going to her apartment; I pictured it as cluttered and small but warm. A European's apartment! The old world! I'd lie on her bed and she'd be moving about the room, maybe making us something to eat, and maybe I'd spend the night.

Sometimes when I make love I want to tell the woman that I love her. My affection and need and love all feel so strong in my chest that I want to say it, that I want to just break down and give the woman everything, but I always stop myself. But it seems to me that it would be so amazing to tell a woman that you loved her while you were inside her. What would happen? Would I feel free?

And when my chest first lay against the prostitute's back and she held on to that tree, I wanted to say, "I love you." So I went back to the woods the next night, prepared to shower her with money. I wanted to go to her apartment, to be let into her home. And then when we made love, I'd tell her. I'd pay to be with her so I could tell her that I loved her.

I arrived at the woods at exactly the same time of night, but she wasn't there. There were three or four transvestites, but not my woman. I walked up and down the path and hid at the edge of the woods for two hours, hoping to see her light in the trees. But she never came. And I was leaving the next morning, I wouldn't be able to return. It seemed crazy to change my ticket, what if she wasn't here the following night?

Finally, I gave up and talked to a tall, pretty black transvestite. She was from the West Indies and spoke English with a colonial accent. Her price was the same as the woman's the night before. What I wanted was completely different but the cost was uniform, and I thought this was interesting.

The West Indian, regal with good posture, led me for several minutes through the woods to a small abandoned building. It was a concrete square, missing a roof. What had been its purpose in the middle of the woods? And why did she bring me there—to kill me? Rob me? I didn't think so—I trust my intuition when it comes to these things, but it has to fail me some day.

So in the shadow of the building—she must have liked it for its privacy—I gave her the money and then knelt in front of her. She lifted her dress and pulled down her panties and out came her long, elegant black cock. That's always a nice moment when it comes out. The shock of it. She put a condom on and I sucked her while I knelt in the mud. I undid my pants and put my hand on myself. I liked having her in my mouth; it was comforting. A phallic pacifier. But I think it pacifies me because it kills me. Says I'm not a man. Erases me. Must be why I do it. I want to disappear. Give up. Then she said sweetly, "Let me see your bum."

I lifted my coat so she could see it. She bent over some to get a good look and I kept sucking her and touching myself. Then I came on the mud. It was over. Maybe it lasted two minutes. We walked out of the woods together for safety. Then she kissed me on the cheek goodbye. She was kind. I have good luck that way. In the most unkind settings, I meet the kindest people. I go to them to die but they don't really let me. So I only die a little.

I took the metro back to my hotel. It was a long ride, especially after what I had done—it's shameful when you're not homosexual to take another man's penis in your mouth, even if it's the shame I'm after. And, too, I felt very sad because I had touched yet again how desperate I really am, how lonely, how without answers.

I looked down at my knees and saw that my pants were dirty from the mud, but nobody on the train looking at me would think I'd been kneeling in some woods. How could it occur to them? Then I looked in the black window of the metro. It was like a mirror and I recognized my face. These things don't really change you. I wished they did, but they don't.

FROM you shall know our velocity

Dave Eggers

W E RAN INTO the Chilean-American tennis man in the lobby—

"What's his name again?" I whispered.

"Raymond."

"Thanks."

"Hey Raymond!" I said.

"Hello my friends!"

—and had a taxi take us all the six blocks to the Italian place he liked. The streets were narrow and dark. We opened the windows and the warm air touched us with coarse hands. The buildings looked like buildings I'd seen before—they had straight lines and neat corners and windows in between—but they seemed closer to something imagined and built by architects of another world. We flew beneath their roofs and I grinned to the wind, because we'd at least come this far and that meant we'd won.

The cabbie asked for the equivalent of fifty cents and I gave him ten dollars; he said thank you thank you, and that he'd

wait until we were done to take us back, or anywhere else, anytime, while we stayed in his country, you friends!

The restaurant was empty but for four drunk and round
Italians at the bar talking to the drunk Italian hostess.

"She's gorgeous, isn't she?" Raymond said. "That's why I had
to come back."

Hand agreed. "She *is* nice. But I'm really starting to have a
thing for Senegalese women."

"You too?" said Raymond. "I know. They are superb." Raymond raised his finger, about to make a point. "But," he said,
closing his eyes slowly and raising his chin, "they are all
whores."

"What do you mean?" Hand asked.

"You will see," he said.

Hand and I stared at Raymond and blinked slowly. We were
stuck with this man for a while, even though it was becoming
obvious that he was not of our stripe. Friendships, even tem-
porary ones like this, were based on proximity and chance, and
so rarely made any sense at all. We knew, though, that we'd
part with Raymond tonight and never likely see him again, so
it made it bearable.

The music piped in was a short, ever-repeating loop of Dire
Straits, Pink Floyd, Eagles and *White Album* Beatles. We had fet-
tuccine and Senegalese beer. We learned that Raymond
worked in cellphones. Something involving GPS and cellphones and how, soon enough, everyone would know—for
their own safety, he insisted, with a fist softly pounding the
table, in a way he'd likely done a hundred times before—
where everyone else in the world was, by tracking their cell-
phone. But again: for good not evil. For the children. For the
children. For grandparents and wives.

It was the end of an epoch, and I didn't want to be around
to see it happen; we'd traded anonymity for access. I shuddered. Hand, of course, had goosebumps.

•   •   •

AFTER DINNER HAND asked the cabbie, who'd been waiting without radio or newspaper, to take us to see live music. "You know," said Hand, "like Youssour N'Dour." We'd read in the hotel lobby guidebook that Youssour N'Dour lived in Dakar and owned a club. The cabbie seemed to understand, began driving, and a few minutes later pulled up in front of an outdoor café.

"Here is the location of the music that is live?" asked Hand.

Raymond looked at Hand. Hand needed reining in.

"Yes, yes," said the driver, waving us out of the car. "You like, you like." We got out.

It looked fine, a French café sort of place, outdoor seating, inside warmly lit. But there was no music at all; just wrought-iron tables and a floor of white tile, a black slate bar with a bowl of Manet oranges. We walked in anyway. We'd get a drink and leave.

All eyes jumped to us. There were groups of men and groups of women. The men were tourists and the women were local. I went to the bathroom. In the cool small space, walls like a cave's wet, and brown, I washed my hands with a small piece of round scallop-shaped soap that smelled of home.

I found Raymond and Hand at a table outside, with two women, lighter than most Senegalese, both with long braided hair. Raymond stood and gave me his chair and grabbed another for himself. The girls surveyed me briefly and looked away. I wanted to tear my face off.

There were drinks for everyone. I was introduced to the two, whose names I pretended to understand and whose limp hands I held momentarily and dropped. They looked about twenty, twenty-two. They were sisters and I felt again, as so many times with Hand and Jack, like deadweight, alone.

"They're from Sierra Leone," said Raymond.

"Refugees," added Hand.

They were just short of glorious, with large dark eyes and crooked, oversized teeth. Raymond and Hand were trying to speak French with them.

"We speak little French," the older one said. "Speak English. In Sierra Leone we speak English."

"So you are liking it here in the Dakar?" Hand asked.

Raymond looked at him like he was nuts.

"What?" said the younger. The younger was taller.

"Dakar. Do you like it," Raymond said, annoyed.

"Yes. It's good."

The older one nodded. Hand ordered more drinks and then leaned toward them. He was about to dig in.

"So what's the situation like in Sierra Leone now? Is Charles Taylor still lurking around? I should know this, I guess, but it's been a while since I read about it. Have you seen any of the violence around the diamond trade?"

They looked dumbfounded, turning to Raymond for reason, as if he might translate. Hand continued:

"What did you do for a living? Are you students? When did you guys leave? I mean, are your parents still there?"

The sisters looked at each other.

"What?" the older said, smiling.

"Your parents? In Sierra Leone?"

"Yes. Live there."

"So how old are you two?" Raymond asked.

—Raymond, you're callous and cheap.

—I've seen more than you.

—That means nothing.

—It means everything.

—It's the laziest excuse of all.

"What?" the girl said.

"How old are you?" Raymond repeated.

The older one, to whom Raymond had directed the question, laughed and looked at her sister. Her sister shook her head. She didn't understand.

"How many years are you?" Hand tried.

The older held up her hands in a "Stop" sort of motion, closed them, then did it again.

"Twenty," Hand said.

She nodded.

"And her?" Hand motioned to the sister.

She did it again, with eight fingers on the second flash.

"Eighteen."

She shook her head vigorously, laughing. Then she flashed the fingers again. Eighteen.

"Eighteen."

"No!"

This went on for a while. Raymond laughed.

"Your English is not very good, is it?" Hand said.

"What?" she said.

Raymond said it in French. His French was amazing.

"Speak English!" the girl said. "We are from Sierra Leone!"

Where was this going? No one could know. I wasn't listening anymore, and each girl began concentrating on one man—the younger on Hand, the older on Raymond.

I watched the sidewalk over the café's low hedge. The place was stocked with chubby European or American men, mostly middle-aged and cheerful, patient. Some had garnered the attentions of the available women, others waited with friends, hands cupped around tall glassed beers. By the door was a man with no legs, sitting on a mat.

Now the younger sister was laughing about something Hand said, making a point of grabbing his arm with both hands and burying her head in his shoulder to demonstrate the great mirth he'd generated. Hand rolled his eyes to me like a cat had jumped into his lap. More drinks were ordered.

"So we go to disco now?" the older said to Raymond.

Hand and Raymond looked at each other, then at me. I shrugged. They reminded me of twins I'd known at La Crosse, sisters who knew their skin was more perfect than the rest of ours, and who were very forgiving of the white boys' many fumbling entreaties. These sisters, the Sierra Leonians, had the same bright but complicated smiles.

"No," said Hand, "I think we'll go home. To the hotel." It was clearly a lie. He extended his hand to his younger one.

She and her sister stood up and glared at me and went back to the bar.

"Let's go," said Raymond.

When we'd been all together, and when I'd assumed Hand would ask me if it was okay to spend some time alone with one of the girls and that Raymond would follow, I'd hated them all. I'd felt for the girls, but then realized, uncharitably, that they all deserved each other. Now, though, we were leaving, Hand and Raymond were letting them off the hook, or rejecting them, and now I loved the sisters, and wanted to save them from the violence of rejection. I wanted to be with them alone. I wanted to sit with them, laugh at other people with them.

But what did I do? I gave them the tight, smarmy smile I give to homeless people when I have nothing for them, always with a slight, quick shoulder shrug, and we were gone.

I FOLLOWED HAND and Raymond the two steps to the taxis and we were groped by the man without legs. He wanted money. Then an old woman, middle finger crooked through an actual tin cup, placed herself in front of us, sticking the cup a few inches from my mouth. One of the other women from the bar appeared before us—what she wanted she didn't say. We were surrounded. We backed into the cab. Raymond got in the front seat and closed his door. Hand got in the rear and I sunk in after him, but the no-legged man was now halfway in the car and the door wouldn't close. I could smell his breath, worlds contained within. Why wasn't the cabbie doing anything? He was supposed to tell us not to pay the man. He was supposed to push the man away but he was watching. Everyone in the café was watching.

"Just give him something," said Raymond, laughing. It wasn't funny. This was some kind of thing that happened in India, or the Bible.

I gave the man the coins in my pocket and while counting them he backed away long enough for us to get the door closed. The old woman appeared at the open window, thrusting her head inside. The car was moving, but her head was fully in our cab. Raymond's hand was on her shoulder, pushing her away. He shoved but too roughly—she fell back into the shrubbery with a shriek.

We were off.

"Jesus," I said.

"That was wretched," said Hand.

"These people are poor," said Raymond, without turning around, talking through the wind pouring through his window.

"Listen," Raymond continued, now turning his shoulders to us. "You're here. You came here. You left the hotel. You walk these streets, you allow your path to be chosen by me, by [jerking a thumb toward the cabbie] this driver. You invite things to happen. You open the door. You inhale. And if you inhale the chaos, you give the chaos, the chaos gives back. You know this?"

I felt my forehead tighten, indicating I was thinking—often my forehead starts thinking before I do. I committed what he'd said to memory—it was a jigsaw dumped on a rug but I was hoping I could put it back together, later.

We rode in silence for a few minutes.

"That didn't even make sense," Hand muttered.

"The imbalance is there," Raymond continued. My tolerance for Raymond was waning. "It is just that we don't acknowledge it. We know we're stronger but we ignore this. We don't know our strength. You watch *Star Trek*, how they—what's the word for their beaming up and down—"

"Teleporting," I said, shocked at this train of thought, and how it had just plowed right into my own backyard.

"Right," Raymond said. "They teleport in and out of those troubled planets?"

"Wait," Hand said, actually raising his palm to Raymond's face. "You get *Star Trek* in Chile?"

"Of course."

Hand snorted, impressed. "Okay, go on."

"So this teleporting was based on a Cold War mentality. This was the American foreign policy model then. This was based on the American strength, the American ability to move and change the worlds they touched onto."

The cabbie asked where to and we told him again: Youssour N'Dour's place. Raymond and the cabbie were arguing about something. I clenched and unclenched my fists. They tingled wildly, as if they'd just woken up. Hand noticed.

"You know," he said, "you could go to a hospital here. It'd still be anonymous. No one could track it back here."

"They could."

"C'mon. Really. You should. Get all your shit checked out."

I'd never gone to the hospital after Oconomowoc. We'd decided that if I went in, told the story and made some kind of official record of it, they'd know it was us if we went back some-day and killed all three of them. But getting fixed up here, in Dakar, sounded almost feasible. The cabbie took a few more turns and pulled up in front of a club called Hollywood.

"Is this the live music?" I asked.

"Yes, yes, yes—you love it there!" he said, shooing us inside. "I wait here."

Low-ceilinged and horrible, it was a small disco, pink and purple, full of large, framed movie stills in black-and-white— the decor of an antique auto museum. Life-sized pictures of James Dean and Marilyn Monroe, two or three of each, and one each of Tom Selleck and Sandra Bullock and Charlie Sheen, but also, strangely, seven different shots of Val Kilmer in *Top Gun*. The place was empty beyond ourselves and twelve young white men with crew cuts. Sailors.

"I could do that," Hand said.

"Be a sailor? You're high," I said.

"For a year I could do that."

"Just for the pants. That's why you'd do it."

Raymond ordered drinks and began talking to the bar-tender, a young Senegalese woman in a lace top glowing violet-white in the black light. She came around the bar and was by his side, touching his chest. She looked at me and sniffed. I reached over for my beer and waited for Hand to get back from the bathroom. The place was confusing me. I was sick of looking like a leper.

Hand emerged from the back but was intercepted by a tall thin woman in a halter top and pleather pants. She was built like a fetishist's fantasy—her legs would reach my armpit and her rear (I can't say *ass* in this context; could never say *ass*) was so round and full it looked like it would pop if lanced. She was leading Hand to the small dancefloor in the back, lit from below and facing a mirror. Debbie Harry was singing "Heart of Glass" and the world stood listless.

There was another couple dancing, a sailor and a Senegalese woman, but they were dancing with their reflections more than with each other. The man was staring at himself in a way, if directed at anyone but his own mirror image, would have to be considered lewd.

The other sailors were talking with each other, uninterested in the bartenders or dancers. Who was Hand's woman? I watched them dance, Hand doing a moonwalk and then a kind of samba, laughing. Hand is the kind of guy who has rhythm and can move, but is ashamed of this, so has to goof his way through every song. Now he was doing the sprinkler. Then the shopping cart. He was teaching his new friend the shopping cart.

After the song he came back with the woman, who was huge, easily six feet tall. She was too thin on top for me, but still, she was magnificent. Senegal: who knew?

"This is Engela," Hand said. Something like that. "She's studying to become a lawyer." Hand bought shots for them both. He drank his, she left hers alone till he drank it himself.

I shook her hand and her eyes met mine, scanned my nose and cheeks, and she winced. She played with Hand's ear.

I was bored. If more people were dancing I could watch or join, but this wasn't working. Now two sailors were on the dancefloor, without women, admiring their own legs moving inside their tight tapered delicately bleached jeans.

"It is a shame," said Raymond, watching the sailors with half-closed eyes. "This country does not allow its women dignity."

I thought he might be overgeneralizing, but I didn't really know enough to comment either way.

"There's Burma," he continued, "there's Thailand, there is Russia. All sell their women. Their souls are sold when born. The men are mice and the women are cattle."

I drank two vodka-sodas. Soon Raymond didn't like his new friend anymore and wanted to go. Hand's date whispered something to him and he shook his head and whispered back, hand cupped around her ear. She jogged behind the bar and came back with a pen and a little notebook. He wrote something down.

I went to the bar for a shot of anything. The woman serving me was wearing a white sports bra that looked like it had been mauled by tigers—desert isle chic. I turned again. Hand was showing his friend something. A piece of paper. A picture. What was it?

I grabbed it.

"What the fuck are you doing?" I yelled. It was a picture of Jack. Hand stood and looked at me, heavy-lidded with pity.

"I told her we were looking for our friend," he said.

"What does that mean?"

He was drunk already. He couldn't be, so soon.

"You know what it means," he said.

"That doesn't even make sense," I said.

"So what the fuck?" he said.

"You're disgusting."

"I can show him to anyone I want, fucker."

"I don't know you."

He scoffed. He was such a messy drunk.

"Don't ever show that picture to some random waitress again," I said.

"I'll do whatever."

"You fucking *won't*."

"Guys!" Raymond said, with an arm between us. "Easy."

I walked out and waited in the cab. I wanted an hour alone in the cab in the cooling air but they followed me out seconds later.

HAND ASKED AGAIN that we be taken to the jazz club, and I wanted Hand back in St. Louis. He was the wrong guy to have brought. The picture. What kind of—? I couldn't go home, couldn't leave him, though, because we were in Dakar and only had this week.

Five minutes through deserted streets and the next place was precisely the same but worse and without Val Kilmer. "In every part of the world," explained Raymond, "cabbies are trained to bring men to clubs like this. We go in, the cabbie gets a kickback, everyone's happy. We are merely cargo. The way you guys are traveling, you're gonna be targets everywhere. You're perfect prey."

This time, immediately upon entering, we were all attacked in a very real way—women pushing each other to get closer to us, throwing jagged looks at each other, one grabbing Hand's crotch in a way less erotic than territorial. Raymond wound up next to a large woman with bursting eyes and Hand ran to the bathroom. I was being left more or less alone so ordered a drink and saw, across the bar, the two Sierra Leonian sisters, in the corner, beyond the dancefloor. They saw me too and laughed a warm and commiserative laugh.

They were still on the make. The place was full—more French sailors, three dozen hungry Senegalese women, and the rest a hodgepodge of Italians and older European businessmen sitting alone, still waiting, waiting. We watched the dancefloor crowd, clear and change and at one point the Sierra Leonians were dancing alone and I decided then to give them the contents of my left sock, about $400, before we left.

Hand returned from the bathroom with a story. Apparently there had been a few French sailors inside and they'd asked him his nationality. American, he said. "America!" they said, "you pay for the world!" Then they both cheered and patted him on the back. He probably made it up.

"The crazy thing is," Hand said, "I think they were serious."

"You show them any pictures?" I asked.

"Fuck you," he said.

"They're young. They'll learn," said Raymond.

"Learn what?" Hand asked.

"Derision," he said.

I was impressed by Raymond. He could break out a word like *derision*, in his second language, and even better, he was an aphorism kind of man, who could conceive of such things—*We are merely cargo*—and slip them into conversation—*You give chaos, chaos gives back*. I always wanted to be a guy like that.

I watched the dancefloor, full of slack shoulders and heads hung and swinging, arms reaching passively up, up. Women tucked their hair behind their ears and men pecked their heads to the beat, hands as fists.

What was wrong with Charlotte? Nothing. Every complaint now seemed ridiculous. She had long dark hairs that swirled around her nipples and I'd seen this as problematic instead of loving her indifference to them. And I'd disliked her sighs. She sighed too much, I announced to myself one day, and worse, her sighs were too sad. Too full of sorrow. When I held her she sighed, and her sighs were weary, were groaning and exhausted, the sigh of an old person who'd seen everything and couldn't believe she was now being held, at the end of a journey she could never describe. The sighs were withering, were mood-killing, and finally I complained about Charlotte's sighs, to no avail. She'd responded with another sigh and that, I know now, was the end of the end.

I was a fool. She was full of soul and now I was in this place, and the women here assumed I needed them.

"Let's go," said Hand. "This is too sad."

We moved for the door. A huge woman with enormous fingernails, not just long but wide, was tugging on me. I was flattered by the attention but it was unclear what she wanted. Another woman, her friend, smaller and with red-ringed eyes, patted my crotch like you would the head of a muzzled dog.

Hand was ready, close to the door.

But I wanted to unload the cash on the Sierra Leonians. They were harmless and hopeful next to the rest of these women. I slipped past the clawed woman and to the bathroom—just a hole in the floor in a room like a closet—to secretly retrieve the bills, wrapped around my ankle like a manacle. The wad stifled within my closed fist, I walked across the dancefloor and found the two young women sitting on a watcher's ledge, bored, and said "Sorry" to them while stuffing the bills in the older one's hand. She didn't even look at the wad; she felt it but kept her eyes on mine. It was, I realized in a shot, the first time any of these women had really looked at me. I jogged across the dancefloor, getting a running start before the throng of grabbing women at the bar.

Raymond was outside. The street was crowded and the bouncers said goodnight—that was nice, I thought—and we waited in the taxi in the dark. Hand was not with us.

"Sven's inside," Raymond explained.

Hand emerged with the Sierra Leonian sisters kissing him on the cheeks and rubbing his chest—he'd taken credit for my gift—and he left them on the steps. He crossed the street and strode to the cab smiling grandly. He opened the door and got in with me and tried to close it but jesus—a body, again!—a body stopped the door from closing, prevented us from moving. It was my huge clawing prostitute. She had seen me give the money to the Sierra Leonians and wanted her share. She was enormous. I tried pushing her back but she was strong, at least as heavy as me, and was halfway in the car, preventing us from leaving or even closing the door. Her hand was out and she was talking quickly, in French. Then English: "Give me I see you! Give me I see you!"

I found a 50 dirham note and threw it to her. It fell to the street. She picked it up and I closed the door, narrowly missing her head. She turned around quickly and walked back into the bar, stuffing it in her pants as we drove away.

FROM serenade

James M. Cain

*Until this moment Johnny Sharp and Juana Montes have shared only
one fateful but anticlimactic night, during the course of which Johnny
had bought Juana a "billete"—a lottery ticket—with one of his last
three pesos. It is now some two months later and Johnny has responded
to Juana's urgent summons. He's driving her new car—"the newest,
reddest Ford in the world. It shone like a boil on a sailor's neck."*

"THE AUTO—YOU like, yes?"

"It's a knockout." We were coming
up the Bolivar again, and I had to keep tooting the horn,
according to law. The main thing they put on cars for Mexican
export is the biggest, loudest horn they can find in Detroit, and
this one had a double note to it that sounded like a couple of
ferryboats passing in an East River fog. "Your business must be
good."

I didn't mean to make any crack, but it slipped out on me.
If it meant anything to her at all, she passed it up.

"Oh no. I win."

"How?"

"The billete. You remember?"

"Oh. My billete?"

"Yes. I win, in lotería. The auto, and five honnerd pesos. The auto, is very pretty. I can no make go."

"Well, I can make it go, if that's all that's bothering you. About those five hundred pesos. You got some of them with you?"

"Oh yes. Of course."

"That's great. What you're going to do is buy me a breakfast. For my belly—muy empty. You get it?"

"Oh, why you no say? Yes, of course, now we eat."

I pulled in at the Tupinamba. The restaurants don't open until one o'clock, but the cafés will take care of you. We took a table up near the corner, where it was dark and cool. Hardly anybody was in there. My same old waitress came around grinning, and I didn't waste any time. "Orange juice, the biggest you got. Fried eggs, three of them, and fried ham. Tortillas. Glass of milk, frío, and café con crema."

"Bueno."

She took iced coffee, a nifty down there, and gave me a cigarette. It was the first I had had in three days, and I inhaled and leaned back, and smiled at her. "So."

"So."

But she didn't smile back, and looked away as soon as she said it. It was the first time we had really looked at each other all morning, and it brought us back to that night. She smoked, and looked up once or twice to say something, and didn't, and I saw there was something on her mind besides the billete. "So—you still have no pesos?"

"That's more or less correct."

"You work, no?"

"I did work, but I got kicked out. Just at present, I'm not doing anything at all."

"You like to work, yes? For me?"

". . . Doing what?"

"Play a guitar, little bit, maybe. Write a letter, count money, speak *Inglés*, help me, no work very hard. In Mexico, nobody work very hard. Yes? You like?"

"Wait a minute. I don't get this."

"Now I have money, I open house."

"Here?"

"No, no, no. In Acapulco. In Acapulco, I have very nice friend, big politico. Open nice house, with nice music, nice food, nice drink, nice girls—for American."

"Oh, for Americans."

"Yes. Many Americans come now to Acapulco. Big steamboat stop there. Nice man, much money."

"And me, I'm to be a kind of a combination professor, bartender, bouncer, glad-hander, secretary, and general bookkeeper for the joint, it that it?"

"Yes, yes."

"Well."

The food came along, and I stayed with it a while, but the more I thought about her proposition the funnier it got to me. "This place, it's supposed to have class, is that the idea?"

"Oh yes, very much. My político friend, he say American pay as much as five pesos, gladly."

"Pay five—what?"

"Pesos."

"Listen, tell your político friend to shut his trap and let an expert talk. If an American paid less than five dollars, he'd think there was something wrong with it."

"I think you little bit crazy."

"I said five bucks—eighteen pesos."

"No, no. You kid me."

"All right, go broke your own way. Hire your político for manager."

"You really mean?"

"I raise my right hand and swear by the holy mother of God. But—you got to get some system in it. You got to give him something for his money."

"Yes, yes. Of course."

"Listen, I'm not talking about this world's goods. I'm talking about things of the spirit, romance, adventure, beauty. Say, I'm beginning to see possibilities in this. All right, you want that American dough, and I'll tell you what you've got to do to get it. In the first place, the dump has got to be in a nice location, in among the hotels, not back of the coconut palms, up on the hill. That's up to your político. In the second place, you don't do anything but run a little dance hall, and rent rooms. The girls came in, just for a drink. Not mescal, not tequila. Chocolate ice-cream soda, because they're nice girls that just dropped in to take a load off their feet. They wear hats. They come in two at a time, because they're so well brought up they wouldn't dream of going in any place alone. They work in the steamboat office, up the street, or maybe they go to school and just came home for vacation. And they've never met any Americans, see, and they're gigling about it, in their simple girlish way, and of course, we fix it up, you and I, so there's a little introducing around. And they dance. And one thing leads to another. And next thing you know, the American has a room from you, to take the girl up. You don't really run that kind of place, but just because it's him, you'll make an exception—for five dollars. The girl doesn't take anything. She does it for love, see?"

"For what?"

"Do I know the Americano, or don't I?"

"I think you just talk, so sound fonny."

"It sounds fonny, but it's not just talk. The Americano, he doesn't mind paying for a room, but when it comes to a girl, he likes to feel it's a tribute to his personality. He likes to think it's a big night for her, too, and all the more because she's just a poor little thing in a steamboat office, and never had such a night in her life until he came along and showed her what life could be like with a real guy. He wants an adventure—with him the hero. He wants to have something to tell his friends. But don't have any bums sliding up to take their *foto*. He doesn't like that."

"Why not? The fotógrafo, he pay me little bit."

"Well, I tell you. Maybe the fotógrafo has a heart of gold, and so has the muchacha, but the Americano figures the foto might get back to his wife, or threaten to, specially if she's staying up at the hotel. He wants an adventure, but he doesn't want any headache. Besides, the *fotos* have got a Coney Island look to them, and might give him the idea it was a cheap joint. Remember, this place has class. And that reminds me, the mariachi is going to be hand-picked by me, and hand-trained as well, so maybe somebody could dance to the stuff when they play it. Of course, I don't render any selections on the guitar. That's out. Or the piano, or the violin, or any other instrument in my practically unlimited repertoire. And that mariachi, they wear suits that we give them, with gold braid down the pants, and turn those suits in every night when they quit. It's our own private mariachi, and as fast as we get money to buy more suits we put on more men, so it's a feature. The main thing is that we have class, first, last, and all the time. No Americano, from the time he goes in to the time he goes out, is going to get the idea that he can get out of spending money. Once they get that through their heads, we'll be all right."

"The Americanos, are they all crazy?"

"All crazy as loons."

IT SEEMED TO be settled, but after the gags wore off I had this sick feeling, like life had turned the gray-white color of their sunlight. I tried to tell myself it was the air, that'll do it to you at least three times a day. Then I tried to tell myself it was what I had done, that I had no more pride left than to take a job as pimp in a coast-town whorehouse, but what the hell? That was just making myself look noble. It was, anyway, some kind of work, and if I really made a go of it, it wouldn't make me squirm. It would make me laugh. And then I knew it was this thing that was drilling in the back of my head, about her. There hadn't been a word about that night, and when she looked at me her eyes were just as blank as though I'd been some guy she was talking to about the rent. But I knew what those eyes could say. Whatever it was she had seen in me that night, she still saw it, and it was between us like some glass door that we could see through but couldn't talk.

She was sitting there, looking at her coffee glass and not saying anything. She had a way of dozing off like that, between the talk, like some kitten that falls asleep as soon as you stop playing with it. I told you she looked like some high school girl in that little white dress. I kept looking at her, trying to figure out how old she was, when all of a sudden I forgot about that and my heart began to pound. If she was to be the madame of the joint, she couldn't very well take care of any customers herself, could she? Then who was going to take care of her? By her looks, she needed plenty of care. Maybe that was supposed to be my job. My voice didn't quite sound like it generally does when I spoke to her.

". . . Señorita, what do I get out of this?"

"Oh—you live, have nice cloth, maybe big hat with silver, yes? Some pesos. Is enough, yes?"

"—And entertain the señoritas?"

I don't know why I said that. It was the second mean slice I had taken since we started out. Maybe I was hoping she'd flash jealous, and that would give me the cue I wanted. She didn't. She smiled, and studied me for a minute, and I felt myself getting cold when I saw there was the least bit of pity in it. "If you like to entertain señoritas, yes. Maybe not. Maybe that's why I ask you. No have any trouble."

FROM **on the road**

Jack Kerouac

THE CITY OF Gregoria was ahead. The boys were sleeping, and I was alone in my eternity at the wheel, and the road ran straight as an arrow. Not like driving across Carolina, or Texas, or Arizona, or Illinois; but like driving across the world and into the places where we would finally learn ourselves among the Fellahin Indians of the world, the essential strain of the basic primitive, wailing humanity that stretches in a belt around the equatorial belly of the world from Malaya (the long fingernail of China) to India the great subcontinent to Arabia to Morocco to the selfsame deserts and jungles of Mexico and over the waves to Polynesia to mystic Siam of the Yellow Robe and on around, on around, so that you hear the same mournful wail by the rotted walls of Cádiz, Spain, that you hear 12,000 miles around in the depths of Benares the Capital of the World. These people were unmistakably Indians and were not at all like the Pedros and Panchos of silly civilized American lore—they had high cheekbones, and slanted eyes, and soft ways; they were not fools, they were not clowns; they were great, grave Indians and they were the source of mankind and the fathers of it. The waves are Chinese, but the earth is an Indian thing. As essential as rocks in the desert are they in the desert of "history." And they knew this when we passed, ostensibly self-important moneybag Americans on a lark in their land; they knew who was the father and who was the son of antique life on earth, and made no comment. For when destruction comes to the world of "history" and the Apocalypse of the Fellahin returns once more as so many times before, people will still stare with the same eyes from the caves of Mexico as well as from the caves of Bali, where it all began and where Adam was suckled and taught to know. These were my growing thoughts as I drove the car into the hot, sunbaked town of Gregoria.

Earlier, back at San Antonio, I had promised Dean, as a joke, that I would get him a girl. It was a bet and a challenge. As I pulled up the car at the gas station near sunny Gregoria a kid came across the road on tattered feet, carrying an enormous windshield-shade, and wanted to know if I'd buy. "You like? Sixty peso. *Habla Español? Sesenta peso.* My name Victor."

"Nah," I said jokingly, "buy señorita."

"Sure, sure!" he cried excitedly. "I get you gurls, onnytime. Too hot now," he added with distaste. "No good gurls when hot day. Wait tonight. You like shade?"

I didn't want the shade but I wanted the girls. I woke up Dean. "Hey, man, I told you in Texas I'd get you a girl—all right, stretch your bones and wake up, boy; we've got girls waiting for us."

"What? what?" he cried, leaping up, haggard. "Where? where?"

"This boy Victor's going to show us where."

"Well, lessgo, lessgo!" Dean leaped out of the car and clasped Victor's hand. There was a group of other boys hanging around the station and grinning, half of them barefoot, all wearing floppy straw hats. "Man," said Dean to me, "ain't this a nice way to spend an afternoon. It's so much *cooler* than Denver poolhalls. Victor, you got gurls? Where? *A donde?*" he cried in Spanish. "Dig that, Sal, I'm speaking Spanish."

"Ask him if we can get any tea. Hey kid, you got ma-ree-wa-na?"

The kid nodded gravely. "Sho, onnytime, mon. Come with me."

"Hee! Whee! Hoo!" yelled Dean. He was wide awake and jumping up and down in that drowsy Mexican street. "Let's all go!" I was passing Lucky Strikes to the other boys. They were getting great pleasure out of us and especially Dean. They turned to one another with cupped hands and rattled off comments about the mad American cat. "Dig them, Sal, talking about us and digging. Oh my goodness, what a world!" Victor got in the car with us, and we lurched off. Stan Shephard had been sleeping soundly and woke up to this madness.

We drove way out to the desert the other side of town and turned on a rutty dirt road that made the car bounce as never before. Up ahead was Victor's house. It sat on the edge of cactus flats overtopped by a few trees, just an adobe crackerbox, with a few men lounging around in the yard. "Who that?" cried Dean, all excited.

"Those my brothers. My mother there too. My sistair too. That my family. I married, I live downtown."

"What about your mother?" Dean flinched. "What she say about marijuana."

"Oh, she get it for me." And as we waited in the car Victor got out and loped over to the house and said a few words to an old lady, who promptly turned and went to the garden in back and began gathering dry fronds of marijuana that had been pulled off the plants and left to dry in the desert sun. Meanwhile Victor's brothers grinned from under a tree. They were coming over to meet us but it would take a while for them to get up and walk over. Victor came back, grinning sweetly.

"Man," said Dean, "that Victor is the sweetest, gonest, franticest little bangtail cat I've ever in all my life met. Just look at him, look at his cool slow walk. There's no need to hurry around here." A steady, insistent desert breeze blew into the car. It was very hot.

"You see how hot?" said Victor, sitting down with Dean in the front seat and pointing up at the burning roof of the Ford. "You have ma-ree-gwana and it no hot no more. You wait."

"Yes," said Dean, adjusting his dark glasses, "I wait. For sure, Victor m'boy."

Presently Victor's tall brother came ambling along with some weed piled on a page of newspaper. He dumped it on Victor's lap and leaned casually on the door of the car to nod and smile at us and say, "Hallo." Dean nodded and smiled pleasantly at *him.* Nobody talked; it was fine. Victor proceeded to roll the biggest bomber anybody ever saw. He rolled (using brown bag paper) what amounted to a tremendous Corona cigar of tea. It was huge. Dean stared at it, popeyed. Victor casually lit it and passed it around. To drag on this thing was like leaning over a chimney and inhaling. It blew into your throat in one great blast of heat. We held our breaths and all let out just about simultaneously. Instantly we were all high. The sweat froze on our foreheads and it was suddenly like the beach at Acapulco. I looked out the back window of the car, and another and the strangest of Victor's brothers—a tall Peruvian of an Indian with a sash over his shoulder—leaned grinning on a post, too bashful to come up and shake hands. It seemed the car was surrounded by brothers, for another one appeared on Dean's side. Then the strangest thing happened. Everybody became so high that usual formalities were dispensed with and the things of immediate interest were concentrated on, and now it was the strangeness of Americans and Mexicans blasting together on the desert and, more than that, the strangeness of seeing in close proximity the faces and pores of skins and calluses of fingers and general abashed cheekbones of another world. So the Indian brothers began talking about us in low voices and commenting; you saw them look, and size, and compare mutualities of impression, or correct and modify, "Yeh, yeh" while Dean and Stan and I commented on them in English.

"Will you d-i-g that weird brother in the back that hasn't moved from that post and hasn't by one cut hair diminished the intensity of the glad *funny* bashfulness of his smile? And the one to my left here, older, more sure of himself but sad, like hung-up, like a bum even maybe, in town, while Victor is respectably married—he's like a gawddam Egyptian king, that you see. These guys are real *cats.* Ain't never seen anything like it. And they're talking and wondering about us, like see? Just like we are but with a difference of their own, their interest probably resolving around how we're dressed—same as ours, really—but the strangeness of the things we have in the car and the strange ways that we laugh so different from them, and maybe even the way we smell compared to them. Nevertheless I'd give my eye-teeth to know what they're saying about us." And Dean tried. "Hey Victor, man—what you brother say just then?"

Victor turned mournful high brown eyes on Dean. "Yeah, yeah."

"No, you didn't understand my question. What you boys talking about?"

"Oh," said Victor with great perturbation, "you no like this mar-gwana?"

"Oh, yeah, yes fine! What you *talk* about?"

"Talk? Yes, we talk. How you like Mexico?" It was hard to come around without a common language. And everybody grew quiet and cool and high again and just enjoyed the breeze from the desert and mused separate national and racial and personal high-eternity thoughts.

It was time for the girls. The brothers eased back to their station under the tree, the mother watched from her sunny doorway, and we slowly bounced back to town.

But now the bouncing was no longer unpleasant; it was the most pleasant and graceful billowy trip in the world, as over a blue sea, and Dean's face was suffused with an unnatural glow that was like gold as he told us to understand the springs of the car now for the first time and dig the ride. Up and down we bounced, and even Victor understood and laughed. Then he pointed left to show which way to go for the girls, and Dean, looking left with indescribable delight and leaning that way, pulled the wheel around and rolled us smoothly and surely to the goal, meanwhile listening to Victor's attempt to speak and saying grandly and magniloquently "Yes, of course! There's not a doubt in my mind! Decidedly, man! Oh, indeed! Why, pish, posh, you say the dearest things to me! Of course! Yes! Please go on!" To this Victor talked gravely and with magnificent Spanish eloquence. For a mad moment I thought Dean was understanding everything he said by sheer wild insight and sudden revelatory genius inconceivably inspired by his glowing happiness. In that moment, too, he looked so exactly like Franklin Delano Roosevelt—some delusion in my flaming eyes and floating brain—that I drew up in my seat and gasped with amazement. In myriad pricklings of heavenly radiation I had to struggle to see Dean's figure, and he looked like God. I was so high I had to lean my head back on the seat; the bouncing of the car sent shivers of ecstasy through me. The mere thought of looking out the window at Mexico—which was now something else in my mind—was like recoiling from some gloriously riddled glittering treasure-box that you're afraid to look at because of your eyes, they bend inward, the riches and the treasures are too much to take all at once. I gulped. I saw streams of gold pouring through the sky and right across the tattered roof of the poor old car, right across my eyeballs and indeed right inside them; it was everywhere. I looked out the window at the hot, sunny streets and saw a woman in a doorway and I thought she was listening to every word we said and nodding to herself—routine paranoiac visions due to tea. But the stream of gold continued. For a long time I lost consciousness in my lower mind of what we were doing and only came around sometime later when I looked up from fire and silence like waking from sleep to the world, or waking from void to a dream, and they told me we were parked outside Victor's house and he was already at the door of the car with his little baby son in his arms, showing him to us.

"You see my baby? Hees name Pérez, he six month age."

"Why," said Dean, his face still transfigured into a shower of supreme pleasure and even bliss, "he is the prettiest child I have ever seen. Look at those eyes. Now, Sal and Stan," he said, turning to us with a serious and tender air, "I want you par-ti-cu-lar-ly to see the eyes of this little Mexican boy who is the son of our wonderful friend Victor, and notice how he will come to manhood with his own particular soul bespeaking itself through the windows which are his eyes, and such lovely eyes surely do prophesy and indicate the loveliest of souls." It was a beautiful speech. And it was a beautiful baby. Victor mournfully looked down at his angel. We all wished we had a little son like that. So great was our intensity over the child's soul that he sensed something and began a grimace which led to bitter tears and some unknown sorrow that we had no means to soothe because it reached too far back into innumerable mysteries and time. We tried everything; Victor smothered him in his neck and rocked, Dean cooed, I reached over and stroked the baby's little arms. His bawls grew louder. "Ah," said Dean, "I'm awfully sorry, Victor, that we've made him sad."

"He is not sad, baby cry." In the doorway in back of Victor, too bashful to come out, was his little barefoot wife, with anxious tenderness waiting for the babe to be put back in her arms so brown and soft. Victor, having shown us his child, climbed back into the car and proudly pointed to the right.

"Yes," said Dean, and swung the car over and directed it through narrow Algerian streets with faces on all sides watching us with gentle wonder. We came to the whorehouse. It was a magnificent establishment of stucco in the golden sun. In the street, and leaning on the windowsills that opened into the whorehouse, were two cops, saggy-trousered, drowsy, bored, who gave us brief interested looks as we walked in, and stayed there the entire three hours that we cavorted under their noses, until we came out at dusk and at Victor's bidding gave them the equivalent of twenty-four cents each, just for the sake of form.

And in there we found the girls. Some of them were reclining on couches across the dance floor, some of them were boozing at the long bar to the right. In the center an arch led into small cubicle shacks that looked like the places where you put on your bathing suit at public municipal beaches. These shacks were in the sun of the court. Behind the bar was the proprietor, a young fellow who instantly ran out when we told him we wanted to hear mambo music and came back with a stack of records, mostly by Pérez Prado, and put them on over the loudspeaker. In an instant all the city of Gregoria could hear the good times going on at the Sala de Baile. In the hall itself the din of the music—for this is the real way to play a jukebox and what it was originally for—was so tremendous that it shattered Dean and Stan and me for a moment in the realization that we had never dared to play music as loud as we wanted, and this was how loud we wanted. It blew and shuddered directly at us. In a few minutes half that portion of town was at the windows, watching the *Americanos* dance with the gals. They all stood, side by side with the cops, on the dirt sidewalk, leaning in with indifference and casualness. "More Mambo Jambo," "Chattanooga de Mambo," "Mambo Numero Ocho"—all these tremendous numbers resounded and flared in the golden, mysterious afternoon like the sounds you expect to hear on the last day of the world and the Second Coming. The trumpets seemed so loud I thought they could hear them clear out in the desert, where the trumpets had originated anyway. The drums were mad. The mambo beat is the conga beat from Congo, the river of Africa and the world; it's really the world beat. Oom-*ta*, ta-poo-*poom*—oom-*ta*, ta-poo-*poom*. The piano montunos showered down on us from the speaker. The cries of the leader were like great gasps in the air. The final trumpet choruses that came with drum climaxes on conga and bongo drums, on the great mad Chattanooga record, froze Dean in his tracks for a moment till he shuddered and sweated; then when the trumpets bit the drowsy air with their quivering echoes, like a cavern's or a cave's, his eyes grew large and round as though seeing the devil, and he closed them tight. I myself was shaken like a puppet by it; I heard the trumpets flail the light I had seen and trembled in my boots.

On the fast "Mambo Jambo" we danced frantically with the girls. Through our deliriums we began to discern their varying personalities. They were great girls. Strangely the wildest one was half Indian, half white, and came from Venezuela, and only eighteen. She looked as if she came from a good family. What she was doing whoring in Mexico at that age and with that tender cheek and fair aspect, God knows. Some awful grief had driven her to it. She drank beyond all bounds. She threw down drinks when it seemed she was about to chuck up the last. She overturned glasses continually, the idea also being to make us spend as much money as possible. Wearing her flimsy housecoat in broad afternoon, she frantically danced with Dean and clung about his neck and begged and begged for everything. Dean was so stoned he didn't know what to start with, girls or mambo. They ran off to the lockers. I was set upon by a fat and uninteresting girl with a puppy dog, who got sore at me when I took a dislike to the dog because it kept trying to bite me. She compromised by putting it away in the back, but by the time she returned I had been hooked by another girl, better looking but not the best, who clung to my neck like a leech. I was trying to break loose to get at a sixteen-year-old colored girl who sat gloomily inspecting her navel through an opening in her short shirty dress across the hall. I couldn't do it. Stan had a fifteen-year-old girl with an almond-colored skin and a dress that was buttoned halfway down and halfway up. It was mad. A good twenty men leaned in that window, watching.

At one point the mother of the little colored girl—not colored, but dark—came in to hold a brief and mournful convocation with her daughter. When I saw that, I was too ashamed to try for the one I really wanted. I let the leech take me off to the back, where, as in a dream, to the din and roar of more loudspeakers inside, we made the bed bounce a half-hour. It was just a square room with wooden slats and no ceiling, ikon in a corner, a washbasin in another. All up and down the dark hall the girls were calling, *"Aqua, agua caliente!"* which means "hot water." Stan and Dean were also out of sight. My girl charged thirty pesos, or about three dollars and a half, and begged for an extra ten pesos and gave a long story about something. I didn't know the value of Mexican money; for all I knew I had a million pesos. I threw money at her. We rushed back to dance. A greater crowd was gathered in the street. The cops looked as bored as usual. Dean's pretty Venezuelan dragged me through a door and into another strange bar that apparently belonged to the whorehouse. Here a young bartender was talking and wiping glasses and an old man with handlebar mustache sat discussing something earnestly. And here too the mambo roared over another loud speaker. It seemed the whole world was turned on. Venezuela clung about my neck and begged for drinks. The bartender wouldn't give her one. She begged and begged, and when he gave it to her she spilled it and this time not on purpose, for I saw the chagrin in her poor sunken lost eyes. "Take it easy, baby," I told her. I had to support her on the stool; she kept slipping off. I've never seen a drunker woman, and only eighteen. I bought her another drink; she was tugging at my pants for mercy. She gulped it up. I didn't have the heart to try her. My own girl was about thirty and took care of herself better. With Venezuela writhing and suffering in my arms, I had a longing to take her in the back and undress her and only talk to her—this I told myself. I was delirious with want of her and the other little dark girl.

Poor Victor, all this time he stood on the brass rail of the bar with his back to the counter and jumped up and down gladly to see his three American friends cavort. We bought him drinks. His eyes gleamed for a woman but he wouldn't accept any, being faithful to his wife. Dean thrust money at him. In this welter of madness I had an opportunity to see what Dean was up to. He was so out of his mind he didn't know who I was when I peered at his face. "Yeah, yeah!" is all he said. It seemed it would never end. It was like a long, spectral Arabian dream in the afternoon in another life—Ali Baba and the alleys and the courtesans. Again I rushed off with my girl to her room; Dean and Stan switched the girls they'd had before; and we were out of sight a moment, and the spectators had to wait for the show to go on. The afternoon grew long and cool.

Soon it would be mysterious night in old gone Gregoria. The mambo never let up for a moment, it frenzied on like an endless journey in the jungle. I couldn't take my eyes off the little dark girl and the way, like a queen, she walked around and was even reduced by the sullen bartender to menial tasks such as bringing us drinks and sweeping the back. Of all the girls in there she needed the money most; maybe her mother had come to get money from her for her little infant sisters and brothers. Mexicans are poor. It never, never occurred to me just to approach her and give her some money. I have a feeling she would have taken it with a degree of scorn, and scorn from the likes of her made me flinch. In my madness I was actually in love with her for the few hours it all lasted; it was the same unmistakable ache and stab across the mind, the same sighs, the same pain, and above all the same reluctance and fear to approach. Strange that Dean and Stan also failed to approach her; her unimpeachable dignity was the thing that made her poor in a wild old whorehouse, and think of that. At one point I saw Dean leaning like a statue toward her, ready to fly, and befuddlement cross his face as she glanced coolly and imperiously his way and he stopped rubbing his belly and gaped and finally bowed his head. For she was the queen.

Now Victor suddenly clutched at our arms in the furor and made frantic signs.

"What's the matter?" He tried everything to make us understand. Then he ran to the bar and grabbed the check from the bartender, who scowled at him, and took it to us to see. The bill was over three hundred pesos, or thirty-six American dollars, which is a lot of money in any whorehouse. Still we couldn't sober up and didn't want to leave, and though we were all run out we still wanted to hang around with our lovely girls in this strange Arabian paradise we had finally found at the end of the hard, hard road. But night was coming and we had to get on to the end; and Dean saw that, and began frowning and thinking and trying to straighten himself out, and finally I broached the idea of leaving once and for all. "So much ahead of us, man, it won't make any difference."

"That's right!" cried Dean, glassy-eyed, and turned to his Venezuelan. She had finally passed out and lay on a wooden bench with her white legs protruding from the silk. The gallery in the window took advantage of the show; behind them red shadows were beginning to creep, and somewhere I heard a baby wail in a sudden lull, remembering I was in Mexico after all and not in a pornographic hasheesh daydream in heaven.

We staggered out; we had forgotten Stan; we ran back in to get him and found him charmingly bowing to the new evening whores, who had just come in for the night shift. He wanted to start all over again. When he is drunk he lumbers like a man ten feet tall and when he is drunk he can't be dragged away from women. Moreover women cling to him like ivy. He insisted on staying and trying some of the newer, stranger, and more proficient señoritas. Dean and I pounded him on the back and dragged him out. He waved profuse good-bys to everybody—the girls, the cops, the crowds, the children in the street outside; he blew kisses in all directions to ovations of Gregoria and staggered proudly among the gangs and tried to speak to them and communicate his joy and love of everything this fine afternoon of life. Everybody laughed; some slapped him on the back. Dean rushed over and paid the policemen the four pesos and shook hands and grinned and bowed with them. Then he jumped in the car, and the girls we had known, even Venezuela, who was wakened for the farewell, gathered around the car, huddling in their flimsy duds, and chattered good-bys and kissed us, and Venezuela even began to weep—though not for us, we knew, not altogether for us, yet enough and good enough. My dusky darling love had disappeared in the shadows inside. It was all over. We pulled out and left joys and celebrations over hundreds of pesos behind us, and it didn't seem like a bad day's work. The haunting mambo followed us a few blocks. It was all over. "Good-by, Gregoria!" cried Dean, blowing it a kiss.

Victor was proud of us and proud of himself. "Now you like bath?" he asked. Yes, we all wanted wonderful bath.

whores

James Crumley

FROM WHORES

On long summer afternoons when our idle time lay as heavily upon our minds as the torpid South Texas air, often my friend and colleague, Lacy Harris, and I would happen to glance across our narrow office into each other's eyes. Usually we simply stared at each other, like two strangers who have wandered into an empty room at a party, ashamed of solitude amidst mirth, then we turned back to the disorderly stacks of freshman themes, heaped uncorrected upon our desks. Occasionally, though, the stares held; one would shrug, the other suggest a beer, and in silence we would rise and go out, seeking a dark and calm beer joint.

Sometimes French's, a nigger place south of town, where a cool highyellow bartender, Raoul, let us bask in the breeze of his chatter, as ceaseless and pleasant as the damp draft roaring from the old fashioned water-cooled window fan. Sometimes the Tropicana to joust with an obtuse pinball machine called the Merry Widow, while off-shift roughnecks slept drunk at the various tables scattered among the fake tropical greenery. Easy afternoons, more pleasant and possible than hiding in the air conditioned cage of our office, where the silences had no meaning. Dusty air, dark bars. Outside, the sun, white hot upon the caliche or shell parking lots, reminding us how pleasant the idle afternoon. Dim bars, cold beers, our mutual silence for company. Harmless.

Or so they'd seem until I'd catch Lacy's hooded blue eyes slipping toward the heated doorway. His wife, Marsha, was already prowling the town like a lost tourist, looking for him in the bars. Almost always she found us. One moment the doorway would be empty, the next a slim shade stood quietly just inside, perhaps a glint of afternoon sunlight off her long blond hair, her dark brown eyes like holes in her face. Somehow I always saw her first. When I said "Lacy," he never moved, so I would walk to Marsha, welcome her with the frightened ebullience of a guilty drunk. She seldom spoke; when she did, in a hushed murmur, too quiet for words. She moved around me to Lacy's side, slipped her hand into the sweaty bend of his elbow, led him away. At the doorway, framed in heated light, his face would turn back to me, an apologetically arched eyebrow raised.

On those rare occasions when she didn't find us, we drank until midnight, but without frenzy or drunkenness, as if the evening were merely the shank of the afternoon. Then I drove Lacy home, let him out in the bright yellow glare of his porch light. As he sauntered up the front walk, his hands cocked in his pockets, his head tilted gently back, his tall frame seemed relaxed, easy. A tuneless whistle, like the repeated fragment of a birdsong, warbled around his head as he approached that yellow light. At the steps he'd stop, wave once as if to signal his safe arrival, then go inside the screened porch. Sometimes, glancing over my shoulder as I drove away, I'd see him sitting on the flowered pillows of the porch swing, head down, hands clasped before him, waiting.

On the mornings after, he never spoke of the evenings before, no hangover jokes shared, never hinted of those moments before sleep alone with Marsha in their marriage bed. And on the odd chance that I saw Marsha later, no matter how carefully I searched that lovely, composed face, no matter how hard I peered beneath her careful makeup, I caught no glimpse of anger. Unlike most of my married friends, the Harris' kept their marriage closed from view, as if secrecy were a vow. Aside from her sudden intrusions into our afternoons, his too casual saunter toward the bug light, as casual as a man mounting a gallows, and a single generality he let slip one night—"Never marry a woman you love"—I knew nothing about their marriage.

On rare and infrequent summer afternoons, when the immense boredom that rules my life stroked me like a cat and the heavy stir of desire rose like a sleepy beast within me, when our eyes met, I would say *Mexico*, as if it were a charmed word, and Lacy would grin instead of greeting me with a wry smile, a boy's grin, and I could see his boy's face, damp and red after a basketball game, expectant. On those afternoons, we'd fill a thermos with gin and tonics, climb into my restored 1949 Cadillac, and head for the border, bordertown whorehouses, the afternoon promenade of Nuevo Laredo whores coming to work at the Rumba Casino or the Miramar or the Malibu, the Diamond Azul or Papagayo's.

Perhaps it was the gin, or the memory of his single trip to Nuevo Laredo after a state basketball tournament, whatever, he maintained that grin, as he did his silences, all the way across the dry brush country of South Texas, my old Caddy as smooth as a barge cresting the swales. Or perhaps it was the thought of Marsha driving from bar to bar, circling Knight until full dark, then going home without him. He never went intending to partake of the pleasures, just for the parade.

Sometimes it seemed the saddest part, sometimes the most pathetic, sometimes the most exciting: the dreadful normalcy of the giggling girls. Dressed in jeans and men's shirts knotted above their brown dimpled bellies, they carried their working clothes, ruffled froth or slimy satin, draped over their young and tender shoulders. Although they chattered in Spanish, they had the voices of Texas high school girls, the concerns of high school girls. Dreadfully normal, god love them, untouched by their work, innocent until dark.

Occasionally, because I knew the girls more intimately than Lacy—unlike him, I'd never married either the loved or the unloved—I could convince one or two to sit with us a moment before they changed clothes. But not too often. They seemed shy, unprotected out of their whoredresses, like virgins caught naked. If the mood seemed right, the shyness touching instead of posed, I'd have one then, slaking my studied boredom on an afternoon whore as the sun slanted into the empty room. Afterwards, Lacy often said, "I'll have to try that again. Someday." I always answered, as if wives were the antithesis of whores, "You've no need. You've a lovely wife at home." To which he replied, "Yes, that's true. But someday, some summer afternoon, I'll join you . . ." His soft East Texas accent would quaver like a mournful bird call, and a longing so immense that even I felt it would move over him. Even then I knew he'd want more than money could buy.

Most whores in Nuevo Laredo are carefully cloistered in a section of the city called, appropriately, Boys Town, a shabby place with raucous bars spaced among the sidewalk cribs, but the better-class whores worked in the clubs we frequented, outside of Boys Town. By *better-class* I don't mean more practiced, for Mexican whores don't go in for the precision of the Japanese or the studied depravity of the Germans. I mean more expensive, less sullied by the hard life. More often than not, they're just good old working girls, pleasant and unhurried in bed, not greedy, and sometimes willing to have fun, to talk seriously. Many were sold into the business as young girls, many are married, making the most of a bad life. And then there are the rare ones, girls a man can fall in love with, though I never did, never will. Whores help me avoid the complexities of love, for which I am justly grateful. But even I have been tempted by the rare ones. Tempted.

One afternoon in Papagayo's in the blessed stillness after the parade—the waterfall silent, the jukebox, dead—Lacy and I sipped our Tecates. A moist heat had beaten the old air conditioners. Behind the bar one bartender sliced limes so slowly that he seemed hardly to move; the other slept at the end of the bar, his head propped on his upright arm. Lacy's whistle seemed to hover about us like a swarm of gnats. All of us composed, it seemed, for a tropical still life, or the opening act of a Tennessee Williams play. Absolute stasis. And when Elena came in, moving so slowly that she seemed not even to stir the hot air with her passing, she seemed to hold that moment with her lush body. As I turned my head, like some ancient sleepy turtle, she too turned hers toward me. A slack indifferent beauty, eyes always on the verge of sleep, the sort of soft full body over which frenzy would never leap. Otiosity sublime. Surely for a man to come in her would be to come already asleep.

I clicked my Tecate can lightly on the tile bar as she eased past us. The sleeping bartender, knowing my habits, looked up. I nodded, he asked her if she would join us for a drink. Halting like a tanker coming into dock, she nodded too, her eyes closing as she lowered her head. A life of indolence is really a search, I thought, a quest for that perfect place to place one's head, to sleep, to dream . . . but behind me, Lacy whispered, "This one, Walter." So I let her go. Walter Savage, perfect Languor. Habits can be restrained; passions should not.

After the preliminaries, an overpriced weak brandy, an unbargained price—local airmen had ruined the tradition—Lacy left with his prize ship, walking away as casually as he wandered into the force of that yellow porch light, hands pocketed, loafers shuffling, head back, his aimless whistle. But as he held the door for Elena with one hand, the other cradled itself against her ample waist. I meant to warn him, but in the languorous moment all I could think was, "You've a lovely wife at home," and that seemed silly, the effort too much.

They were gone quite a time, longer than his money had purchased, so I knew it had to be an amazing passion, impotence, or death. Afternoon slipped into evening, the waterfall began flushing. Two students from the college came timidly in, then left when they recognized me. The girls returned in bright plumage. I took the gaudiest one, ruffled her as best I could, but when I came back, Lacy hadn't returned. The bartender cast me a slimy smile. I drank.

When Lacy finally came back, Papagayo's hummed with all the efficiency of a well-tuned engine, and I would have stayed to watch the dance, but Lacy said, "Let's go."

"Why?" Though I could guess.

Hesitating, unable to meet my eyes, he shook himself as if with anger, a flush troubling his pale face. Then he answered, "I don't want to see her working."

Not just impotence, but love, I thought, wanting to laugh.

More silent than usual on the trip back, he drank beer after beer, staring at the gray asphalt unwinding before us. Outside of Falfurrias, I ventured, "Impotent?" To which he answered, with hesitation, "Yes."

"It happens," I said. "Guilt before the deed. With whores and wives and random pieces . . ."

"Don't," he said, almost pleading.

"Hey, it doesn't matter."

"Yes," he whispered, "I know."

When I dropped him at his house, he said goodnight, then walked into that yellow haze quickly, as if he had unfinished business.

During the twenty years or so I've been beating love with bordertown whoring, I've had it happen to me—drink or boredom or simple grief—and I knew most of the techniques with which whores handled the problem. Those who took simple pride in their work, those honest tradeswomen of the flesh, usually gave the customer his best chance, along with motherly comfort and no advice except to relax. Then they would try to laugh it off. Others, working just for the money and those few natively cruel, would pointedly ignore or even scoff at the flaccid gringo member. Or, as happened to me once, they would act terribly frightened, whimpering as if caged with a snake or a scorpion instead of a useless man, occasionally peeking out of the corners of their sly brown eyes to see if you'd left yet. Whatever the act was meant to do, it did. Perhaps because of my youth, when it happened to me, it kept me away from the whores for months, nearly caused me the grief of marriage with a rather chubby woman who taught Shakespeare very badly.

But Elena did none of those things. She was after all only a child, in spite of that woman's body, so she just started talking aimlessly, in her child's voice, winding her black hair with her fingers. What she did was, of course, more cruel: she talked to him, told him about her life. The dusty adobe on the Sonoran desert, the clutch of too many children, both alive and dead, the vast empty spaces of desert and poverty. When their time was up, he asked if he might pay for more, to which she shrugged, lifted a shoulder, cocked an eye at his member. And she answered, *why not*, she covered her breasts with a dingy sheet and smiled at him. God knows what she had in mind. When I told her, months later, of his death, she also shrugged at me, slipping into her dress.

Although Lacy and I were both in our thirties and both knew that, except for a miracle, we were going to ease out the rest of our academic careers at South Texas State trying to make them as painless as possible, I accepted my failure more gracefully than he. I'd been born in Knight, still lived in a converted garage behind my parents' house, and I taught because it was a respectable way to waste one's life. Unlike my mother's attachment to morphine and my father's to the American Conservative Party, teaching is respectable. The salary may be insulting, the intellectual rewards negligible, but when I tried doing nothing at all, the boredom drove me to drink. So I teach, my U.T. PhD a ticket to a peaceful life.

But Lacy, like so many bright, energetic young men, once had a future. Articles published in proper journals, one short story in a prestigious quarterly, an eastern degree, that sort of thing. And he came to South Texas State for the money, just for the money. When he came, he thought that, like a boulder tumbling down a hillside, he had only lodged for a moment, a winter's rest perhaps, and when spring came with heavy rains, he would be on his way once again. By the time he realized that no more showers were going to fall, he had been captured by the stillness, the heavy subtropical heat, the endless unchanging days of sun and dust. He hadn't accepted his defeat, but it didn't matter. By the time of this last summer, he had stopped writing letters of inquiry, had ditched his current Blake article, replacing somehow his fiery vision with Elena.

II

THEY SAY THE second acts of all boring plays take place at parties, where truth looms out of the drunkenness with all the relentless force of a tidal wave. But in Knight the parties were dull, deadly dull, and whatever shouted insults rose above the crowd like clenched fists, whatever wives were hotly fondled by whomever in dark closets or under the fluorescent glare of kitchen lights, were beside the point. The truth lay in the burnished dullness, not in the desperate cries of hands clutching at strangely familiar bodies. The last party at the Harris' seemed no different, perhaps was no different, despite the death of our chairman.

Even Lacy had risen from his torpor long enough to become a bore. Each time he found me near enough to Marsha for her to overhear him, he would remind me loudly of our golf game the next day, suggesting earlier and earlier tee-offs. But he had El Papagayo's in mind, not golf. We had been back three or four times in less than a month, more often than was my habit, and his love remained unconsummated. He had passed through acceptance to sorrow to rage, and on quiet midnights in my apartment I had begun to think of Lacy and Marsha abed, he cursing his errant virility, she pliant upon their bed. His untoward passion had begun also to disturb the tranquility of my life, and when he reminded me about our golf game the fifth or sixth time, I answered queruously, "I don't think I'll play tomorrow, I think I'll go to Mexico and get fucked." Then I left him, his stricken face like a painted balloon above the crowd.

It was then I noticed our chairman, a pleasant old gentlemanly widower who asked no more of life than I did, leaving the party. He wore a tweed jacket, as if fall in South Texas were autumn in Ithaca, that smelled slightly of pipe smoke, paper, and burning leaves. We chatted a moment, the usual graceful nothing, then bid each other good night. He suffered a coronary thrombosis just off the porch and crawled under the oleander bush at the corner of the Harris' house; slipped away to die, I like to think, without disturbing anyone. The party continued, somewhat relieved by his absence, until those wee dumb hours of the morning. Shortly before noon the next day, Marsha found him as she worked in the flower beds. On his side, his head cradled upon his clenched hands, his knees lifted toward his chest, the rictus of a smile delicate across his stubbled face, the faint stink of decomposition already ripe among the dusty oleander leaves. She brushed bits of grass and dirt from his face as she knelt beside him; she began crying and did not stop.

In an ideal, orderly world, on this day Lacy would have performed his necessary act, a final act of passion before we went home to his mad wife, but the world is neither ideal nor orderly, as the life we forge from the chaos must be. Elena, who was I can attest a very dull girl despite her interesting beauty, decided that day to become interested in Lacy's failure. She no longer babbled about her past but promised to cure his problem, if not with her antics, then surely with a *curanderas potion.* Of course, neither worked, and Lacy's life was complicated for the next month with an infernal dose of diarrhea. Even now, even in my grief, I know he deserved better.

When he returned that night, we both noticed the absence of the porch light. He took it as a favorable omen, I thought it an oversight. Even as I unlocked my apartment door—unlike most folk in Knight, I lock my door; I have a small fortune in medieval tapestries and Chinese porcelain, two original Orozco's—the telephone's shrill cry shattered the night. Lacy.

After the bodies had been disposed of, our chairman's beside his wife, Marsha into a Galveston hospital, instead of driving Lacy back to Knight, I made him stop with me in Houston, not so much to cheer him up as to hold him away from the scene of disaster for a few days. We stayed at the Warwick, drank at the nicest private clubs, where my father's money and name bought us privacy. Finally, on our third night, as we were sipping Scotch at the Coronado Club, our nerves uneasy in their sheaths from seventy-two hours of waking and sleeping drunk, Lacy began to talk, to fill in the gaps, as if by breaking his silence he could restore his shattered life.

His mother, as she often said, had made only one mistake in her life, she'd fallen in love with a Texas man and followed him out of Georgia and into exile in East Texas. In exile her native gentility grew aggressive, proud. No girls in Tyler met her standards, none quite good enough for Lacy, so except for one wild trip after a basketball tournament his senior year, a single fling to the border, Lacy knew nothing of girls. Where he found the courage to remove his clothes before a strange dark woman in a dank cubicle behind the 1-2-3 Club, and how he overcame his disgust long enough to place his anointed body upon hers, I'll never know. What guilt he suffered, those days he carried himself carefully around Tyler as if a sudden knock would unman him, he never said. I like to think of that first time, Lacy's body, lean and as glossily hard as a basketball court, yet tender, vulnerable with innocence, a tee-shirt as white as his buttocks, flapping as he humped, his wool athletic socks crumpled about his ankles, his soul focused on the dark, puffy belly of a middleaged whore with an old-fashioned appendix scar like a gully up the center of her stomach.

In college, his career as young-man-about-campus kept him so busy that girls were just another necessary accessory, like his diamond-chip KA pin, his scuffed bucks and chinos with a belt in the back, and it wasn't until he began graduate school at Duke, where all the other teaching assistants seemed to have thin, reposed women at their elbows, that he discovered the absence of women in his life. Then too he looked over a freshman composition class and mistook that dark quietness in Marsha Long's wide eyes for intelligence, mistook her silence for repose.

The brief courtship could only be described as whirlwind, the wind of his stiffled passion whirling around her pliant young body. Surprised that she wasn't virgin, he forgave her nonetheless, then confessed his single transgression in Mexico. Marsha nodded wisely, just as she did when he suggested marriage, expecting her to hold out for magnolia blossoms and fourteen bridesmaids. But she didn't. They were married by a crossroads justice of the peace on the way to South Carolina to tell her parents.

They lived on the old family plantation on the Black River in a columned house right off a postcard, and as he drove up the circular way, Lacy thought how pleased his mother would be. But inside the house he found an old woman, perfumed and painted like a crinolined doll, who called him by any name but his own and confused Marsha with her long dead sister. In Marsha's father's regal face he saw her beauty, larded with bourbon fat. Everywhere he turned, each face—black, white, or whitetrash—every face on the place had the same long straight nose, the broad mouth, the wide dark eyes. Only the blacks still carried enough viable intelligence in their genes to maintain some semblance of order. Marsha cried ten solid hours their first night, only shaking her head when he inquired as to why. By dawn he expected a black mammy to waddle in from the wings and comfort the both of them, but none came. At breakfast, Marsha had redrawn her face, and stare as he might through his own haggard eyes, he could see neither hint nor sign of whatever endless grief lay beneath her silence.

They left later that morning, since nobody seemed to mind. Mr. Long ran wildly out of the house, spilling whiskey, and Lacy, fearing now for both sanity and life, just drove on. But he heard the shouted, "Congratulations, son." He looked at this mad child, now his wife, seeing her now, dumb, painted, pliant. Perverse marriage vows followed; he made her silence his, vowed to love her.

"They were so old, old enough to be her grandparents, they didn't have her until they were in their forties. God knows what her childhood must have been like, locked on a movie set with those mad people, and every face she saw for ten miles in any direction, every club-foot, humpback, cross-eyed genetic disaster, was her face. She thought she was ugly. You know that, ugly. In all the years we were married, I saw her without make-up just twice. Once, when she had the flu so bad that she couldn't even crawl to the mirror. I found her like that, on her goddamned hands and knees, mewling and crying and holding back the vomit with clenched teeth. When I tried to carry her back to bed, she fought me like a madwo . . . fought like a wildcat, hiding her face from me as if she'd die if I saw her . . . Listen, I shouldn't be here, I should be back in that room, room, shit, cage with her. She needs me, she needed me and I wasn't there . . . And all those niggers in that house, so goddamned servile, so smug butter wouldn't melt in their assholes. Listen, drive me back to Galveston, will you? This isn't helping."

I led him out of the club, holding his elbow as if he were an elderly uncle. And it had helped. In the car he slept, quiet, not mumbling or twisting or springing awake. Slept really for the first time in days. I checked us out of the Warwick, drove us back to Knight on benzedrine—bordertown whorehouses are filled with more vices than those of the flesh. When I woke him in front of his house, dawn flushed the unclouded sky as birds chittered in the mimosa trees of his yard. He mumbled a simple thanks, grabbed his grip, and went into this empty house, his toneless whistle faint among birdsong. I thought he'd be all right.

III

HE SEEMED ALL right for the next few months, more silent perhaps, uninterested in afternoons at French's or jousting with the Merry Widow, but accepting his life on its own terms. I hadn't the heart to suggest a trip to Nuevo Laredo, and Lacy didn't invite me to accompany him on the frequent weekends he spent in Galveston. So we began to see less of each other. He had his grief, I had a spurt of ambition and energy that threatened to destroy my wasted life. I handled it, as usual, by spending a great deal of my father's ill-gotten money. Christmas in Puerto Vallarta. An antique Edwardian sofa. Two Ung Cheng saucers in *famille rose* that made my father take notice of me and suggest that I was worse than worthless, expensively worthless. I even gave a party, a Sunday morning champagne breakfast, fresh strawberries, caviar, an excellent brie, and although Lacy didn't come, those good folk who did, didn't make church services that morning, not even that night. For reasons beyond me, I made the mistake of resuming my affair with my chubby Shakespearian, an affair it took me until spring to resign.

Spring in South Texas lacks the verdant burst of those parts of the world that experience winter, lacks even the blatant flowering of the desert, but it has its moments. A gentle mist of yellow falls upon the thorned *huisache*; tiny blossoms, smaller than the hooked thorns of the cat-claws, appear briefly; and the ripe flowers of the pricklypear, like bloody wounds, begin to emerge. And the bluebonnets, sown by a grim and greedy highway department, fill the flat roadside ditches.

On a Sunday when he hadn't gone to visit Marsha, I took Lacy out into the brush country north and east of Alice to show him the small clues of our slight season. But it only works for those who take pride in the narrowness of their vision, who stubbornly resist boredom, whatever the cost. By one o'clock we were drunk in the poolhall in Conception; by three, drinking margaritas at Dutch's across the border in Reynosa; at seven, stumbling into the waterfall hush of Papagayo's in Nuevo Laredo, giggling like schoolboys.

Lacy, standing straight, asked loudly for Elena, but she wasn't working that night, so he collapsed into his chair, morose and silent for the first time that day. I, ever-present nurse and shade, bought him the two most expensive girls in the place, sent him with them to find Elena's room. *Dos mujeres de la noche.* Where love had failed, some grand perversion might work.

And of course it did. When we met at the dry fountain in the courtyard afterwards, Lacy had a bottle of Carta Blanca in each hand, a whore under each arm, his shirt open to the waist, and a wild grin smack on his face.

"Hey, you old son-of-a-bitch, you set this whole fuckin' thing up, didn't you?"

I smiled in return, trying to look sly, but failing. My eyes wouldn't focus. "I'm responsible," I said. "How was it?"

"Ohhh, shit, wonderful," he said, stumbling sideways, his two ladies holding him up with a patient grace that my father's money hadn't purchased. "Listen," he said to them, "I want you to meet my best friend in the whole damned world, he's a good old boy." He lifted his arm from the right one's red satin shoulders, gathered me into his fierce grasp. "Stood by me, held me up, laid me down, introduced me to the woman I love . . ."

"We've met," I said, putting my arm around the abandoned whore. Her skin, warm and sweaty from the bed, smelled like all those things that men seek from whores: almonds and limes, dusty nights, cheap gin, anonymous love. I buried my face in her neck, had a moment's vision in which I bought both girls and fled south across the desert toward some other pleasantly idle life, a Yucatan beach, a mountain village, Egypt. But even as it came, it passed like a night wind. Lacy began to shout and shuffle our circle around.

"Ohhhh, what a great fucking night." The girls slipped out of the circle, whores again, leaving the two of us. Lacy hugged me until my breath faltered, repeating, as if it were a litany, "Ol' buddy, ol' buddy, little ol' buddy."

It had been years since I'd been frightened by a man's embrace, or ashamed, or I must add in all honesty, aroused, but Lacy held me with such a fierce love, so much drunken power and love, that I clutched him, hugged him back, and for a few seconds we whirled, stumbling about the dark courtyard. Then—perhaps he thought it a disgusting revelation, perhaps he responded, I'll never know—he flung me from him as if I were a sack of dirty laundry. My knees hit the fountain wall, my head the fountain.

IV

THE NEXT MORNING I woke in the back seat of my car, not a great deal worse for the night. A bit stiff and sore, but no more. Because I am terribly responsible about the way I exhaust my life, I cleaned up, made a thermos of bloody mary's and went to my office. Lacy was already there.

"Listen," he said as I sat down, "I'm sorry."

"Hey, it doesn't matter."

"I know, I know."

He smiled once, nearly grinned, then raised his hand and left the office, walking with a bounce and energy that I'd never seen, striding as he must have onto the hardwood courts of his youth. I never saw him again. Elena says he was drunk, but I doubt it. She thinks he was drunk because of the wad of bills he offered her to flee across the border with him, because of the wonderful grin on his face. When I asked her answer, she shrugged, slipping into a yellow frothy dress that gave her skin a touch of jaundice, *"Casada."* She held up her ring, not as if it were a trophy, but as if she had been born with it on her finger.

"Did he make it?" I asked.

She shrugged again, not knowing what I meant until I showed her. Then her whore's face brightened, like a cheerleader's welcoming home a winner. *"Bueno,"* she said, *"Muy bueno."*

I tried to excuse her, telling myself that the craft of whoredom is lying; I tried to excuse myself, blaming my grief. But it didn't work. I paid her for another time, and as she slipped out of her yellow dress, she shrugged once again, as if to say *who knows about these gringo men*. Inside her, I slapped her dull face until she cried, until I came.

I don't go back to Nuevo Laredo anymore: I satisfy my needs up or down the border. Of late my needs are fewer. I visit Marsha occasionally. We sit in her room, I talk, she nods over the doll they've given her. Her parents would rather have her back than pay for her keep, so I pay; that is, my father pays. Even in her gray hospital robe, without a trace of makeup left on her face, she is still lovely, so lovely I know why men speak of the face of an angel. She neither ages nor speaks; she rocks, she nods, she clutches her painted doll. I believe she's happy. When I told her about Lacy, just about the accident, not the cause, she smiled, as if she knew he were happy *too*. I didn't tell her that it took a cutting torch to remove his body from the car.

As they say, the living must live. I don't know. From my parents' house I can hear them living; my mother's television tuned to an afternoon soap opera, the volume all the way up to penetrate her morphine haze: in the kitchen my father is shouting at a congressman over the telephone. I don't know.

I'll marry my chubby Shakespearian, or somebody so much like her that the slight differences won't matter. I'll still go bordertown whoring, and it will never occur to her to complain. And we'll avoid children like the plague.

tijuana
Michael Hemmingson

NEVER CARED much for Tijuana. The few times I'd been down there, across the border, a forty-minute drive from San Diego, I didn't like the atmosphere. There was one time in high school—my friend Maurice and I drove down in his Mustang, hoping to check out the strip clubs, the hookers. In one, a sad-looking blonde danced and she didn't seem to be into it (nor were her tits). In another, the Unicorn Club, a skanky dark-haired woman with hardly any breasts squat down on a beer bottle. I watched it go inside her and it didn't arouse my teenage libido one bit.

"Where's the donkey show?" I wanted to know.

TWO SUMMERS AGO, my feelings about Tijuana changed. Maybe because I'd had a few sleazy sexual encounters in my world travels—whores and loose women alike—and I was desiring more. I was desiring *something*. I didn't have a girlfriend at the moment, and the woman I was interested in didn't seem to be interested in me any longer.

I was feeling dark and I wanted something dark, so I

decided to go down to the Mexican-American border. I took the southbound trolley from downtown. I walked across the bridge. I got into a taxi cab and said, "Take me to where the women are."

"The who?" said the Mexican cab driver.

"The whores."

"Ah, prostitutes!"

"Yeah," I said, "those."

"What do you want? The cheap? Or quality?"

"Well," I said, "quality."

He nodded and drove. He took me to a place called Madonna's, off of Avenida Revolucíon. The cab ride cost me $5. It cost me another $5 to get into the club.

It was classier than the strip joints I remembered in Tijuana—clean booths, lots of lights, waiters, bouncers, and pretty young women. There was one I had an eye on—she wore a green dress that didn't quite cover her ass; her hair was braided; her skin was light-brown and she had large eyes. I wasn't quite sure how to approach her; she spent most of her time at a table with a skinny man in his sixties, being friendly with him. I didn't like how friendly she was with him.

She got up to do her three dances. The music was loud and got inside my guts. I felt a yearning for—what? I don't know. For my twenties, perhaps; I was thirty-three and feeling stupidly old.

She knew how to work that pole; she was a pro, and she had a nice, nimble body.

She was a pro all right. Dressed back in the green dress that didn't quite cover her ass, she returned to the old man. Several other dancers tried to entice me into a private booth. I wasn't interested. I watched, instead, the girl in the braids and green dress as she led the old man into the back, to the area of private booths, his hand in hers.

Two songs later, the man returned. He had a smile on his face. I figured I'd have a smile on my face, too, if I were him.

I wanted to have that smile.

I saw the girl leave the booth, hands covering her breasts,

heading toward the back—the dressing room I guessed. She had a disgusted look on her face. Her expression made me feel sick, and I left the place.

I spent $15 in drinks and tips there.

I walked south of the Hard Rock Cafe; two blocks down I found the red light district, packed with rowdy cantinas and whores that lined up and down the streets, shoulder to shoulder, waiting for business.

This is where I wanted to be. I should have had the driver drop me here. This was the darkness I sought.

Most of the whores looked like clones of one another—dark-skinned Mexican women in colorful tight spandex pants and tube tops; five-foot-four in heels and too much makeup. Many of them appeared bored, and they probably were; some would meet my gaze as I walked by, others looked down at the ground. Then there were the aggressive ones—they grabbed at me, jumped in front of me, said, "Hey, honeeeee, what you say? You like what you see?"

I spent half an hour walking up and down several streets, trying to decide which one I wanted. I couldn't decide. I stopped at one with white-and-black striped spandex pants and said, "How much?"

"For fuck," she said, "$20."

"Okay."

She led me upstairs to one of the many run-down hotel rooms. An elderly woman sat behind a glass booth. "$3 for room," she said. I paid her. The woman gave my prostitute a roll of toilet paper and said, "23."

The room wasn't locked. There was no lock. The room was small and stank and there were bugs and I thought how wonderfully seedy this was—and that I could easily be robbed or murdered up here.

I handed the whore a $20 bill. She put it in her purse. She sat on the bed and took off her pants and underwear. I took off my shoes and pants. She motioned for me to come over to her. I hesitated. I could hear the thumpa-thumpa of Mexican can-tina music on the street. I went to her. She took my cock in her hand. I thought she was going to suck it so I moved closer; she looked up at me with disgust and pushed me back. She had a condom in her hand. She was putting it on my dick.

She leaned back on the bed and spread her legs.

"I want to do you doggie-style," I said. "Turn over."

"No," she said.

"Well maybe you can get on top."

"Cost you another $20," she said.

"Why not," I said. "Okay."

"Give me the money first."

I reached for my wallet and gave her another bill.

She said, "Lay down."

I did, and she got on top of me, spat in her hand, rubbed her vagina, bounced a few times, then said, "Now the other way."

She lay on her back and spread her legs. She spat in her hand again, and rubbed the saliva on her cunt.

Her pussy was dry despite her spit. She didn't make a sound, and her face was still. I knew she didn't want to be here with me, I knew she needed the money, I knew she was a product of some geo-socio-political condition that I was ignorant of. Weren't all whores? She stared at me with hate. "Why are you looking at me like that?" I said. She didn't reply. She stared. Her eyes were saying *how dare you do this to me.* "You're a whore," I said, "so take it like a whore."

I came, and I left.

I WENT BACK to Tijuana six months later. I was seeking another dark and sleazy experience. I returned to Madonna's, hoping the girl with braids and the green dress would be there. She wasn't.

I spotted a blonde standing in a corner. She wore a white thong and a white see-through blouse and held a small lunch pail. She had the little-girl look, she was eighteen or nineteen but looked younger. She noticed me staring at her and smiled. I waved at her. She stayed where she was. I asked one of the waiters that I'd like her to sit with me. The waiter fetched her.

She was a bit plump, with a small top; she held her weight well. She smiled as she approached, and sat at my table.

What interested me was that she wasn't Hispanic. She was white, she was American.

"What would you like?" she asked.

"I'm not sure."

"My name is Tanya."

"Hi Tanya. Mike."

"Mike," she said, "there's a two-for-one special—you can have me for two songs, for the price of one."

"And how much would that cost?"

"$60."

"What do I get?"

"You get to touch me all over, wherever you want, except for my pussy," she said.

I said, "Okay."

She took my hand. She led me back to the area of private booths. We went into one. It was very small. I sat down. She stood before me and removed her top. I reached for my wallet.

"You can pay me after," she said.

She started to sway to the music. I reached out for her. She pressed herself into me.

A well-muscled man with a flashlight kept passing by every other minute. He would look at us, then leave. I knew he was there for the women's protection, but it was annoying. I tried to ignore him. I tried to get into feeling up Tanya.

I closed my eyes and listened to the music. She smelled very nice, and her young body in my hands was tactically wonderful. I loved her body—her little tits, her round ass, her soft tummy. She kissed me on the forehead. She danced and danced in my lap. She pulled her panties down. There was very little blonde pubic hair down there. I broke the rule, I ran my finger, quickly, across her pussy lips. She didn't protest. My finger made its way over there again and lingered. I slipped it in and was surprised to discover how wet and warm her cunt was. Was she actually getting into this? She slapped my hand away and giggled.

michael hemmingson 219

"These are long songs," she said.

"How much to fuck you?"

"What?"

"Or a blow-job."

"We don't do that here," she said.

I didn't believe her.

I left Madonna's and walked down the streets lined with whores. Again, I couldn't make up my mind. I saw a very young-looking one. She was fifteen or fourteen. She stared at the ground. The whores around her were grabbing at my jacket and trying to get my attention.

"How much?" I asked the young one.

The other whores went, "ahhhhh," and one said, "He like them young."

The young one said, "$20."

I nodded. We went down the street to a hotel. The room was $2 here.

In the room, she would not look at me. She took her pants off and lay on the bed. Her legs were skinny and her bush was bushy. The notion of fucking a whore this young excited me.

She glared at me when I stuck myself in her. There was more hate and loathing in her eyes than the one last time. Her eyes said *how could you do this to me?*

I TRAVELED DOWN to Tijuana two months later. I arrived at the border at noon. I wanted to make a day of this, I wanted to whore my way through the city until midnight. How many prostitutes could I fuck in a twelve-hour period?

First, I went to the Unicorn Club. I was hoping I might see a woman squat on the bottle the way I did in high school.

The place was nearly empty. The music was loud. I sat at a table and ordered a Bohemian.

An overweight woman in a yellow dress approached my table. "Buy me a drink?" She had a high-pitched voice.

"No," I said.

She pouted. "Why not?"

"You don't need a drink," I said, "I know the drink scam."

"You want to fuck then?" she said. "I have a nice big pussy." She pulled up her dress and showed it to me. "You see, big pussy! Big pussy!"

"Yeah, it's big."

"So, what say? You wanna go somewhere and fuck?"

"Well," I said, "why not."

She led me upstairs to a room. In the light, I could see that she was in her forties. She was a sad sight. What a way to start out the day.

"$40," she said.

"That's a bit expensive."

"It's what it is."

I shrugged. I had set aside $200 for the day. I handed her the money.

She gave horrible head, and I couldn't get it up. She disgusted me.

"How am I doing?" she asked.

"Great, but I have to go."

"Did you come?"

"Didn't you notice?"

She tossed the condom into the trash.

I walked down to Madonna's. I was hoping Tanya would be there. She wasn't. I watched several of the dancers. One of them looked like—reminded me of—an ex-girlfriend: she had the same hair, same body-type. She sat next to me and asked if I wanted a private dance.

"The $60 one," I said, "for two songs?"

"There's the $80, for two songs," she said.

"What do I get?"

"I get naked and you can touch me anywhere."

She took my hand and led me not to the booths, but to a small room with a see-through black curtain at the door. She got naked and danced in my lap. That same well-muscled guy kept walking by and peeking in, but I ignored him this time. I was amazed that this woman not only resembled a certain ex-girlfriend, but her body felt just like my ex-girlfriend's. This wasn't my imagination. I started feeling that lonelyache you get when you miss the women you once loved and had.

This one let me touch her pussy, let me stick a finger into her. She bent down, her ass in my face, and slipped her middle finger into her asshole. She pulled it out and licked it. I put my finger in her ass, moved it in and out. She took that finger and sucked it.

"Having fun?"

"Oh yeah," I said.

"We can go to another room," she said, "you can fuck my cunt and butt."

"How much?"

"$200."

"Exceeds my budget," I said.

So Tanya did lie to me.

"Too bad," she said, "it would be fun."

"I bet."

From there, I walked down to the red light district. There were fewer whores standing on the street during the day, but they were there.

I crossed paths with an American girl with dirty, flat brown hair. She wore loose jeans and a t-shirt. She looked at me and I looked at her.

"Hey," she said.

I stopped and turned around.

"You look like you need a blow job," she said.

"I do."

"$10."

"You're on."

She led me to a motel. The room was $4.

The girl was a mess. I guessed she was twenty or so. She looked like she was on something, like she'd been around the road one too many times.

"Lay down and take your dick out."

She didn't use a condom. She sucked me. She wasn't very good at it but at least she made me come.

She spat my semen out on the floor. "How about a tip?" she said.

"A tip for what?"

"For the good head."

I gave her $2.

I had some lunch, some beers, checked out a few cantinas. I didn't want to dance with any of the girls. It was getting dark out. I went back to Madonna's. Again, I was hoping for Tanya. There was a whole new set of women here. I sat in the club for an hour and a half, drinking, watching, and finally went back into a room with a dancer that had silicon implants. Her tits were big and hard and fake. The hairspray in her puffy hair made me sneeze. I had another $80 special—she got naked, I touched and squeezed her body.

It was nine o'clock when I left Madonna's. I had $30 left. I figured I could get in another fuck and have at least $5 for a cab and $2 left to take the trolley back to downtown San Diego, where I lived alone in what they call an "urban miniloft."

Again, I perused the many street whores, looking for one that I wanted to spend money on. I spotted a woman in her thirties who looked out of place—baggy white pants and a sweater, she was very thin and something about her reminded me of another ex-girlfriend.

She seemed nervous when I approached her, but smiled at me. She was new to this, I thought.

"I'd like a blow job," I said.

"$5," she said.

A bargain. "Let's go."

We went upstairs, the room was $3. I lay down on the small dirty bed. She did wonders with her mouth. I hadn't had a blow job like this since the girlfriend she reminded me of.

She pulled her pants down. She was wearing a purple thong. She began to finger herself.

I grabbed her boney ass and said, "I think I want to fuck you."

"Another $5," she said.

She took her clothes off. Her skin was very brown, and she had stretch marks on her stomach. Not only did I know this was probably her first night as a prostitute, she was probably doing this to feed her children. I imagined she had three of them, small ones, future whores or criminals. To her, $10 would feed those kids for several days.

Her cunt was ready for me. She really got into the sex. She wrapped her legs around my ass. She had several orgasms. She resisted my kisses at first, but then she kissed me.

She kissed like the ex-girlfriend; she fucked like the ex-girlfriend. This had to be my imagination. I closed my eyes and imagined that I was, again, fucking the ex in question, and this made me sad.

There was an electricity between us that surprised me, and must have surprised her. Our bodies fit well; I came inside her and wanted more.

If I had money left, I would have asked her to join me in a better motel for the whole night. We could screw and love each other until dawn.

We both got dressed. There were fireworks outside, people laughing.

I looked at her. She smiled, came up to me, and kissed me on the lips.

"My name is Laura," she said in strained English.

I told her my name.

"That was . . . very nice," she said.

"Yes," I said. I owed her $10. I gave her $15. "Thank you," I said.

"*Thank you*," she said, kissing the bills.

I left the room and returned to the streets of Tijuana, my body glowing, my soul dimming; I felt dirty and very alone.

whores

Luis Alberto Urrea

Let me burn you, let me burn you,
let me burn you Down.
—Front 242

IT'S TWELVE HUNDRED miles south of Tijuana and about an hour inland from the sea. It lies on the western lip of the town, near a small cemetery and the old rail line. The town itself is a classic rural Mexican community, with cobble and dirt streets, a small square with a gazebo, and such new developments as marijuana and *cholos* and graffiti. Sometimes, gringos make their way here, but few stick around long enough to be impressed. Once in a while, they even make their way to this place, called *El Club Verde Para Hombres*—"The Green Club for Men."

It's not as exciting or evil-hearted as some of the places in Tijuana. Most of the clients here are skinny farmhands or well-fed minor urban functionaries or fat off-duty cops. A few of the women are too old for work in a more fancy house, and the other ones are just lucky that this is as far down as they'll go.

It's a big structure, and it presents a blank wall to the street. Concrete blocks slathered over with slapdash Mexican stucco and a green paint job last touched up in the 1950s. The relentless sun has faded it a sort of watercolor yellow. If you listen at the wall, at night, you will hear the forced sounds of partying emanating from within—trumpets, laughter, jukeboxes, bad live *rocanrol*. And the women, every night, can be heard shouting naughty jokes and risqué insults.

I am in a car with the most macho young men of the Urrea family, cousins I first met when my father decided I was queer. Third grade, perhaps. Tough Mexican boys brought up to the United States because I was being raised gringo. I was speaking Spanish in too *pocho* a manner: not enough rough edges in the words, not enough disdain and wit inherent in my pronunciation. My *R*'s were not hard enough, the *G* and *J* sounds lacked the heft of phlegm at the back of the palate to really sizzle. I had learned, to my utter shock, that the wrong emphasis on the wrong consonants could lead to humiliation, insults, even violence. I remember one of these cousins giving me tequila in fifth grade, then cigarettes, in order to roughen the far borders of my words. I, apparently, had a garden on my tongue, and the men were demanding a desert.

They were doubly worried about me because I had made the deadly error of announcing, in first grade, that I wanted to be a priest. My father said, "But you won't want to have women." What did I know of women? I'd had visions of the plaster Christ on the cross opening His eyes and looking at me. I wanted the stigmata. I wanted to work miracles and save the sick. "You want to wear a black dress? You'll be a faggot!"

What's that? I remember wondering.

OUTSIDE THE WHOREHOUSE, looking like they've been beamed up from 1970, a small group of Mexican males gathers nervously. They're mostly young, but one of them is too young. Fathers regularly bring their sons to the Green Club for their first sexual encounter. The cop at the door smiles like an uncle when a terrified twelve-year-old comes under the wing of his dad. But solo, you'd have to be at least eighteen. And one of these boys is only fourteen. But he's tall, and without his glasses he looks maybe old enough.

They have gathered to buy him his first sex.

Their names are Jaime, Fausto, El Gordo, Fu Manchu, and Blondie. Blondie's other nickname is Pigfoot. But tonight, his lighter hair is more visible than his stubby feet. He's the fourteen-year-old.

It is a law: Mexican males must have nicknames. Jaime, in this group, is called El Red. There are others in their circle known as Dracula, Frankenstein, Taras Bulba, and El Chino Cochino ("The Dirty Chinaman"—he's one of the many Mexican-Chinese who inhabit the Norte). The best nickname in town belongs to a man they all fear. He's called El Quema-pueblos, and I agree that it's the best nickname I've ever heard. Its pithiness can't be translated into English. The best I can do is "The Man Who Burns Down Cities."

Thank God he doesn't figure in this story, I think.

MY FATHER IMPORTED these strange, rangy boys to intensify the manhood factor around the house. One of them—I'll call him The Bull, a nickname he was awarded for the size of his penis—was a boxer and an athlete. Something I definitely was not. In my memory, The Bull is ten feet tall and muscular, evil, self-satisfied enough that he even sleeps with a smirk. Years later, wandering into the whorehouse, I realize with a start that he's just a little Mexican government weasel. Another God-damned wiseguy, picking the meat off the bones of the poor, sliding illegal funds sideways into his various bank accounts. He has matted hair, jug ears, and dresses like a bad scene from an old episode of *Charlie's Angels*. All petroleum-product materials. He's only five foot eight.

I start to laugh.

"What?" he says, half-smiling but worried, afraid there's a joke somewhere that he's not in on, already partially angry that

I might be laughing at him, when it has always been his right to take ferocious aim at me.

"I could break your neck," I tell him, "with one hand."

His face flushes.

His blush, in Club Verde's frosty tube lights, looks purple.

The Bull's legendary good looks have rotted and turned the color of half-cooked liver.

HE IS VISITING his father, my uncle. We have all gathered for a family holiday. Their home is stately by village standards. It sits atop a small stationery store with the only Xerox machine in town. The machine is so old, however, that it produces weird, Cold War Xeroxes. The kind where the paper is black and the text is white—a negative copy of your document.

Over supper, he has told me, "We've got to go to the *bule* tonight. They've got a deaf-mute girl!"

He beams at this news—it's the most exciting thing he's thought of all day. I can only suppose it's the exotic nature of it that has him in a lather. It's the only new thing to do in town except for the movie, which is showing John Wayne's old nugget, *The War Wagon*, dubbed into German, with Spanish subtitles. As we talk, hundreds of little birds tumble through the air like leaves on a sidewalk.

"She's even cute," he enthuses. "And she charges thirty thousand pesos."

At the current exchange rates, I'm thinking, what—ten bucks at most.

"Just," he intones, "don't tell my wife we went."

I'm not telling anyone anything. It's my plan to get him in the graveyard and beat him senseless. I feel the rocks in my hands: I hide them under the table. I want to bury him alive out there, pour dirt in his mouth, listen to him underground as the scorpions descend.

WE FOLLOW THE boys inside. I feel like Blondie's father. He could be me at fourteen. The entrance is off a small courtyard.

Around this courtyard, six shacks are arrayed. On the front step of one, a child plays.

"Whores' houses," my host quips.

"They live here?"

"You can't expect them to go into town! They keep to themselves."

A river of shit has run out of the spectacularly noxious toilets near the door. We all make our crossing in single file. The open door of the Green Club belches smoke and discordant electric guitar. Too metaphorical. A cop stops the boys and frisks them. He doesn't even look at Blondie. They're in.

I grab a table near them and look around.

Three women are visible. The deaf-mute, who is heartbreakingly cute, with a short hairdo and no makeup. She is using a crude sort of sign language to indicate lust to a table full of drunk men. She grabs her crotch, makes a pained face, writhes. She pantomimes masturbation as the farmers giggle like little boys and poke one another with hard black forefingers. I can see dolls in her face, and excitement over Popsicles. She looks like she's selling lemonade at a sidewalk stand in La Jolla. And masturbating.

The other woman has a face like a friendly turtle and a brassy voice that brays louder than anything in the room. My host asks, "Are you mute, too?"

She points to her ass.

"This isn't mute!" she reports. "It cuts loud farts!"

She smiles at me.

"*Hola, guapo,*" she says.

"Good evening, *señorita,*" I reply.

She stares at me like I've said something exceedingly strange. Stops smiling.

He tries to touch her, and she yanks her arm away.

She starts to dance with a small ranchero. They look like the two ends of a horse having a seizure. The song is a Mexican version of "Rock Lobster." Some idiot on the record is bellowing: "*¡Langosta! ¡Langosta* Rock!*"

The third woman, the one the young boys at the next table have obviously come for, is terrifying. She's Tina Turner—even has the same wig. Her massive eyelashes are the size and shape of tarantulas. When the boys goad Blondie into touching her—he timidly taps her on the arm with one finger—she glares at him. I'd swear she's hissing. He pulls his hand away fast and looks at the floor.

"¡Ay ay ay!" they note.

THE BULL AND his invasionary force came into my life with a promise of companionship and adventure. I was a Boy Scout. The scouts were the only escape from the eternal race war between my gringo mother and my *mexicano* father. It was also the only way I, raised on dirt and outhouses and barrio sadism, could hike up a mountain, see coyotes, drink from waterfalls. The cousins informed me that Boy Scouts were pussies.

If I really wanted to be *un hombre*, I'd learn to box.

Then they slapped me silly. I learned fast that my bloody noses were *funny*. I was supposed to wipe the blood off on my forearm and laugh.

I also learned an unspoken lesson about machismo.

All the toughest males, every *muy macho chingón* from deep Mexico who entered my house, was obsessed with forcing the younger children to suck his dick. Each one wanted to push his hard-on up the asses of the boys and girls of our family. But mostly, these men who were to rescue me from the unforgivable queerness of serving God wanted to ride the backs of little boys. Little boys like me.

BESIDE THE BAR there is a small shrine to the Virgin of Guadalupe. Votive candles burn at her feet, and some wilted carnations are strewn at the statue's sandals. The center of the room is a big concrete dance floor. The walls all have two doors. They are so cheap you could, if you really wanted to, look through the slats and watch the action inside.

Each door opens onto a small room. In each room, one bed

and one chair. One small table holds a bowl and a jug of water, a bar of soap and a rag. Above the beds hang crucifixes.

Once, the police captain of the town fell in love with a woman who worked here. He got so jealous—and drunk on tequila—that one night he burst into the Club Verde, kicked open her door, and shot her and the unfortunate beer salesman on top of her. The Green Club didn't know what to do with the room. They considered closing it in honor of the tragedy, but ultimately changed the mattress and went on as usual.

The deaf girl—she can't be more than eighteen, I've decided—comes up to me and offers me the brother handshake. We clench hands. She looks like one of my English students. But suddenly, she gets a flushed expression, then pantomimes something going up her. She stands there and grinds at my table, hands on crotch. She's doing her little dance for me now. The Bull punches me on the arm and laughs appreciatively. Then she opens her eyes and grins at me and nods. I shake my head. She has dimples. She points at me, at my crotch, then holds her hands about two feet apart and makes an "Ooh" with her mouth.

I shake my head.

I laugh.

I hold up two fingers and hold them about one inch apart and look sad. This cracks her up. She shakes my hand and rushes off to the next table.

"You had her," my host says. "You could have fucked her up the ass!"

THE MAN WITH the Macho Box comes around to the boys' table.

He's called El Maestro, "The Master," as are all workmen in the places where the old Mexican ways are still practiced. Mexico is rapidly becoming as rude as the United States, but in courtlier days, mastery was honored. Shoeshine boys, barbers, or violin virtuosos were all *maestros*. And this *maestro* brings the Macho Box, a device known to anyone foolish enough to hang out in Mexican bars for very long.

It's basically a torture device. A box with a couple of dials, a trillion batteries inside, and wires attached to two metal rods. For some reason, Mexican men can't resist holding these rods and trying to prove how much shock they can withstand. Think of it: The *maestro* actually gets paid to turn his knobs and torture men—and the torturees are the ones who pay! The really brilliant *maestros* offer, as a prize, free shocks. This is pure capitalism at its best.

Blondie has been anesthetized by his first serious gulps of tequila. He has confided to me what his friends don't know— he's too afraid of Tina Turner to try to make love to her. His buddies hook him to the machine and the *maestro* cranks it up. Blondie hangs on. After a while, he *has* to hang on because his fists are cramped onto the rods. "Not. So. Bad," he says. His arms curl and rise above his head. The *maestro* really lets him have it. But he can't give up now—everybody, even Tina, is watching. His knuckles clack together above and behind his head. He is either smiling or frozen in an electrified rictus.

THE TURTLE-FACED Woman comes up to me.

"Writer," she says. "Look at this."

I put down my notebook and look up.

The Bull says, "*Pinche maricón. Puto. Joto.* Writing in your little diary all night."

A beer delivery man had been pestering me. He was overwhelmed with drunken filial love, you know—the kind that immediately precedes a mass slaying. He shook my hand about ten times, hanging on my table, insisting, "*Tú, amigo mío.*"

She cuts him off and pulls a Polaroid out of her blouse. She's standing there naked. Smiling like she's in front of the flamingo exhibit at the zoo. In the photo, her nipples are black.

"For you," she says, "five hundred pesos."

The Bull announces, "I love this shit!"

OVER AT THE next table, Blondie has followed his Macho Box challenge with a drinking contest with a local stud named

Mauser, after the German rifle. I never ask, but I draw my own conclusions. He wins seven hundred pesos on an impromptu bet as he and Mauser chug tequila from eight-ounce tumblers. I will later learn that Blondie will spend the night with his head in a plastic bucket, convinced his bed is flying around the room, uplifted by demons. He will beg Jesus, in the classic drunk's prayer, to sober him up, and he will *never drink again.*

With the winnings, and the money pitched in by the boys, Blondie's got about enough for sex.

Tina whips her wig in the near distance, curls her lip, goes *"Chk"* with her mouth to show her disdain. But keeps her eye on him.

I watch Blondie. He's breaking out in a sweat, and it's not just the booze. Fu Manchu is almost asleep. He's lost his bridge somewhere, and his upper lip blows in and out of his mouth like laundry on a line. Fausto is fairly sober, Jaime is doing cricket imitations with his mouth. El Gordo hates his nickname. Who'd want to be called "Fatso"? His real name is Gilberto.

He leans over to Blondie and makes a drunken confession: "You're lucky," he says, "to have so much love from these guys."

"What do you mean?" says Blondie.

"You're only fourteen!" Gilberto cries. "I am twenty-one! And *I've never been laid!"*

He bangs the table.

Blondie is no fool. I can see it in his face. Inspiration.

"Boys," he says. "Boys!"

They drag their attention away from the dance floor, where everyone is wiggling around to "El Fatolito."

"I love you all," says Blondie. "I do."

Drunken promises of undying love and brotherhood come from their lips in response.

"I love it that you have brought me here and given me this."

He shows them the money.

They agree that they have given it to him.

"But brother Gilberto here . . ." He touches El Gordo. "My dearest friend."

They take it in stride—in Mexico, when you're drunk, everybody's your dearest friend or deadliest enemy. Gilberto, through the magic of intoxication, is suddenly *everybody's* dearest friend.

"Fucking Gordo," they say.

"And Gilberto is twenty-one years old to my fourteen!"

This is clearly Blondie's Gettysburg Address. He will, I suspect, live longer in the town's mythology for this act than for anything having to do with Tina Turner.

"And Gilberto is a virgin!"

"No!" they say as Gilberto hangs his head in sorrow.

"It's true," Gilberto says.

"I," Blondie says, "have time. Gilberto does not."

He's a hero! The boys can't believe his loyalty to El Gordo. They buy him a beer and slap him on the back. One of them signals for Tina. She storms across the dance floor at them, looking like she's going to slap somebody. They push Gilberto at her. He holds out the money. She takes it, sinks her nails into his forearm, and pulls him away.

The little door slams.

AS WE LEAVE, the deaf prostitute signs something that I can't figure out. She repeats her gestures until I understand. She is saying: "I want to come with you."

The Bull says, "You're not writing about me, are you?"

"Yes," I say, smiling.

"What?" he demands.

I continue to smile.

Bloody noses are funny, after all.

"*Oye, cabrón,*" he warns.

"I only," I whisper, "write the truth, you son of a bitch."

He moves away from me.

Outside, the boys wait for Gilberto. When he finally comes out, his hair is a mess. He looks very sad. As they walk away, he keeps looking back at the Club Verde.

The little prostitute tugs at my arm. She gestures at herself, at me, away, to the north. She places her hands before her heart, as if she were praying. Her eyes are wet.

"Don't tell my wife about this," The Bull pleads.

My God—he's terrified of his wife. The top of his head reaches my nose. I look into the dark—the cemetery wall is barely visible across the road. A thousand dogs are barking at the moon. I put my hand on the back of his neck. It's skinny. I imagine the blows. I squeeze lightly. He winces.

"Do you remember when we were boys?" I ask.

His eyes, huge with worry, rotate in their sockets. Are they looking for escape? Then they settle on my face.

"We had fun, right?" he says.

"Not really."

The color is draining from his face.

I hug him.

He relaxes against me.

"You taught me to be a man," I say into his ear. I hug him harder. "I'm a writer now," I remind him. "And I will make you famous." I slap him on the back. "I don't need to kill you, cousin. I can make you immortal."

He pulls away.

"¿Qué?" he says.

"All of you. Every bit of you, *Bull.*"

I push him away.

I walk out the gate.

She is watching me. He stands between her and me. The boys are laughing in front of me. Gilberto is talking quietly. As I catch up to them, he finally says, "Do you think she would go out on a date with me?"

I stop, halfway between the graveyard and the whorehouse. The Bull is running toward me. The little whore turns and walks back inside. The boys move away, gray as ghosts. I can hear them, laughing at Gilberto all the way home.

FROM clara

Luisa Valenzuela

TRANSLATED BY Hortense Carpentier
and J. Jorge Castillo

OW BORING TO wait. Her left foot scratched her right leg in a gesture of resignation. Her name was Clara, and she had had it. Who else would have thought of wearing new shoes, knowing all along she'd have to stand around and wait, and why had she agreed to meet him on a corner where there was no place to sit down?

And Victor telling me to be here before eight to avoid the crowd. Now it's almost eight-thirty and there's still no sign of him. I should know him better by now: he talks about tranquillity all the time, but there's no tranquillity. If I reproached him he'd swear he didn't even remember we had a date.

As usual, Clara had been on time. She had been waiting since before eight, while he, she was sure, sat at some bar talking to some stranger or other, endowing words like "silence" with great significance so he could savor the silence he himself had imposed.

In Victor's life, monotony and boredom had nothing to do with one another. He repeated his repertoire so often that even from miles away, Clara could follow his conversation with anyone who happened to be sitting next to him.

"Well, you have to take life with a grain of salt," the man next to Victor would conclude, tired of the harangue.

Victor would never allow himself to be put off by an irrefutable platitude, nor miss the chance to have the last word.

"Not with salt, my friend. Salt makes fissures, it deceives and distorts. Life, you see, has to be taken with its own pure flavor, a flavor that satisfies hunger."

Unfortunately, Clara knew Victor's priceless clinchers very well; what she didn't know was when he would use them. In the beginning, she had listened to him attentively, expecting to be initiated into what he called the secrets of harmony and balance. However, she soon discovered that he said the same things to everyone and that he had no special mystery to reveal to her. So now she preferred to wait patiently and let him upset others with his need to be thought profound.

One by one, the streetlights went on around the square, the clock hands of the Torre de los Ingleses pointed pitilessly to eight-thirty, and, above Clara's head, the Parque Retiro's big neon star flickered as if it were real. The sky had turned a deep blue; it made her think about the sea, and for an instant she felt happy. It was that flash of happiness which at times redeems a day, a month, a year of indifference and insularity; for Clara, the sea was one of her fondest memories.

Through a scrim of wet haze, the people running toward the railroad station had the ponderous appearance of subterranean beings. Although the Southern Cross had not yet appeared in the sky, Clara's eyes were fixed at the exact point where it was hidden, and she tried not to move or be distracted for fear of missing it.

In that confused weariness, the weariness that comes of waiting, she expected everything. She even expected Victor—not with a great deal of hope, it's true, because everything came to her too late. Once, to console her, a friend had said, "Happiness never comes too late." The only words that had stayed with her were "late" and "never," permanently fused into a single, irremediable reality. It was that way with Victor. He remembered things at the wrong time, when they no longer mattered.

She raised her left hand to look at her watch, but suspended the gesture in mid-air; she remembered that three days earlier she had pawned the watch. Parting with it had been a great sacrifice, but they needed money, and Victor was a gentleman and would not let her walk the streets as she had done before. Victor was always there to tell her that he was a gentleman, and a gentleman would never allow his wife to be a prostitute.

As if we were married, Clara said to herself, but she chose to remain quiet, because with Victor no one was ever right. To avoid hopeless arguments, she pawned her watch and the silver maté gourd her grandfather had given her. She did take the precaution of carefully hiding the pawn tickets for the day when she could redeem her treasures. She had learned her lessons well from Lady Experience, and did not trust Lady Luck.

The enormous Torre de los Ingleses, with its brick body and circle of light, didn't allow her to forget that time was passing. The grass squares of the park were no longer visible, and the water had stopped spurting from the slow-turning sprinklers. Victor, naturally, was nowhere in sight. He was fated to be late, just as he had been the night they met: she was, by then, imprisoned behind a wall of anguish that had built up slowly over the years and that no one could tear down now. She asked herself if it would not be too simple to blame everything on fate and in that way free herself of responsibility, but she realized her anguish was not of his making.

No, nor was it because her old work disgusted her or because she liked it: she did it without thinking, like when she came from Tres Lomas and got off the train at Once Station. Back home, they had told her that in the capital the most beautiful place was the Palermo woods, with its lakes, its swans, and its neatly trimmed rose gardens. But when she descended the short flight of stairs from the station, she found herself facing a square and an inhospitable plaza with an inhospitable monument. She saw more people than she had ever seen before; they rushed along the wide avenues, breathing the fumes of millions of big and small buses, and for the first time she saw streetcars and heard them screech as they rounded a curb.

Carrying her suitcase, she took a walk around the plaza. Thinking of the woods she yearned to see, she asked an elderly man with a kind face how to get to Palermo. The man, thinking she meant the Palermo railroad station, told her to take the red minibus. When Clara arrived at Palermo, there were no trees, no lakes with swans, and the only roses were the ones wilting in the window of a flower shop that smelled like a cemetery. Next to the flower shop, though, there was a window filled with silk and lace blouses and flouncy skirts. She stood there looking at the window.

Her father had told her she was old enough to go to the city and find a good job. She hadn't the time to object, because her father had immediately locked himself in the bedroom, where Clara had once discovered him with the butcher's wife. There was nothing else for her to do but take off her apron, put on her coat, and meekly leave the house without waiting for her mother, who might return any day from her long trip to Quemú-Quemú. She walked the mile and a half to the station and boarded the eleven forty-five train. Now that she was in the city, however, the blouses were tempting her, keeping her in front of a shopwindow.

From a distance, a sailor with sparkling eyes had been watching her. He waited a little while before approaching her.

"Alone?" he asked; and then, "The blouses are pretty, aren't they, honey?"

"Uh huh."

"But you're even prettier."

She laughed. The boy seemed nice. He was in the navy, his uniform was blue, not a murky green like some she had seen. So Clara agreed to have a drink with him in the café across the street. Besides, she was hungry, although she didn't know how to go about asking for the dinner special. She drank the Martini in one gulp so she could get quickly to the olive. She kept sucking on the pit. Hunger, however, couldn't be fooled by a morsel, and she was afraid the bubbles she felt in her stomach would start to rumble. She asked a question to forestall that possibility.

"Is the sea pretty?"

"Believe it or not, I don't know. I've been in the navy for a year and we haven't left port once. The fellows say the ship's too tired to go to sea and it only stays afloat because the river's thick with muck."

He laughed. He was missing two teeth, which somewhat diminished his charm; also, it was rather depressing to meet a sailor who had never seen the sea. Without feeling guilty, she accepted a second Martini and a third. Then she took courage and asked for the dinner special, but he had a better plan.

"What do you say we take a little stroll upstairs? There're some nice, cozy rooms. . . ."

Clara's elbow was on the table, her chin resting in her hand. Outside, the cold fell with the night, and inside, the café was warm and inviting, with its many mirrors and curtains—dirty perhaps, but inviting all the same. She looked indifferently at the sailor. Everything seemed at once so beautiful and unimportant, and she had the sensation of floating. She shrugged, smiled wryly out of the corner of her mouth, and answered, "If you feel like it . . ."

On the second floor, the room with an iron bed wasn't pretty at all. It was cold. The man who had gone up with them ran to close the window. "Have to air out the place between one and the next, right?" And he left them alone.

Clara didn't even realize she was being undressed. Once they got into bed, she asked the sailor his name, but the question was lost in moans. In the morning, he rose at five to return to his ship. Pleased that he had taken her virginity, he left a hundred pesos on the night table and ran off to tell his buddies about the great catch he'd made on Plaza Italia.

Clara, on the other hand, woke up late, with a terrible

headache and a strange dry taste in her mouth. Slowly she recalled what had happened, but the money under the lamp saved her from shame. She got dressed and, looking in the mirror, settled on a vague expression which she thought would serve to get her out of the elevator and through the café with dignity. But just as she passed the cash register, the owner approached her and she lost her composure.

"Nice of you to honor our modest establishment, miss. You'll find all the necessary comforts and discretion here, if you want to come again."

He cleared his throat, straightened his tie, and unobtrusively slipped thirty pesos in her coat pocket. Frightened, Clara looked around her, but there were only a few customers at that hour of the morning, and no one seemed to notice what had just occurred. She left the café thinking that, after all, life in the city wasn't too pleasant, but it wasn't as bad as she had been told. She went into another café to have a hot chocolate and a sweet roll while she counted her money. Then she walked to the shopwindow where the blouses were, and this time she looked at the prices.

She lingered there to make sure the hundred and thirty pesos she had earned—she hesitated at the word "earned"; she preferred "gotten"—plus the twenty-six she had brought from home could not pay for something that cost the fabulous sum of one hundred and ninety-nine pesos and ninety cents. She remained looking at the window and peering down the street, secretly hoping to spot the sailor again. Finally, she grew bored and walked toward the center of town, studying the uniforms that passed.

She forgot about shopwindows until she came to a German restaurant with a large sign that said "Indoor Garden." It was noon, and a cup of chocolate and a sweet roll weren't enough to fill the stomach of a person with a physically demanding occupation. Besides, the garden might very well turn out to be the park with the lake and swans she had heard about. She decided to go in.

The garden was small, but there were several tables in the sun with red tablecloths, and the steak and French fries were almost as delicious as the caramel-and-whipped-cream dessert. She did not miss Tres Lomas at all. When she left the restaurant, she realized her capital had been considerably reduced, but she wasn't too worried. She had enough money to last her through the night.

AT LAST THE Southern Cross appeared, dotting the clear sky, and there was no longer any reason for Clara to continue gazing upward, dwelling on her past. Victor was still not there. Her legs were hurting, and she was afraid impatience would win out. She always brushed aside negative feelings and refused to be carried away by anger or despair.

To shake off her unhappy thoughts, she decided to walk. She was rewarded when she came upon a low wall in front of a souvenir stand where she could sit down. There, at least she could be comfortable.

I hope Victor takes a little longer, so I can rest, so I can take off these tight shoes. I've walked too much since I came to the capital, or rather since the fourth customer I had on my own, the one who wore that battered hat he wouldn't take off even when he jumped into bed. I remember asking him, before we went upstairs, if we could have a drink, something to make it a little easier.

"A drink? Like hell," he had answered. "I pay to have you in bed, not sitting at a bar. Do you think money grows on trees?"

The customer is always right. Besides, you have to finish what you start, so Clara forgot about the drink. She would go to the sacrifice with a clear mind, like cows she had seen going to the slaughterhouse, surely knowing they were about to die.

The man didn't waste a moment with her. He finished his business quickly, leaped up, zipped up his fly, and clapped on the hat, which had fallen off his head in an involuntary gesture of courtesy. He shook Clara's arm.

"Get up, lazy. It's time to leave."

"You leave. I'm going to sleep."

"You think I'm paying for you to snore?"

"Don't get excited. It's the same price anyway." Clara yawned and covered her face with part of the pillow.

"Same price, your mother's ass! At this hour, I'm paying for every extra minute. Get up by yourself or I'll get you up!"

It was useless to argue with this fellow, so Clara chose to dress slowly and to go downstairs, doing both with her best expression of disgust.

As she passed the front desk, the man behind the register—the one who had given her the thirty pesos and who smiled whenever she came to the café—felt pity for her, a pity that had ulterior motives: he called her into the coatroom, felt her breasts, then tapped her cheek consolingly with one hand while patting her behind with the other.

"Take this key, child. Go up to Room Five and wait. I'll cheer you up."

When Clara arrived at Room Five—a luxurious room she had never seen before—she realized that it must belong to the owner. There were curtains, a flowered coverlet, and a wardrobe of shiny wood. She sat down on the edge of a chair facing the sink; she clasped her hands in her lap and lowered her eyes. One had to savor these moments of hope: the owner had asked her to his own room; someday, perhaps, he would marry her.

A few minutes later the man arrived. He immediately switched off the overhead light and switched on the bedside lamp—"to make it more intimate," he said.

He reclined the beautiful Clara on the bed and disappeared behind the half-open wardrobe door. When he finally reappeared, stark naked, all Clara's hopes vanished. He was as white and blubbery as those strange creatures she had seen mornings in the fish market—God knows who had told her they were called squid. She secretly christened him "The Squid," and when he forced her to place her open hand on his belly, she was surprised that it was neither slimy nor cold.

She woke up the following morning and opened the Venetian blinds like a good housekeeper. The light that suddenly brightened the room brought her back to reality and, as always happened, to disenchantment.

Like hell he's the owner!

The man who had gone to bed with her couldn't be important in the hotel, because he didn't live in that elegant room: the wardrobe door was open and she could see that it was empty. The few hangers there seemed sad not to have clothing to support.

Dreaming's a waste of time. No one's going to want to marry me, ever: for that you have to say no, show restraint. I can't play those games any more.

A short while later she heard a gentle knock at the door and, without waiting for an answer, the man entered carrying a tray.

"Don Mario has breakfast for his precious. . . ."

So your name is Don Mario. So I'm your precious. You're bringing me breakfast. It's not all bad.

Modestly, she covered her breasts with the sheet and smiled back softly. Don Mario placed the tray on her knees, and she began to sip the hot café au lait, which pleased her senses more than all the love-making. But The Squid, of course, kept annoying her, and that destroyed all the charm.

"I don't understand how a fine girl like you can go around doing these things. . . ."

She soaked a croissant in the coffee. "Out of necessity."

"Where do you live?"

"Here, for the time being."

A few drops of coffee fell on the sheet, which smelled of bleach.

"Mother of God! I can't have you here. Don't you know the boss doesn't want to have anything to do with regulars? He says he has enough headaches already with the ones who come and go; he needs customers, he says, but not that bad. . . ." He touched her naked back with a caressing hand.

"Don't worry about anything, señor. I just sleep with men. . . ."

During the day she didn't like to talk about those things. She preferred to walk around the zoo or go to the movies. Near the hotel there was a theater with a continuous show, which was exactly what she needed, for at the end of three viewings there wasn't a detail left undiscovered. The first time, she simply looked at the images; the second time, she read the subtitles; and the third time, she tried to do both at once and figure out what the story was about. The last time was always the most moving, but she couldn't explain that to The Squid. Instead, she decided to repeat, "I just sleep with men."

"You're a dreamer, woman. If I wanted to exploit you, I'd get rich. But I don't take advantage of people," he sighed. "And besides, nowadays, this business has gotten very risky. But I won't hurt you, you'll see. I'm going to protect you like a father."

What good are fathers? If you only knew my story. . . .

"Yes, like a father . . ." Don Mario repeated to keep the conversation alive. "How old are you?"

"Twenty-one."

"Thank God, at least you're of age. You don't look it, though. I would have said eighteen, at the most. Tell me, how long have you been around here? You said you're twenty-one, right? You're already a woman. . . . Gee, I thought you were just a kid. I even told myself you couldn't be more than seventeen. It's a pity, isn't it?"

Who can understand men? First they say one thing and then they say another; first they say it's better to be almost of age, and then they pretend you're seventeen.

To please him, she wanted to tell him that until five days ago she had been what is called a virgin, but she didn't know how to phrase such a delicate matter.

"Well, don't you worry. I'll help you all the same. Do you have a little savings?"

"No."

"See, see? Just what I said! You don't even know the basics

of life, my girl! Do you think you can spend the rest of your life like this? Without thinking about tomorrow, without a roof over your head or a penny in your pocket? If you count on those poor fish you catch at Plaza Italia . . . The one last night left you in the lurch. Besides, you can't live on what you get from one man a night; you have to find two, three, four, I don't know how many. Some find as many as ten. Don't look at me that way; you'll get used to it soon. But you'll need a corner where you can rest. . . . Look"—he went on as if he'd had a sudden inspiration—"look, I'll work it out with the boss to rent you a little room for a special price, and in exchange you can bring me customers. On the days when you hook more than three who have a few drinks, I won't charge you. Don't tell them you live here. Make them take another room. Then they have to pay, right? Don't be a fool."

Clara nodded in agreement, although she realized she was going too far along a path she hadn't chosen.

Maybe that's how things happen in life, whether you like it or not; probably because it's already written, as they say.

"The little room will cost you almost nothing . . . if you do me a little favor once in a while, of course."

To save time and to seal the pact, Don Mario wanted a little favor immediately; he lay on the bed almost fully dressed. Clara did what she could, but the pact was only half sealed, and that same morning she discovered that while any time is good for going to bed, there are men who are not so good at any time. It was a relief.

IT'S SAD TO think of Don Mario; he turned out to be all right, really; a squid with a heart of gold. . . . And I am all woman now, just as he said. And without having come too far along in life. It's a change, having someone to wait for, but it's not the same as getting ahead. Most of all I'd like to have someone waiting for me, like ladies do. One day my time may come. Who knows? Right now, though, the ledge of the wall is hard and narrow, and my feet hurt.

She walked to the corner, just for something to do, and she heard arrogant steps.

"Excuse me, miss. Your papers, please."

It was the voice of a hoodlum speaking out of the corner of his mouth. Clara turned around sharply, frightened, and found herself looking straight at a well-trimmed mustache.

"Oh, Officer. I don't have my papers. I left them at home."

"Sergeant," he corrected her, throwing his head back. Clara laughed in a high-pitched voice to show that she wasn't afraid and that she liked strong men.

"So you forgot them, eh? And what are you doing, walking around here all alone?"

"Waiting for my boyfriend, Sergeant."

"Has he kept you waiting long?"

"Well, long enough . . ."

"Come off it, kid. That boyfriend story is older than Methuselah. You've been sitting here forever. If you're looking for a real man, come with me. I'm the best in town." He laughed, showing a row of large white teeth.

"You're mistaken, Sergeant. I'm not what you think, believe me. I'm waiting for my boyfriend."

How maddening! Don't forget Don Mario's advice just because of a small blond mustache. Stay away from cops.

She had learned about cops soon after she had been given her own little room. Deciding to make the most of her new position, she had taken a handsome young rookie to the hotel café. To show him she wasn't a beginner, she sat at the table sideways and summoned the waiter with a nod. She was as well known there as anyone walking around, and the waiter would certainly give her a big hello. But he gave her no sign of recognition. Nothing. He came toward them, scrupulously wiping his metal tray with the towel he always carried under his arm, and asked, "What would you like?"

The rookie ordered a beer, and Clara was about to say, "The usual for me," when she noticed Don Mario gesturing desperately from behind the cash register. The cop saw Clara frown, but she could only look beyond him at Don Mario's frenetic hands alternately motioning her to the door and pointing at her as if they held a gun. At last she understood. She managed to smile at her companion and ordered a rum and Coke.

A few minutes after the drinks arrived, she looked at the clock on the wall and, like a perfect actress, exclaimed, "God! it's seven-thirty. My mother must be worried." She picked up her purse, jumped up, and, with her sweetest smile, said, "Officer, it was a pleasure to meet you. See you again, I hope."

If she had been on the stage her exit would have received a long ovation, but this was life and she was not at all pleased to disappear while the poor boy, with his mouth open, watched her infinitely repeated image finally vanish from the café mirrors.

She was on the street again. It was Don Mario's fault; after all, that young cop was the most promising customer she had found. Young, handsome, just the right sort to help her find out if the business of going to bed could be more pleasant. She thought of Eulosia, the crazy one, as she was called in Tres Lomas. Eulosia had raved about going to bed.

She felt sorry for herself.

It's terrible, a young girl like me having to work all the time. And not a moment of pleasure. Horrible Squid, you forced me to get rid of the cop. Tonight I won't bring you a single customer. Drop dead, for all I care; you won't get anything from me.

An hour later she returned to the café, sat at a table, and angrily ordered a double brandy. From his watching post behind the cash register, Don Mario noticed she was upset and came over to comfort her.

"You know, it's better not to get mixed up with the police. When you least expect it, they'll ask for a permit we don't have and then lock us all up. Especially you. Us, we can pay a bribe and everything will be fixed, but you'd be lost. I did it for your own good."

My own good, my own good, jealous pig.

"You don't have to jump at the first guy who comes along. Someday you'll meet a prince of a fellow, you'll see. Come on, cheer up." He made her drink another brandy and then, followed her upstairs to her room on the third floor.

"Are you going to invite me in?" he asked as they reached her door. Clara nodded.

"Don't play with the bulls," he went on. "Uniforms are beautiful but dangerous. First they take advantage of a woman and then, bang! They finish it off by putting her in jail. Whatever path you follow, modesty is the best virtue," he concluded.

Pompous ass.

Nevertheless, Clara had absorbed that lesson and promised herself never again to be impressed by a double row of silver buttons or the little stars given after five years of active service.

But, my God, this one at Parque Retiro is stickier than chewing gum . . . even though I he does have a golden sword and shiny boots.

However, when Clara made a decision, she was as firm as rock.

"But my boyfriend will be here any minute."

"Don't try to kid me, baby. Don't give me that innocent act. I like my women simple and straight."

If only Victor would show up. Waiting isn't too bad when you can stir up memories you've set aside for years; but waiting when you're face to face with a blue uniform doesn't leave you a moment to think of anything else.

She leaned against the wall, and the sound of the Cuban orchestra playing on the other side reached her in slow waves. The sergeant said a few more things to her, but she didn't hear him because she was concentrating so intently on the hands of the tower clock. Victor obviously wasn't coming, and here was this other man, entrenched in his arrogance.

She looked at her nails, pretending to be distracted. Another woman passed by, almost touching her. The sergeant whirled around.

"Miss, may I see your papers, please. . . ."

Clara felt lighter when he left, as if the sergeant's solid body had been weighing on hers.

. . .

AT TIMES, WAITING is as tiresome as working; muscles become tense, contracted. Clara found it difficult to understand why she was tense about Victor. They had been living together for more than three months, enough time for her to have become accustomed to seeing him arrive at the most unlikely hours.

Let your whole body relax, like in bed, beginning with your face to prevent wrinkles. Don't make fists. Don't dig your nails into the palms of your hands. Think about something else, anything else. Victor will never surprise me by arriving on time, not even once.

She had met him on the night when all her optimistic notions and good faith had forsaken her. The only consolation she had had was the pleasure of hateful thoughts, which made her feel stronger but which were also tearing her apart. She wanted to strike at something with her bare hands, to twist something, to rip it into shreds, to strangle it. Once she had believed in goodness, but she no longer had the strength to believe; all the dsperation of her life was focused now on destructive desires, and she looked at the passing subway cars in search of some way to restore indifference.

He got off one of those cars, just in front of her, and stared at her. For a long while, he stood there staring at that woman, so pale, with such big eyes, so lost. She had a vague beauty, like an old engraving he had seen in a bookstore window. Her hair was straight and long, like that engraving. Finally, when the platform was almost empty, he approached her.

"I don't like tunnels, either," he said. "Let's go look at the stars."

Clara smiled bitterly, but someone was offering her a hand and it was difficult to refuse that hand. They went up the escalator and found themselves facing a dull, starless sky.

"The Three Marys must be there, behind the Coca-Cola sign, and the Southern Cross over there, near the church steeple," Clara said. But he wasn't listening.

"My name is Victor. And yours?"

"Clara."

"A pretty name. Transparent, like peace must be. You couldn't be called anything else. That's why I liked you. I had to take you out of there. I hate closed-in places and crowds and noise. You hate them too, I'm sure. What were you doing in the subway?" He didn't give her time to answer. "Life should be an open space, where everything is clear, Clara. Clear without chlorine, clear as clear water."

The phrase seemed perfect to her, and she relished it in silence. But then she thought he was waiting for her reaction, so she said, "I don't understand anything about life, but it seems to me that . . ."

He took her hand. "Shhh . . . Don't talk. The moment is too delicate, too rare to shatter with sounds," and he remained sniffing the air to inhale the moment.

They had just met, but Clara knew that with him it would be useless to open her mouth. The idea of not being able to talk didn't worry her too much, for no one could prevent her from continuing an inner monologue, silent but intense. That same night, sitting on the steps of the new church, they decided that since Clara didn't have a place of her own, she would move to Victor's house for a while.

The apartment was old and small, with a tree that grew so close it almost came through the window. Victor felt proud showing her the matrimonial bedroom suite he had just bought, as if he had had a premonition. The enormous wardrobe and double bed, the two night tables, and the chair cluttered the one room. The narrow passageway had nothing in it yet—a blessing, Clara thought, because there was no room for anything else, except possibly a mirror and a clothes tree. The kitchen was long and narrow and also served as a dining room. Victor told her he would have it painted green to keep flies away. She looked at him admiringly.

"Then you're rich, with new furniture and everything. . . ."

"Well, I have a little nest egg. I'm also thinking of selling that old radio and buying a new one; you know, one of those small ones with a golden dial."

Clara settled into her new home, happy to have a man who gave her socks to mend and shirts to wash. That way, at least, she could say she was a true homemaker. She also had dishes to wash and new saucepans, which Victor had brought home one afternoon because he was tired of eating ham and cheese sandwiches.

Clara did a lot of scrubbing because there was nothing else to do. Victor never allowed her to talk. By now she had lost the use of her voice, but she could still dream. Her favorite fantasy was the one about marriage. She had perfected it all the way, to its very ending—no winners and no losers. The truth was that she didn't want to marry Victor any more than he wanted to marry her. On days she had nothing to do, she would stretch the daydream to the infinite; when she was tired, though, she would sum it up in a few words: it wasn't worth marrying and having children, because, as Victor said, "it's too complicated."

Victor did have crushing arguments, and it was better to agree with him, even in thought. Besides, Victor was making an effort to be good to Clara, a fact she couldn't ignore. She was already too weary from wrestling with his defects to attack the few virtues he had left.

When their life together was going smoothly, he would call her Clarita and take her out for an evening. But when some problem arose, it was invariably her fault, and he would refer to her as "my wife." At those times Clara would tell herself how much better off she was not being married to Victor, even if it meant not having children.

Usually, though, their life together went well. Clara learned how to haggle with the butcher to get the most meat for the least money, and Victor appreciated her boiled dinners. Sometimes, it's true, she did dream of the blouses and necklaces she used to buy, and, feeling despondent, she would go for a walk around Plaza Italia. But it was her vocation as homemaker that would win out, and instead of buying the pretty lace-trimmed slip she wanted so badly, she would come home with a chicken and a bottle of good wine. Since men's minds are conquered through their stomachs, Victor never took the trouble to ask how these delicacies reached their table.

The inevitable day arrived when Victor confessed to her that his savings were spent and that lately he hadn't been able to sell even one refrigerator. Clara told him not to worry, she would find some customers, but that infuriated him.

"Are you crazy? I wouldn't think of using you that way. Do you believe I've sunk so low? Do you expect me to send you back to the gutter I took you out of?"

He fell silent, and then his fury changed to humility.

"Look here, Clarita, the best thing we can do is pool our strength to weather the storm. Everything will be all right soon, you'll see. I'll pawn my cuff links and my pearl tiepin. The new radio, too, if you think I should, although I don't think that'll be necessary. You . . . well . . . would you have something to add?"

"Yes," she sighed, and went to get her grandfather's silver maté gourd. Then she took off her wristwatch and handed it to Victor.

She didn't care much about her grandfather's maté gourd: it only brought back memories of her fifteenth birthday, a day as boring as any other. The watch, though, was as much hers as her feet or her mouth. It was her medal, won in a moment of courage she might never repeat. One of her greatest pleasures was to watch the tiny wheels spin around while she told herself that she had managed to escape without too many scars from machinations as fiendish as those she was watching.

Of course, luck had been on her side.

OVER AND OVER, Don Mario had told her in that special tone he used when, as he said, he was trying to protect her from the evil of the outside world, "Never go after men with cars. Cars are very nice, and men wearing gold chains are attractive, but they're bad. Who knows where they'll take you and what they'll do with you. Your profession isn't one of the easiest, right? And if you give in to someone who won't stop until he has sucked your soul dry, don't come crying to me. I'm telling you now: no cars or men flashing a fat roll of bills."

Clara decided to follow Don Mario's sound advice to the letter. It's good to have someone guide your early steps. But she couldn't get the car out of her mind. She wanted to get ahead, and she knew there was a vast difference between a man with his foot on a gas pedal and one with his foot on the curb. There was a social difference, too. Besides, she dreamed of seeing the sea, and a car was necessary for that, one with soft reclining seats to set the mood for foamy blue waters. The sea couldn't have a train filled with fat women and snoring men as its prologue.

She had never brought up the subject of the sea with Don Mario. She enjoyed having secrets to ponder as she sat in the solitude of her room on the top floor, facing the window that looked out on a black roof spotted with the pigeon droppings. Sometimes she hoped the pigeons would change into sea gulls that would eat from her hand. And every morning she threw out bread crumbs, just in case.

Don Mario had also advised her not to get mixed up with the hotel employees. "They're a bunch of alley cats. You're going with the manager. That gives you a certain position in life. One has to have dignity, my girl."

He smiled with pleasure then, and remained still. She would take advantage of such moments to close her eyes and imagine that the man next to her was not Don Mario at all, but Carlos, one of the waiters on the afternoon shift.

Clara's dreams were divided between Carlos and the sea. Carlos was tall and dark, and when one looked at him closely she could see golden spots in his eyes. Every once in a while, Clara would ask him to bring up tea and pastries at five in the afternoon, the fashionable hour, but he would stay only long enough to greet her and place the tray on the night table. She always promised herself that next time she would receive him with her robe slightly open, but she never did, because Carlos was shy and she didn't want to make a bad impression on him. For the same reason, she went out to work after nine, after Carlos had left the café.

But one afternoon her confinement became more than she could bear, and she left her room before eight, dressed in her new lilac dress even though it was too low cut for the cool October night. But if she had felt confined in her room, on the street she felt worse. She stood in front of the café windows watching the neon lights changing colors. Suddenly a voice tickled the flesh on the back of her neck.

"Are you waiting for somebody, Señorita Clara?"

She turned her head, startled, and whispered, "Oh no, no."

"Are you busy?"

"No."

Now that she faced him, she didn't know what to do, but she ventured to say softly, "The night is so beautiful. . . ."

"A beautiful night to be enjoyed. 'Ambition rests . . . ' " he said, quoting the words of a tango. "Since neither of us has anything to do, why not have a drink together?"

Clara looked at him as if she were dreaming. "Yes," she answered in a voice thin as thread, and she moved toward the café door.

"No, not here, Clara. May I call you Clara? Let's go someplace else. Change the setting. I know a nice bar in Rosedal, facing the lake. We could even take a twirl around the dance floor."

"I don't dance very well. . . ."

"That doesn't matter; they keep the lights dim there, so no one will be able to see us."

They looked at each other and laughed. It was the first time Clara had laughed with a man. Usually, she would laugh at a man before he could laugh at her, or she would laugh to please him if he said something intended to be funny. But she and Carlos laughed together, and when she spoke, it was without watching her words.

"All right, the bar by the lake, and if no one can see us, we'll have fun."

He took her by the arm firmly, and they turned into a dark street. They walked in silence. Carlos was holding her arm and she was afraid to break the enchantment. "We can call each other Clara and Carlos," he ventured. "We've known each other for months."

"Thats true."

But they continued to walk in silence, with the lights of the avenue dwindling into small white spots.

They strolled at an easy pace, their steps marking the rhythm of the night. Carlos let go of her elbow and put his arm around her shoulders; Clara felt stiff and clumsy, her arms hanging at her sides. As they were crossing a street, Carlos stopped her in the yellow circle of light that fell from a street lamp.

"You are too pretty," he said.

Clara shivered as he pressed her against his chest.

"Are you cold?" he asked, and she shook her head, which she rested on his shoulder as they went on walking.

First he caressed her forehead and then he took her hand.

"Is the bar much further?" Clara asked, although she never wanted to get there, despite the lake and the swans.

"You're tired, let's rest a bit," he said, as he sat down on a low wall that bordered a garden. Carlos drew her to him gently and sat her on his knees. She lowered her head, afraid that the feelings hammering inside her temples would escape, and he took advantage of the moment to kiss the hair at the nape of her neck. Then Clara raised her eyes and found the little golden spots in his eyes.

With a tremendous effort, Carlos pulled himself away from her and put his arm around her shoulders again as they moved on. He whispered into her ear words that were full of magic.

The lights of a new street stunned her eyes. There were no streetcars or buses, only cars that sped by. Clara let Carlos decide the right moment to cross the road, and she let herself be led, eyes closed, enjoying the sensation of being cared for.

On the other side, the woods were barely lit by the street lamps. Beyond, there was the thick darkness of blooming trees.

Carlos led her to the darkest part of the map drawn by the shadows of tree trunks. He took his jacket off and spread it flat on the ground, under a big eucalyptus tree. He stretched Clara out on the jacket and lay upon the soft mattress of her body.

Disarmed with passion, Clara was afraid of what she was and of what she was no longer, the part of herself that she had given up without regrets when she came to the city. A moment of fear as he separated from her, that long emptiness so full of man and earth, a step closer to the gods and, at last, after so many rehearsals, closer to happiness.

Back at the hotel, Clara wanted to feel forever as she felt now, with the sensation of Carlos's body floating on hers. She sat at the bar and ordered a cognac, smiling blissfully and looking at Don Mario without seeing him.

"Clarita, my girl," Don Mario called from behind the cash register. "You look strange. You must have been out drinking. Go up to your room and get some sleep. In the morning I'll bring you a nice hot cup of coffee and an aspirin and you'll see how much better you'll feel."

Don Mario kept his promise and brought her an aspirin along with the coffee, but Clara had never felt better. She was radiant. But then Don Mario shattered the enchantment into a thousand pieces.

"How many times have I told you not to go out with anyone who works at the hotel? A pretty mess you got me into! Last night Carlos's wife came in like a madwoman, looking for her husband. Pichi told her he had seen him with you. Imagine what an uproar there was! And I got all the screaming. To make matters worse, now we're without a waiter. That bitch won't let him come back here."

Those few words had the taste of death. Clara leaned against the pillow, drank the coffee, and swallowed the aspirin, trying to understand why she had to pay so dearly for every minute of happiness.

Now, with Victor, she at least lived quietly: she was not excessively happy, but then again she was not afraid that the relentless judges who rule life would make her pay for these monotonous days. At the most, they would give her the penance of waiting without a show of impatience, of facing the enormous clock that intensified the awareness of time. It wasn't like the time she had waited for Carlos: three days and nights without eating, without sleeping, without leaving the hotel. She hadn't wanted anything to distract her from her waiting.

She consoled herself by telling herself that he had deceived her—after all, he had never told her he was married. But she also blamed herself.

I deceived him, too. I never told him how I earned my living. I'm to blame for everything. Yes, he'll come back; he hasn't come yet because his wife is an ogre and has him locked up. But he'll escape. It doesn't change the fact that he deceived me, though. At least I wasn't betraying anyone, but he had his own woman. Maybe even children.

Even so, she waited. But Carlos never appeared again.

On the last night, as they were putting the chairs on top of the tables in order to wash the floor, Don Mario took her by the arm and said, "I'm going to put you to bed. You need it."

Clara let him lead her out of the café and into the elevator. He didn't even try to fondle her between floors.

When they got to the room, he forced her to sit next to him on the bed and said reproachfully, "I told you not to go out with waiters, but you didn't listen. Those kind of men play with women and then disappear. I hope you've learned your lesson. Now you won't disobey old Mario again, eh?"

He helped her to undress and tucked her into bed; he turned off the light and sat down on the chair at her side. He wanted to make love to her, but he knew that Clara needed sleep; then she would forget everything and things between them would be the same.

Obedience. Lots of obedience, but if it weren't for you, old Squid, Carlos would still be here and I could see him as much as I wanted.

She slept until the next evening, when Don Mario had one of the maids bring her a cup of hot chocolate and a ham sandwich.

An hour later she went down to the café and, as she passed the bar, she realized that she could not longer live there. The despair sat hard in her gut, and she left the café resolved to give up the life at Don Mario's and find a man who would take her to the sea in his own car.

She began to study the long cars that went by, the fancy two-toned ones with tail fins, but most of them were driven by uniformed chauffeurs and she knew that an important man couldn't reveal to a subordinate that he needs a hooker.

He has to pretend he can have all the women he wants by simply lifting his little finger. Of course, there are some ladies who are too difficult and some who are too easy, but unfailingly they are also too expensive and full of airs. That's why every so often these proper gentlemen have to look for a woman whose price is fixed, but they can't do that in front of everyone, and least of all in front of their own chauffeurs.

Nevertheless, Clara continued waiting for the right car. She even refused a blond sailor, and sailors were usually the best customers around Plaza Italia. Each time she saw a car with a man alone in it, she bent down to smile, but they were all in too much of a hurry to notice her. Finally, a car pulled up at the curb in front of her. She hadn't smiled at that one because it was an old-fashioned model, but the driver said "Get in!" with such authority that Clara obeyed.

As she settled into the car, she noticed that the seats were fairly comfortable, and they might even be able to get as far as the ocean if the motor didn't break down. It occurred to her that perhaps the front seat could be pushed back to make a bed, like that drawing on the cover of a magazine that the Catholic Action in her town had condemned as immoral.

Ridiculous! How can a drawing of a car ever be moral or immoral?

She had not dared to defend it before the Committee, but when she went to confession the following Sunday, she told the priest about her bad thought. She still remembered how he had admonished her:

"My daughter, bad thoughts are like flies on candy: one alone seems inconsequential, but soon others are attracted, and they accumulate and cling to one another until they form a putrid body. Say six Hail Marys and three Our Fathers. . . ."

Clara tried to think of other bad thoughts she had had since; she could find none. Until now, as she again wished for a car that would change into a bed and take her to the sea. Therefore, she concluded, if she hadn't had bad thoughts, she couldn't have a putrid body. That idea was soothing, and she smiled.

She casually ran her fingers through her hair and said to the stranger, "Let's to go the Almafuerte bar. It's very pleasant there."

Awful habit. If I go back there, I'll think about Carlos again and I'll never be able to make this one take me away.

The man seemed to read her thoughts. "You think I'm a taxi that'll take you wherever you want to go?"

Clara looked at him, wide-eyed. The stranger lit a cigarette and brought the lighter perilously close to her face.

"Do you have an obligation to go there?"

"No, no obligation."

"Who's in charge of you, honey? This isn't the first time I've seen little innocent you cruising around here."

"Nobody's in charge of me."

Clara thought that was the right moment to sigh, to be elegant and sad at the same time, but she never had the chance because the car shot ahead. "Then let's go where I want to go."

A few blocks farther on, they had to brake to let a truck go by.

"What's your name?" the man asked.

"Clara."

"I am Toño Cruz. My buddies call me Devil Cruz."

Clara never knew that that was only a half-truth: his classmates in the second grade had called him Devil Cruz, but no one since then had used the nickname. Certainly not at the bank where he had been working for fifteen years at the same job, and where he was considered quite respectable. Nevertheless, he repeated, "Devil Cruz, ha ha!" and slapped her on the back.

He stepped on the gas again and kept his foot pressed hard on the accelerator until they stopped abruptly in front of an austere building with a brown marble façade. The car moved slowly toward a garage door, which opened automatically to admit them. When Clara turned around to see how the door worked, it had already closed behind them and they were surrounded by darkness. The shadow of a man approached, making such obsequious gestures that Clara didn't have to be coaxed to get out of the car and to follow Toño Cruz and the porter into the somber, carpeted corridor.

When they were alone inside the apartment and the bright light was turned on, Clara saw that Toño Cruz was shorter than she had thought, and that there were white streaks in his hair. His chin came to a sharp point, and the top of his head was flat, *but Clara knew that the perfect prostitute doesn't worry about her customer's physical appearance.* He was studying her, too, but that was fine, because a customer can waste his time in foolish games; after all, he's paying for it.

When he finished inspecting her from a distance, he approached to touch her, rolling his tongue over his lips.

"All right, undress. Now we'll try you out."

Clara undressed meekly and made a move to turn off the light, but he told her to leave it on. She came toward him slowly, like a cat, and rubbed against his body.

When they finished, Clara figured that playing the cat had pleased Toño, because he had tried to please her. She decided she would play the cat with all men from now on. Don't think of Carlos, don't think of Carlos, she told herself. The phrase was lulling her to sleep when a roar cracked the air.

"What's that?" she asked, startled.

"Nothing, woman . . . a boat whistle . . ."

"Are we near the sea?"

She knew very well that you had to travel at least five hours to reach the sea, but they had driven so fast . . . A city-educated boy from her town had explained to her once that if one goes very fast, time no longer exists. She hadn't understood him, she had been afraid of him, and she never wanted to see him after that, even though he had asked her to marry him. That had only made her more afraid, sure that he would fill her head with peculiar ideas simply to make it easy to abuse her and forsake her. Now everything was different: no one could abuse her and she could clearly understand that they had moved so fast toward the sea that they had escaped time.

But Toño, Devil Cruz, brought her back from her comforting illusions.

"What sea are you talking about, dummy? We're near the harbor. Don't you know the harbor?"

"No."

"And the Rio de la Plata?"

"No."

"And this neighborhood?"

"No."

"Then what *do* you know?"

"Well . . . very little."

Toño Cruz decided to play his trump card. "The best thing you can do for yourself is come with me. I'll teach you everything you need to know."

"Seriously? But I have a room in a hotel. . . ."

"You're alone, aren't you? Then what the devil do you care? Come to my house and make yourself at home. A classy apartment on Junin Street, lined with shops."

"And leave my work?"

"Your work? You're not a maid, are you?"

"Oh, no. This is my work."

"Ah, this isn't work. It's a pastime. Don't give it a thought. You'll be much better off with me. When you have time to relax, I'll keep you company. I'll get you organized and you'll even be able to save. What do you say?"

Clara thought of Don Mario, and of his advice. She thought of the hotel, and the bar where Carlos no longer was. She felt an urgent need for change, and she asked Toño, "Will you take me to look at the sea?"

"During your vacation, maybe, if you behave . . ."

"What do I tell the people at my hotel?"

"Don't tell them anything. You'll get your things early in the morning. I'll wait for you in the car. Do you have much?"

"A few things, but I don't have a suitcase to put them in."

She had thrown away the one she brought from Tres Lomas because it was old and shabby. Later, she had bought some blouses and skirts and two dresses, but not a new suitcase. I don't really think ahead, she said to herself, and she laughed at the thought that when she left the hotel she also would leave behind all her sad memories, and, in addition, she would finally be taking a step forward.

Undoubtedly she took a step, but it was more sideways than forward. Things were neither better nor worse than before. It had pained her to see the hurt expression on Don Mario's face as she was leaving, carrying a clumsy bundle.

"So you're going," he had said, simply. "I guess I couldn't keep you forever. I'm an idiot."

But his humility irritated him, and he screamed:

"Go, just go! If you prefer living with a pimp, what do I care! But don't ever put a foot in this door; I never want to see you again!"

Toño's apartment was on the ground floor, in the back. It was a good size and had a small private patio, although that turned out to be useless since the sun never reached it and the neighbors threw garbage out of their windows. Soot fell like black rain and stuck to the freshly washed clothes Clara hung there to dry.

Nevertheless, the hope she felt in those first days there compensated for the disappointments of the past. With the exception of some details, Clara worked as before; she was acquiring a great ability to handle her customers more efficiently. The hotel she went to most often was ugly and small, not like Don Mario's. She missed her old neighborhood of Plaza Italia, and all those young boys and service men. There were even times when she would allow herself to think nostalgically of Carlos.

She remembered, back at Don Mario's, the time a group of tourists had arrived, such happy people, singing and playing guitars, and she had heard their music and laughter from the rooms below. What she missed most, though, was Don Mario's encouraging smile when she would arrive with an old or ugly man. Hoping to find another smile that would give her the courage to go on, she once asked Toño:

"Wouldn't it be better if I brought my customers here? It would be much more elegant, and we could charge them the price of a hotel room. . . ."

Toño looked at her, astonished.

"Are you crazy, woman? What will the neighbors think? What will the janitor and his wife and daughters think? And that woman in 1C is a real lady! She'd be horrified to learn she lives one floor above a prostitute. She's a friend of the landlord and could have us thrown out. You can't offend the modesty of ladies."

So as not to offend anyone's modesty, Clara had to keep going to a dirty hotel and give Toño all the money she earned. First he had asked for it to pay the rent; later it was for the gas; after that, food, until one day Clara screamed.

"Toño, what I give you is enough for you to pay the food bills, the rent, the gas, the electricity, the hot water, and to keep a car running for all our neighbors!"

But he wasn't intimidated. "I knew you'd be ungrateful. Didn't I give you some class? Didn't I give you a home? Of course, you have to complain! You know, I'm not stealing from you; I'm investing your capital in stocks and someday you'll be rich. If I let you do whatever you want with your money, you'll spend it all on junk. Well, I think for you: with the stock, you'll have a magnificent pension. A whore can't keep on working forever, you know. The time comes when the body is worn out and nobody wants it."

To hell with the stocks!

While that was a comfort, she was much more impressed with the threat of her worn-out body. When she finished that night, she rented the hotel's most luxurious room and looked at herself for a long time in its only mirror, which was on the ceiling. It wasn't too easy to look at herself lying down, but she could tell that it would be many years before her body was worn out. That made her happy, and thanks to Toño's stocks, she could retire from her profession while her body was still good.

She worked more eagerly and with more hope until Toño told her that he had quit his job at the bank—although he continued to leave the apartment every morning, freshly shaved and wearing a tie. She was too tired to get dressed and follow him. She didn't even have the strength to ask him where he was going until he returned home one day wearing a pair of gold cuff links with big topaz stones.

"I'm sick and tired of working for you!" she cried. "I can't buy myself a pair of earrings and you go around like a big shot, and at my expense! But this is it! Give me my stock now. I'm getting out. Do you hear me? I'm getting out!"

Toño stuck out his chest and raised himself to tiptoe. "Go ahead, beat it. I'll just go to the police and turn you in! Are your papers in order? Do you think you have the right to do the work you do? You're not going to get rid of me as easily as that!"

Clara closed her eyes, and as his words spun around her head, she realized that this was not the right moment to force the issue. But she wanted to force a promise out of him.

"All right, I'll go on working for you. But you have to take me to the beach for a few days."

"You've got to be kidding! Gas is expensive, and I'm not here to play around."

Tears rolled down her cheeks, and Toño felt pleased. He told himself that the way to handle women was to mistreat them; from now on he could do what he wanted with her because he had command of the situation. He began to abuse Clara and to scream at her from that day on.

"Two hundred pesos! Two hundred pesos! You've been out for twelve hours and you bring me two hundred pesos! You're nothing! What do you expect me to do with your lousy two hundred pesos? I need money, money!"

Or: "Why're you back so early? You think you've done what you're supposed to do? Well, in case you're interested, you haven't done anything. Rain is no excuse to come back after two customers. Or is the baby tired?"

He screamed so much and his voice was so resonant that Clara thought he must be hollow inside, like a drum. To get some relief from him, she went out one day earlier than usual and returned later. As she undressed in the dark, Toño saw a sparkle on her wrist.

"What's that you have there?" he shouted as he switched on the light.

"A wristwatch."

"Oh? So now you go around buying gold jewelry without my permission, eh?"

The watch was solid gold, with fifteen rubies inside. It had a one-year guarantee. Thinking of the guarantee, made Clara smile with satisfaction, and that smile so angered Toño that he jumped out of bed and slapped her.

Clara stared at him, wide-eyed, but she didn't even raise her hand to rub her smarting cheek.

Pleased with her reaction, Toño returned to his bed. "Man, do I know females!" he said to himself. "This'll quiet her down for a while." Aloud, he added, "Tell me where you bought that ridiculous watch and I'll go tomorrow and exchange it for something I can use."

Clara didn't have the slightest intention of exchanging it, and the following day, when Toño returned from his daily visit to the lady in 1C, the landlord's friend, he found that Clara had left for good, taking with her all her clothes and even a handsome imitation crocodile-skin suitcase that belonged to him. Toño was alarmed and ran to the wardrobe to search among his winter underwear. Also missing were the thirteen hundred pesos he had hidden there to pay the smuggler who was going to bring him French perfume for the lady in 1C.

"A PLACE FOR everything, and everything in its place," the man who had snatched her from Toño's hands had said when he wanted to put her in a brothel. Waiting by the side entrance of the Parque Retiro railway station, Clara felt as out of place as a mouse in a rainstorm, staring at a brick clock tower wouldn't let her ignore the waste of time.

Years ago, during a long summer siesta, she would say to the daughter of her mother's employer, "Let's listen to time go by." But that had been a small town, where lost hours are not important. She and the other girl would shut themselves in the dark living room and lie under the table to look up at the sheet-swathed furniture and listen to the ticking of the pendulum clock. Back then, time was a man with a cane and a wooden leg who walked in circles while he slowly grew old. But in front of the gray station, there was no man with a wooden leg; it was simply adult time, an elusive and irksome time slipping away as Clara waited for a man with legs of flesh and bone, who should be arriving at any moment.

Twenty to nine, and the clock hands keep moving, without worrying about me. Of course, time itself is strange. There were no problems about that with Toño; he used to let me come and go as I pleased—as long as I handed over the cash, of course, fresh bills, one by one. It was a way of buying time and of being able to use it any way I liked.

But that was so only until she decided to buy herself time seriously, in palpable form, in the shape of a wristwatch.

After leaving Toño, her big experience with time cost her dearly. Her birthday was approaching, and she didn't want to face it. Though she tried, she couldn't delay it for more than forty-eight hours. She wandered about the streets, went into tearooms, window-shopped, and when her conscience told her it was time to do something, she would look at her watch, which she hadn't wound since she left Toño. It always showed the same time—ten past four. Eventually she grew bored and wound the watch. An hour later, she was angry that the time had moved so quickly, so she turned the hands back a half hour. She continued to do this whenever the hands advanced toward her birthday faster than she wanted them to.

Lavalle Street had become her passion: people hurrying by, and scores of movie houses. She wanted to hurry along, too, but the movie posters were irresistible, and she would cross from one side of the street to the other just to look at them. Occasionally a man would approach her and ask, "Alone?" in a confidential tone.

At one-fourteen it was really nine-thirty. Clara was hungry, so she went into a cafeteria. Then she decided that she wanted to sleep, so she did something she had always wanted to do: she rented a room in a hotel with revolving doors.

As she was going to bed, she thought that being twenty-one was all right, but twenty-two was an adult, a painful age. Although she had seen "May 22" printed on the register at the hotel desk, she assured herself that she wouldn't become twenty-two on the twenty-fifth of May, because, thanks to her little watch, that day would never come.

The thirteen hundred pesos once set aside for French perfume evaporated in other ways. Clara ate as much as she wanted and slept as long as she liked. She even saw the same film three times in a movie house where she had to leave and then pay to get in again. But she only gained two days in her fight against growing older. On the third morning, it was obvious that Clara's efforts had failed. All the houses were decorated with flags, and the music of military bands was driving the pigeons away from the square. No doubt about it, it was Liberation Day, the twenty-fifth of May. Schoolchildren were self-conscious in their immaculately starched white smocks, each with a badge pinned on at the left side.

The fatherland on your heart, the teacher used to say. I really liked the big pleated badges with the tiny metal circle in the middle, and Mother insisted that I wear that horrible one she had made, with the narrow pleated ribbon. Year after year I wore that same badge so we wouldn't have a useless expense. If you think about it, though, useless expenses are the only ones worth having—everything else is a necessity.

She thought the moment had come at last when she could buy the badge of her dreams, and right at the corner was a man who sold flags and other patriotic items. But she changed her mind; first she should straighten out her situation. After all, she had until Independence Day, the ninth of July, to buy a thousand badges, and also to make herself a necklace, white and sky blue, and an eagle in the sky with wings as blue as the sea.

She opened her purse, unfastened the pin in the lining, and took out a scrap of paper she had hidden there, with the name and address of a very distinguished lady who would find Clara a job.

Her suitcase in hand, she boarded a streetcar. There was nothing more pleasant than a trip by streetcar, Clara thought. On hot days, with the cool air racing through the windows, it gave her the feeling of being out in the open. When the weather was cold, it seemed like a glass cage carrying her along, enclosing her in its ringing bells and groans.

Clara was pleased. A job was waiting for her, in a fine house facing a park. "Just the right place for you," the man had said, and she thought perhaps he meant a job taking care of children. She would take them to the park across the way; ever since that night with Carlos, she longed to be surrounded by trees.

When she arrived, she was told that the woman had gone away.

FROM suspicious river

Laura Kasischke

"SMITH," HE SAID, "Gary."

Sure enough, it wasn't in the ledger.

I looked up at him. His smile was a flinch on one side of his face—a smirk, a wink—sexy, I thought, experimental. He smoked a cigarette and the smoke weaved around his head like a web, the way an egg white, cracked, swirls and rises in a glass of water. Then he started to cough, rattling and wet, and he said through it, eyebrows raised in a question, "You don't got my reservation?"

"No," I apologized, "but it's O.K. We have plenty of empty rooms."

Luckily he didn't seem to care. Some people will get upset that you don't have their names even if the whole motel is empty. They'll stand around fretting long after you've checked them in, room key safely in their hands, wanting to know exactly what went wrong, looking as if some piece of themselves had been lost, like a greasy playing card disappeared from the deck without which the game could not go on. It seemed to be proof to them of an insecure universe, proof that they might barely even exist if they didn't insist on it. I'd want to comfort them, to say *It's just Millie, she writes nothing down,* but I couldn't.

"I called last Saturday," he said. "Morning."

His leather jacket was thin, a starched white shirt under it, and there was rain on the shoulders and the slick sleeves. He was small, but nice-looking. Thin. His hair was brown and short, wavy—sparse on top, and he had a scruffy beard that might have been new, accidental, or both. He scratched at that stubble as if to make sure it was still on his chin.

"Hmm," I said, looking at the open book again, though I knew his name wouldn't be in it—Saturday morning, Millie's shift. "Well," I said, trying to change the subject, "Fortunately it's not a problem at all. How many nights?"

"One for now," he said, and I noticed his accent then. East Texas. Or Tennessee. And thick. A little like humidity between us.

I took a check-in card out of the drawer under the adding machine and began writing the date on it, then *Smith, Gary.* He flipped his wallet open onto the counter and handed me his Visa—small slice of plastic silver like a homemade knife. But the name on it was Jensen, Gary.

I glanced back then at the guest book, still open on the counter. And there it was, in Millie's handwriting—Jensen, G.

He'd lit another cigarette and leaned, smoking it, with his elbow on the counter. He was watching me write. I picked his credit card up off the counter between us with fingernails painted shell pink, and ran it. A long string of numbers and Jensen, Gary—smudged and permanent imprint on a piece of paper.

I wrote $60.00 under Payment. $2.40 under Tax. $62.40 under Total. Then I turned the paper toward him and watched as he signed his name: Gary W. Jensen. Then he looked up.

"Forgot my own name," he laughed. "Forgot I wasn't gonna use the credit card, and then I forgot whether or not I'd put the reservation in my real name. Sneaky guy, huh?" He tugged on his shirt collar and smiled. "Guess you caught me," he said. His eyes were brown and clear. Forty, I guessed. He smelled like soap mixed up with smoke.

"Guess so," I said, and I held his eyes in silence until he started to look nervous.

It works every time. They think they're bigger than you, bigger than some girl behind a motel counter, that God made them that way. But if you don't flinch, and it's sex that's being negotiated, they wither under it like a hot light and start to sweat.

"Well." He looked behind him, and I could see the inch of neck exposed between his hair and the collar of his coat. The skin looked just shaved, a bit naked, scraped. There was no one behind him, and he looked back at me with his eyebrows raised and his face seeming younger for a moment than forty, with a teenage boy's shy deception, charming and inept, and he said, "Reason for all the shenanigans is I was looking for a girl my buddy told me about. In addition to needing a room, of course. You wouldn't happen to be her?"

I leaned forward, wrist close to his fingertips. "Might be," I said, singsong.

He cleared his throat and straightened a bit. His voice was scratched. "So, I guess you know where my room is, don't you?"

I reached under the counter then and took 42 off the rack of plastic hooks and tossed it to him gently across the counter. It landed at his elbow.

"42," I said.

Maybe he looked worried then, like a man in a restaurant who wasn't sure how to eat what he'd ordered for dinner.

Here's your flaming rack of lamb, sir, I might have said.

I could see him swallow. He had the cigarette burning a small orange eye in one hand and with the other he smoothed the thin brown hairs on top of his head.

"How much?" He opened his eyes wider when he asked it.

"Sixty."

"Now?"

"I'll give you some time to get settled in your room, Mr. Smith," I said, teasing him, feeling powerful and innocent as a child lying straight to your face.

He forced a smile, but it wasn't easy for him.

As he was leaving, I could see he was wearing blond cowboy boots, his nearly new blue jeans tight around the ankles. The boots made a sharp sound on the linoleum, and the bells on the office door jingled tinny and cheap as he stepped out.

THERE ARE DIFFERENT kinds of men, I thought then, but not many different kinds. There are men who aren't as strong as they think they are, trying all the time to prove something. And there are men who are stronger than they think they are, trying all the time to prove something. It all adds up to the same thing in the end, until all men seem the same. But, I thought, Gary W. Jensen Smith looked like a man who was stronger than he thought he was, though he would never find it out for himself. He had the body of a boy—and the boots, the leather jacket, the jeans. *Rascal*, I imagined his mother saying under her breath about him until he turned forty and was still a boy.

When I left, I set a plastic sign on the front desk that said RECEPTIONIST WILL BE RIGHT BACK.

The rain had stopped, but it was dark. Only five o'clock. But the days were getting shorter, and this one had been dark to start. The air was damp, and it gave me a chill that began in my hair and crept down my back as I stepped over the puddles of rain, which were shallow and swirled with peacock colors from old oil. They smelled like tarnish, like the inside of an empty tin can. Iodine, or was it indigo, in the dusk.

A cool steam rose ghostly from the hoods of the few parked cars, and I thought the silver Thunderbird must be his. Nice. Florida plates. I passed it on my way to 42 and touched the hood briefly with the palm of my hand. It was warmed from within, like an electric blanket, or a big cat.

The metal railing vibrated, and it felt solid, heavy, but hollow under my hand as I walked up the stairs. Mrs. Briggs had hired a blond high school boy the summer before to paint it aqua blue, and the paint had already begun to peel, leaving ovals of rust like elbow patches where the smooth gloss was gone. My shoes were red—they matched my purse, back in the office, but they looked too bright to me on my feet that evening against the gray slab stairs.

Gary Jensen's door was open about an inch.

This is common. Maybe they're afraid you won't wait if the door is closed tight and locked, but they don't want to leave it gaping open either, especially in the evening, especially if it's damp. I knocked.

The week before, I'd walked in, and the man was already naked. Hard. Pumping his thing with one hand, a little plastic glass of whiskey and ice in the other. A big celebration. He must have wanted to shock or impress me, I thought, but he did neither. I just wondered to myself how it was I hadn't noticed that he was fat back in the office, and bald. Maybe he'd been wearing a hat, I couldn't remember. I just looked at him, blank. His own expression was wide-eyed and full of crazy hope. When I sighed, he frowned and stopped pumping. He put his drink down on the chest of drawers. When I held out my hand for the money, he said, "What?"

"The money," I said.

His jaw dropped a bit and then he covered himself up with a towel—suddenly shy—while he fished through the pockets of his black pants, which were laid out carefully on the bed, to find the money for me.

"Here." He shoved the three twenties toward me like a disgruntled tenant. He wouldn't look at me.

I didn't ask him what he wanted, just got on my knees and took it in my mouth. He whimpered when he came but never touched me. His arms were straight down at his sides, fists gripping and ungripping nothing, and I kept the soft cash in my own left hand the whole time.

Remembering him, I wondered if that man might have been Gary W. Jensen's buddy, the one who'd told him about me.

Probably not.

Maybe the trucker from Milwaukee. He'd left real happy and said he'd send his friends.

"COME IN." FRIENDLY.

Gary W. wasn't undressed, though it seemed to me he'd changed his shirt. This shirt was starched stiff and light blue. Hadn't the other one been white? He was sitting on the edge of the bed, smiling, a bottle of Rolling Rock in his hand, and now that he had his leather jacket off, I could see that his shoulders were no wider than my own. He was only a few inches taller, couldn't even have weighed much more, but he looked solid, scrappy—a thin tough man.

"Here," he said, holding the green bottle toward me. I saw another one, then, between his knees, and I thought he must have mistaken this for some kind of date—strangers getting to know each other better, something like that. But that's not what this was about.

"I can't," I said, gesturing behind me, "I'm working."

He started to laugh at that. His eyes were true brown. "Oh," he said. "You can come up here and give blow jobs to total strangers, but they won't let you drink a beer."

It wasn't angry, the way he said it, just honest—pointing out a contradiction, sharing an absurdity. I wasn't offended. I laughed, too. I liked his smirk, his accent, which seemed sarcastic, consciously a little stupid.

"Well," he stood up and put the two bottles of beer on the dressing table, which was blond and shiny, made of wood pulp and sawdust pressed into boards—fake, like everything in the motel room. The drywall was smooth and freshly painted, and the partition that separated the bathroom from the rest of the room was covered with metallic wallpaper that reflected the light from the window. It all seemed identically, eternally, fresh and sterile from room to room.

He hadn't closed the curtains.

"Well, here." He fished through the pockets of his jeans and handed me the money politely, then stood facing me, seeming happy, not nervous at all, just excited in a shrugging, boyish way.

I looked at the money in my hand. Two twenties. Two tens. I slipped my foot out of my shoe and bent a bit to slip the bills in under my heel.

The slap surprised me as I was standing up again, lifting my eyes back toward him.

We were both still smiling.

Just the flat surface of his hand made contact with my face, and it knocked me off balance. He stood in the same place, looking.

I hadn't wanted to gasp, but I knew I had by the way he laughed, that smirk, at my shocked face. It stung. It must've gone very red, burning, or drywall white. Then he hit me again, leaning into it more deeply this time, taking a step toward me as if he were pitching a baseball game, and then he pulled me forward onto the floor, onto my back.

I closed my eyes and heard a jet pass over the Swan Motel. Someone going somewhere fast. It took him a long time, a lot of scrambling, to get my skirt up and himself between my legs, and after he did, he kept one hand pressed at my neck the whole time, one on my wrist. I opened my eyes, and he stared into them while I stared out. It didn't hurt at all, though I supposed from the look on his face that he was hoping it would.

Gary Jensen lowered himself over me until the side of his jaw was against my mouth, and I could feel the sparse dark beard, a bit of sweat beading between the whiskers. I could have bitten him then, but I closed my eyes again instead.

I supposed he was hoping I'd fight, or whimper. But I wouldn't: Smelling his neck I realized without surprise that I'd been wrong about what he was, completely wrong—the skin there smelled like boots. And whatever he'd expected of me, I wanted him to have the opposite of it, too. For instance, what's the point of hurting someone who doesn't mind being hurt?

I only worried about the curtains being open. I worried someone might be waiting at the front desk for me. There were six other guests on their way to the Swan Motel in the fog and tinny drizzle that night, if Millie's calculations were anything close to correct.

BUT THE OFFICE was empty when I got back.

I slipped the sixty dollars out of my shoe and into my red purse behind the counter. The bills were warm and moist from my skin. Maybe I counted them one more time before I put the purse down again, beside my jacket.

22. I KNOCKED. The door was the usual half-inch open. The curtains had been closed.

He said, "Come in."

The room was cold. His maroon suitcase was open on the floor. Black socks and gray underwear spilled out of it. I said, "You could turn the heat on."

"Well," he said, shrugging, "I couldn't figure out how."

"Here," I said, going to the radiator under the window, turning the dial to ON. Twisting the knob in the direction of the red arrow pointing to WARM.

He looked over my shoulder as I did this. "Wow," he said, "great. Is that all? Hmm."

Then he handed me a twenty and a ten, which he'd already had in his hand. I leaned down to slip it in my shoe, and I could smell him. Old Spice and Listerine. He was standing close to me in his undershirt and blue polyester pants. I could see black hairs on his chest sprouting out of his T-shirt. His belly was soft behind his belt, and he was breathing hard.

I could hear country music drone above us. Someone singing O-O-O over and over. Twang and thump. Gary Jensen stomping in his cowboy boots over our heads while I undid the buckle of this man's belt, unsnapped his pants and pulled them down.

He was trembling, practically screaming, "Oh my god. Oh. Oh my god."

When it was over, he wanted more. I told him I had to go,

but he held onto the sleeve of my blouse. "Please," he said, "just let me see your titties."

"No," I said.

When I got back to the office, Gary W. Jensen was leaning on one elbow with his back toward the counter, smoking a cigarette. He wasn't wearing the leather jacket, and he looked lean. His brown hair was combed now. The thin beard looked darker. He looked like someone vaguely familiar from a TV show—maybe the deputy on *Gunsmoke*, but sexy, clever.

I didn't look at him, just walked around the counter, took the money out of my shoe and reached under the cash drawer to put it in my purse, checking first to make sure the rest of my money was still where I'd left it. Then I stood back up and said, "Can I help you, Mr. Jensen?"

"You sure are a busy little beaver, ain't you?"

"Yes." I looked straight at him. "So what can I help you with now?" Not a hint of anything in it—sex, fear, anger, nothing.

"Well." He cleared his throat, which led to a long cough, and then he said, "To be honest, I wanted to apologize. I know I'm really a bastard. I should never've hit you."

"It didn't hurt," I said. It hadn't.

He looked surprised. "I'm glad of that, at least, but I still feel so damn bad about it." The Texas accent made him sound sincere, and his eyebrows were knitted together. His eyes were dark and sad. He dragged on his cigarette and looked hard at me, though he didn't look for long. My fingers felt cold and thin to each other.

"Forget about it," I said, and meant it. I'd gotten the money, he'd hit me, so what? It was just my body, and it was over.

"Thank you," he said. "You're real sweet, you know that? You shouldn't be doing what you're doing. I know it's none of my damn business, but you're real pretty and nice, and it's just wrong. It could be dangerous, too, with fools like me running around loose."

I felt my throat tighten, near the spot he'd held me down against the floor.

Here he was, someone else again, and what role was left for me to play?

I swallowed and said, quieter than I'd meant to, "Why'd you hit me then?"

He leaned across the counter and whispered, as if it were the most astonishing fact I'd ever hear, "Sweetheart, I have no idea." He shook his head and looked at his thumbnails lined up next to each other on the counter, then he looked up at me again with damp eyes. "That's the truth," he said. "I don't have the slightest damn idea. Just something sick in me, I guess."

"I guess you're right," I said, and my own eyes went stupidly damp. I felt myself step back a bit then, away from my body or out of it, and I could see myself as if in a mirror. Embarrassed, sentimental, blurred.

Gary Jensen began to fish for another cigarette in his shirt pocket and handed one to me, too. The flame was warm near my face when he lit it, and I didn't look up again.

Outside now it was deep blue, though the October sky had begun to clear with just a bruise of old light, the sun already sunk like a shipwreck to the west, where Lake Michigan sloshed sloppy with dead fish and weeds.

The office felt too small and hot, a dull fan scrambling the heat, blasting dust into the air, and I imagined the dry mummies of mice stuck in the electric furnace duct, crumbling and blowing mouse ash into the air. Us sucking it into our lungs. The cigarette smoke filled my mouth with soot.

"You saw that woman then, the one who came looking for me?" he asked.

"I guess so."

"She's got a good heart, too, and I've broke it to pieces. She's the mother of my child, for chrissakes, and I've treated her worse than dirt. Worse than dirt." He shook his head, seeming baffled by himself. "Who knows why a guy like me does the kind of stuff he does. Who knows?"

I shrugged and said, "I don't," exhaling a banner of gray hair over his shoulder.

He grinned. "No, hon, I suppose you don't! But I just want to tell you I have never been sorrier in my life for anything I've done than I am for hitting you. There's just no excuse for hitting a pretty little girl like you. A total stranger. And I just had to have you know that. Especially since, you know, you were being real nice to me, and we were doing something—intimate. You know? The way I behaved was just plain wrong. I am one evil guy. My mama would just roll over in her coffin if she knew what kind of man I have become."

"O.K.," I said, putting the cigarette out in the ashtray near his elbow, "but I need to get back to work." I felt annoyed, familiar, myself again.

He straightened up then, as if I'd caught him in a lie. "I understand. I understand." He cleared his throat. "Listen, I hope this isn't going to make matters even worse. But money is not a problem for me right now, though I suspect it is for you. Here." He handed me a wad of drab green. "I want you to have this as a gift from me."

I took it without looking at it and slipped it into the front pocket of my skirt.

"Thanks," I said, looking at the wall behind Gary W. Jensen's head as he turned to go. His boots squealed over the linoleum and, before he stepped out of the office into the damp curtain of dusk, he turned at the door to its K-Mart Christmas jingling: "Bye."

I tried to smile.

I didn't know why.

The clock said twenty-five past eight, and the river sounded sloppy and fast outside, like someone running away with a bucket of cold black water.

I LOOKED AT the check-in sheet and saw what I already knew, having seen his silver Thunderbird in the parking lot when I pulled in. Jensen, Gary, with Smith in parentheses next to it. How had he explained that to Millie?

I emptied an orange ashtray into the wastebasket under the

counter. The ashtray was heavy, for plastic, and shaped like a kidney. It felt strange and dangerous in my hand, heavy enough to explode if it slipped to the floor, or if it was thrown.

I lit a cigarette then and watched the clock on the wall across the counter. There was no second hand, but the minute hand jerked forward hard and mechanical, with only a small clicking sound like someone pulling the trigger of a pistol without any ammunition in it.

I DIDN'T LOOK at him at first when he came in, but he stooped a little, a friendly dance step in his blond cowboy boots, a blue baseball cap shading his face, and he tried to catch my eye. "Howdy," he said, mostly twang.

Gary Jensen was wearing another shirt—also light blue and starched so stiff it would've stayed standing even if he'd suddenly melted to nothing in it. Same stiff jeans. His face looked leaner, maybe a little mean now, with that baseball cap over his high forehead. And he could've been a baseball player, too. I could see the hollows from his cheeks to his jaw like slashed scars or a boy's dimples gouged too deep when he smiled, even under the scruffy stubble of his beard. I could imagine him spitting on a mound.

"You mind if I smoke a cigarette with you?" he asked, reaching into his breast pocket for the package. But his hand froze over his heart like a pledge, and he looked at me with his eyebrows raised for my O.K.

I inhaled and nodded my head slightly, maybe I rolled my eyes, and I mumbled, "I don't mind."

Gary Jensen relaxed then and lit a cigarette without offering one to me, striking two matches to light it. The first match popped and snuffed itself in midair before he got it to the cigarette, and it left a puff of gunpowder in the air between us, hanging. He didn't lean on the counter this time.

"Sure is a beautiful day," he offered, and I nodded, twitching my lips in a kind of automated smile—like the minute hand of the clock, that mechanical snap. That smile could have meant anything at all, I hoped. I hoped it confused him a little—but again he stooped to catch my eye and said, "You seem like a real sad girl, though. I sure wish I hadn't done nothing to make you even sadder."

"You didn't," I said, as if by now I'd grown impatient with apologies and compliments from him, though I'd only met him the day before.

He sucked on a front tooth with his tongue and thought about that before he dragged again on the cigarette and said, "Yeah, I did. Don't lie. It's not O.K. for some asshole to come along and slap you for no reason, is it? Twice!" as if he couldn't believe it himself. "That's got to make you feel pretty awful, sweetheart. That would make anybody feel like shit."

I wished then that the radio in the office still worked or that we had an aquarium stocked with small, panicky, kissing orange fish. Fluorescent aqua rocks. A slimy ceramic castle and a snail sucking up the glass. I remembered seeing one like that in the office of the Blue Moon Inn on the other side of town—four, maybe five years before. But I'd been offered the job here first. I thought at that moment I'd tell Mrs. Briggs about the aquarium at the Blue Moon Inn and offer to pay for the fish myself. Even the fish food, the water purifier, the fake decorations. Money was not a problem.

"Look," he said, "you're probably afraid of me now, and I don't blame you—"

"I'm not," I said, honest. And then, sarcastic, "Sorry, but I'm not."

I shrugged.

And I wasn't. I'd gotten my money, I thought, even the extra, and it hadn't hurt. Not even for a moment had I feared for my life.

Naturally, death scared me as much as the next person—a big, white room with shelves and shelves of books, all with blank pages—and the ambulance screaming down the street bright and blanched while a glitter of steel and needles flashed from the small back window as it passed. I hated that surprise, could never hear the sirens until that thing was right behind me. But I wasn't the least bit afraid of being slapped by a strange man in a motel room. Not in the least. Plus, I'd been paid.

Gary Jensen seemed pleased about that, and he inhaled smoke before he said, "Well, I was going to say I'd like to give our little rendezvous another try"—he held his palms up facing me—"*if* you'd even consider it, after what I done. The money's no problem." His palms were pale and empty. "I'd pay you whatever you want."

I sighed, as if at a child.

He glanced out the glass window to the parking lot, then back at me, and whispered, "You name it. I'd just like to be alone with you again and do it right this time."

"Two hundred dollars," I said fast, looking straight in his eyes, and I felt a rush of wind when I said the number, as though a speeding car had brushed the right side of my face— wings, or a slap. There was a big white semi pulling into the circular drive, and the wheels and engine rumbled under my feet, in my stomach, up my legs.

"Great," he said, putting a hand over his heart, smiling. "I sure do appreciate this."

GARY W. JENSEN was leaning against the hood of his car when I stepped out of 22. He was smoking a cigarette, looking down at his blond boots. I walked by him without speaking, but he grabbed my elbow in his hands. Lightly, but I stopped.

"Jesus," he said and bit the inside of his lower lip, shaking his head. "Sweetheart," he said, still looking at the boots. Then he looked up at me. "How often're you doin' this anyway?"

I let a moment pass while I tried to decide how to speak to him. He wasn't as easy as the man with the maroon suitcase in 22. I liked his boots and jeans, his easy laugh. He reminded me of a happy con man, the kind you cheer for in the movies— slick, but tenderhearted, with a sense of humor about his own, inevitable death. I'd felt small and clumsy the second time in Gary Jensen's bed. Naked, I thought I looked skinny and uncooked under his solid body, a piece of white fish on a white plate, and nothing to eat with it.

But he'd been shaking, touching me, cooing about *so beautiful, so beautiful.* And it was hard to keep my eyes open. I'd gotten used to being treated like a plaster statue by then, and didn't mind. Just my body, I thought, you can do whatever you want. I'd gotten used to treating the men themselves as if they'd hired me to complete a menial domestic chore, one they'd started themselves and hadn't had time to finish—their couch spot-cleaned, their knickknacks dusted and rearranged.

But this was different. Gary Jensen had been trying to please me—circling, kissing. He wouldn't let me take him in my mouth. He wanted to rub my back instead, which made the inside of my skin feel like static—an electric crackling along my spine beneath his hands, red sparks snapping from my nerves. He said *Relax, relax,* but I couldn't. He wanted to touch my hair, get on his knees between my legs.

His body was thin, but his skin was smooth. A feather-ridge of dark hair at his breastbone, as if there had once been wings, as if they'd been surgically removed. He moved his face down to my stomach, and the whiskers felt like a small fire there. I touched the top of his head, where the hair was thin, and I felt how soft it was, like a child's. He begged me to let him kiss me there, and I imagined he was trying too hard to make up for hitting me the day before, that now he felt he owed me the way I felt I'd owed him for the money I'd slipped into my shoe, and, therefore, didn't fight back when he hit me. So I let him, and he never even came, just tongued and touched me until I couldn't stand it anymore, coming under his warm mouth.

Afterward, he kissed me over and over on the ear while I tried to catch my breath. Smiling, he said he was done, that's all he'd wanted to do, and I put my clothes back on. Maybe it had felt good, that attention, I wasn't entirely sure, but walking back down the concrete steps from his room, I'd felt crushed and numb where he'd tasted my heartbeat between my legs. Foolish and defeated, like a kid. I felt like a child who'd asked for a toy my parents couldn't afford to buy, and they'd bought it for me anyway:

What you want for yourself, and what you dread being given.

"HUH? HOW OFTEN?" He nudged me, squeezing my elbow. Not hard, but I looked up.

"I'd have to say that's none of your business," I said. Then I moved my leg between his legs, my light blue jeans against his dark blue ones, and I pressed my knee into his. "Unless you're saying you'd like to do it again," I said.

He threw his cigarette into the rock garden, and a thin string of smoke rose from the ruined petunias, wadded as they were now, like used tissue, facedown and done. He took his hand off my elbow and slipped his arm around my waist, pulling me into him. Kissing my ear. "Yeah," he said into my hair, "I want to do it again."

22 opened then. Someone looked out from a dark split in the doorway, a man with small bird eyes, and shut the door again.

GARY JENSEN CAUGHT my tongue between his teeth, gentle, and undressed me without moving his mouth from mine. This time my heart beat hard against the cage of my ribs. I came with him inside me, which had never happened before, not with any man, and the coming fluttered improbably and like a bird dying between my legs. I hadn't imagined it would be like that, and it made me open and close around him like the mouth of something underwater and warm, something not yet born.

Afterward he kissed my nipples again. My neck. My lips and the lids of my eyes, and then he seemed to start to cry.

"God," he said, "Leila—I can't believe, after what I done to you the other day that you're so damn sweet to me. You come up here again like you're not afraid of me at all, and you make the nicest love to me anybody's ever made."

He put his fingers in my hair, and they got tangled and lost in the copper of it.

I noticed a thin scar under the stubble of his beard, stretching thin and red from his neck to his ear. It was white at the edges, as if someone had sewn the skin together neatly with a needle of light. I put my hand, then, on his narrow chest. It was no wider than my own, and, while we'd made love, it had felt soft against me, gently crushing my breasts beneath its bones. I said, "I should get back down to the office. God, what if Mrs. Briggs has been trying to call or there's a bunch of guests down there?"

Gary Jensen propped himself up on his elbow and said, "Don't go yet, Leila, please. I got to look at you some more." His eyes were brown and dry.

I let him look.

"God," he said, touching the side of my face with two fingers, "I can't believe I hit you, baby. I can't believe I did. What the hell is the matter with a man like me?"

I looked hard at his face. His eyelashes were also dark. A scattering of faded freckles on the bridge of his nose was left behind by the agitated boy he used to be. Soft hair. I touched it where it curled behind his neck, and he kissed me again.

"Leila, I got to tell you why. Something about me, so you don't hate me. Because I feel like I could fall in love with you," he said, squeezing my nipple between his thumb and forefinger when he said it. He swallowed. "My daddy used to beat my mama bad." He swallowed again. "And I used to see that all the time. Probably since I was only just born. I bet I never saw him do anything *but* beat her, I guess. And even though I swore I'd never, never treat a woman that way as long as I lived, there's just this thing in me that's him, that's what I seen him do to her, and there I go. I done it again, Leila, before I even knew what I did."

I didn't want to cry, but it seemed like a true story, the way he told it, and I saw myself leaning over the seat of a car, some boy straining into my mouth, his hands in my hair, and I said in a whisper, looking away from him, "I know how that is."

That sentence, as it scrolled out of my mouth, stunned me itself like a slap. I'd never thought of it like that before, and then I closed my eyes, saw myself suddenly in a bright flash against my eyelids at the kitchen table on my sixth birthday. My mother had baked a cake. A plastic Raggedy Ann was stuck in the middle, into the chocolate frosting like a birthday sacrifice. Six candles blazed around Raggedy Ann's orange braids.

My father was on the road, and my uncle had come over with a jewelry box for me, a bottle of red wine for my mother. They'd played some slow jazz on the record player while they drank it and toasted my birthday, knocking their gory glasses together full of red, ringing like old bells. The saxophone sounded scratchy and full of breath, obscene.

I was wearing a petticoat, a velvet dress like a girl in a story-book. It scratched, too, and shuffled, prickling and stiff around my thighs. They both insisted that I laugh—my mother leaning into me with that purple sweetness on her breath like a spleen, clapping, singing, *Leila, Leila, Happy Birthday Leila.*

I wanted to smile to make her happy.

I blew the candles out in one deep gasp, one long forced breath, but I couldn't eat the cake. My stomach hurt. They put me to bed when I started to cry, and my mother and uncle sat at the edge of the bed and smiled.

Make Leila smile, my mother said, and my uncle did a magic trick then, waved his hands in the air, and then he pulled a long silk scarf from my ear. Red. I closed my eyes, and I heard red wind as it passed out of me into his hands. It spun my heart like a plastic top. My mother pretended to gasp, but I knew where he'd gotten it from, and my heart sparked loose and blurred against my ribs:

When Gary Jensen put his face next to mine and kissed my ear, I remembered that. Something deadly yanked out of my body for everyone to see, and now it was in his hands.

Something scarlet, secret, like the wish to die or kill.

His fingers circled my nipple. He moved down to kiss it, then he looked up at me again. "I know you know what I mean," he said, "that you been damaged, too. I could tell that about you from ten miles away."

He sat up in the bed and leaned over the side of it to pick his shirt up off the floor. He slipped his arms in, shrugged it to his shoulders, straightened the collar and started to button. My body felt soft and exhausted, like something left to soak too long in too-warm water. I couldn't move, though I knew I needed to put on my clothes and go back to the office. I knew I should be in a hurry, but I couldn't be anymore.

He stood up and put his pants on. We'd never even pulled the bedspread down. He was looking at the whole bare length of my body on the bed. "Clean yourself up," he said, and left.

He hadn't given me the money, and I knew I'd never ask.

555

Linh Dinh

FROM *FAKE HOUSE*

THE PACK OF 555 was a sure giveaway.

"Give that guy a shot on me, Fergie," I said, gesturing toward the scowling man sitting by the cash register, a pack of 555 in front of him. It was a Saturday afternoon, in the summer, and most of the ten people sitting at the bar had their face tilted toward the TV. Lenny Dykstra, going against Maddux, was working the count to 2 and 2. There was no score in the third. The bases were empty.

In fifteen years of going to McGlinchey's, this was only the third or fourth time I had seen a Vietnamese there. Koreans and Chinese, yes, but almost never a Vietnamese. I walked down the length of the bar and sat next to him. I began, in Vietnamese: "I'm Bui."

"I'm Thanh."

"First time here?"

"Yeah."

"The drinks are cheap in this place."

"It's not an issue," the man replied, somewhat oddly. He was about forty-five, brown-skinned, sturdy-looking, with a perpetual squint on his face, betraying a catatonic form of concentration.

"Want a shot?" I asked.

"Sure."

"What do you drink?"

"It makes no difference."

"What was that you just had?" I pointed to the empty shot glass in front of him.

"I don't know."

"Then how did you order it?"

"I pointed to that old guy across the bar and said: 'Shame!' "

"Two Jamesons, Fergie."

Thanh looked at me, squinting. "How long have you been in America?"

"Since I was eleven," I said, "since 1975. How about you?"

"Seven months."

"Seven months!"

"Look," he opened his mouth wide, "I got no front teeth." And he really didn't.

"What happened?"

"Prison."

"They rotted?"

"No, punched out!"

"V.C.?"

"V.C."

I felt elation, then shame. To chase this feeling away, I offered, "Two more shots?"

"I'll buy this time," Thanh countered.

"Two more Fergie."

I thought of a man I had met once who, after the war, was imprisoned for thirteen months in a tiny underground cubicle. He used the cotton lining from his flak jacket to wipe his ass. When Fergie came back, Thanh gave him a five-dollar tip.

"That's too much," I whispered as the bartender walked away.

"Money is not an issue when I'm out partying," Thanh sternly said. He snuffed out his cigarette, then lit up another 555. He handed me a dollar. "Could you put music on the jukebox?"

"Any preference?"

"Doesn't matter."

I went to the jukebox and punched in Nina Simone, Patsy Cline, Sam Cooke, and Dylan, bypassing the grunge. When I came back, my friend said, "I came to town today to fuck a whore."

"What?"

"Fuck a whore in Chinatown."

"Oh."

"There's a massage parlor at Eleventh and Arch. You pay forty dollars for a massage, then twenty dollars for a blow job, or fifty dollars for a lube job."

"A what?"

"A lube job. You've been away from Vietnam too long."

I had once paid a red-headed girl in Washington. "So how was it today?"

"I didn't fuck her. The girl I picked was Vietnamese, but I didn't know it at first."

"The girls are usually not Vietnamese?"

"No, they are all Koreans. Some of them are Chinese, but never a Vietnamese.

"I've been going there every other payday—once a month, for about five months. The girls there are not so pretty, but they are pleasant, and the place is clean."

THE PLACE IS clean and the girls are pleasant. You find it by word of mouth. It is on a second and third floor, over a travel agency with posters of Hong Kong, Seoul, and Ho Chi Minh City in the plate-glass window. Next door is a Cantonese restaurant serving dim sum on Sundays. At street level, above a dirty glass door, is a tiny red sign with a single Chinese character for *Gym*. There is nothing to see beyond this glass door but the green-carpeted stairway. A surveillance camera browbeats you from its stanchion. You ring the doorbell, wait for the Korean bouncer to buzz you in.

Thanh sat on the green couch, fidgeting with his complimentary midget-size can of Coke. It was noon outside, but inside, with the windows painted over, it was always evening. Three nearly naked girls, returning from their assignments upstairs, were arrayed on a row of folding chairs against the opposite wall. One of them had to stifle yawns. Up all night, they were waiting for another hour so that they could go home. The burly Korean bouncer, with a quarter in his left ear, chewing on a toothpick, was sitting at his desk meticulously cleaning a .22. Thanh was not satisfied with the current selection, and neither were the other two customers. On the couch with Thanh was a cook from Ho Sai Gai, in his white uniform, yellowed by old grease. To his right was a baby-faced guy, not bad-looking, about twenty-two, sitting on an easy chair. He didn't lean back but was hunched forward, with his forearms resting on his thighs. He was sniffling and wiping his nose periodically with the back of a hand. He stank of beer. *Why,* Thanh thought, *would a kid like this go to a whorehouse and pay almost a hundred bucks to get laid? Can't he find a girlfriend?* A new girl entered the room: short, small-breasted, with a cheery, innocent face, wearing a green silk blouse. She smiled. As the cook and the baby-faced guy hesitated, Thanh stood up, nodded at the girl, and walked to the desk. He forked over his forty dollars, took his sneakers off, and followed her upstairs. She led him down a corridor, stopping at a linen closet to pick up a white towel. The fact that these transactions were often carried out with little or no conversation suited him perfectly. He never picked the same girl twice. The idea of fucking a complete stranger appealed to him morally. No dissimulation—that's what he liked about it—only intimacy.

The room had a queen-sized bed and a chair, to put your clothes on. It was lit by a single red bulb. There was a shower stall, but no toilet. Thanh promptly took his T-shirt off, stepped out of his jeans, and walked into the shower. The girl stuck a hand under the jets of hot water, fidgeting with the knobs. It was a bit too hot, but he said nothing. Still in her blouse and panties, she stood to the side and ran a new bar of soap all over his wet body. Then she rubbed him with a big sponge, lingering for a long time about his privates. Although her movements were efficient and perfunctory, like a man washing his car, or a mother her child, he was genuinely touched by this attention. He watched her small, bent figure, and thought of an incident from the night before: Someone had thrown an egg at him from a passing car. It landed at his feet, spattering his sneakers with yolk. He saw a blond girl in the passenger's window. She was yelling something.

The water was turned off and she dried him with the towel. She held his hand and walked him to the bed. "I must sleep," she said, "I've been up all night. I must sleep for five minutes, then we can fuck."

She lay down on her stomach, closed her eyes, her face turned away from him. Thanh, erect, lay next to her. He wanted to sniff her hair but dared not. He stared at her white panties, pink in that light, for a moment before deciding to peel them off. She yanked them back on. "My ass is cold!"

"Du Me!" He cursed.

The girl turned around, frowning. "You're Vietnamese!" she said in Vietnamese.

"And so are you."

He grabbed the towel to cover his prick, which had suddenly gone limp.

"What's your name, Brother?"

"Thanh."

"Nice to meet you, Brother Thanh."

"And your name?"

"Huong."

"Your real name?"

"That is my real name."

They laughed. Her face brightened up.

"How old are you, Huong?"

"Why should I tell you?"

Huong looked about seventeen. Thanh said, "Are you in school?"

Huong nodded.

"What are you doing in a place like this?"

"What do you think?"

"You should be home studying."

Huong stared at Thanh, expressionless. In two quick motions she pulled her blouse and panties off. "Let's get this over with," she said. "I've got to go home."

Thanh did not move, the white towel still covering his prick.

"What do you study at school?"

Huong, becoming irritated, said, "Five more minutes and I'm going back downstairs."

"I don't want to, uh, fuck anymore," Thanh said, "but I'll pay you for your time."

Huong cheered up. "I study history, biology, English, and French."

"Conjugate the verb *être* for me."

"You must think I'm stupid."

"I'll give you fifty more bucks if you can conjugate *être* for me."

Huong's lips were pressed together in consternation. She thought it over, then said, "I'll conjugate *être* if you promise never to come here on the weekend again."

"Why?"

"Because I'll never want to see you again."

"It's a deal."

"Je suis," Huong blurted, with vehemence, accenting each syllable, *"Tu es. Il est. Elle est. Nous sommes. Vous etes. Ils sont. Elles sont."*

FROM memoirs of egotism
Stendhal

TRANSLATED BY Hannah and
Matthew Josephson

T HROUGH BEING IN love in 1821 I acquired a very comic virtue: that of chastity.
Against my will, my friends Lussinge, Barot and Poitevin,
finding me low in spirits, arranged a delightful evening at a
bordello for my benefit in August 1821. From what I have
learned since, Barot is one of the best qualified men in Paris
to organize an entertainment of this kind, a somewhat delicate
business. A woman is a woman for him only once: the first
time. He lives on 30,000 of his 80,000 francs a year, and of this
30,000 he spends at least 20,000 on wenches.

Barot therefore made all the arrangements for an evening at
the establishment of Mme. Petit, one of his former mistresses,
to whom, I believe, he had recently lent some money to set up
a house of pleasure (*to raise a brothel*)[1] in the Rue du Cadran, at
the corner of the rue Montmartre, on the fourth floor.

We were to have Alexandrine—who six months later was
being kept by the wealthiest Englishmen in town—then only a

---

[1] *Thus in English in the text.*—Ed.

novice of two months' experience. We arrived at eight o'clock in the evening, and toiling up four flights of stairs found a charming reception room, champagne in ice buckets, hot punch . . . At length Alexandrine was led in under the surveillance of a lady's maid. I have forgotten now who had engaged this lady's maid, but she must have had considerable authority, for I saw on the bill for the evening's entertainment that she was put down for twenty francs. When Alexandrine appeared she surpassed everyone's expectations. She was a tall lass of sixteen or seventeen, already well-formed, with the same black eyes that I found later in the portrait of the Duchess of Urbino by Titian in the museum at Florence. But for the color of her hair, she was the image of Titian's portrait. She was a gentle, healthy creature, a bit shy but cheerful, and decorous withal. The eyes of my colleagues started from their heads at the mere sight of her. Lussinge offered her a glass of champagne, which she refused; he then retired with her. Mme. Petit brought in two other girls. They were not bad, but we told her that she herself was a prettier woman. She had indeed a very trim foot. Poitevin carried her off. After a frightful interval Lussinge returned, his face quite pale.

"Your turn, Beyle. Good luck!" they cried.

I found Alexandrine stretched out in bed, a little wan, in almost the same costume and in precisely the same position as the Duchess of Urbino in Titian's portrait.

"Let's chat for a few minutes," she said sensibly. "I'm a bit tired. Let's talk. In a little while I'll regain my former ardor."

She was adorable. I doubt that I have ever seen anyone so lovely. She was not too wanton, except that gradually her eyes began to light up with excitement, one might even say with passion.

I failed her completely; it was a perfect *fiasco*. I then tried to make amends in another way, and she seemed to countenance it. Not knowing exactly what to do next, I tried to go on with my sleight of hand, but she put a stop to it. She seemed astonished at my behavior. I then said a few words to cover my confusion and left the room.

Barot had scarcely succeeded me when we heard shouts of laughter that reached us from the other end of the apartment. Suddenly Mme. Petit dismissed the other girls and Barot led Alexandrine into the room, dressed

. . . dans le simple appareil D'une beauté qu'on vient d'arracher au sommeil.[2]

"My great admiration for Beyle," said Barot, roaring with laughter, "makes me want to imitate him. I come to fortify myself with champagne." They could not stop laughing for ten minutes. Poitevin rolled on the floor. Alexandrine's wide-eyed astonishment was priceless to behold. It was the first time anyone had failed the poor girl.

My friends expected me to feel mortally ashamed, and tried to persuade me that this was the unhappiest moment of my life. But as a matter of fact, I was merely surprised, nothing more. Somehow the thought of Metilda had come to me as I was entering the room so charmingly adorned by Alexandrine.

At any rate, I doubt if I resorted to harlots more than three times in the ten years that followed. The first time after my encounter with the delightful Alexandrine was in October or November of 1826, in a moment of great despair.

Thereafter I frequently ran into Alexandrine driving about in the sumptuous equipage she acquired only a month later, and she always had a glance of recognition for me. But after five or six years of that kind of life her face grew coarse, like all women of her class.

From that moment on I passed for a *Babillan* in the minds of my three boon companions. My fine reputation became a subject of gossip in society, and endured in one form or

[2] *"In the simple costume of beauty just wrenched from sleep." From Racine's* Britannicus.—Ed.

another until Mme. Azur was able to give a different account of my powers.[3]

My relations with Barot, meanwhile, were improved by the events of that evening. I still like him and he likes me. He is probably the only Frenchman with whom I can enjoy passing two weeks in his country place. He has the most loyal heart, the frankest disposition, and at the same time the least discernment and education of any man I know. But in two fields he is supreme: that of making money without playing the stock market, and that of striking up an acquaintance with strange women on the street or at the theatre, above all in the second department.

This is an absolute necessity for him, because any woman who once gives him her favors thereafter means no more to him than a man.

One evening in Milan Metilda was speaking to me of her friend Mme. Bignami. Of her own accord she began to tell me of one of Mme. Bignami's love affairs, adding: "Imagine her hard lot; every evening after her lover bade her goodnight he went off to a harlot."

Only after I left Milan did I realize that this moral observation had nothing to do with the story of Mme. Bignami, but was intended as a rebuke to me.

In truth, every evening after I had accompanied Metilda to the house of her cousin, Mme. Traversi, to whom I had boorishly refused to be presented, I used to go to pass the rest of the evening with the charming, the divine Countess Kassera. And here I made another blunder, of a piece with my conduct toward Alexandrine, for I once refused to be the lover of the Countess Kassera, who was one of the most delectable women I have ever known, only in order to merit the love of Metilda in the eyes of God! In the same spirit and for the same reason I refused the advances of the celebrated Mme. Vigano, who, as

[3] *Babillan: one who is impotent, a eunuch, a word possibly of Italian origin. Beyle here recalls Mme. Azur's testimony on his behalf in 1829. This may have been verbal, but the letters of Clémentine de Curial of earlier date, found among the Stendhal papers, furnish written testimony of his claims to normality.*—Ed.

she was descending the stairs[4] with all her retinue—and among her courtiers was that witty and reasonable fellow, Count Saurau[5]—dropped behind them to say to me:

"Beyle, they say that you are in love with me?"

"They are mistaken," I answered very coldly, without even kissing her hand.

Such infamous behavior to a woman who was accustomed to having her own way, earned me her implacable hatred. She would never greet me again, even when we met face-to-face in one of the narrow streets of Milan.

Those are my three great blunders. I shall never forgive myself for my stupidity with regard to Countess Kassera (today she is the most respectable and most respected woman in her country).

I AM A sensible man about everything but certain memories of the past, I quickly grasped the absurdity of the forty-eight hours of toil imposed on the English workingman. A poor Italian, dressed in rags, is far happier. He has time to make love, and he devotes between eight and a hundred days a year to the observance of a religion which is all the more amusing because it instills fear in him, etc.

My companions made no end of fun of me for entertaining such opinions. And yet my supposed paradox is fast coming to be recognized as the truth, and will be a commonplace by 1840. My friends also called me a fool when I added that the excessive and crushing labor of the English workman was our revenge for Waterloo and the four coalitions. We at least have buried our dead, and those of us who survive are better off than the English. But as long as they live Barot and Lussinge will regard me as a stubborn fellow. Even now, ten years later, when I try to shame them by saying: "You see, today you hold the same opinions that I did in London in 1821," they deny it,

[4] *Of the Scala Theatre in Milan.*—Ed.
[5] *Count Saurau was governor of Lombardy, grand chancellor of the Austrian Empire, etc.*—Ed.

and my reputation for obstinacy persists. Imagine what I suffered whenever I had the ill-luck to talk to these men about literature. My cousin Colomb for a long time thought I was really consumed by jealousy because I told him that M. Villemain's *Lascaris* was as dull as ditchwater. And great God, what a clamor they made when I broached general principles!

One day when I was speaking of the great labors of the English, our smug little valet protested that the honor of his country was impugned.

"Quite right," I said to him, "but you must understand that we are in an unfortunate position; we don't know any amusing people here."

"Sir, I will see to that for you," he answered. "I will make all the arrangements. Don't apply to anyone else; they will make you pay through the nose, etc."

My friends laughed. Thus as a result of poking fun at the valet's honor, I was lured into an affair with some wenches. Nothing could have been more disagreeable, more repulsive, in fact, than the way in which our man, while directing us about London the next day, made us listen to all the details of the bargain he had struck.

In the first place, the girls lived in a lonely quarter of town, out on Westminster Road, the kind of place where Frenchmen might well expect to be set upon by a gang of sailors or pimps. When we mentioned the matter to an English friend, he said:

"Watch out for an ambuscade!"

Our valet told us that he had haggled a long time to obtain the privilege of having tea served to us in the morning when we got up. At first the girls refused to grant us their favors and tea as well for only twenty-one shillings (twenty-five francs and five sous) but at last they had consented. Several Englishmen tried to warn us:

"An Englishman would never fall into such a trap. Do you realize that you will be several miles out of London?"

It was agreed among us that we would not go. But when the appointed evening came, Barot looked at me inquiringly. I knew what he meant.

"We are strong," I said, "and we have arms."

Lussinge dared not come with us.

We took a cab, Barot and I. The road led across Westminster Bridge, and then through streets without dwellings, shut in between garden walls.

Barot laughed.

"Considering how brilliantly you conducted yourself with Alexandrine, in an elegant establishment, in the middle of Paris, what do you expect to accomplish here?"

I was indeed very depressed. If not for the dullness of London after the dinner hour, especially when the theatres were closed, as happened that day, and if not for the slight element of danger in the affair, Westminster Road would never have seen me. After almost going off the road several times into unpaved lanes, the driver, swearing all the while, finally pulled up in front of a three-story house that altogether was no more than twenty-five feet high. I have never seen such a tiny house in all my life.

Certainly without the thought of possible danger I would never have entered that house. I expected to find three vicious trollops, but instead we were met by three shy little girls, very pale and eager to please, with beautiful chestnut hair.

The furniture was absurdly tiny. Since Barot is tall and portly, and I too am stout, we literally could not find a seat. It was like being in a doll's house, and we were afraid we might crash through the chairs. When the little girls saw our distress, their own increased. Happily Barot was inspired to mention the garden.

"Oh yes, we have a garden," they said, not with pride, but as if delighted to show us something a bit more luxurious. We went down into the garden, carrying candles to light the way. It was all of twenty-five feet long and ten feet wide. Barot and I burst into laughter. All the domestic utensils of the poor were there: a little wash-tub, a little vat with a spiral device for brewing beer.

I was touched, but Barot was so disgusted that he said to me in French: "Let's pay them off and clear out."

"But they will be so humiliated," I replied.

"Bah! Humiliated! Little do you know them! If it's not too late, they will simply send for other customers, or for their lovers, if this is anything like France."

These sound observations made no impression on me. The girls' obvious poverty, their toy furniture, so old and yet so clean, had touched my heart. Before we had finished drinking our tea I was on such intimate terms with them that, in my broken English, I confessed our earlier fears of being murdered. This disconcerted them completely.

"But after all," I added, "the proof that we trust you is that I am telling you all this."

We sent our valet away. And then I felt as if I were with warm friends from whom I had been parted for long years.

Not a door in the house could be closed properly, another cause for suspicion when we went to bed. But what was the use of having doors and strong locks, when any of the partitions would have crumbled under a blow? You could hear whatever was said all over the house. Barot, who had gone up to the third floor, shouted to me:

"If anyone tries to murder you, call me!"

I wanted to keep the light on, but my modest little friend, otherwise so gentle and submissive, would not allow it. When she saw me lay out my pistols and dagger on the night table beside the bed, facing the door, she gave a great start of fear. She was charming, small, pale, but well-formed.

No one murdered us. The next day we dispensed with their tea and sent the valet to fetch Lussinge, telling him to bring cold meat and wine. In a short time he drove up with an excellent lunch in tow, quite astonished at our enthusiasm.

June 26.

THE TWO SISTERS sent for one of their friends. We left them some wine and cold meat, of finer quality, apparently, than any they had ever seen.

When we told them that we would return, they thought we were making fun of them. Miss . . . , my little friend, took me aside and said:

"If I were sure you would return this evening, I would not go out. But I suppose our house is too shabby for men like you."

All day long I looked forward to the pleasant evening that awaited me with my gentle, quiet friends (*full of snugness*[6]).

The play that afternoon seemed long drawn out. Barot and Lussinge wanted to have a good look at all the shameless hussies who crowded into the lobby of Covent Garden. At last Barot and I set out for our little cottage, where the poor girls opened their eyes wide when they saw us unwrap bottles of claret and champagne. I have a notion that they had never before been confronted with a bottle of *real champagn*[7] that had not already been broached.

Fortunately the corks of our bottles popped in the approved manner, thereby rendering their happiness complete. Their transports were, however, quiet and decorous. In fact their whole behavior was marked by extreme decorum.—But we already knew this.

The amusing thing is that during my entire stay in England I was always unhappy unless I could finish the day with a visit to that little house.

This relationship was the first real consolation I found for the misery that was poisoning my hours of solitude. It is apparent that I was no more than twenty years old in 1821. If I had been thirty-eight, as my baptismal certificate would seem to indicate, I could have tried to find similar consolation among the respectable women of Paris who had shown some sympathy for me. Sometimes, however, I doubt that I would have succeeded there. What goes by the name of the highest breeding, an air that supposedly distinguishes the manners of Mme. de Marmier from those of Mme. Edwards, often strikes me as damnable affectation, and at once seals my heart hermetically.

[6]*In English,* sic.—Ed.
[7]Sic—*Beyle's idea of how the word was spelled in English.*—Ed.

This is one of my great afflictions. Does the reader share my sensibility in this regard? I am always mortally offended by the slightest nuances in behavior.

When I see the grand airs displayed in high society I cry out inwardly: *Bourgeoise! or Puppet of the Boulevard Saint-Germain!* and I promptly turn disagreeable and ironical to the next person I meet.

One can understand everything except oneself, to which one of those polished products from the aristocratic quarter of Paris would add, in order to avoid any possibility of ridicule: "I am far from believing that I understand everything." My doctors always enjoy treating me when I am ill, because they consider me a rare example of *nervous irritability*. On one occasion I caught a chill from an open window in the next room, whose door was closed. The slightest odor (except bad ones) takes all the strength out of my left arm and leg, and tends to make me fall over on that side.

"But what detestable egotism you show by mentioning all these details!"

"To be sure, and what is this book if not a work of detestable egotism! And what good would it do to display the grace of a pedant in a book of this kind, like M. Villemain in yesterday's article on the arrest of M. de Chateaubriand?"

If this book of mine is tedious, two years after publication it will be used to wrap up parcels of butter at the grocer's; if it is not tedious, it will prove that egotism, that is, *sincere egotism*, is one way of describing the human heart, in the knowledge of which we have made giant strides since 1721, when Montesquieu, that great man whom I have studied so faithfully, wrote *Les Lettres Persanes*.

The progress we have made since that period is so amazing that sometimes Montesquieu seems crude in comparison.

TRANSLATED BY Frank Wynne

WENT OUT AND walked round the lobby.
It was 7 P.M.; no one from the group was
around. For about four hundred baht, those who wished could
have dinner and a show of 'traditional Thai dance'; those
interested were to assemble at 8 P.M. Valérie would definitely be
there. For my part, I had already had a vague experience of traditional Thai dance, on a trip with Kuoni three years previ-
ously: 'Classic Thailand, from the "Rose of the North" to the
"City of Angels".' Not bad, really, but a bit expensive and ter-
rifyingly cultural; everyone involved had at least a masters
degree. The thirty-two positions of the Buddha in Ratanakosin
statuary, Thai-Burmese style, Thai-Khmer, Thai-Thai, they
didn't miss a thing. I had come back exhausted and I'd constantly felt ridiculous without a *Guide Bleu*. Right now, I was
beginning to feel a serious need to fuck. I was wandering
round the lobby, with a sense of mounting indecision, when I
spotted a sign saying 'Health Club,' indicating the floor below.

The entrance was lit by neon and a long rope of coloured
lights. On the white background of an electric sign, three

bikini-clad sirens, their breasts a little larger than life, proffered champagne flutes to prospective customers; there was a heavily stylised Eiffel Tower in the far distance—not quite the same concept as the fitness centres of Mercure hotels. I went in and ordered a bourbon at the bar. Behind a glass screen, a dozen girls turned towards me; some smiled alluringly, others didn't. I was the only customer. Despite the fact that the place was small, the girls wore numbered tags. I quickly chose number 7: firstly because she was cute, also because she wasn't engrossed in the programme on the television or deep in conversation with her neighbour. Indeed, when her name was called, she stood up with evident satisfaction. I offered her a coke at the bar, then we went to one of the rooms. Her name was Oôn, at least that was what I heard, and she was from the north somewhere, a little village near Chiang Mai. She was nineteen.

After we had taken a bath together, I lay down on the foam-covered mattress; I realised at once that I wasn't going to regret my choice. Oôn moved very nicely, very lithely; she'd used just enough soap. At one point, she at length caressed my buttocks with her breasts; it was a personal initiative, not all the girls did that. Her well-soaped pussy grazed my calf like a small hard brush. I was somewhat surprised to find I got hard almost immediately; when she turned me over and started to stroke my penis with her feet, I thought for a minute that I wouldn't be able to hold back. But with a supreme effort, tensing the abductor muscles in my thighs, I managed.

When she climbed on top of me on the bed, I thought I would be able to hold out for a long time yet; but I was quickly disillusioned. She might have been very young, but she knew what to do with her pussy. She started very gently with little contractions on the glans, then she slipped down an inch or so, squeezing a little harder. 'Oh no, Oôn, no! . . . ' I cried. She burst out laughing, pleased with her power, then continued to slide down gently, contracting the walls of her vagina with long, slow compressions; all the while looking me in the eyes in obvious amusement. I came well before she got to the base of my penis.

Afterwards we chatted a bit, entwined on the bed; she didn't seem to be in any hurry to get back out on stage. She didn't have many clients, she told me; the hotel was aimed at groups of terminal cases, ordinary people, who were pretty much blasé. There were a lot of French people, but they didn't really seem to like body massage. Those who patronised the place were nice enough, but they were mostly Germans and Australians. A few Japanese too, but she didn't like them—they were weird, they always wanted to hit you or tie you up, or else they just sat there masturbating, staring at your shoes; it was pointless.

And what did she think about me? Not bad, but she would have liked it if I'd been able to hold out a little longer. 'Much need . . . ' she said in English, gently shaking my sated penis between her fingers. Otherwise, she thought I seemed like a nice man. 'You look quiet . . . ' she said. There she was somewhat mistaken, but I suppose it was true that she'd done a good job of calming me. I gave her three thousand baht, which, as far as I remembered, was a good price. From her reaction I could tell that, yes, it was a good price. 'Krôp khun khât!' she said with a big smile, bringing her hands together in front of her forehead. Then she took my hand and accompanied me to the exit; at the door we kissed each other on the cheeks several times.

As I climbed the stairs I ran into Josiane, who was apparently hesitating about whether to go downstairs. She had changed into an evening dress, a black shift dress with gold piping, but it didn't make her the least bit more appealing. Her plump, shrewd face was turned toward me, unblinkingly. I noticed that she'd washed her hair. She wasn't ugly, you might even say she was pretty—I had fancied Lebanese women like her—but her basic expression was unmistakably nasty. I could easily imagine her trotting out tired political positions; she hadn't a flicker of compassion that I could make out. I had nothing to say to her, either. I lowered my head. A little embarrassed, maybe, she spoke: 'Anything interesting downstairs?' I found her so infuriating that I nearly said: 'A bar full of hookers,' but in the end I lied, it was easier. 'No, no, I don't know, some kind of beauty salon . . . '

'You didn't go to the dinner and show . . . ' the bitch remarked. 'Neither did you,' I snapped back. This time her response was slower in coming, she became snotty. 'Oh no, I don't really like that sort of thing . . . ' she went on, curving her arm like an actress playing Racine. 'It's all a bit touristy . . . ' What did she mean by that? Everything is touristy. Once again, I stopped myself from putting my fist through her fucking face. Standing in the middle of the stairway, she was in my way; I had to show patience. A passionate letter-writer on occasion, St Jerome also knew how to display the virtues of Christian patience when circumstances called for it; that is why he is considered to be a great saint and a Doctor of the Church.

This 'traditional Thai dance' show was, according to her, just about Josette and René's level, people she thought of, in her heart of hearts, as white trash; I realised, rather uncomfortably, that she was looking for an ally. True, the tour would soon head deep inland, we would be divided into two tables at meals; it was time to take sides. 'Well . . . ' I said, after a long silence. At that moment, like a miracle, Robert appeared above us. He was trying to get downstairs. I smoothly stepped aside, climbing a couple of steps. Just before rushing off to the restaurant, I turned back: Josiane, still motionless, was staring at Robert, who was walking briskly toward the massage parlour.

Babette and Léa were standing next to the trays of vegetables. I nodded in minimal acknowledgement before serving myself some water spinach. Obviously they too had decided that the 'traditional Thai dance' was *tacky*. As I went back to my table, I noticed the tarts were sitting a couple of feet away. Léa was wearing a *Rage Against the Machine* tee-shirt and a pair of tight denim shorts, Babette something unstructured in which different coloured stripes of silk alternated with transparent fabric. They were chattering enthusiastically, talking about different hotels in New York. Marrying one of those girls, I thought, that would be *radically* hideous. Did I still have time to change tables? No, it would have been a bit obvious. I took a chair opposite so that at least I could sit with my back on them, I bolted my meal and went back up to my room.

A cockroach appeared just as I was about to get into the bath. It was just the right time for a cockroach to make an appearance in my life; couldn't have been better. It scuttled quickly across the porcelain, the little bugger; I looked around for a slipper, but actually I knew my chances of squashing him were small. What was the point in trying? And what good was Oôn, in spite of her marvellously elastic vagina? We were already doomed. Cockroaches copulate gracelessly, with no apparent pleasure; but they also do it repeatedly and their genetic mutations are rapid and efficient. There is absolutely nothing we can do about cockroaches.

Before getting undressed, I once more paid homage to Oôn and to all Thai prostitutes. They didn't have an easy job, those girls; they probably didn't come across a good guy all that often, someone with an okay physique who was honestly looking for nothing more than mutual orgasm. Not to mention the Japanese—I shivered at the thought, and grabbed my *Guide du Routard*. Babette and Léa could never have been Thai prostitutes, I thought, they weren't worthy of it. Valérie, maybe; that girl had something, she managed to be both maternal and a bit of a slut, potentially at least, I mean; for the moment she was just a nice friendly, serious girl. Intelligent, too. I definitely liked Valérie. I masturbated gently so I could read in peace, producing just a couple of drips.

If it was intended in principle to prepare you for a trip to Thailand, in practice the *Guide du Routard* had strong reservations about, and as early as the preface, felt duty-bound to denounce, sexual tourism, that 'repulsive slavery.' All in all, these backpacking *routards* were belly-aching bastards whose goal was to spoil every little pleasure on offer to tourists, whom they despised. In fact, they seemed to like themselves more than anything else, if one was to go by the sarcastic little phrases scattered throughout the book, in the style of: 'Ah, my friends, if you had been there back in the hippy days! . . . ' The most excruciating thing was probably their stern, dogmatic, peremptory tone, quivering with repressed indignation: 'We're far from prudish, but Pattaya we don't like. Enough is enough.' A bit further on, they laid into 'pot-bellied Westerners' who strolled around with little Thai girls; it made them 'literally puke.' Humanitarian Protestant cunts, that's what they were, they and the 'cool bunch of mates who had helped to make this book possible', their nasty little faces smugly plastered all over the back cover. I flung the book hard across the room, missing the Sony television by a whisker, and wearily picked up *The Firm*, by John Grisham. It was an American bestseller, one of the best; meaning one of those that had sold the most copies.

IT ALL CAME to a head over the sticky rice. It was a light golden colour, flavoured with cinnamon—I think the recipe was original. Taking the bull by the horns, Josiane decided to tackle the question of sex tourism head on. For her, it was absolutely disgusting, there was no other word for it. It was a scandal that the Thai government tolerated such things. The international community had to do something. Robert listened to her with a half-smile which I didn't think boded well. It was scandalous, but it was hardly surprising; it was obvious that most of these places (brothels, that was the only word for them) were owned by generals; that told you what kind of protection they had.

'I'm a general . . . ' interrupted Robert. She was speechless, her lower jaw dropped miserably. 'No, no, I'm only joking . . . ' he said with a slight grimace. 'I've never even been in the army.'

She did not find this funny in the least. She took a moment to pull herself together, then launched back into the fray with renewed energy.

'It's absolutely shameful that fat yobs can just come over here and take advantage of these girls' poverty with impunity. Of course you know they all come from the north and the northeast, the poorest regions of the whole country.'

'Not all of them . . . ' he objected. 'Some of them are from Bangkok.'

'It's sexual slavery!' screamed Josiane, who hadn't heard. 'There's no other way to describe it! . . . '

I yawned a little. She shot me a black look, but went on, calling on the others to give their verdict: 'Don't you think it's disgraceful that any fat old yob can come over here and have it off with these kids for next to nothing?'

'It's hardly next to nothing . . . ' I protested modestly. 'I paid three thousand baht, which is about what you'd pay in France.' Valérie turned and looked at me, surprised. 'You paid a bit over the odds . . . ' observed Robert. 'Still, if the girl was worth it . . . '

Josiane's whole body was trembling, she was starting to unsettle me a little. 'Well!' she shrieked in a very shrill voice, 'It makes me sick, that any fat pig can pay to shove his cock into a kid!'

'Nobody's forcing you to come with me, madam . . . ' Robert replied calmly.

She got up, trembling, her plate of rice in her hand. All conversation at the next table had stopped. I really thought she was going to chuck the plate in his face, and in the end I think it was only fear that stopped her. Robert looked at her with the most serious expression, the muscles under his polo-neck tense. He didn't look like the sort of person to let himself be pushed around; I could well imagine him punching her. She viciously slammed down her plate, which broke into three pieces, turned on her heel and vanished into the darkness, walking quickly toward the chalets.

'Tsk . . . ' he said softly.

Valérie was stuck between him and me; he stood up gracefully, walked around the table and sat where Josiane had been sitting, in case Valérie, too, wished to leave the table. She, however, did nothing; at that moment, the waiter brought the coffees. After she had taken two sips, Valérie turned to me again. 'So is it true you've paid for girls? . . . ' she asked gently. Her tone was intrigued, but without any real reproach.

'They're not as poor as all that, these girls,' added Robert; 'they can afford mopeds and clothes, some of them even have their tits done. It's not cheap getting your tits done. It's true they help their parents out, too . . . ' he concluded thoughtfully.

AT THE NEXT table, after a few whispered comments, everyone quickly left—doubtless out of solidarity. We remained the sole masters of the place, in a sense. The moon now bathed the whole pontoon, which gleamed a little. 'Are they that good, those little masseuses? . . . ' asked René dreamily.

'Ah, monsieur!' exclaimed Robert, deliberately grandiloquent, but, it seemed to me, basically sincere, 'they are marvellous, positively marvellous! And you haven't been to Pattaya yet. It's a resort on the east coast . . . ' he went on, ' . . . completely dedicated to lust and debauchery. The Americans were the first to go there, during the Vietnam war; after that, a lot of English and Germans; now, you get a lot of Russians and Poles. There, they have something for everyone, they cater for all tastes: homosexuals, heterosexuals, transvestites . . . It's Sodom and Gomorrah combined. Actually, it's better, because they've got lesbians, too.'

'Aaah, aaah . . . ' the former pork-butcher seemed thoughtful. His wife yawned placidly, excused herself and turned to her husband; she clearly wanted to go to bed.

'In Thailand,' Robert concluded, 'everyone can have what they desire, and everyone can have something good. People will talk to you about Brazilian girls, or about Cubans. I'm well-travelled, monsieur, I have travelled for pleasure and I have no hesitation in telling you: in my opinion, Thai girls are the best lovers in the world.'

hot sex in bangkok

Gary Dunne

ONE OF THE highlights of being a resident of Bangkok is observing the tabloid tourists doing Patpong, the red-light area. These mixed packs of large colourfully dressed westerners can always be seen late at night cruising around in search of something really awful. They usually end up in one of those laminex bars where Thai women, each with a plastic number pinned to her scanty costume, dance on small stages. By the time the ice has melted in their one grossly overpriced drink, they've seen some man pay the bar for the right to take one of the women upstairs or home for the night. Everyone is in agreement that it's absolutely terrible, degrading, and someone, maybe *Sixty Minutes*, ought to do something about it. And they leave, armed with a great story to liven up the slide show when they get back to the real world.

Whenever I mix with foreigners, I keep hearing the same story again and again. The sex bars are shockingly lurid and not to be missed. The English queen can't believe that I've never been inside one.

"It's the moral outrage," I explain. "I'm no good at moral outrage."

"Look at it this way," he replies. "Do you really want to leave Bangkok without having seen at least one live sex show full of tacky sleaze?"

"It's not my style. I don't care how far a girl can fire a ping-pong ball from her cunt."

"They do have *boy* bars. I know just the place, The Shark Tank. If you're interested, we can go there tonight."

He can be very persistent but this time it isn't necessary.

"OK. Let's do it."

I don't apologise. Being totally honest, I guess there's a touch of the tabloid in even the nicest of us.

ONCE OUR EVENING classes have finished we retire to the nearby open-air bar. After a bottle or so of Mekhong, he decides it's late enough and we catch a taxi to Suriwong Road. From there it's a short stroll down a laneway and up a flight of stairs to a cosy, ultra-airconned bar.

We seem to be the only foreigners in the place. Then I notice two Japanese businessmen near the back wall. They are being quietly chatted up by three G-strung boys, each with a plastic number tag (13, 24, and 32) pinned prominently to his open dressing gown. A number of older Thai men sit nearby in arm-chairs, intent on conversation with each other. The front tables and bar stools are occupied by late-teen Thai yuppies, mainly straight couples, all knocking back over-garnished cocktails and ignoring the American gay porn on the video screens on the walls.

My guide orders G&Ts. To our left, at the end of the bar, is a small stage on which three boys in see-thru briefs are dancing. It's strange dancing, maximum effect for minimum move-ment. Their feet seem glued to the stage. Every five minutes or so another trio replaces them, each boy's plastic number either in hand or pinned to his thin costume.

"My dear, it improves after midnight," I am advised. "Just watch out for the manager, she's pushy."

He is. He hovers at my elbow, a large Chinese-Thai person of indeterminate gender with a round face, permanent smile and two prominent gold teeth. His sales pitch is slick and unavoidable.

I make a fatal opening mistake by admitting this is my first time. He launches into an explanation of the bar fee system. It's as the tabloid tourists foretold. You pay the bar 150 baht so that you and your intended can leave. Later you "make private arrangements" which include "a gift". The amount is "up to you". When pushed he suggests, "maybe 300 baht".

"My boys," he assures me, "are best in Bangkok. All young, hot sex. All good boys, show much respect, hundred per cent honest. All have test, hundred per cent very clean."

I suggest that I'll have a drink or two and think about choices later.

The hard-sell, however, isn't over. The manager brings out a thick photo album and insists I view every page. It's filled with glossy colour nude shots. Each boy is splayed centre-stage in exactly the same unimaginative pose, clearly showing off his teeth, his erection, and his plastic number tag. None look very happy.

My guide has slipped away to an armchair near the back wall and keeps toasting me and winking as the manager continues.

I'm being asked about my personal sexual predilections. My reply is vague. I don't want him fixing me up with a date. He explains that all tastes are catered for here from "kings and queens" to "all-'merican kinky sex fun". Anything is possible. Nothing is too much trouble.

I apologise, ask directions to the toilet and make my escape.

While crossing the bar, I realise that I'm probably a bit drunk. We should have had a meal before coming here. I also realise that I'm disappointed. I was expecting a voyeuristic thrill or two with maybe some intimate audience participation, lap dancing, or its Thai equivalent. Not that I was planning on doing anything really sexual, I'm not the type who pays for it, but hot sleaze was what I envisioned, not this cold, clean, neon-lit bar with the carnal ambience of a Pizza Hut and a manager who should be selling Amway.

Of late, erotic disappointment has loomed large in my life. I now have a Thai boyfriend, Lek. We go to the movies as a couple. We go to dinner as a couple. We go nightclubbing with friends as a couple. We do everything most couples do, except fuck. I'm sure we will, eventually. It's all a matter of time. It took him a month to agree to go to the movies. A week later we were kissing good night at my front door. Another week later we kissed horizontally while on a picnic in the park. It was obvious that we were both aroused, but unzipping was still out of the question. One weekend, as soon as we're both free, we're going away, overnight, to Ayuthaya, the old capital, about 100 kms north, and, as always, I have great expectations. Which is a long-winded way of saying I'm sexually frustrated.

The Men's is spectacularly tacky. There are spotlights above every plastic gilt-edged mirror and gaudy fixture. The attendant, a svelte queen with over-permed hair, jumps to his feet and greets me with a big friendly smile and polite bow. It occurs to me that he and the manager are the only staff in the whole place who are wearing pants.

I register the hot towel oven, blow driers, jars of gel and body lotions, cans of hairspray, and a whole shelf of familiar designer-label colognes and aftershaves. His vanity units each have two taps. I beam a grin right back at him. I haven't experienced hot running water in months. I intend to indulge myself. I may go home sexually disappointed (what's new) but at least I'll feel and smell totally fabulous.

The attendant massages my shoulders and neck while I pee. I moan encouragingly and he works harder. I undo my shirt and almost bathe in the basin. He lets me use extra hot towels and go to town on all the beauty products. My enthusiasm is infectious. He wants to blow-dry, spray and style my hair, but I know a zooshy-do practitioner when I meet one, so I don't let him. He seems genuinely disappointed. I leave a generous tip and exit, red-faced and reeking of fake Eternity.

(Tourist Tip #29: Sniff any designer-label scents *before* liberally applying.)

The manager, thankfully, is nowhere in sight. There's a cute young Thai in pure white Y-fronts perched on the arm of the English queen's chair. I saunter over and take the armchair next to them. His tag says 47, his briefs say Calvin Klein, and, his name, he says, is Nik. Up close, he's even better looking.

Nik thinks her majesty is a "very sexy man" who will, he suggests, buy the three of us a drink. I say no, it's my shout, and Nik signals to the barman. Any remnants of a grumpy mood evaporate as I watch my friend ever-so-politely resist the wandering hands and erotic hard-sell. I love observing Brits under fire, their manners are always so impeccable. And Nik's brilliant at his trade, constantly flattering, prick-tempting and teasing, a right little heartbreaker. The drinks cost a fortune and I don't mind at all.

Onstage a new performance is beginning. Nik explains that it's called *The Big Cock And Masturbation Show*. The same trios of young men, now naked and wanking, are still dancing without moving their feet. It's pretty unerotic, given their blank expressions and the audience's complete lack of interest. The yuppies' tables are littered with cocktail debris, paper umbrellas and lemon twists; the air thick from their imported Marlboros, puffed not smoked. The Japanese leave discretely, taking numbers 13 and 32 with them. Their places are taken by a pair of Thai suits who look like they too are only after a quick take-away before supper.

Nik finally establishes that the queen and I are an item. He suggests a "sexy threeway," which my friend firmly rejects. Nik politely thanks me for the drink, bids us both a friendly farewell and moves on to try his luck with the Thai businessmen.

"He'll tell the others we're a couple and we should be left alone."

"You don't fancy him?" I ask with suitable fake incredulity.

"Of course I fancy him but I've got an equally hot Thai boyfriend waiting in bed at home. Do *you* fancy him?"

"Maybe," I reply cautiously. "But I've got a boyfriend too."

"Your yuppie disco accessory?"

"His name is Lek."

"So she's now your *boyfriend*. Congratulations. Obviously I was quite wrong about her."

"Indeed."

"And you're totally satisfied? You don't fancy a quick fuck on the side, no strings attached."

"Correct."

"It's simply that as your guide, it's my job to see that you're aware of all the possibilities."

"I'm fine thanks."

While he's ordering another round of drinks, I watch one of the Thai businessmen pay the bar fee and leave with Nik.

I sulk in silence through *The Big Suck And Fuck Show,* a bland combination of gymnastics and gay sex. Each position is repeated at various locations on the stage so everyone can see what's going where. No one, including the performers, seems that interested.

We are being hassled to buy drinks by numbers 7, 9, and 24. They begin classic Suzi Wong conversations. 'What your name?' 'You sexy man. How long you stay Bangkok?' 'What country you come?' 'I know Australia. Have good Sydney friend, Mr Daryl. You know him?'

They don't have Nik's disarming looks or charm. I answer in equally fractured Thai that maybe lowers their enthusiasm and expectations. It's surprising sometimes how much conversation can be drawn out of a working vocab of twenty words in another language. Obviously enough for a one-night stand.

Number 24 is babbling in a mixture of English and Thai about the highlight of the next show that is about to begin. I whisper to my friend that perhaps it's time to go. I've seen enough for one night.

"Quite right, my dear. Perfect timing. I always leave before they bring on the Alsatian."

. . .

BANGKOK'S HUMIDITY SEEMS worst whenever you exit anywhere air-conditioned. Stepping out onto the footpath is like entering a sauna filled with compost and exhaust fumes. We adjourn to the nearest greasy wok for supper.

"Well, at least I can say I've seen it," I announce flatly.

"And how's your moral outrage?" he asks, pouring me a glass of Mekhong.

"It wasn't what I was expecting. The hard sell makes it kind of unreal. It's too easy, too sterile. We're buying, we've got money. They're selling, they need money. I can't imagine myself actually throwing 150 baht on the bar and ordering a number 69 to go, hold the anchovies. I think I was expecting something less businesslike. It certainly wasn't erotic."

"Raw capitalism rarely is."

"I'm glad I'm a socialist."

"You Australians and your socialism. Everyone has to be equal. You always have to split every bill. Thais don't think like that. The richest person picks up the tab. We're foreigners, ergo we're rich, ergo we pay. Your real problem is pride. You simply don't like the idea of having to pay for sex. What do you think your affair with Lek is based on? Who pays the big bills when you two go out to those expensive nightclubs?"

I'm tempted to try justifying things like love and commitment, but I suspect he'd demolish a romantic argument in seconds flat. Plus I'm not so sure I really believe in it myself.

"My relationship with Lek is based on more than just money." I reply. "I merely happen to earn a lot more of it than he does."

"Exactly. Which is why I keep telling you, you can do better than an upwardly mobile prick-teaser. For a similar weekly investment, in cash rather than cocktails and restaurants, you could have a hot young Thai living with you. All the rich queens have one, expats and locals alike. Even the former PM, Old Mother Prem, has that hunky chauffeur he takes everywhere with him. Think about it. Your own well-mannered, well-hung houseboy. No middle-class scruples, no expensive tastes.

With luck he might even cook or clean. Mine, unfortunately, refuses. That's why we hire staff when we entertain."

"You've seen my place. It's not a huge apartment like you two have. It's a hovel, barely suitable for one," I reply. "I don't need, or want, a paid houseboy."

"If that's too morally offensive, for the cost of a round of cocktails you can pick up a boy for the night. Lek will never know, not that he's being faithful to you anyway. You only see him once or twice a week. You can bet he's out and about on the other nights. And before you start talking about exploitation, try looking closer to home. Ask yourself if someone like Nik would trade places with that young kid who cleans our classrooms and toilets every evening for 300 baht a month. I don't think so. Not when he can make that much in an hour.

"And you aren't going to try and tell me you didn't find young Nik the slightest bit attractive. When he and that banker left, your tongue was hanging out with jealousy. I know. I could see it, even from way over at the bar. And believe me, it wasn't a pleasant sight. Mind you, he was a cut above the usual trash we ferungs attract around here. Even I was sorely tempted."

"You win," I admit, mainly because he has. "Like I said, I'm no good at moral outrage. I'm too easily corrupted. Maybe next time. I did like the bathroom up there. You should have checked it out. Unbelievable. It would be worth a return visit just for another round with their beauty products."

"Next time go easy on their fake colognes. If anyone stinks like a whore around here, it's . . ." He pauses midsentence and starts waving furiously at a passing Thai student, "Speak of the devil."

It takes me several seconds to realise that it's Nik, casually dressed and carrying a small backpack, presumably returning to the bar up the laneway. He comes over and greets us both by name.

"Do you have time for another drink," says the English queen, offering him the stool next to me, then the bottle of Mekhong.

"No problem," says Nik, and, in Thai, asks the proprietor for a Pepsi, then sits down.

"You not find boyfriends in the bar?" he asks.

"We had to leave, it was too cold," I reply.

"My friend Tui says ferung countries all very cold. Ferungs like very cold."

"Not all ferungs," says my friend. "Some like it hot . . . That's why we live in Bangkok."

"How long you live in Bangkok?"

"I've been here too long," he replies. "Simon, maybe a few months. I told a big lie back in the bar. We work together, teaching English, but we aren't a couple. I've been living with my Thai boyfriend for over a year. But my colonial friend here is very single. And available. She's really not my type. Two queens together, no good. It would never work. Too much gossip, no sex."

Nik laughs.

"Are you from Bangkok?" I ask.

Nik is Isaan, from Udorn Thani up near the Lao border. He learnt English hanging around the local US military base as a child. He's in Bangkok to complete a uni degree in economics and commerce, and also attends an advanced language class early evenings. It's a school we haven't heard of, which makes sense when he explains that he's studying Japanese.

Throughout this conversation I'm aware that Nik's knee is rubbing against mine under the table. He's quietly flirting with me. At last, familiar gay territory. I flirt back. The eye contact is immediately reciprocated.

I tell him about the joys of teaching English, the casual conversation videos we are about to star in, and I list my favourite nightclubs.

"I love The Palace. I dance same same Michael Jackson," says Nik. "But Palace very expensive for poor student. Maybe you take me there?"

"Good heavens, is that the time?" says the English queen,

glancing at his watch and faking a huge yawn. "I must be on my way. The boyfriend turns frigid if I stay out after midnight."

He shakes Nik's hand, "It's been a real pleasure meeting you Nik. Good luck with the Japanese." And he adds a paragraph in rapid-fire Thai that I don't catch.

Nik smiles and responds, promising something, but again my Thai isn't good enough to understand.

"And you my dear, you comprendez le franglaiz?" he asks while shaking my hand.

I nod and he continues in a fast flat monotone, "Donnez votre hot trade, um, trios centenaries, not prior, but après la grande bonk. OK?"

"Mercy madam," I reply and nod again.

We watch a very happy man head off down the street.

Nik finishes his Pepsi, smiles, and takes my hand. "We go your apartment now."

I pay the bill and we leave.

I'M ALMOST NERVOUS as I open my front door. It's been two or three years since I brought trade home. I've been travelling, and before that, in Australia, I spent a year or so being too neurotic about Aids to successfully score anything but minor tranquilisers. There has been the odd, occasional fuck while on the road, but it's always something serendipitous, never a full-on pickup like this.

Nik shuts the door and starts kissing me.

"You go washroom at bar?" he asks. "Sexy aftershave."

I laugh. "Too much sexy aftershave. But it's great. I had fun there."

"Tui my good friend. He always fun. He makes my haircut. Much style. He teach me washroom massage."

Nik begins massaging my shoulders and neck. I moan theatrically and he starts tickling me under the arms. Soon we are rolling on the mattress, undressing each other. I'm surprised to discover big candy-striped boxers beneath his loose cotton slacks.

"Where are your Calvins?" I ask.

He looks confused.

"Your white underpants?" I explain.

"Very sexy briefs," he replies. "Very small. I only have in bar. I like boxer shorts."

"They're very sexy too," I say, unconvincingly.

"We go washroom now," he replies and pulls them off. He already has an erection.

My bathroom is very primitive, nothing like the facilities at the bar. There's a squat toilet, a drain, and two cold water taps; one low, one high. I've connected a showerhead to the top tap and it's functional, water goes everywhere but eventually ends up running down the drain or toilet.

We wash each other. His body is almost hairless, a rich dusty brown, quite dark for a Thai, and he's slim and lithe, built like a dancer. Up close I realise that his small rectangular patch of pubic hair is too small and too rectangular.

"You shave?" I ask, looking up.

"Tui makes haircut," he explains. "Tui makes all boys haircut at bar. He says ferungs like boys very young, no cock hair. Good for business."

"How old are you?" I ask. Going by his verbal CV, I guess early twenties. Going by his body, he could be anything from late teens upward. It's really hard to guess a Thai person's age.

"Sixteen."

One good lie deserves another. "I'm twenty-two," I say.

Back on the bed we kiss and romp. Nik's playful, exploring what turns me on and what doesn't. He's harder to read, mainly because he's had a bone-hard erection ever since he kicked off those trashy extra-large boxers. He's a passionate kisser and his other oral skills are as finely honed.

"We fuck now," he finally says and rolls over, unzips his backpack and pulls out a tub of Crisco.

"Not necessary," I suggest and get up. "I have plenty of condoms."

I hand him the creature comforts post-pack I received a month or so ago from The Salbutamol Kid in Sydney. The

Chocolate Koalas, Vovo biscuits, Vegemite, and other uniquely Australian delicacies, all since consumed, were buried within this huge assortment of sachets of lube and condoms: plain, ribbed, and coloured.

"You always do safe sex?" I ask, wondering if now's the time for a lecture.

"No problem," says Nik. He rips open an orange condom, unrolls it, blows it up to balloon size and lets it go. It jets out over the low balcony wall and into the night. He pushes me onto my back, kneels between my knees, opens a black condom and giggles as he rolls it on himself.

"Big black cock. Same same Michael Jackson."

"I think his is smaller," I reply.

I lift my legs and apply some KY. He takes his time. We maintain total eye contact as he fully penetrates me. Then we begin slow fucking. We kiss deeply. I notice that his eyes are still open and for some unclear reason this means a lot to me.

It's as if we've been lovers for years. We pulse together with an intensity that keeps on building. Just when I think he's about to come, he stops, changes our position, and the intensity starts all over again. He won't let me touch myself, concerned, accurately I guess, that any direct stimulation and I'll come in seconds flat. He keeps me in this quivering state seemingly forever.

Finally I'm on my back yet again, my knees as earrings, and he's really pumping. Without loosing momentum he slips one hand between us and begins wanking me. His timing is perfect. We orgasm in unison.

Bliss.

Eventually he withdraws, throws the condom at the bedside bin and lies down next to me. His body has an erotic sweaty sheen. I'm dripping like a collapsed marathon runner.

"You number one, Simon. Very sexy man," he whispers in my ear.

"Phew . . . Nik," I reply breathlessly. "Phew . . . That was . . . incredible. Thank you."

"Your friend say you need long time hard fuck." He nods at

the bedside alarm clock. It's 1:52. "We fuck thirty-two minutes," he says proudly. "You like?"

All I can do is nod.

Nik kisses my cheek, reaches over and grabs a towel. After wiping us both off, he gathers the other towel and his backpack.

"I go washroom now," he says.

I heave a long sigh, get up and consider changing the bed linen which is dark with sweat, all of it mine. Nik's good. The best sex I've had in years. I pick the black condom up from the floor and drop it into the bin. It isn't loaded. Nik's better than good. I check my wallet then raid the emergency cash supply in the wardrobe for 100 baht notes.

He spends ages in the bathroom. I wrap on a sarong, make a pot of tea, and sit on the balcony smoking the best cigarette I've tasted in years, listening to the sound of him brushing his teeth and gargling.

Nik finally emerges and dresses quickly. He doesn't want tea. He styles his hair in my small mirror before returning his brush, comb, and gel to his pack.

"I go home now," he says and kisses me on the cheek.

"Any chance I can see you again?" I ask.

"I'm always at the bar Friday and Saturday nights. Maybe other night. Always Friday and Saturday."

He pulls his wallet from his back pocket and extracts a business card which he hands to me. On one side it has a simple map showing how to get there from Suriwong Road. On the other, the bar's name, address, phone number, and hours are printed in English and Thai, along with the name NIK clearly handwritten below a quick sketch of a number 47 bar tag. It looks like a rough coat of arms.

This is not exactly what I was expecting. I hand him the money, four one hundred baht notes, and, remembering the manager's euphemism, say, "For you Nik. A gift."

Nik formally thanks me in Thai, bowing, his hands together as if praying, the full traditional wai. He then drops to his knees and touches his forehead on my bare feet.

I'm mortified.

He stands up, kisses my cheek yet again, and opens the front door.

"Friday," he says, "Come to bar Friday, early, before nine clock. You talk manager. Order number forty-seven. No talk to other boys. I come. We go dinner and nightclub. The Palace. We dance same same Michael Jackson. We make long time sexy love all night."

A final kiss and he's gone.

I sit on the balcony, sipping tea and wistfully calculating the potential cost of such a night of long time sexy love: the bar fee, his 'gift', one classy meal, two Palace tickets, three or four taxis, maybe supper afterwards and certainly drinks at every venue. It comes to well over US$150, half a week's wages or a month's rent for this concrete box.

But economics can't touch my mood. I've been thoroughly laid and I'm euphoric. The scent of fake Eternity lingers. I smell and feel totally fabulous.

watermelon in a shanghai whore house

Rachel DeWoskin

KNEW THAT MY male acquaintances frequented massage parlors. Usually they did so
when on vacations in South East Asia, notorious for its complicated buffets of services. I was aware that such services were
available in China as well, but never gave it much thought.
Prostitution was flirty and rampant there; I saw it in high heels
and miniskirts, discos, and hotel lobbies. But as a girl, and
a foreign one at that, I was never mistaken for a hooker
or approached by one. Hence, I never really had an insider's
view, until I made a strategic error during my last business trip
to Shanghai.

I was staying at the Park Hotel, which, although somewhat
run-down and state run, was a thirty second walk from my
office. I opted for convenience over glam, and was pleased with
that until I decided one day after sixteen hours in the office
that I needed a massage. I had gone for a hideously awkward
business dinner, and dragged ass back to the hotel in a taxi,
thinking miserably about my decision to stay somewhere with
no health club. I even gave a moment of sarcastic thought to

the late night phone calls I knew hotel prostitutes made to single businessmen (the girls were tipped off by the concierges, to whom they gave kickbacks), "good evening sir, would you like a massage?"

Hence, when I noticed a sign in an upstairs window only a block from the hotel, I read it with a certain lack of perspective: "24-Hour Massage." I figured I'd get out there and go in. I had nothing to lose, except my innocence, and since I lost that a decade ago, I'd get a massage and let other people do their own things around me. I didn't care. I felt reckless.

There was a winding staircase leading up to "24-Hour Massage," covered in a shred of tattered velvet so stained it had a kind of road-kill flavor. Perhaps I'll sit during the massage, instead of lying down, I reasoned. There were "erotic" paintings as I climbed further up the stairs, thick, swirling oil paintings with too-brightly flesh-colored women. Most of them had long ropes of hair, covering half nipples. Were they supposed to be Western? Yes. The hair was curly, tied back in baby blue ribbons. Their eyes were blues and greens. I blinked.

At the front desk, I felt a surge of relief. The women working there were in their 50s at least. They must be masseurs, I thought. "Hello, Aiyi," I said to one of them, using a formal and sweet term of respect. She stared at me.

"What service do you need?" she asked.

"Massage," I said.

There was a moment of silence, during which I considered my options. Chinese are not about confrontation or confession. There was no chance of their saying to me, "I'm sorry, stupid white girl, but this is a whore house." I felt safe for that reason; it couldn't get too awkward, since they were Chinese and I knew the rules. Nobody would embarrass anyone else; I would get a massage, and we'd all be happy and not lose face.

They looked at each other with resignation. "OK," the stunned one said. "Come right this way and change clothes."

She led me into a locker room, and stood there staring at me while I changed into a thin polyester robe with pink flowers on it. I opened one of the lockers and a cockroach scurried around and slipped into a metal crack at the bottom of the locker. I hung my suit anyway. I have no idea why I didn't run right then. Maybe I wanted to prevent the aiyi or the establishment from losing face. More likely, I was still on my own dare and/or feared I would lose face if I admitted how stupid my whole stubborn midnight massage plan had been. I put my shoes upside down, hoping that the foot mouths would be covered and cockroaches wouldn't be able to climb in and wait for my feet. I kept my cell phone with me, tucking it between the flaps of the robe.

The aiyi and I didn't speak to each other. When I was entirely clothed in the scratchy, dirty frock, she led me back out past the front desk. There were a few young women at the desk now, whispering. When I walked by, the silence buzzed. I held the robe flaps together in the front and thought about my suit, besieged by roaches.

"First rest a minute," the aiyi said to me. "You can stay here while we find the massage doctor."

She swung open a large red door, and gestured to me to walk in front of her. I inhaled. The room was huge, and lined with two hundred chairs of a variety I'd never seen. They were like lawn chairs, except padded and covered with cotton doilies. In almost every one of them reclined a fat businessman. We were all wearing the same robes. Most of theirs were hanging open.

I thought of the "Little Engine that Could," and walked across the room, finally settling on a recliner in the corner. There were televisions hanging from the ceiling, and the collective gaze immediately shifted from the screens to me. I felt the oxygen supply in the room deplete instantly as everyone inhaled. There was an audible gasp, followed by a dark current of conversation, which included, "what the fuck is that foreign miss doing here?" I arranged myself on the chair, paralyzed with horror, and then remained expressionless. I was unwilling to acknowledge either that I spoke Chinese or that I could hear. All the men were all eating watermelon and sunflower seeds; there was a soundtrack of shells and seeds being spit onto little end tables next to the recliners. I set my cell phone down on my table and kept my eyes pinned on a TV. A moment later, the aiyi walked over and handed me a slice of watermelon on a stained plate.

"Xie xie," I said, and my voice was high pitched and false, coming from a hundred miles away. "Uh," I continued, interested to hear my voice again. "The massage doctor?"

"First rest a minute," she said, and I knew I was in trouble.

I bit into the watermelon as noisily as I could, and made a show of enjoying it as much as everyone else.

She brought me tea.

The men continued to stare.

Eventually, two tiny women in black miniskirts and red blouses came out. They sat on footstools in front of various fat men and began foot massages. The men groaned. Were these places collectives? Did everyone go at the same time? I tried to flag the aiyi down. I had been sitting there at least eight minutes, and had begun to shift around miserably in the chair. She avoided looking at me, and I felt a kind of flutter spread and fan out into my chest. I picked up the cell phone and called my friend in Beijing. My voice must have been super quiet and strained and weird because he said, "Where the fuck are you?"

"I'm not sure," I said, in English. Every head in the room whipped around toward me. "I think I'm in a whore house." I wondered how many of them spoke English. Probably a fair number, I guessed. No one said anything; they just stared. I couldn't help looking at some of their stomachs, and feeling a sense of indignation and anger that they couldn't close their robes on my behalf. I wondered how the foot-massaging girls must feel.

"What?" he said. "What are you doing? It's one in the morning? Where are you really?"

"I wanted a massage," I told him.

"And?"

"So I came to one of these all night places."

"Rachel, get up and walk out."

"I can't," I told him.

"Why not?"

I was whispering now.

"Because my clothes are in a locker."

He paused, collecting himself.

"What does that mean exactly?"

"There are a hundred naked Shanghai businessmen in this room," I said, "and I'm wearing Chinese pajamas." I could feel a hint of hysterical laughter beneath the surface of everything I said. I wondered whether I would suddenly shout with laughter and run from the room, screaming with delight and waving my arms.

"Ok," he said, "Stay on the phone with me."

I did.

"Stand up and walk to the door.

I did.

"Now go get your clothes, and get the fuck out."

"Where are you going?" the aiyi asked, loud from the middle of the room.

I hung up the cell phone accidentally.

"I'm leaving," I told her.

The men were staring at us. There was a ripple of incredible tension and quiet through the room. Were we going to admit how nasty this was?

She watched me, expectantly. The girls in red blouses looked up from their men's feet.

I dropped my voice. "This isn't a massage place," I told her, idiotically. "You don't even have massage doctors here."

I waited for her to deny it, hoping, because it would have been familiar and comforting, that she would. I thought she would say, "yes, we do, they're just sick today," or "yes, just wait a few minutes more," and I'd leave anyway and we'd both be OK with our versions of the truth.

"Yes," she said, "I'm sorry. We're very embarrassed."

I ran. I was so horrified by her confession, and at such a loss for a response, that I started running before she even had the last syllable of "embarrassed" out (it has four distinct syllables in Chinese: bu hao yi si). She was still on "yi" when I took off. She spun around.

I went straight for the locker room, grabbed my clothing from the still open locker, banging the door, exchanged my shoes for the plastic slippers I had on, and bolted down the stairs. One of the young women at the desk screamed after me about the pajamas, but I tore down the slimy velvet staircase and busted out onto the street. I kept running until I was panting back at the Park Hotel. The concierge in there knew better than to give me a second look. I ran directly past the desk in my suit shoes and the nasty flapping robe, and into the first elevator that opened. The elevator had mirrored walls and a mirrored ceiling. I saw myself reflected all over the place, flushed, half naked, breaking a record for walks of shame. There was watermelon juice smeared from the upper side of my right lip almost to my cheek. As I mopped at it with the back of my hand, I realized I had left my cell phone in the locker room. I called from my hotel room and cancelled the service.

police and mama-sans get it all

Nelson Algren

FROM THE LAST CAROUSEL

THE STREET CALLED Huong-Dieu slants through a slum pervaded by the yellowish scents of raw fish, urine, and charcoal fires. You push your way through throngs of yam-and-mango vendors, Vietnamese veterans still wearing their field uniforms the better to beg, women between the shafts of donkey carts, and small girls who tug your sleeve but speak not a word; from one sunstriped alley to the next until you reach 22 Huong-Dieu.

Up a stairwell so worn its wood looked gnawed, I passed into a narrow passage, made narrower by heavy red draperies, and into a room where women sat or lay upon a dozen beds. Some wore slacks, some miniskirts and some were in their slips. Above, several candles burned in Buddhist altars. Only one had a Christ impaled above her. I favored Jesus as being the lesser fire hazard. I was in a camp of refugee whores.

An upended container, marked US ARMY in rusting white paint, held water for both washing and drinking. Yet the room was so spacious that 22 Huong-Dieu, I surmised, must once have been a luxurious French hotel; there were still gas fixtures from that long-gone time. Now the water was off and lights were out and all the carefree times were done.

"Where Xuong?" I asked one of the women.

"What numba?"

I'd first spoken to Xuong in the Central Market. I'd been shopping for oranges. Not the little green-skinned lumps that pass for oranges in Saigon—I wanted those big yellow California Sunkist dandies imported from the nearest American commissary.

A foreigner pays half a dollar each for them; a Vietnamese gets them for a quarter. Moreover, when a foreigner buys six, he winds up with five. These market women are really deft.

I asked Xuong to buy a dozen for me and gave her the piastres. When she returned with oranges *and* the change, I was impressed; it was the first time I'd seen a Vietnamese return change to a foreigner. I gave three oranges to her eight-year-old boy to show my appreciation.

"O, me wuv *you* too *much*," she thanked me, and added, indicating the boy as we walked out of the market, "him Hiep." I would have walked her further but she seemed embarrassed.

"Me Xuong," she told me, "2 Huong-Dieu," and walked away.

When I ran out of oranges I went to find her. Had she told me her number instead of her name she could have saved me a troubled search. In a troubled season.

"What numba?"

Then Hiep jumped out of some cranny, put his arms about me and his head against my chest, and bummed me for a cigarette. He wouldn't lead me to his mother until I'd given him a light. Then he pocketed the matches.

Xuong was sitting cross-legged on Bed 16 with neither a Christ nor a Buddha above her. Her nose had no bridge and her right cheek bore a long slant scar that must once have been livid but had long since turned ash-grey.

"Numba-One Mama-san co*dock*," she explained instead of saying hello; touching a safety-razor blade to her temple with a slanting motion to show me how Numba-One Mama had co*docked* her. "O, me wuv *you* too *much*," she remembered; and put the thin blade down. Two middle-teeth of her uppers were gold. Her skin was unblemished nonetheless.

The girl on the next bed put on shades, though the light was dim, and turned up the volume of her transistor as though to raise a sound curtain between the beds. Some of the beds had drawstring curtains. One woman took her laundry off the curtains and drew the strings. The Mama-san, a woman in her seventies, no bigger than a child, was led in by Hiep.

"Short-tam?" the old woman wanted to know. "Long-tam? Numba One gel."

The girl on the next bed took off her shades, turned down the volume and came out flat against Short Time: "Short tam didi fast. Long tam Numba One." A girl lying on her back in a far corner agreed and added, indifferently, "Me wuv you too much too." Then Mama came out, independent of the opinions of anyone else, for Long Tam.

The only dissenter was Hiep, who kept pulling the bed's drawstrings and trying to push his mother onto the bed. He was plainly afraid that unless it was Short Time, it might be no time at all. A bird in the hand was Hiep's thinking.

A quorum having finally been attained, the girl on the next bed put her shades back on and turned up the volume while Xuong began to get dressed for the street. She had a slight limp, yet she never went out on the street without looking neat.

Mama-san took me aside to tell me her sorrows. She had been, when young, she assured me in a mixture of French and GI English, a dancer in Paris. I gave her the benefit of the doubt. Perhaps she *had* danced a step or two down the Boulevard Sebastapol *circa* 1917. Up from some Cambodian hamlet to the lights of Montmartre, then down to the alleys of Saigon. Where now she raced curfew, corner to corner, night after night, upstairs and down on her seventy-year-old legs.

Xuong came out of the curtains wearing a white blouse and a dark pleated skirt. But Hiep clung to her and wouldn't let her leave him.

"Give cigarette," Xuong explained.

"Eight years old and pimping your mother," I congratulated the child, "here, son, take the whole pack."

On the street I gave Xuong cab fare to my hotel. I walked in the opposite direction to be certain I wasn't being checked by one of the White Mice. Then took another cab to the hotel.

What a lovely city this once must have been, I reflected, driving north on the Rue Pasteur, when it was still flowered and wooded. Now its gardens are sandbags and barbed wire. If you want a flower you can buy an artifical one in any market.

Xuong left her ID card at the hotel desk under the eyes of four bellboys. Before the night-chameleons had fled the walls, one of them would be rapping my door for 500 piastres for entertaining a guest. But there wouldn't be a tip in it for him. I always knew they'd like me in Saigon.

"*Beaucoup* piastres," was Xuong's first reaction to my second-class yet air-conditioned nest. "How much for *all*?"

"36,000 P. a month."

Xuong rolled her eyes at a sum so fantastic. "Hundred P. a day for me and Hiep," she filled me in on what it cost her and her son to survive. Her rent comes out of her own half of her fees. The other half, she assured me, is divided between the Mama-san from the Rue Sebastopol and the First District Police.

Police—the White Mice—and mama-sans alike are terribly hard on these village women. Country girls sometimes have a tough and sinewy pride; so co*docking* them becomes more or less routine. If a mama-san's razor doesn't subdue one, the First District will be happy to take her in hand. After living in darkness a month, on rice cooked in muddy water, never knowing at what moment she's going to be slapped silly again, then being turned back to mama with her head shaven, the girl may wish she'd settled with mama out of court.

Mama doesn't feel she's asking too much of the girl—just to hold up five fingers or 10, meaning 500 piastres for short time or 1000 for long.

Each holds up her fingers in the end: police and mama-sans get it all.

Around the Hotel Caravelle and the Continental Palace, women are available who are never co*docked*. Who never hold up five fingers or 10, and are never shaven by police. These are city women from Vung Tau, Dalat, Danang, Saigon, and Hué. Generally, they're better looking than the refugee women, and always better dressed. Most are Catholic and have had some French schooling. The village women are commonly Buddhists and speak no French at all.

These restaurant courtesans, more mistresses than whores, don't sleep with a man because he pays for a dinner. They pick and choose and take no chances on the common soldier. Most dress in the traditional *aodai*, and are, essentially, conservative women. They are for men with bank accounts in New Delhi, Cincinnati, Athens, Stockholm, Hamburg, Buenos Aires, Paris, and Manila.

Some of them must marry a bank account in Cincinnati: anything to get out of Saigon.

Xuong came out of the bathroom holding a bar of soap.

"How much?"

"Fifty P."

"Fifty for you, fifteen for me," she informed me smugly, and returned to experimenting with hot and cold running water. Then gave a yelp of surprise and came out drying her neck, looking both pleased and rueful. She'd gotten an unexpected sprinkling from the shower. Xuong was a fast learner; even if she was a little heavy around the hips.

The refrigerator was a lesser mystery; some of its contents curiosities. "What name?" she'd want to know, holding up a can or jar. I had to open instant coffee, soluble chocolate, powdered orange juice, and let her taste them all before she could be satisfied. Now she had a tea-bag in her hand. "What name?" When I brought a cup of hot water, she tore open the bag and poured the leaves into the water. She had the right combination anyhow.

Then she discovered a manicure scissors. She pushed me back on the bed, pulled off my socks, and I had to submit to a toenail paring. She enjoyed the work so I let her go on, meanwhile watching a bug on the wall above her head. He'd been living in the room before I'd moved in, and my thinking had been that if he didn't bite me, I wouldn't bite him. Live and let live was how I'd looked at it. Because if he were the kind of bug I suspected he was, he was The King. Now watching Xuong working on my big toe, he began applauding with his feelers. The rascal was growing bold.

Xuong transferred her scissors to her other hand, smacked the brute with her palm, and went back to paring. Five gets you ten that the stain The King left on that wall remains there to this day.

Xuong was older than most of Saigon's refugee whores. For her own refugee time had begun when her father had been killed fighting against the French, or fighting for the French; or for refusing to fight anybody; it all depended on who Xuong was talking to.

Some of these women have been made homeless by B-52s and some by bulldozers. Some by search-and-destroy, and others by search-and-cordon. Some fled the NLF. Some the Americans. Some because a father said a plague on both your houses; or because he rowed down a river nobody had told him was no longer his own. Some are lost because a pilot had to lighten a bombload; others for revealing a cache of rice. Some because a brother informed to the NLF; others because someone informed to the Americans. And some by the defoliant called Blue Bamboo.

Some by knives and some by mines; some by fire and some by water. One says her husband would not have been killed had he not been bareheaded in the paddy. The war has been going on so long, the woman has sold her grief to so many, it is no matter now whether she herself did the informing or was informed upon. Nor upon whose side her father died while being pacified. All she knows is that her name was once

Xuong-thi-Nhan; and that it is now Number 16. It all comes under the general heading of winning hearts and minds.

Xuong was a big girl and a resolute one. My fingernails had to be manicured, too. I tried to get free while she was shining my bedroom slippers and almost made it. But she put the slippers down and began to massage me.

Later she showed me needle-marks, on her arms, with pride. She wanted me to know that she took anti-VD shots every week. She was reassuring me. Then she splashed about in the tub like a great baby. I fell asleep hoping she wouldn't drown.

In the middle of the night, I wakened to find the lights still on, the radio going, and something still transpiring in the bathtub. I rolled out of bed.

Xuong, naked in the tub, was stomping the hell out of every shirt, pair of socks, shorts, and tops I owned, regardless of fabric, fast colors, or condition of cleanliness. She'd found it unthinkable to let all that lovely bathwater down the drain without putting it to some use first. Her hips may have been a bit heavy; but she made up for that in frugality.

Personally, I felt it was a little early in the day to be getting out a laundry. Yet, by the way her big breasts bounced as she stomped, it was plain she was having a ball. So I turned off the radio and went back to bed. When I woke in the morning, Xuong was gone and so were most of my clothes. She'd left me one shirt, one pair of pants, and my shoes.

I didn't want company that evening. I got a knock all the same. Xuong, with laundry ironed and my pants pressed. I went for my wallet.

She looked hurt. "No money," she reproved me. And kicked off her shoes. I would have preferred paying her. I didn't think I could stand another toenail paring this soon.

A lot of good it did me. So what do you know; instead of a Numba One Gel, what I had on my hands was a pedicurist, laundress, masseuse, bodyguard, nurse, cook, seamstress, market-woman, vermin-exterminator, economist, pants-presser, shoe-shiner, and bed-warmer. At the least a mistress; at the most a wife. I didn't have a shirt-button missing. And clean underwear has its own appeal. I just wasn't prepared to set up housekeeping.

"I find Numba One hou' for you," she seemed to read my mind, "you come see."

Now she was in real estate.

So we went down a walk so narrow that no light had even fallen across its walls, into a passage littered with droppings of children and dogs, down a hall, then up a ladder to a floor that sagged beneath my feet. Into a room about 8 × 10 containing an iron cot bearing a mattress stained with rust or blood. We were home.

Xuong switched on a floor fan and looked at me as much as to say, "Didn't I tell you it would be great?" Well, we had electric power at least.

I just sat on that beat-up bedspring and boggled; this was how people actually lived in the world, born into rooms like this: eat, sleep, pray, make love, and die in such kennels. Whole lifetimes. The floor fan creaked and skreaked. It didn't like the place any more than I did.

"Numba One!" Xuong assured me.

"Numba Ten!" I assured her.

"Numba Ten for you, Numba One for me," she reminded me.

When she knocked the following evening, I didn't answer the door. She knew I was there all the same.

"*You* Numba Ten!" she denounced me from the other side of the door.

A chameleon on the wall fled for cover.

The night before I moved, Xuong caught me in. My bags were packed and my escape-route plain. I let her stay. She bathed but didn't splash about. And wouldn't turn out the lights until I'd turned off the ceiling fan.

"Make bad wind," she explained her superstition: death comes on a night-wind.

ILL WIND STRIKES SOLDIER

A soldier slept soundly in his home at Trinh Minh The Street, but alarmed his wife when she heard him uttering indistinct cries. She sped him to a hospital but he died upon arrival. There was speculation that the soldier had died of an ill wind.

—Vietnam Guardian

We had breakfast in a Chinese noodle cafe. When she rose, I glanced up. Then let her go. She didn't turn and look back at the door. She didn't look back from the street. She didn't look back at all.

Those shots she took ought to help one of us, I reflected glumly.

I'll say this much for Xuong: she fought with all she had to get out of a whore's bed and back into a wife's.

FROM **more benadryl, whined the journalist**

William T. Vollmann

One obvious question concerning the ultimate
reproductive success of males is whether it is better
for a male to invest all of his sperm in a single
female or else to copulate with several females.
HÖLLDOBLER AND WILSON, *The Ants* (1990)

1

ONCE UPON A time a journalist and a
photographer set out to whore their
way across Asia. They got a New York magazine to pay for it.
They each armed themselves with a tube of cool soft K-Y jelly
and a box of Trojans. The photographer, who knew such essential Thai phrases as: *very beautiful!, how much?, thank you* and *I'm*
gonna to knock you around! (topsa-lopsa-lei), preferred the extra-
strength lubricated, while the journalist selected the non-
lubricated with special receptacle end. The journalist never
tried the photographer's condoms because he didn't even use
his own as much as (to be honest) he should have; but the pho-

tographer, who tried both, decided that the journalist had really made the right decision from a standpoint of friction and hence sensation; so that is the real moral of this story, and those who don't want anything but morals need read no further.—Now that we've gotten good and evil out of the way, let's spirit ourselves down (shall we?) to the two rakes' room at the Hotel Metro, Bangkok, where the photographer always put on sandals before walking on the sodden blue carpet to avoid fungus. As for the journalist, he filtered the tap water (the photographer drank bottled water; they both got sick). There was a giant beetle on the dresser. The journalist asked the bellboy if beetles made good pets.—Yes, he grinned. It was his answer to every question.—Good thing for him he doesn't have a pussy, said the photographer, untying his black combat boots with a sigh, putting foot powder on; and the journalist stretched out on his squeaking bed, waiting for the first bedbug. The room reminded him of the snow-filled abandoned weather station where he'd once eked out a miserable couple of weeks at the North Magnetic Pole; everything had a more or less normal appearance, but was deadly dangerous, the danger here being not cold but disease; that was how he thought, at least, on that first sweaty super-cautious night when he still expected to use rubbers. The photographer had already bought a young lady from Soy Cowboy. In the morning she lay on the bed with parted purple-painted lips; she put her legs up restlessly.

Last night *tuk-tuk* fifty bhat, she said.* Come back Soy Cowboy, thirty bhat.

So you want some more money for the *tuk-tuk* ride, is that what you're trying to tell me? said the photographer in disgust. Man, I don't fucking believe it. You know, she only let me do her once. And then she wanted a thousand bhat—that's why I had to get that five hundred from you.

---

*In 1991 a U.S. dollar was worth about 25 Thai bhat, or 1,000 Cambodian riels.

The woman's teeth shone. She slapped her thigh, yawned, walked around staring with bright black eyes.

Where do you come from, sweetheart? asked the journalist, flossing his teeth.

Me Kambuja.

Cambodia?

Yes. Kambuja.

We go Kambuja, said the journalist. You come Kambuja?

No.

Why?

She grimaced in terror.—Bang, bang! she whispered.

Outside, the *tuk-tuks* made puffs of smog. Men huddled over a newspaper by the Honey Hotel.—You want Thai food I wait for you, she said.

Oh, that's all right, said the photographer. You go on back to Soy Cowboy. We'll find our way around.

You come Soy Cowboy me tonight?

Sure. Sure, honey. You just go back to Soy Cowboy and sit there and hold your breath.

You like? You like me?

Sure. Now beat it.

You come tonight I have friend she go hotel with you, the girl said to the journalist.

O.K., he said. He smiled at her. She smiled and darted into a *tuk-tuk.*

Well, I guess we go get her and her friend tonight, right? said the journalist.

Are you crazy? said the photographer. There are thousands like her, twice as nice for half the price. She had the nerve to ask me for a thousand bhat! I've *never* paid more than five hundred before. You don't have to give 'em anything after you buy 'em out. I remember one time this bitch kept pestering me for money; I sent her away with *nothing,* man. She was *crying;* it was GREAT!

So what did you pick her up for?

Her? She really stuck out—her long hair, her shorts up the

crack of her ass; I really liked that. But next time I want a big girl, man. Not one of these fucking little babies that don't know what the hell they're doing.

But later he said: I felt sorry for her. Next time I pick up a girl, I won't screw her.

2

ON THE SLIGHTLY tippy table visited by flies, there were four jars: one with salt, one with capers and vinegar and other things like aquarium plants, one with curry powder, and one with pickled peppers. The photographer and the journalist sat there having lunch, in the alley with colored striped sheets for awnings, and colored umbrellas over the tables. They had noodle soup with vegetables. Roof-water dripped slowly into pools on dirty glazed trestles. It was monsoon season. Motorcycles passed slowly between the tables. The young smoothfaced vendeuses turned and scraped the meat in their woks, looking patient behind their glass bulwarks stacked with eggs, tomatoes, bok choy, sprouts, noodles of all kinds. The vendeuse squirted new oil into the wok, then strolled to a grating, where she reached into her apron and gave someone money; then she made her easy way back, just in time for the oil to bubble. A policeman came by, took out his wallet and bought ice. Water dripped onto mossy benches.

The journalist kept thinking of the hurt look in the Cambodian girl's eyes. What to do? Nothing to do.

3

AT HALF PAST four in the afternoon, the sticky feeling of sweat between his fingers felt like fungus growing. There was an American detective video on: gunfire and smashing glass and roaring cars at maximum volume. He sat reading the *Bangkok*

Post: 'Big Five' see eye-to-eye on Khmer arms cuts. Two girls were sitting at the bar where it curved, playing a game like tic-tac-toe with poker chips in a wooden frame. Their cigarette smoke ascended the darkness of the long mirror. When a man was tortured on TV the girls looked up with interested smiles. Then they clicked the chips back into the board. More girls drifted in, filling out forms, making business calls. The whirling circles of light began to go around. A girl watched a fistfight on TV, her forefingers meeting in a steeple on her nose. A girl came in to refill the journalist's beer glass so that the bottle could be taken away and then she could sell him the next; the web of skin between his fingers continued to stick more with each passing moment. Another gunfight. The girls saw him grinning and grinned back. Bored with their game, they peered through the holes in the gameboard which stood on its end like a grating between them.

A white man came in, rubbing his mouth, checking his wallet, resting his arm on the table.

The smokers raised their hands to their mouths like buglers. One of the girls was playing the game of plastic counters with a white boy, and she smiled much more when she won or lost now than she had when playing the other girl. The boy put a cigarette in his mouth, and two girls' hands reached to light it for him.

Slowly the beer receipts piled up in the journalist's ringed teakwood cup. When a girl refilled his beer, she exhibited the utmost concentration, holding it critically to eye level.

Straight-eyebrowed faces, arch-eyebrowed faces, all gold and oval and framed by straight black hair, watched the gameboard or the TV or themselves in the pink-bordered mirror. Whenever something violent happened on TV, they looked up with calm interest.

Traffic crept outside. A police whistle shrilled steadily, then there came a sound of faraway singing or screaming; a *tuk-tuk* passed slowly enough for the passengers to watch the TV. At a quarter to six, when the next white man came in, they switched on the music for a minute, and a girl started dancing, leaning on the bar, clapping her hands. Outside, the lights were turning red and the girls were standing everywhere in sexy skirts. A middle-aged midget in a double-breasted suit came down the alley, walked under one girl's dress, reached up to pull it over him like a roof, and began to suck. The girl stood looking at nothing. When the midget was finished, he slid her panties back up and spat onto the sidewalk. Then he reached into his wallet. The music was getting louder everywhere, and the lights were coming on; girls grinned gently in every doorway as the businessmen passed, sometimes hand in hand; a girl leaned against a vegetable cart smoothing her long hair as the motorbikes passed.

The longhaired girl in the burgundy shirt looked up from her calculator and came to put ice in the journalist's beer.

4

THERE WAS A bar aching with loud American music, pulsing with phosphorescent bathing suits. He picked number fourteen in blue and asked her to come with him but she thought he wanted her to dance, so she got up laughing with the other girls and turned herself lazily, awkwardly, very sweetly; she was a little plump.

You come with me? he said when he'd tipped her.

She shook her head.—I have accident, she said, pointing to her crotch.

She sat with him, nursing the drink he'd bought her; she snuggled against him very attentively, holding his hand. Whenever he looked into her face, she ducked and giggled.

You choose friend for me? he said. Anyone you want.

When you go Kambuja?

Three days.

She hesitated, but finally called over another lady.—This my friend Oy. My name Toy.

You come to hotel with me? he said to Oy.

She looked him up and down.—You want all night or short time?

All night.

No all night me. Only short time.

OK.

5

IN THE BACK of the taxi he whispered in her ear that he was shy, and she snuggled against him just as Toy had done. She smelled like shampoo. She was very hot and gentle against him. Knowing already that if he ever glimpsed her soul it would be in just the same way that in the National Museum one can view the gold treasures only through a thick-barred cabinet, he tried to kiss her, and she turned away.

Please?

She smiled, embarrassed, and turned away.

No?

She shook her head quickly.

6

HE REACHED OVER her to turn out the light, and she cuddled him. He sucked her little nipples and she moaned. He kissed her belly, and eased his hand in between her legs. She'd shaved her pubic hair into a narrow mohawk, probably so that she could dance in the bathing suit. He stuck his mouth into her like the midget had, wondering if she'd push him away, but she let him. He had to suck a long time before he got the cunt taste. She started moaning again and moving up and down until he could almost believe in it. He did that for awhile until she pushed his face gently away. He got up and opened her with two fingers to see how wet she was because he didn't want to hurt her. Not surprisingly, she wasn't very wet. He reached under the bed and got the tube of K-Y jelly. He squirted some in his hand and smeared it inside her.

What's that? she said.

To make you juicy, he said.

When push came to shove, he didn't use a rubber. She felt like a virgin. When he was only halfway in she got very tight and he could see that she was in pain. He did it as slowly and considerately as he could, trying not to put it in too far. It was one of the best he'd ever had. Soon he was going faster and the pleasure was better and better; she was so sweet and clean and young. He stroked her hair and said: Thank you very much.

Thank you, she said dully.

He got up and put on his underwear. Then he turned on the light and brought her some toilet paper.

She was squatting on the floor in pain.

Look, she said.

Blood was coming out of her.

I'm sorry, he said. I'm really sorry.

No problem, she smiled . . .

I'm sorry!

Maybe I call doctor.

He got her some bandages and ointment. She prayed her hands together and said thank you.

He gave her one thousand bhat. She hadn't asked for anything.—Thank you, sir, she smiled.

Enough for doctor?

This for taxi. This for *tuk-tuk.*

He gave her another five hundred and she prayed her hands together again and whispered: Thank you.

He gave her some ointment and she turned away from him and rubbed it inside her. When they finished getting dressed she hugged him very tightly. She turned her face up to let him kiss her if he wanted. He kissed her forehead.

She hugged him again and again. When he'd shown her out to the *tuk-tuk,* she shook his hand.

Well, he said to himself, I certainly deserve to get AIDS.

7

I CAN'T HELP but feel it's wrong, he said.

Well, we're giving 'em money, aren't we? said the photographer very reasonably. How else they gonna eat? That's their job. That's what they do. What's more, we're payin' 'em real well, a lot better than most guys would.

8

WHAT DID THE journalist really want? No one thing, it seemed, would make him happy. He was life's dilettante. Whatever path he chose, he left, because he was lonely for other paths. No excuse, no excuse! When the photographer led him down the long narrow tunnels of Kong Toi (they had to buy mosquito netting for Cambodia), he got bewildered by all the different means and ways, but everyone else seemed to know, whether they were carrying boxes on their shoulders or hunting down cans of condensed milk, dresses, teapots, toys; it was so crowded under the hot archways of girders that people rubbed against each other as they passed, babies crying, people talking low and calm, nothing stopping. How badly had he hurt Oy? He had to see her. Lost, the two vampires wandered among framed portraits of the King, greasy little blood-red sausages, boiled corn, fried packets of green things, oil-roasted nuts that smelled like burned tires, hammerheads without the handles . . . But it was equally true that the vampires felt on top of everything because they were fucking whores in an air conditioned hotel.

9

IN THE BAR after the rain, the girl leaned brightly forward over her rum and coke with a throaty giggle; everyone was watching the gameboard, smoking cigarettes while the TV said: Jesus Christ, where are you? and the girl said to the photographer: Tell me, when you birthday?

She said to the journalist: You smoke cigarette? so he bit down on his straw and pretended to smoke it, to make her laugh . . .

The girls leaned and lounged. The photographer's girl was named Joy. She kept saying: Hi, darling! Hi, darling!—Her friend's name was Pukki.

Come here, darling, said Pukki. What you writing?

I wish I knew. Then I'd know how it would turn out, said the journalist.

He likes to write long letters to his mother, said the photographer.

The girls had brought the photographer a steak. He didn't want the rest of it, so he asked Joy if she wanted to eat it. Pukki cut pieces for her, nice and fat; she screamed teasingly because it was hard to cut.

You buy me out please, Pukki cried to the journalist.

I love Oy, he said. Tonight I buy Oy.

(That's real good, said the photographer admiringly. That's the way to show 'em!)

The journalist got a little loaded and made the bar-checks into paper airplanes and shot them all over the room. Patiently one of the girls gathered them all up so that he was ashamed; she smoothed them and put them back in his cup and he said: You boxing me? and she giggled no. More girls swarmed around, cadging drinks (he bought them whatever they asked for), sliding their arms round him, snuggling their heads on him, stroking his money pouch slyly.

The photographer squeezed Joy's butt and Pukki's tits and all the other girls cried in disgust real or feigned: You butter-fly man!—He bought Joy out, and Pukki screamed at the journalist: *Please* you no buy me out *whaiiiiieee?*

I'm sorry, he said. I promised Oy. I'm really sorry.

He slipped her a hundred bhat and she brightened . . .

10

SO THEY WENT to Oy's bar, the photographer, the journalist and Joy. Toy said: She no work today.

Is she OK? said the journalist. I worry about her. I hurt her pussy. I'm sorry, I'm sorry . . .

She no work today, Toy smiled.

11

THE MANAGER CAME and said: Oy? Which Oy?—Evidently there were so many Oys . . .

The photographer went and looked (he was very good at picking people out), but he couldn't find her.

12

RACING THE UNHAPPY accelerator in stalled traffic, the taxi driver ignored the treeleaves wilted down into balls in the air that smelled like a black fart. The journalist sat up in front with him so that the photographer and Joy could fondle privately. The letters on the bus beside him swirled in white flame. Wet noises came from the back seat. The driver stared from the righthand window, disapproving, envious, appalled, or indifferent.

He say me where you go I say Metro Hotel, Joy announced.

Finally the light changed, the driver shifted gears so that his weird mobile of shells tinkled as the taxi sped past dogs and cornstands. A big canvas-covered truck loomed in the darkness. The driver looked ahead when they stopped again; his lips were wide and rounded. Raindrops shone like dust on the other cars' windshields. A foreigner made chewing motions in back of a *tuk-tuk* and then he was gone forever as the taxi driver made a roundabout and rushed between twisted pillars, honking his horn in the fog. He took them down secret-arrowed alleyways to the hotel . . .

13

ALL NIGHT THE TV went aah! and oi! to dubbed movies while the prostitute lay wide-eyed in the photographer's bed, bored and lonely, snuggling her sleeping mealticket while the journalist, unable to sleep on account of the TV and therefore likewise bored and lonely, could not ask her to come even though the photographer had offered because he didn't feel right about it the way she snuggled the photographer so affectionately (when he got to know her better he'd understand that she wouldn't have come anyway) and besides he was worried about the growing tenderness in his balls. He jerked off silently to Joy; it didn't hurt yet, just felt funny, so he could still pretend that it was nothing; as soon as he was done he wanted to get inside Joy as much as before, and then he had to piss again; that was a bad sign; as soon as he pissed he felt the need to piss again.

14

IN HIS SLEEP he listened, and every time he heard the rustle of her in the sheets he woke up with his penis as hard as a rock, aching. It was a little before six. His desire seeped like the tropical light coming slowly in, first illuminating the white valleys in the curtains, next the white barred reflections of the curtains in the mirror, then the white sheets, his white sheets, her white sheets folded back down over her shoulders, the black oval of her head on the white pillow (could he see her fingers on the sheet?) Now the outline of the grating grew behind the window, now a white belly of light on the ceiling, the white upper walls, black wainscotting, the white closet shelf's black clothes. Her silhouette was sharpening; he began to see the shape of her hair, his socks and underpants hanging to dry on the curtains. He could see the outlines of leaves through the grating. Now the wall-blacks weren't quite black anymore. The frame of the TV had differentiated itself from the screen. The bathroom door detached itself from the wall-mass. Clothes and luggage were born on the tables. He could see her shoulder now separating from the sheet, the white bra-straps leaping out; her head was turned away, toward the photographer; he could see her neck, ear and cheek begin to exist as separate entities from her hair. He could see the border of paleness around the edge of her blanket. He could see her breathe.

15

THE WHITE HAZY morning air was humid with the smell of fresh Brussels sprouts, not yet too thickened by exhaust. Little piebald dogs yapped on the sidewalk. Two policemen motorcycled by. The *tuk-tuks* were mainly empty, the buses only half full.

The sun was a red ball over the canal whose violet-grey fog had not begun to stink much; a motorboat wended feebly down the middle of its brown water, which was thick like spit, and spotted with oil, trash, leaves; the boat vanished in the fog below the bridge long before its sound was lost, and birds uttered single notes from the vastly spread out-trees that resembled the heads of broccoli; aluminum-roofed shacks, siding and boards walled the canal as it dwindled past piers and banana trees; beneath an awning a little brown boy squatted and shat while his mother dressed; a long tunnel of boards and siding ran along the canal, and in it people were going about their business; a brown dog and a white dog bit their fleas; a man in a checkered sarong dipped water from a barrel; a baby cried; a boy was washing his clothes. The dogs left wet prints on the sidewalk. The sun was whiter, higher and hotter now. The air began to smell more acrid. Another motorboat came, very quickly, leaving a wake; other boats started up. The man who'd been in the sarong came out of his shack, putting his wet shirt on. He walked barefooted. Other men got into their boats. This morning run of business reminded him of the evenings at Joy's bar when the girls gathered gradually.

16

AT BREAKFAST THE photographer sat on pillows, a sweet brown arm sleeping around his waist. Eighty percent of the Pat Pong girls had tested positive for AIDS that fall. Probably she'd be dead in five years.

17

SHE WATCHED THE TV's cartoons as wide-eyed as before. Coffee was all she ordered from room service, giggling rapt with head on chin, while in the hotel's humid halls the maids in blue stood folding towels and talking, leaning elbows on the desk, and the *tuk-tuks* went by and the clothes dried from windows across the courtyard, barely moving, and rainwater dried on the tiles while one of the hotel's men in red livery went out to smoke and scratch his belly, and across the courtyard a brown man naked to the waist flickered past a window of shadow.

The journalist's balls glowed faintly. The soles of his feet stuck itchily to his rubber sandals.

Suddenly the sun came on like a dimmer knob turned rapidly up to maximum, and it began to get hot.

18

WHEN JOY LEFT, she was dressed conservatively, smiled blandly; she shook each of their hands. Did she become that way in the morning, after the photographer fucked her up the ass, and she saw that he was like the others? (The photographer told him that she'd pointed to her vagina and said: Here OK condom OK and then to her anus and said: Here OK no condom OK.) Or was her affection just an act? Or was this public demeanor of hers an act? The journalist's heart sank. He'd never know.

19

AND WHAT'S *THIS* injection? he asked.

The doctor's glasses glinted.—Pure caffeine, he said enthusiastically.

If I wear a rubber from now on so that I don't infect the other girls, can I keep having sex, starting today?

I think it would not be good for you, said the doctor. You see, the disease has already migrated far into the spermatic cord . . .

20

RECEIPT NO. 03125 (two soda waters, 60 bhat) was already in the cup, and fever-sweat from the clap ran down his face. At the bar, the two girls watched King Kong, plump-cheeked, wide-eyed, almost unblinking. (Joy wasn't there yet; probably she was still sleeping in some other place of narrow alleys . . .) A girl in a blindingly white T-shirt came in, and then another. They leaned on the bar on that hot afternoon, talking, while the spots of disco-light began to move and the fan bulged round and round like a roving eye. No-see-ums bit his feet between the sandal straps, so he put some mosquito repellent on; business stopped as all the girls watched. The two plump-cheeked girls looked catty-corner at opposing TVs as King Kong roared; then, when it was only helicopters again, they went back to the click-

click-click of red and yellow counters, thinking hard as the pattern built up, six by six, click by click; in their concentration they lowered their noses almost against the wall of that gameboard, hair long, cheeks smoother than golden nectarines, so young, so perfect; perhaps it was just to a coarse-pored Caucasian that they appeared perfect. Click, click. Soon the meaningless game would be finished (meaningless since they weren't betting ten bhat against each other as they did when they played the journalist; he always lost), and then one woman would pull the release and the plastic counters would clatter into the tray below with a sound like gumballs. Then they'd start again, smoothing back their hair, reaching, showing hand-flesh through the holes.

The journalist was working, and the girls sometimes gathered around to watch him write. Lifting his head from the bar, the photographer explained to them: My friend likes to write long letters to his balls.

In Oy's bar the Western video was repeating and dinner had closed because it was six-o'-clock now, Oy's hour to come to work as the photographer had kindly ascertained; and paunchy white guys grinned. The staff was getting ready for dancetime. Someone was chopping ice, and a girl in a beige miniskirt sat spread-legged by the register where the glasses were, scratching a mosquito bite on her thigh, and the great green ceiling grid was activated; then the blue fluorescents came on, then the yellow and green spotlights at angles, then the multifaceted ball, and a girl with a lovely face like all the others (who seemed increasingly ghostly) smiled encouragingly at the journalist and drew her arm grandly down as if to yank the ripcord of a parachute and went into the Ladies'.

The journalist's teeth chattered with fever.—Man, I hope you make it, said the photographer, and there was love and worry in his voice.

I'm all right, the journalist said. Do you see Oy around?

You wait here. I'll ask around.

Well, he said after a moment, they say she'll be in at seven or seven-thirty. You want to wait?

Sure.

At seven, Toy came. She said hi, smiling; she said no Oy today. She smelled like perfumed excrement. There was something so sincere about her that the journalist almost said to hell with it and asked her, but she would only have said no. He wrote her a note for Oy, showing her each of the note's words in the English-Thai dictionary: *Oy—I worry you blood that night. Are you OK?*

Will Oy come today? he asked her again, just to be sure.

Toy patted his arm.—Not today.

You come hotel me, Toy?

No, sir.

You my friend?

OK friend OK.

Oy is sick?

Oy no today.

Then Oy came, smiling. Toy went off to dance.

He bought out Oy, saying: I just take you back. Just sleep watch TV no fucking just sleep you know OK?

OK, laughed Oy.

She seemed in perfect health. That annoyed him after all his anxiety. Oy? he said. Oy? I'm *sick* from you. From your pussy.

Oy hung her head smiling . . .

The photographer went back to the other bar to buy Joy, and the four of them walked down the hot narrow alley, the two boys in faded clothes a little dirty, the two girls in fancy evening wear; what a treat!—Oy went to a store to buy condoms (and it never occurred to him until much much later that she might have been doing it for him); he said no need and she was happy. They got a taxi to the hotel. Joy rode in front with the driver. Oy pressed against him. He held her hand, gave her leg a feel; her dress was drenched with sweat.—You hot? he said.—She nodded; she'd always nod no matter what he said.

How long have you worked in Pat Pong? he said.

Six month.

How long has Toy worked there?

Ten month.

(Toy had told him that she'd worked there for six months.)

The photographer grinned.—So, how do you know she worked there for ten months if you only worked there for six months?

Oy blushed and ducked her guilty head.

He led Oy into the hotel while the photographer paid off the driver.

The journalist went grandly up to the desk.—Two-ten, please.

All the Thais in the lobby watched silently. Oy hung back, ashamed. They began talking about her. She raised her head then and followed her owner up the stairs, into the humid heat and mildew smell . . . At the first landing, when she could no longer be seen, she took his hand and snuggled passionately against him . . .

He told her again that she'd gotten him sick, but that it was OK.

I go doctor; doctor me in here! she giggled, pointing to her butt. Later, when he'd gotten her naked, he saw the giant bandage where she'd had some intramuscular injection. It did not give him confidence that while her disease must be the same as his her treatment had been different.—Best not to think about it.

The photographer came in.—Same room? said Joy on his arm.

It's OK, the journalist told her. No sex. Don't worry.

That was truly his plan—just to lie there in the darkness with Oy, snuggling and watching Thai TV while the photographer and Joy did the same. Needless to say, once the photographer took a shower and came out wearing only a towel and cracking jokes about his dick, the journalist could see how it would actually be. He took his shower . . .

The photographer laughed.—You should really get back in the shower, he said. You finished, man?

The journalist just nodded. He was feeling dizzy. He wandered out with his shirt around his waist; the girls laughed; Joy shook her head saying *you baah* which means you crazy and he hopped into bed sopping wet. Obedient Oy snuggled up to him in her fancy clothes . . .

You take shower, he said to her.

Finally she did, wearing the other towel. The light was still on. Every time anyone flushed the toilet the floor always flooded; he could see the comforting sparkle of that water on the bathroom tiles . . . She crawled in, snuggling him, and he slid a hand between her legs and was happy to feel her narrow little bush.

I go ten-o'-clock, she said. Toy birthday party. Toy my sister.

Whatever you say.

He lay sucking her tits while she held him. She let him kiss her a little but she didn't like it. Her body was slender, her nips just right. Her face looked rounder and older tonight; her voice was hoarser. She kept coughing. After awhile she started playing with his penis, probably to get it over with. He had an erection, but no desire to use it; his grapefruit-swollen balls seemed to be cut off from the rest of his body. He still didn't plan to do it, but when he got up to go to the bathroom with just the shirt around him, the two whores sitting eating room service (the bellboy had carefully looked away when he brought it into the half-darkened room, the photographer and the journalist lounging like lords with their half-naked girls beside them), the head of his dick hung down below the shirt and they started laughing and then he started getting wild like the class clown. First he began tickling Oy. Then he started lifting her around, and pulling the covers down to show her off naked; she laughed (probably thinks you're a real pest! said the photographer, shaking his head); she kept rubbing against him to make him do something, and then she'd look at the clock . . .

Eventually she rubbed against him in just the right way, and then he knew he'd have to do it. What a chore! But life isn't always a bed of guacamole. He squeezed K-Y into her cunt, handed her the rubber, and then she said she didn't know how to put it on . . . Wasn't that SOMETHING? She tried sincerely, but she just didn't understand it. He did it and then thrust into her. She pretended to come and he pretended to come; he didn't care. In the carpet of light from the half-open bathroom door the other two were doing it in the far bed; Oy lay watching the photographer pedaling slowly like a cyclo driver high between three wheels, and she clapped her hand to her mouth and snickered softly; meanwhile Joy suddenly noticed that Oy was on top of the journalist and rolled off her trick and went into the bathroom and turned the shower on loud for a long time.

He really enjoyed playing with her body, lying there relaxed and feverish, doing whatever he wanted while the TV went ai-ai—if he felt like sticking a finger up her he'd just grease it and pop it in!—*I have the clap!* he announced to himself, and he felt that he'd won some major award. Lightheaded and distant, he enjoyed snuggling up to her and smelling her, sucking her shaved armpits, pursuing with kisses her face which sought to evade him; every now and then he'd catch her and kiss her lips and she'd laugh. Whenever he'd touch her between her legs she'd start going um um and begin swinging her hips as if in ecstasy, but her cunt stayed dry and her face didn't change and her heart didn't pulse at all faster beneath his other hand. . . . He lounged, played, stroked in a delightful fog of disease like the foggy sprawl of Bangkok he'd be leaving in four hours, soaring east over big grey squares of water going into greyness, riding the hot orange sky. At the moment it was still dark. She tried to get him off again and he let her play with his useless and meaningless erection; later he lifted her onto his neck and ran around the room in his underpants with her on his shoulders clinging and laughing in fun or terror while the photographer and his whore laughed themselves sick . . .

He kept saying: Oy, you want go Kambuja?

No want! No want! Kambuja people is bad people! Thai people like this (she prayed); Kambuja people like *this!* (she saluted fiercely). The journalist saluted her in return, and she cowered back . . .

21

OY WAS FEELING fine from her injection.—But what if she wasn't? What if she'd been in terrible pain that first time and then the other time; what if she'd just done it for the money to pay the doctor or for rent?

22

JOY STAYED WITH the photographer until the last minute, of course. Joy had class. The photographer had class. The whole time he was in Thailand, the journalist (poor slob) could never get any but short time girls . . .

23

GREY-GREEN AND beige squares like a flaking dartboard showing its cork beneath; these and the other squares of grey water absorbed the plane's shadow as it sped through the morning, cooled patches of trees and rectangles of various greens and greys all shining wet . . .

Cambodia seemed a no-nonsense country. There was a line of soldiers on the runway, each soldier directing the photographer and the journalist on to the next.

24

HE WENT INTO the hotel lobby and took a few stacks of riels out of the paper bag.—Help yourself to some money, he said to the concierge . . . and shot past the big traffic island with the monument to independence from the French. He was hot, weak and dizzy. Thanks to the caffeine injection, he hadn't slept for two nights. In the wide listless courtyard and porticoes of the Ministry of Foreign Affairs, which seemed almost empty like the rest of Phnom Penh (how many people had been killed off?), he and the photographer sat playing with their press passes, waiting for their fate to be decided.—*In our country, at the moment, the militia plays more of a role than the army,* an official explained, and the journalist wrote it down carefully while the photographer yawned.—A tiled roof was flaking off in squares of pink like weird rust or lichens. The afternoon smelled like sandalwood. An official led them into one of the rambling yellow buildings and told them to come back tomorrow. They took a cyclo back to the hotel, and the photographer went outside to snap some land mine beggars while the journalist lay down on the bed to rest. As soon as he rolled over on his stomach, something seemed to move in his balls, weighing them down with a painless but extremely unpleasant tenderness, as if they were rotting and liquefying inside and slowly oozing down to the bottom of his scrotum. Thinking this, he had to laugh.

It was evening now, just before curfew. The boys were shooting cap guns and everyone was cheering. A boy in sandals, a dark blue shirt and a dark blue Chinese cap peddled a cyclo slowly down the street. The photographer brought some takeout from the French restaurant across the street—steak and fries. The journalist appreciated it very much.

25

THE MORNING SKY was a delicate grey, cats stalking along the terraces, ladies puttering among potted plants, the rows of cool doors all open in the four- and five-storey apartment blocks, rows of x-shaped vents atop each square of territory, gratings on the windows. The journalist lay in bed, clutching his distended balls. It was warming up nicely. His underpants steamed against his ass. The hotel maid came in and cleaned. She made seven thousand riels a month. The

Khmer Rouge had killed her father, grandfather, sister, and two brothers. She'd worked hard for the Khmer Rouge in the fields . . .

26

A CLOUD BLEW over the street. Papers started to swirl. The vendors ran to cover their stands. Suddenly came a hiss of rain. A militiaman dashed. The almost naked children danced laughing. Potted plants shook on the terraces. Now as the rain slanted down in earnest, people braced themselves between the almost shut gratings, watching. A cyclo driver pedaled on; his two lady passengers held red umbrellas over themselves. Power wires trembled; the rain shivered in heavy white rivers. A boy prayed barefoot to Buddha in the street, then clasped his hands and danced, water roaring from his soaked shirt. A clap of thunder, then rain fell like smoke; rain spewed from the roof-gutters . . .

27

THE ENGLISH TEACHER wrote *sixteen* in standard and phonetic orthography on the blackboard while the children wrote *sixteen* in their notebooks, and the English teacher got ready to write *seventeen* but then the power went out and they sat in the darkness.

Your English is very good, said the journalist.

Yes, the teacher said.

Where did you learn it?

Yes.

What is your name?

Yes. No. Twenty-two.

Well, that's *real* good, said the photographer brightly. That's *real* nice. Do you know what the word pussy means?

28

STEAMY-FRESH, THE sandalwood night neared curfew while water trickled down from the balconies and orphans sat down on bedframes on the sidewalk, huddled over rice. The grilles were drawn almost closed now. Only one was open. A lady stood with her child in yellow light, guarding rows of blue bicycles whose wheelskins caught a glow of gold. On the sidewalk, boys were carving a deer. Its head hung from a hook. The rest, now flensed to a snakelike strip of steak, red and white ribs, danced as their knives stripped it down. The journalist went to watch, and everyone crowded to watch him, crying: *Number one!*—He hadn't picked up any whores yet; they still liked him.—Another long strip peeled off—scarcely anything but bone now. A boy with muscled brown arms held the swaying backbone like a sweetheart; another fanged the cleaverblade down. Skinny-necked like a bird, the carcass tried to flail against a grating, but the strong boy wouldn't let it.

29

HOW HAPPY HE was when on the third day of the antibiotics something popped like popcorn in his balls and he started feeling better! The tenderness was now in his lymph nodes, but it would surely go away from there, too—

To celebrate, he showed all the hotel maids his press pass.— You very handsome, they said—

30

THEY HAD AN engagement with the English teacher who couldn't speak English. The small children were silhouetted in the dark, singing *A, B, C, D, E, F, G* . . . On the blackboard it said THE English ALPHABET. The teacher pointed at this, and the children said: *Da iii-eee aa-phabet.*

Why does the alphabet only go up to S? asked the journalist.

Yes, the teacher replied.

The journalist pointed to a photograph that concentrated darkness like an icon.—My father is die by Pol Pot regime, said the teacher simply. He go to Angkor Wat to hide Buddha. They die him by slow pain . . .

For a moment the journalist wanted to embrace him. Instead he stared down at the floor, and the sweat dripped from his nose and forehead. As soon as he wiped his face it was wet again.

The English teacher and his friend took the journalist and the photographer to someone's house. The room was dark. Someone lit a candle and connected a gasoline generator outside. Then the lights flickered on. The wall-gratings looked out on darkness. The journalist sat in a corner consuming cool tea and cakes; the photographer sweated wearily. It was very hot. After a few minutes they thanked their hosts and went to dinner.

They sat at an outside table on the rainy streets, while everyone watched them from underneath lighted canopies or leaning against trees; the rain gleamed on bike lights. There was a pot of cold tea on the table. One-legged beggars kept approaching, some in soldiers' uniforms; the journalist gave each one a hundred riels because he and the photographer still had plenty of money. The English teacher ordered Chinese noodle soup with organ meats and peppers. Then they went for a walk. The English teacher's friend suggested a movie, which proved not to be a Chinese story about angry ghosts as the poster had suggested but a dubbed American thing; lizards crawled up and down the cement walls, and it was sweltering. After five minutes the journalist was ready to go. After ten minutes he slid out of his seat and walked down the dark stairs, knowing that the English teacher and his friend would be hurt, feeling guilty, but only a little; after all, he'd bought them dinner. At least the photographer wouldn't care.

The night was lovely at curfew time, the rain just barely condensing out of the hot black sky like drops of sweat, motorbikes purring with considerable deliberation down the street. A woman pedaled slowly in the rain. It was very nice to see how her wet blue skirt stuck to her thighs. He passed the new market and saw a disco's dark doorway evilly serendipitous; I'll have to tell the photographer about that, he thought. (He didn't go in. The gaggle of taxi girls and motorbike drivers sitting hands on thighs, or looking sweetly, palely, over their shoulders, daunted him like pack-ice black and grey and all in a blue of mystery.) Every little chessboard-floored restaurant had become a movie theater of chairs packed with mothers and children raptly watching a TV screen placed high in the corner; two naked children, brother and sister, sat on the sidewalk staring in through a grating; every cell in the honeycomb was a cutaway world made expressly for the journalist to stare into and long to be taken into, just as the TV screens were for everyone else. Crossing a pitchdark street he dodged cyclos and bicycles (all headlightless, almost silent). No one paid much attention to the curfew anymore; even so, as the hour shrank, more and more steel accordion-diamonds stretched taut to meet and lock everything into darkness. Girls leaned out of their terraces; doors opened to show darkness or brightly turning fans. The girls put both hands on the railings and leaned, their watch-dials white like fire; they gossiped across at each other, enjoyed the hot night's raindrops, watched the street where a boy crossed with long slow steps, the scrape of his sandals a continuous sound, his blue shirt glowing like a night aquarium. Lizards waited head down on hotel walls. The girls looked at the journalist and waved; he waved back. A black dog scuttered across the street like a moving hole.

31

IN THE HOTEL there were paintings of bare-breasted girls in butterflywinged skirts standing waist-deep in the mist before science fiction palaces. The night was so hot that his face felt as if it had peered into a steaming kettle. He went into the room, turned the air conditioning on (he and the photographer, being boys of high morals, always travelled first class), and took a shower. He was standing naked in the cool water when the photographer came in with two whores.

32

THEY WERE FROM that same disco he'd passed, as he soon learned (the photographer's soul always gushed when he'd made a novel score).—I was gonna take the tall one because I kept thinking how it would be, you know, with her legs around me, but as soon as we got into the street the short one took my hand, so that's that.—I guess it is, replied the photographer, towelling himself off while the girls screamed and looked away.—They went through all his pills and medicines first, sniffing the packets, going *nnnihh!*, giggling at the condoms, whispering and pointing like schoolgirls. The photographer's girl was already in the shower and out, halfway demure in her towel. The journalist's girl stayed dressed. She did not seem to like him very much, but then that didn't seem unusual to him because girls never liked him; was it his fat legs or his flabby soul? Fortunately this was an issue he'd never be called on to write a newsicle about.—Look at 'em! shouted the photographer. They're as curious as fucking *monkeys*, man!—With great effort they mouthed the Khmer words in the dictionary section of his guidebook; they opened the box of sugar cubes, which were swarming with ants, and ate one apiece. The journalists's girl had a beauty spot over one eye. When she opened and closed everything, her eyebrows slanted in elegant surprise. She wore a striped dark dress. There was something very ladylike about her. She intimidated him slightly. He lay sweatily on the bed watching them; when they'd completed their inspection they neatened everything up like good housewives; so that it

took the journalist and the photographer days to find their pos-
sessions. Such *well-meaning* young women, though . . . They
stared with satisfaction into the mirror, the photographer's girl
tilting the purple tube of lipstick and drawing it along her lower
lip like a gentle loving penis while her earrings and necklace
shone gold, her hair spilling black and pure black like squid's
ink. Suddenly she turned toward the photographer, her nose's
beauty spot spying on him, something shiny and watchful in her
eyes and tea-colored face in the darkness as she made her hair
into braids for him, smoothing the electric blue dress down
over her tits; but the journalist's girl never looked away from the
mirror; she smiled into it or she leaned her nose against it so as
not to have to look at anything else; only the gold glitter around
her dark breasts like drops of light in the humid darkness of the
hotel room, her face level or low, maybe satisfied after all; or
maybe the smile was only some resigned grimace.

33

THE PHOTOGRAPHER'S GIRL got ready right away. But after
half an hour the journalist's girl was still silent in the bathroom
with the door closed. She stood staring at the back of her little mirror, which had a decal of a man and woman together . . .

34

HE COMMUNICATED WITH her mainly by signs. She liked to
smell his cheeks and forehead in little snorts of breath, but not
to kiss him; whenever he tried, she'd whirl her head away into
the pillow, so he started Buddha-ing her in just the same way
that Oy had steepled her hands very quickly together for good
luck when he'd bought her out, she probably hoping he
wouldn't see, probably praying that he'd give her a lot of
money; so he did this to the Cambodian girl; he'd seen the

beggars do it; he'd do it to say please, then he'd touch his fore-finger from his lips to hers—and she'd Buddha him back to say please no. Sometimes he did it anyway, and she'd jerk her head away, or let him do it only on her closed lips. Then sometimes he'd steeple his hands please and point from his lips to her cunt, and she'd wave her hand no, so he wouldn't do that; he'd pray to kiss her again, and she'd pray him no; so he'd pray and point from his crotch to hers and she'd nod yes.

35

HE SMILED AT her as affectionately as he could. He wanted her to like him. It just made things easier when the whore you were on top of liked you.—No, that's how the photographer would have put it, but the journalist had a deeper thrust (if you know what I mean). The truth was, he really did like her. He traced a heart on her breast with his finger and smiled, but she looked back at him very seriously. Then suddenly she ran her fingernail lightly round his wrist and pointed to herself.— What did she mean? So many prostitutes seemed to wear religious strings for bracelets; was that what she meant? Somehow he didn't think so . . .

36

GIVE 'EM MORE Benadryl; come on, give 'em more Benadryl, the journalist whined as the photographer's girl turned on the light giggling for the fourth or fifth time that night; he didn't know exactly what the hour was, since his watch had been stolen in Thailand, possibly by Oy . . . The photographer's girl loved to watch the journalist making love. Even when the photographer was screwing her she'd always be looking avidly into the other bed, hoping to see the journalist's buttocks pumping under the sheet; whenever she could she'd sneak up and pull the sheet away to see the journalist naked with a naked girl; then she'd shriek with glee. It was very funny but it got a little less funny each time.—Fortunately they obediently swallowed whatever pills the journalist gave them; the photographer told them that the journalist was a doctor and the journalist neither confirmed nor denied this report, which most likely they didn't understand anyway. So he gave them Benadryl; one for his girl, three for the other, who was hyperkinetic. Even so they both kept turning the lights on to see what time it was; they wanted to leave by the end of curfew.—The journalist's girl lay against him, her cool weightless fingers resting on his chest. Her face smelled sweetish like hair-grease. In the morning she pulled a towel about herself and slid into her gold and purple dress. Then she sat in a chair, far from the bed, making up her lips, using her eyebrow pencil, occasionally uttering brief replies to the other girl's babble. The other girl had a voice like a lisping little child. The girl in the chair ran the lipstick very slowly over the outside of her lower lip. She saw the journalist looking at her and smiled guardedly, then raised the pocket mirror again. She smoothed her hair away from her cheeks and began to apply more of the sickly-sweet cream.

37

ONCE THEY'D LEFT, he told the photographer he didn't want to see her again. Why, she hadn't wanted to do *anything!*—and she'd seemed so sorrowful he'd felt like a rapist. What did she expect anyway?—But as soon as he'd conveyed these well-reasoned sentiments, his heart started to ache. He didn't tell the photographer, of course. They rarely talked about those things. But he remembered how she'd hung his trousers neatly over the chair, how she'd ordered his money in neat piles without stealing any, how before leaving she'd taken each of his fingers and pulled it until it made a cracking noise, then bent it back; this was her way of pleasing him, taking care of him.

38

AT THE DISCO that night he didn't see her. He sat and waited while the crowd stridulated. Finally her friend, the photographer's girl, came to the table. She was slick with sweat; she must have been dancing. He asked the English teacher who didn't speak English to ask her where his girl was. The man said: She don't come here today.—Already they were bringing him another girl. He said not right now, thank you. He tried to find out more, and then there was another girl sitting down by him and he figured he had to buy her a drink so she wouldn't be hurt, and the photographer's girl was biting her lip and stamping her foot, and then his girl came and stood looking on at him and the other girl silently.

39

HE POINTED TO his girl and traced the usual imaginary bracelet around his wrist. (He didn't even know his girl's name. He'd asked the photographer's girl and she said something that sounded like *Pala*. He'd tried calling her Pala and she looked at him without recognition.) Finally the other girl got up, carrying her drink, and began to trudge away. He patted her shoulder to let her know that he was sorry, but that seemed to be the wrong thing to do, too. His girl sat down in her place, and he could feel her anger, steady and flame-white in the darkness, almost impersonal.

40

BUT THAT NIGHT when he put his closed lips gently on her closed lips, not trying to do anything more because he knew how much Thai and Cambodian women hated kissing, her mouth slowly opened and the tip of her tongue came out.

41

YOU GOT HER to french you? laughed the photographer, as the two chauvinists lay at ease, discussing their conquests.—Oh, *good!* She must have been *really* repulsed.

42

SLIDING PILES OF fish empyred the dock, bleeding mouths where heads used to be, heads white and goggle-eyed and wheel-gilled at their new red termini like the undersides of menstruating mushrooms. The heads went into a big aluminum bowl; then the squatting girl with bloody hands and feet started picking through yellow tripe-piles, getting the yellow snakes inside; the dock was red with blood.—Another pile (smooth skinny silver fish) still flapped; the flies were crawling on them before they were even dead.

The rickety boards, which bent underfoot, were laid over a framework of wet knobby peeled sticks. Big fish and small fish flashed in the water-spaces. They were from Siem Reap. The fishers had been feeding them corn for four months. If all went well, they'd make more than a hundred million riels' profit. A big basket of live fish gaped up as sweetly as angels, winged with gills, their lips mumbling a last few water-breaths as their eyes dulled. They stopped shining. The flies were thick on them like clusters of black grapes.

A man tied two live fishes together through the gills with withes. Then he lifted them away.

Boys in dirty white shirts and pants scuttled on the planks. Then they leaped into the water. They began to draw in their nets. A gorgeous leopard-butterfly crowned them.—Why do butterflies love blood? the journalist wondered. The beauty of the butterfly seemed a sort of revenge that left him uncomprehendingly incredulous.

The glistening brown boys came up from the brown water,

squatting on the frames. Fish splashed in the nets. The boys raised the nets a little more. The splashing was loud and furious now; it was impossible not to get wet. The fish were fighting for their lives. The boys began their work. They grabbed each fish by the tail. If it was still too small they threw it back. That didn't happen often. Usually they whacked it on top of the skull with a fat stick. Then they beat its head against a beam until it was still, and blood came out of its mouth.

The butterfly had settled in a drop of blood, and was drinking.

A man with a notebook wrote numbers. He had a stack of money in his shirt pocket. Another man stood by pressing buttons on his calculator. It was like the Stock Exchange.

Dead fish were in a big basket. Two men slid a pole through, and lifted the pole onto their shoulders, carrying it away down the long wagging double planks onto the land, past the photographer who stood scowling like an evil dream, past the sweating journalist, past the people scraping earth into broad half-shell baskets which they dumped up onto the levee so that the pickman could work and tamped it down. (Everyone was worried about flooding.) The two men walked on and finally set the basket down in the back of a truck.

In the square wood-walled cells of water, the boys raised their nets until fins broke water. The squatting girl was already chopping off the heads of the other fish with a big cleaver. Her toes were scarlet with blood.

The disco was stifling hot, and everybody mopped his face with the chemical towelette that the hostess brought. Waves of stupid light rusted across the walls.

You happy? he asked the English teacher who couldn't speak English.

Good! the other replied. I'm berry excited . . .

It was long and low in there with occasional light bulbs. Girls said aaah and oooh and aieee while the crowd swarmed slowly and sweatily. Semen-colored light flickered on men's blue-white shirts and women's baggy silk pajama-pants or dresses; the accustomed smell of a cheap barbershop choked him like the weary

Christmas lights. The barmaid brought a tall can of Tiger beer. Hands clutched all around, as if in some drunken dream—

44

SHE ALMOST NEVER smiled. Once again that night she traced an invisible bracelet around her wrist, then his. He watched her sleeping. In the middle of the night he pulled her on top of him just to hug her more tightly, and she seemed no heavier than the blanket.

45

SHE LAY HARDLY breathing. He could barely hear her heartbeat. Her hands lay folded between her breasts. Her nipples were very long, brown and thin.

46

IN THE MORNING she cracked his finger-joints and toe-joints for him; she stretched and twisted his arms and legs; she slapped him gently all over. Then she made her rendezvous with the mirror, where she stood painting her eyebrows in slow silence. When she was finished he sat her down with his guidebook, which contained a few dictionary pages. He pointed to all the different words for food, pointed to her and then to him. She just sat there. He made motions to indicate the two of them going off together. She followed soundlessly. He locked the door. She came downstairs with him, into the lobby's ocean of staring faces which surely judged him; he could not smile as usual, and the faces watched him in silence. They hadn't even traversed the lobby yet. The faces watched and waited. She was behind him on the stairs, creeping slowly down. He dropped the key onto the front desk and she was far behind him. He let her catch up to him a little, not too much because she might not want that, and went out, into the street that was filled with even more eyes that watched, and she was farther behind than before. He looked back to make sure that she was there. It must be difficult for her to be seen next him. So he went half a block to an outdoor restaurant and sat down. They brought him tea and bread. She had not come; she was gone. He drank a few sips of his tea, paid, and walked wearily back. He said to the cigarette vendeuse: You see my friend?

Market. That way, she said.

You tell her, please, if she go to hotel, she come in.

No, no. You go market. She that way.

He did, but of course he never found her.

47

HE FELT MISERABLE all day. He didn't want to fuck her anymore, only to straighten things out. He'd find someone to speak English to her . . .

Again and again he circled the market's yellow-tiered cement dome. The traffic was slow enough to let jaywalkers stand in the street. He loitered among the umbrellas and striped awnings, under each a vendor's booth or table; and sometimes they tried to sell him things; moneychangers studied him behind their jagged walls of cigarette cartons; but there was only one vendeuse he wanted, and what she had, it seemed, he couldn't ever buy.

The photographer's girl, on the other hand, had stayed. The photographer was getting sick of her. He told her that he and the journalist would have to go to work soon; he pointed to her and then to the door, but the girl tried desperately not to understand. In the middle of the morning she was still there. She wanted him to buy her a gold bracelet. They were out on the street, the three of them, and the photographer said to the journalist: All right. We'll each grab a cyclo and split.

Where to?

Where *to?* cried the photographer in amazement. *Anywhere!* Just as long as we get rid of this bitch . . . Oh, shit, she's getting a cyclo, too!

Finally they went home with her. She took them down a very dark narrow dirt lane, then right into an alley, then up a steep plank ladder two inches wide to a dormitory that smelled like wood-smoke and was rowed with tiny square windows for light and air. It was very humid. Puddles on the floor darkly reflected the ceiling's patchy plaster. Mosquitoes and fleas bit the journalist's feet. The room was filled with beds enclosed by patterned sheets hung from strings like laundry; sturdy beds, neatly made up. People lay one or two to a bed, very quiet, some sleeping, some not. The photographer's girl said that she paid ten thousand riels a year to stay there. She lived with her aunt, in a bed against the wall.

She pulled the photographer down on top of her, tried to get him to marry her—with a gold chain—

How many times has she been married? asked the journalist.

The aunt smiled and fanned him.—Five times.

He heard the sound of a thudding mallet, saw the shadow of a woman's bare legs, darkening the nearest puddle on the dirty-grey cement. The photographer lay listless and disgusted on the bed, his girl on top of him whining, working him slowly but determinedly like a cyclo driver polishing his wheels. The journalist felt sorry for her.

Now they brought another girl for the journalist to marry in the dimness; she'd gone through it three or four times at least from the look of *her* gold chains; she took over the task of fanning him, smiling so wide-eyed that the journalist began to feel sorry for her, too; he already had a girl.—Pala, Pala! he said.— The photographer's girl knew what he meant, and she gnashed her teeth. This rejected matrimonial prospect turned away and put on a new bra, kneeling on her pallet two feet away. The disks of her gold necklace gleamed consecutively when she turned her head, like the bulbs of a neon sign. While she was away the aunt resumed fanning him. Her teeth were perfectly white except for one of gold. She wore a ruby ring from Pailin. Her plump face looked forty-five; she was thirty-five.

I can't stand this anymore, the photographer said. Let's get out of here.

They'll want us to take them out to lunch.

So we'll take 'em out to lunch. Then we'll dump 'em.

The aunt didn't come. So it was only the photographer and his girl and the journalist with two new ladies, each hoping and vying, who went to the nearest sidewalk restaurant. He was a little afraid of one of them, a very pale girl with a Chinese-porcelain face (was she albino, or sick, or just heavily powdered? The longer he looked at her, the more corpselike she seemed . . .); she, noticing how he studied her most frequently, said something in a smug undertone to her rival, who then withdrew her solicitudes. The Chinese-porcelain girl kept lowering her head and smiling, fingering her strings of gold, while the other girl, still hopeful to a small degree, gazed lovingly from time to time into the journalist's eyes. Crowds lined up behind everyone's chairs, staring unhappily. By and large, they did not seem to admire whores or foreigners who whored. But of course there wasn't a damned thing they could do about it, thought the journalist as the Chinese-porcelain girl peeled him the local equivalent of a grape, which had a green rind, an inner sweet grey substance the texture and shape of an eyeball, and then a round seed—did it taste more like a grape or a cantaloupe? Being a journalist, he really ought to decide the issue once and for all—oh, GOOD, he'd have another chance (she'd hardly touched her soup; she looked very very sick; quite suddenly he was sure that she was going to drop dead any minute) . . . She called the fruit *mayen*.

48

SO AFTER LUNCH they dropped the girls, and the girls were very disappointed.

49

THE PHOTOGRAPHER HAD to go back to the hotel to get more ointment for his rash, which had spread from one arm to the other and itched practically as bad as scabies or crabs (which the well travelled photographer had already experienced; of course he'd never had *** GONORRHEA *** so the journalist was one up on him there). The journalist sat waiting for him in an open square of grass riddled with wide walkways and rectangular puddles between which children ran. On the far side (this park was quite large), two-storey houses whose roofs were truncated pyramids strutted stained balconies. Between the roots of a tree, a boy was digging with a stick.

The journalist thought about the gold chain that his prostitute wore about her naked waist. He wondered who'd given it to her, and whether the man had loved her in his heart or whether he'd just paid her. Did he still see her?

There were red lines running down her skin in slanted parallels, from her shoulders to her breasts, three lines on her left side, three on her right, the two triads arrowing symmetrically inward; they reminded him of aboriginal tattoos. Most likely they'd been made with a coin's edge. Someone had told him that Cambodians did that to ease the blood when they were ill. Suddenly he recalled the nightmare pallor of the Chinese-porcelain girl, and he almost shuddered.

50

NIGHT HAVING SMOTHERED the wasted day at last, he set out for the disco while his dear friend the photographer lurked kindly in the rat-infested shadow of the garbage heap, not wishing to show himself to *his* girl, the five-time bride, whom he'd dismissed definitively, and who was in corresponding agonies. The journalist knew very well that by returning to the disco he'd be disturbing her, and the photographer as well, but this was the time to actualize his own reproductive strategies. So he passed through the hot outer crowds alone. Every time he came here they seemed more menacing. It was all in his head, but that was his problem; as the saying goes, he was thinking with the wrong head. As soon as he'd been sucked into the sweaty inner darkness, the photographer's girl came running up, seizing him by the hand, weeping, pleading in a rush of alien singsong. He shook his head, patted her shoulder (this was becoming his stereotyped Pontus Pilate act), and she stamped in a rage. Just as nightshade grows tall and poisonous in American forests, its spider-legged veins hung with red balls, black balls, and milky white putrescences, so grew her fury in that long narrow cavern whose walls dripped with lust-breath. She ran away into the cigarette fumes between the crowded tables and though he'd lost sight of her, her terrible howling made his ears ache. She was back again snarling and grovelling monstrously (did she need to eat so badly as that? what didn't he understand?) and he wondered whether she only wanted him to buy her out so that she could rush to the hotel in pursuit of the photographer, or whether she wanted *him* now, whether he was her fallback; anyhow it was clear that she wasn't Pala's friend (that night she finally took the trouble to tell him that the woman he was falling in love with was not named Pala, but Vanna) because that afternoon she'd tried to get him to go with the girl in the bra, the Chinese-porcelain girl, or failing that the other one (did she get a commission?); she wasn't loyal to Vanna!—Thinking this helped him harden his heart. (In truth, what could he have done? His loyalty lay with Vanna and with the photographer, not with her.)—I want Vanna, he said.—Excuse me, sir, said a low-level pimp or waiter or enforcer, presenting him with two other girls, each of whom slid pleading hands up his knee.—I want Vanna, he said.—The photographer's girl said something, and the others laughed scornfully. Then they all left. (Later the photographer said that he saw his girl come running out, and he hid behind the garbage pile so she didn't discover him; she got on a motorbike and went to the hotel to sniff him out; not finding him, she came back weeping.)—Vanna must be dancing, probably. There was no possibility of finding her if she didn't want to be found. She was a taxi girl; it was her profession to find him. If she wanted him she'd come . . . He sat back down, and a waiter said something in Khmer that to him sounded very eloquent. Evidently it was a question. Tall, white, conspicuous, the journalist sat at his table facing the stares from other darknesses.— Seven-Up, he said. The waiter trotted off, and returned with a long face.—Sprite, said the journalist. The waiter brought him three cans of ice cream soda.—Perfect, he said wearily. The photographer's girl was sitting down beside him again; he slid one can toward her. His own girl came from the dance floor at last, eyeing him with what he interpreted to be an aloof and hangdog look. A man said to him: YES my friend! . . . and began to explain something to him at great length, possibly the causes and cures of hyperthyroidism, while the journalist nodded solemnly and Vanna stared straight through everything. The journalist offered him a can of ice cream soda as a prize for the speech. The waiter remained anxious at his elbow; the two staring girls needed so badly to be taken out . . . —At last the man pointed to Vanna and then to himself, joined two fingers together . . . Then he said something involving many vowels, concluding with the words *twenty dollah*. Buying a girl out was only ten. The journalist reached into his money-pouch and handed the man a twenty-dollar bill. The man rose formally and went behind the bar, speaking to a gaggle of other smooth operators as the journalist took Vanna's hand and tried to get her to rise but she made a motion for him to wait. The man came back and announced: *Twenty-five dollah.* The journalist shook his head and popped up from his seat again like a jack-in-the-box. He was required to stand and sit several more times before the man finally faded. Then he took Vanna's hand. She walked behind him without enthusiasm. Every eye was on them. The photographer's girl made one more attempt, weeping again. He was too exhausted now to feel anything for her. Outside, Vanna shook her hand away from his. He'd already slipped her a stack of riels under the table. She picked out a motorbike and he got on behind her. The hotel was only three blocks away but she didn't like to walk much, it seemed. When they got to the hotel she paid the driver two hundred from her new stack, and they went in. The lobby crowd watched them in silence as they went upstairs.

51

WAIT, HE SAID gently, his hand on her shoulder. He left her in the room and went downstairs.

Do either of you speak English? he asked the desk men.

Yes, they both replied in low voices.

Will one of you please come and help me? There is someone I want to talk to, and I cannot speak Khmer.

There is some kind of problem?

No problem. I just want to talk to her.

I cannot go, one clerk said, and the other clerk said nothing. Maybe if my friend comes I go or I send him. What is your room number, please?

102.

OK. I go with you, the other man said.

That's *great*, the journalist said with all the enthusiasm of his nationality. I sure appreciate it . . .

She was standing in the middle of the room, staring into the mirror.

The journalist said: Please tell her I want to talk to her. I want to find out if she is angry with me.

The man in the yellow shirt said something, and she opened her mouth and began to reply. It was practically the first time he had heard her speak (but as long as he knew her it always seemed that way when she said something; she talked so seldom). He marveled at the lisping syllables, the clear calm childish incomprehensible voice.

Oh, it is only a misunderstanding, the man laughed. She think you are ashamed of her, because you walk in front of her very fast.

Tell her I thought she was ashamed of being with me, because she walked very slowly.

You walk very fast, she walks very slowly; it is nothing. I told her you seem to be a nice person, a good person; she says she likes you very much.

Please ask her what she expects from me.

Well, you know she does not like to ask you for anything. She never ask. But a small gold chain, for a souvenir of you, that would please her very much. To show your . . . —well, it makes her very happy.

Ask her if I should give her the money to buy whichever gold chain she wants.

She says she wants to go with you, to pick it out together with you.

Ask her if she has anything to ask me.

She says she wants to do what you want, to make you happy.

Ask her if she can stay with me tomorrow morning.

How long you want her to stay?

Up to her.

She says she can stay until eleven or twelve. She has a job in the morning. She gets paid by the hour to work in the fields for small wage; that is no problem, to miss that; she simply won't get paid. But after that time maybe her uncle comes looking for her. These taxi girls, you know, they do this work to make money for the family. They never tell the family what they do.

52

THEN THEY WERE alone again. Once more she wasn't really looking at him. Then she smiled a little and got the towel and went into the shower . . .

53

HE'D MADE UP his mind, as I've said, not to fuck her anymore. He just wanted to be with her. When they lay in bed that night he kept his arm around her and she drew him close, drumming playfully on his belly, pinching his nipples; but then she was very still on her back beside him and he could see that she was waiting for him to do what he usually did (as meanwhile in the street the photographer met his former girl, who'd come hunting for him again alongside the girl with the Chinese-porcelain face, who still entertained hopes of majoring in journalism on her back; the photographer's girl was sobbing and screaming in the street . . .) He didn't even kiss her or touch her breasts. He just held her very close, and the two of them fell asleep. All night they held each other. He wanted to respect her. In the morning he could see that she was waiting for it again, so he got up and took a shower and started getting dressed. He couldn't tell if she was surprised. She got up, too, and pulled her bra on, while in the other bed the photographer lay grinning.

You mind if I hop her while you're in the shower? he said.

I don't think she'd like that, the journalist said evenly.

That's a good one, the photographer jeered.

54

HE MADE EATING motions and she nodded faintly.

He took her downstairs, this time holding her hand and introducing her to everyone as his girlfriend, but she didn't look anyone in the eye.

At the restaurant they pretended she wasn't there and asked him what he wanted.

Ask her, he said.

They looked at him incredulously.

He said it again, and she said something.

Uh, they said, she want, uh, only soup, sir.

Two soups, please, he said.

When the soups came she put pepper on his and smiled a little. She picked the meat and noodles out of hers, leaving the broth as people always seemed to do in Cambodia, and then she just sat there. He suddenly wanted to cry.

He drew an imaginary gold circlet on her wrist, and she nodded.

They went out, and he was about to take her by the hand to go to the market where he'd seen some gold things for sale, but she took *him* by the hand and led him to a motorbike and they got on. They travelled far across the city, down shady lanes of coconut palms, past clean white two-storey houses already shuttered against the heat, then a sudden crowded market-place, then a sidewalk lined with the checkerclothed tables of the cigarette vendeuses, ahead more palm trees receding infi-nitely . . . He gripped her shoulders. Everyone was looking at him as usual. He kept expecting to get used to it; instead, every day it got harder to bear. There was a young soldier in fresh glowing green who lounged in sandals, smoking and talking with a friend sitting on a Honda; the soldier looked up sud-denly and locked his eyes on the journalist's face; when the journalist looked back, the soldier was still watching. Two old brown faces leaning close together, smoking Liberation ciga-rettes over a bicycle, peered round and caught him. They stood up slowly, never looking away. A cyclo driver with veined brown pipestem legs saw him, and gave him so much attention that there was almost an accident. The journalist never tight-ened his grip on Vanna's shoulders; he did not want to add to her shame. They vibrated past shady chessboard-floored cham-bers open to the street, their corrugated doors and grilles retracted to let the last of the morning coolness in, glass-fronted shelves not quite glinting in the dimness, people rest-ing inside with their bare feet up on chairs, schools of child-fish watching TV; and the journalist drank them in almost vindictively because so many had drunk him in; everywhere soldiers and gorgeous-greened police rode slowly on motorbikes, looking both ways. At last they reached a video arcade which was also a jewelry store without any jewelry, without anything in the glass case except for a tiny set of scales on top of a cigar box. The Chinese-looking man in the straw hat opened the cigar box and took out three gold bracelets. Vanna gestured to the journalist to choose. He smiled and signed that it was up to her. She smiled a little at him. Already a new crowd was secreting itself, like the swarm of black bees eating the sugar and flour in the market's open bowls . . . —Two of the bracelets were slender and lacy. The third was quite heavy and had three blocks that said A B C. That one would obviously be the most expensive. She took that one. He took a hundred-dollar bill from his pocket and gave it to her. She looked at it as if she'd never seen one before, which she probably hadn't. The man in the straw hat said something to her; the motorbike driver joined in, and they all began to discuss the alphabet bracelet with its every ramification. There was one chair, and she gestured to him to sit down; he gestured to her to do it, but she shook her head. The man in the straw hat gestured to him to sit down; he gave in. The man in the straw hat got a calculator from somewhere and clicked out the figure 30 and said *dollah.* The journalist nodded. I guess I can give Vanna a lot of change, he thought. They all talked some more. The man in the straw hat clicked out 137. They were all watching him to see what he'd do. When he got out two twenties, everybody but Vanna started to laugh. Were they happy, polite, scornful, or sorry for him? What did it matter? The man in the straw hat brought out his miniature scales and weighed the alphabet bracelet against a weight. Then he switched the pans and did the same thing again. The journalist nodded. Vanna took the bracelet and draped it over her left wrist. He realized that everyone was waiting for him to fasten it for her. He bent down and did it, taking awhile because the catch was very delicate and he was clumsy and nervous with his fat sweaty fingers. The man in the straw hat came to help him, but he waved him away. When he'd finished, he looked up. An old lady was standing at the edge of the crowd. He smiled at her tentatively, and she stared back stonily.

Then he looked at Vanna. The smile that she gave him was worth everything. And she took his hand in front of them all.

They got back on the motorbike and went to a bazaar. She paid the driver off with with two of the one hundred hundred-riel notes he'd given her last night, and led him into the awninged tunnels. People stared at them and snickered. A woman with her three young children was sitting on a bed-frame on the sidewalk, eating rice. When they spied Vanna and the journalist, they forgot their rice. Someone called out: *Does you loves her?*—She stared ahead proudly; he hoped that their cruelty did not touch her.

55

SHE WENT TO a bluejean stand and held a pair of black ones against herself and then put them back. (Did she want him to buy her something?) She looked at a white blouse and a yellow blouse. She put them back.

She kept looking at her watch. Had he already used up his hundred thirty-seven dollars' worth of her time? She caught them another motorbike and brought him to a place that looked like a prison. Soldiers were sitting at a table behind a grating, with their pistols lying pointed out. There was a ragged hole in the grating. She put some money in, and a hand reached out and gave her two slips of waste paper with hand-written numbers on them.

Then he realized that they were going to the movies.

Taking him by the hand, she guided him upstairs through the molten crowds and bought them fruit. Then they went into the auditorium. It was almost unbearably hot and stifling, and the shrill screaming crackling echoing movie was interminable.

But he was very happy because she held his hand and snuggled against him, and he could watch her smiling in the dark.

There was a newsreel about the latest floods. She pointed, held the edge of her hand to her throat like rising water.

Then she brought him back to the hotel. People lined up on the sidewalks to watch them pass; he longed for one of those Chinese rockets-on-a-string, to clear the landmined path . . .

Well, what have you been up to? said the photographer, on the bed, nursing his skin rash.

Got married.

Oh. Well, I guess that means I'd better clear out. Is an hour enough?

He still didn't really want to fuck her. He just wanted to be naked next to her, holding her for the last ten minutes or two hours or whatever it would be until she went to work. He stripped and took a shower. While she did the same, he looked for his gonorrhea pills. When she came out he got into bed with her. She pointed to her watch. She had to go soon. She snuggled him for a minute, then pointed to the tube of K-Y jelly. He didn't want to confuse or disappoint her anymore. If that was what she expected, then he'd better do it. She touched his penis, and he squirted the K-Y jelly into her and rolled the rubber on and got ready to mount her, and then something in her face made him start to cry and he went soft inside her and rolled off.—She was not pleased, no two ways about it. After all, it was their honeymoon. She was rubbing him; she wanted him to try again. He put more K-Y jelly inside her and took the rubber off and threw it on the floor. The doctor had said he wouldn't be contagious anymore; sex was only hurting him, not anyone else. As soon as he was inside her, he went soft again. He was crying, and she smiled, looking into his face, trying to cheer him up; he was behaving like a baby. He traced a heart on his chest, pointed from himself to her, and drew a heart between her breasts. She nodded very seriously. He made a motion of two hands joining and she nodded. He said: You, me go America together . . . and she shook her head.

She drew a square on his chest, not a heart, then pointed to a heart-shaped chain of gold that some other man must have given her . . .

She got up and took a shower. He started to get dressed, too, but she gently motioned him back into bed. She dressed very quickly. She came and sat with him for a moment on the bed, and he pointed to the number eight on his watch and signed to her come to the hotel then and she nodded and he said: *Ah khun.**—Then she stood up to go. She clasped her hands together goodbye and he was crying and she was waving and kissing her hands to him and she never came back again.

*Thank you.

the girl from blue hawaii
Samuel Atlee

FROM MEN AT RISK

E DWARD ALLEN WEBBER'S first close-up of Manila was the faux marble floor in his bathroom at the Philippine Plaza, where he lay on his side doubled-up with stomach cramps. It was midnight somewhere when he'd arrived, and jet-lagged and dopey from his sixteen-hour flight, he'd ordered from room service an American-style hamburger and a local soup called *pansit molo*, which contained the offending peppers. Like a fool, he'd eaten them—little inch-long red fuckers that looked like the bloody incisors from some fire-eating beast—and they were pulsing now inside his stomach like pods of nuclear fuel.

Webber finally struggled to his feet, out of the bathroom and onto the bed by the phone. When the hotel doc appeared, he gave Webber paregoric and several liberal swigs of mefloquine. Like the other Filipinos Webber had seen thus far, the doctor was small, black-haired, and toffee-skinned, and seemed eager to please. He wore a white flaxen shirt they called a *barong* outside his slacks. "You are not to eat the peppers," the doctor told him. "They are simply to taste." Then he made Webber take down his trousers and he injected something into Webber's buttock. The effect was nearly instantaneous: a sort of frozen feeling from Webber's knees up through his abdomen, plus a massive erection, with which, at last, he went to sleep.

Eating those peppers his first night proved to be only one of Webber's many miscues. He was out of his element, culturally speaking, in Manila, though his displacement there was entirely intentional. He had taken leave from his law firm, where he was an associate, and if he had the time—that was the senior partner's phrase, anyway—he was going to check out a new plant site for one of the firm's investment clients. But why Manila? He and Jean, his departed wife, had vacationed together often in Europe, so for Webber that was out; instead he'd looked east, hoping for a change. He'd had a number of letters over the years from a college classmate who was living with his family in the Philippines, stationed at the U.S. Embassy as undersecretary for such-and-such affairs—the man had invited Webber numerous times to visit. Yet it was only after Webber had his ticket in hand that he learned by fax that the man had been transferred to Turkey. Well, what the fuck, he thought, he was going anyway. In Manila they spoke English, and money wasn't an issue. Jean had been a hot-shit lawyer herself, the youngest female vice president ever appointed to the SEC, and Webber was sole beneficiary to her life insurance. They had no children, and even if she'd lived they never would, since it was ovarian cancer that had killed her.

What Webber really wanted was for Jean to be alive. Jean, Jean, the chemo-queen, which is what she'd taken to calling herself, after the chemotherapy took her hair. Oh, how she'd diminished! Watching her sleep one night in the hospital, stick-thin and with a face the color of a pumpkin, Webber saw through his tears that she was curled in a ball at the edge of her bed like an animal that had struggled to the farthest end of its burrow.

"When is a person a healthy person?" Dr. Deitch had asked,

repeating Webber's query. Dr. Deitch was the grief therapist Webber's law firm had referred him to back in Washington. Deitch was utterly hairless (no eyebrows, even), overweight, and pink. He was much prone to maxims and fond of quotes. "In order to be reborn, sometimes you have to die first." "Who said that?" asked Webber. "Deitch," said Deitch. "Sometimes it's life that provides the therapy, not the therapy." "Author?" Webber asked. "Freud," said the doctor, sighing in deference to the master.

That had been two months ago, four months after Jean's funeral. All that while Webber, seeking to bury himself too, had continued working. "The answer," Dr. Deitch had said, "is that the healthy person is a person who can love and work. Neither thing, right now, which you can do."

"Maybe I should take some time off, go away somewhere."

"Yes?"

"But what about the office?"

"From what you tell me, you're so distracted you're just making yourself a nuisance. So take a leave, get lost for a little while."

"Like where?"

"Better make it someplace far away. You don't like this world very much right now, so try another. Meet a woman, help you get over things. Someday you'll look back and see that every life has its rough spots. I know that sounds cruel, but there'll come a time, I hope, when you'll see it that way too. Allowing yourself that first step is very important."

Thus Manila. Deitch might be a crackpot but for Webber there weren't many alternatives. As for the city, aside from the high-rise hotels and a few concrete government buildings, the whole place looked like it had been flattened by a typhoon— even the shantytowns Webber saw from his taxi were made of cardboard and corrugated tin.

After a drugged sleep, the next day Webber checked out the view from his balcony. There was blue sky and high humidity. Traffic sped past below on Roxas Boulevard, and there were freighters out beyond the seawall on Manila Bay. There was a keen sense of a strange life going on all around him, but of Webber having no obligation to take part in it.

Downstairs, the lobby was full of Arabs. Not sheiks or diplomats, but dark men in sunglasses with silk suits and expensive jewelry, business types. Webber took a seat and a hawk-nosed man with a chunky Rolex immediately sat down beside him.

"These people," he said, exasperated, indicating an entire race as he spread his hands. "They are never on time."

"What brings you to Manila?" Webber asked.

"I'm here to hire hospital staff, and clerks for a supermarket. Contract laborers. Filipino nurses are very good."

"Where will they go?"

"Saudi Arabia. Overseas workers, they're the chief source of foreign income for the Philippines. No oil." He smiled. "What business are you in?"

"None," said Webber. "I'm on holiday."

"First time here?"

"Yes."

Presently the man rose to his feet. "My colleague," he said, pointing as he looked across the lobby to a Filipino in crocodile slip-ons and a flowered shirt.

"A word of advice?" said the Arab.

"Shoot."

"The little women here, they screw superbly. They'll take good care of you."

Webber returned to his room, to shave and shower. Sex, in fact, had been largely absent from his thinking. Rather, it was very much on his mind that he wasn't giving it any thought. He should, shouldn't he? Something ought to happen, he felt. The last time he'd made love to Jean was some eight months ago, and the memory of it still filled him with sadness. Curled on her side in the hospital bed, Jean had sucked him off as he stood beside her. That was illicit and exciting, but still, this woman with the hungry mouth, his wife, was dying.

"You don't have to do this," Webber told her. "Please."

Jean felt his prick soften, and the look she'd given him was villainous. "I'm not doing it for you," she said. "I'm doing it for me." Then she made Webber come and drank him down like an elixir, and afterwards turned away from him on her side and wept. It was very nearly Webber's last contact with her, with Jean as a human being, because as the days dragged on she retreated deeper and deeper into the narcotic stupor of her nonself, this dwindling nonperson who was mortally ill. Without consulting him, she'd made arrangements for her body to be cremated, so afterwards there had been nothing save an anonymous black urn for Webber to mourn. Where had she gone? Webber tried talking to her, talked to her as he remembered her, discussed with Jean what she might want him to do in this new solitary life of his. They hadn't, in fact, discussed it. "Just try to live," Dr. Deitch had advised him, trying to be helpful. "At dawn, pray for dark. In the dark, pray for dawn."

OK, Webber thought, sure thing. But what help was that?

AT DUSK, HE took a taxi from the Plaza over to Ermita to a bar called Blue Hawaii. It was a warm breezy evening and traffic on Roxas Boulevard was bad, so he sat watching it get dark as the neon signs came on. The air was foul with exhaust fumes.

"Cockfight tonight," said the driver. "Over Taft Avenue."

Thus the traffic jam. Half the city seemed to be named after Americans—the rich vanished lords with their money and their displaced military. Webber watched a street vendor in flip-flops dodge between cars and jeepnies and buses, selling from a tray he wore on a halter hung around his neck. Webber's driver signaled him over, bought a single Marlboro cigarette, and waited while the vendor lit it with an imitation Zippo.

Ermita had a carnival atmosphere, the street jammed with taxis and music blasting from the clubs. Boys scampered about hawking cigarettes and candy. Inside, Blue Hawaii had a low ceiling and a raised stage where women danced. Webber took a seat at the bar and ordered a beer. The music on the sound system was Pinoy rock—Filipino versions of American hits. The girl sitting next to Webber had orchids in her hair and some sort of nasal obstruction, which caused her mouth to hang open like a trout's. She was wearing a sleeveless kimono and was smoking a cigarette, and every time she caught Webber's eye she stopped to sigh ostentatiously, as if she were already burning with desire for him.

"Remember me?" the woman said.

"No."

"I think we met before. You want to buy me Coke?"

"No, thanks."

"You don't like girls?"

"Girls are fine."

"You homosexual, you're in the wrong place," she said. Then she plopped down off her stool and went back to a corner, where she replayed their conversation to one of her girlfriends. Webber flushed under their amused, brazen glances.

Presently a door opened in the back of the bar and there was a tumult in Webber's chest. Here now was a girl! She was tall and dark, wore a white jersey top and blue jeans, and was grave and beautiful. She displayed no interest in Webber, nor in any of the other tourists drinking at the bar—Americans, Australians, Germans. She didn't get up to walk the room in a restless, flagrant attempt to attract attention as the other women did. She didn't have to. She was entirely self-contained, and she was smashingly good-looking. When she gave her short hair a tug the play of muscles in her shoulders was exquisite.

The girl had turned her head away as he approached but now she looked up and offered Webber a minimalist smile. "You want to dance?" she asked.

Webber shook his head. "Talk, maybe."

"You want to buy me drink?"

"Sure."

She extended her hand. "You American?"

"Yes."

"I thought you either American or English."

"Which do you prefer?"

She shrugged. "Doesn't matter. Why were you staring at me?"

"Because you're the best-looking girl I've seen in here."

She was pleased all right but still had her suspicions. "I trust you, maybe then I make a big mistake. Maybe you like me because you have no other girlfriend."

"That's true," Webber said.

The girl changed the subject suddenly by standing up. "I have to work, make money. I have to dance now."

"You can't stay?"

She narrowed her eyes at him. "You want?"

"Sure," Webber said, laughing now, embarrassed.

She leaned in a little closer. "You understand, you have to pay my bar fine?"

"I understand," Webber said, a bit confused.

"I'm Tess." She offered her hand and made him shake it.

Tess returned to him five minutes later, having changed in the back somewhere into a pair of shorts, rose-colored flats, and a white blouse with a smudge of color. Over her shoulder she toted a bulky leather handbag. Webber ordered her an orange juice, for himself another beer. An air of goodwill encompassed them. They talked, though later Webber couldn't recall what about. He had the impression that he was charming and witty and interesting, and that his audience was unusually receptive.

Tess listened and rarely talked. Under the dark canopy of her short, curly hair, her high forehead narrowed downward to the wings of her eye sockets; her cheekbones were high-set and prominent, jutting inward toward her tip-tilted and practically bridgeless nose, which gave her an exotic, Siamese look.

"Maybe we should go now?" she said.

Webber paid and headed out the door with the girl on his arm. The sidewalk was crowded with touts and beggars. Women slept in doorways with two or three grubby infants, an empty cigar box before them for alms.

Back at the Plaza, high up on Webber's balcony, the night-scape spread out before them looked similarly impoverished: the sprawling city with its bleak; tiny tin-roofed houses and shabby high-rise flats. It was like the view from the plane, only passing overhead one had to wonder if it was worth coming down here.

At the moment, yes. Inside the room Tess kicked off her flats and used the toilet, and now they stood together on the balcony smelling the swampy salt breeze blow in off the bay. She leaned against Webber and yawned elaborately.

"You work tomorrow?" she asked.

"I don't work now. Just holiday."

"Lucky you."

"My wife died six months ago," he said, surprised that he'd admitted it.

They went inside and while Tess showered, Webber undressed and drowsed beneath the covers. When Tess came out she was wrapped in a white towel, all thin brown legs and arms. She sat on the side of the bed for a moment looking down at him, alert, but not unlike some placid friendly dog. Then she reached over and snapped off the lamp, and slipped out of her towel and slid under the sheets beside him. Finally, with his fingers Webber felt down her back, felt her skin warm and still moist from her shower. His heart was going like crazy but he made no further move to touch her.

If she was a seasoned professional she hadn't learned yet the art of waking up in a hotel room, because the next morning Tess started up with a violent jerk, then lay tense and rigid beside him. At last she relaxed and with a groan sat up, found the towel on the floor, and wrapping it loosely around herself crossed to the bathroom. She looked at herself in the mirror, first taking a general view of herself and then, thrusting her chin out, a more detailed one of her face. Then she showered and came out again, found her handbag on the chair, and sat down on the bed beside him.

Webber watched as she took out her compact and a jar of cream, then fiddled with the compact on the pillow until the mirror reflected her face. She did up her towel again more securely and began to work the cream into her face and arms. Occasionally she would lean back like an artist from her easel and judge how her work was progressing.

"How old are you?" he asked.

"Twenty-six."

"From Manila?"

"Where did you meet me?"

"I know," he said. "But maybe you didn't always live here."

"Maybe not." She paused to look him over. "My family's down south."

"So you're alone?"

Tess looked over toward the balcony. "Not this minute," she teased.

Webber watched her while she combed her hair. Then she gathered up her underwear from the chair and slipped into her panties, keeping the towel around her until they were hoisted. With her back to him, she took off the towel and then slipped on her bra, squirming like an eel to get her arms through the straps.

"I have another job too," she said. "Not just dancer. Sometimes I work in the office, do secretarial."

"Oh?" he said, rather doubting her.

Tess sat down again and leaned over and kissed Webber on the forehead. "Maybe tonight you want to take me to dinner?"

"I'd love to," Webber said.

While he showered, Tess ordered for them a room service breakfast. When he returned there was fresh mango juice and coffee and toast on a tray. Tess put marmalade on one slice, honey on the other, then handed the slices to him. The movement of her hands was fluid and graceful, the perfect little hostess.

In the afternoon they took a taxi over to Fort Santiago, the old Spanish bastion defending the original city. Filipinos had been, over the centuries, a subservient folk: to the Spanish, the Americans, the Japanese. Tess, too, seemed dependent on the kindness of strangers. In the taxi, Webber wondered for a moment if she really liked him, or if she was just taking advantage before he moved on. Moved on to what? The truth was, Webber wasn't much thinking, because for him thinking hadn't paid off the past few months. "All I want is to take care of someone," Tess had said that morning in their room. "All I want is someone I can look after, who wants to look after me." Had anyone ever put the case to him so bluntly? Did she sense that Webber was someone she could trust? After she'd said that she just looked at him, as accustomed, in all likelihood, to rejection as acceptance.

Fort Santiago was on the Pasig River, not far from Malacanang Palace, which had once been filled with Imelda Marcos's shoes. There was a Spanish cathedral there, in Intramuros: the stones in its floor had come over as ballast in the hulls of old galleons. From the walls of the fort they overlooked the vast Tondo slums.

"Let's have a look," said Webber, pointing.

Tess was shocked.

"I'm a tourist," he said. "Come on."

There were people in Tondo barely living on the brink of existence. Houses lining the street were made of packing cases and cardboard, where entire families lived in places no bigger than a kennel. Even the piled trash hadn't the dense, bulky quality of rich American dumps, but looked picked over, sifted, like mountains of confetti. The place was unsewered and baking in the sun. At a *sari sari* shop on the corner everything was sold on a *tingi*, or piece-by-piece, basis: individual cloves, cigarettes, and sheets of writing paper could be purchased.

Afterward, riding back to the Plaza in a taxi, Webber realized that his little tour had been a bad mistake. Having come from poverty, no doubt Tess associated these places with her own stricken past, and to her his ignorance must seem clumsy.

"Don't ever ask me to take you to a place like that again," she said, once they were back in their room.

"I'm sorry."

"The Philippines is a beautiful country. Why do you want to

look at filth like that? Those people there, they're too stupid to work."

"Stupid?" Webber was shocked by her lack of compassion. "Doesn't anyone try to help them?"

"Why?" she said defiantly. "Anyway, it's none of your business. This isn't your country and it never will be. Just don't take me there to rub dirt in my face."

"Jesus," Webber said, stung. "I'm sorry."

"Forget it," said Tess, "I'm going to shower. Afterward maybe we'll make love."

Startled, Webber said, "I guess we shouldn't waste any time, then."

"What do you mean? I'm hot and dirty."

"Me, too," he said. "But maybe now I'm a little too distracted for fucking."

Tess didn't care for that word. "If you don't want me to stay here then just tell me. If I stay here maybe we'll make love. It's what people do, you know? Or maybe you can just sit here on the bed now and think. Think of what? Is there something about me that you don't find attractive?"

By now she had slipped off her shoes and presented her back to him so he could unzip her dress. She held her hair up from the zipper and the muscles in her neck and shoulders were perfect. She snaked her hand back into Webber's lap.

"Shower first?" she mumbled. "Or not?"

Tess pulled the dress over her head and tossed her bra and underpants on the floor. On her belly, she turned and watched as Webber disrobed behind her. He kissed her then, on the back, and nibbled at her neck. Tess moaned and drew up her legs beneath her. She reached down and guided him into her, then lowered her shoulders and wriggled her backside as she pushed herself against him, impaling herself with a long deep-throated moan. By that time, of course, Webber had climaxed already.

THEY WERE GOOD together. Tess was patient and pleasant and adept at taking care of him, and for Webber it was easy to surrender to her attentions. They talked, though the questions she asked—what job his ex-wife had, did they have any children?—mostly concerned life in the States, which Tess imagined as a vast palace of skyscrapers and shopping malls, where one was likely to run into Sly Stallone or Cindy Crawford. Her lack of sophistication didn't trouble her and charmed him. She had a mother and a sister in the provinces, she said, and had graduated from a junior college in Manila. A boyfriend? "Not anymore," she said, looking shyly away. A moment later she gave Webber her most radiant smile. "Maybe today," she said, "if you're going to be my new boyfriend."

They spent an inordinate amount of time in bed together. Tess was wholly uninhibited about her body, her breasts smallish and thick-nippled and sensitive. Webber made love to her, stupidly, without condoms, and sucking at her small, nearly hairless sex, his mouth filled with something syrupy like sap, and he wanted more.

In short order, there was the issue of money. Once she'd decided to stay, it cost Webber two hundred dollars to buy her out for the week from Blue Hawaii, which was rather unpleasantly like renting a car. Then there was the matter of her debts, for a single room in Mabini on which she was behind, and a loan she had from a girlfriend. Also, when they went out together, it was mostly for shopping. A native-carved chess set and a cotton *barong* for him, two dresses, skirts, blouses, and jewelry for Tess. Not gold, but bracelets and amulets made from coral or the skins of lizards. At home, in their room at the Plaza, in her bare feet Tess modeled her new clothes.

Each time when Tess left the room on some errand, a wad of pesos stuffed into her purse, Webber worried that this view of her, departing, might be his last. What could she see in him, after all, but a bankroll? Sitting on the balcony, waiting for her, as he watched the day fade he felt a familiar despondency settle over him. Behind the mountains of Bataan the sky darkened and the freighters began to twinkle with light. Then along the crescent of the bay all the street lamps suddenly came on. It was easy, wasn't it, just breathing in, then out? When the knock on the door came, at last, it was only Tess returning.

None of which could be explained easily to Jean, if she had been alive to listen. Jean, Jean in her dark vessel back in their Washington apartment, who wasn't there for Webber—and now he had to question whether she ever had been. What would she think, or say? Whenever his union with Tess struck him as incongruous, which it did frequently, Webber wondered if it wasn't due to his own desperation, his newfound taste for the absurd. If there were other Americans around (and there weren't many), would that inhibit him with Tess? Of course the differences between the two of them could be pretty exhilarating, but then Webber wasn't an anthropologist—Tess came from somewhere and so did he.

Still, in the course of paying for her favors he allowed himself to believe that her feelings for him were a lot more than a delusion, and he was happy. Sure, she was a primitive and lived deeply—or maybe just closer to the surface. But Tess had reawakened something in him and for that Webber was immensely grateful. "Bitch," he thought. "My wife was a bitch to leave me." Let's face it, he thought, what thing, other than her dying, could have propelled him into *this* relationship? He hated Jean for dying. But at least now he was making an effort to cast off his piled-up past for this remote idyll where he could be someone different.

As for Tess, she withheld much and in a funny way seemed to resent the intimacy of Webber knowing her secrets, as though that might lock her in somehow, into an identity she couldn't bluff her way out of. Yet she confounded him by showing him how unhappy he had been in the final days of his marriage—and how foolish it was for him to mourn a woman who was no longer alive.

AFTER TWO DAYS Tess's husband showed up at the Plaza. Leaving the lobby one evening for a walk, Webber noticed some Filipinos hanging out around the entrance to the hotel. He thought they stared even more than the locals usually stared at him—they all assumed he had lots of money. Then, coming back later at dusk, he thought he heard someone following him but shrugged it off.

The next night when he returned to the Plaza he found their room in utter darkness and Tess crouched in a corner, weeping. It took Webber half an hour to get any sense out of her, but when he'd heard her story he was frightened for her too. If it had been entirely clear to him what was going on it might not have ended so badly.

The next morning the same Filipinos were waiting for him at the entrance to the hotel—three of them. They said something to him in Tagalog, the native language. No one touched him. "Money you got?" one said in English. "Go away now," said another. Webber understood that much. They let him go then and walked off, joking grimly.

Tess was weeping again when Webber got back to the room. These people had been pushing notes under their door for the past two days, apparently. Tess showed Webber the scraps of paper with their inky messages but was too upset to translate.

"Tess," he said. "You've got to explain."

She turned her head, thrusting her hand away and refusing to answer.

"He's my husband," she said sobbing, finally. "Not those boys in the street, but another. Those are his friends. He's the one sending the letters. I married him five years ago and now he wants my money. He's threatening my daughter."

"Your daughter?"

"Yes."

"You're married?"

"Yes."

Webber felt stunned for a moment, then foolish. "So you lied to me all along?" In his own ears his question sounded petulant and stupid.

"Of course I lied to you."

"But why?"

"You want to go with me if I'm married? If I have a husband and a baby?"

"Just because he says so, you don't have to do what he wants."

"He threatens to take Ja-Ja, or hurt her."

"Ja-Ja?"

"My baby, she's two."

"We'll get her back and we can leave here."

"Cannot."

"Why not?"

Tess wouldn't, or couldn't, answer.

"Didn't you know something like this might happen?"

Tess was silent.

"You set me up," Webber said, finally.

Tess stretched out on the floor, regarding him with narrowed eyes. For Webber it was doubly disquieting: her look was far from amiable, and all access to her was now denied. Sure, she had lied to him—what difference, really, did that make? Couldn't she see that he loved her? Or did this paradise, too, have to vanish?

A SENSIBLE MAN might have called it a day. Just packed up and left, looking back later on his Philippine adventure as one protracted miscue. But not Webber. Because he was made of sterner stuff? He'd been in the Philippines just a week. Seven days of bliss and betrayal.

The final insult came when Webber returned the next afternoon and found the room they'd shared picked clean. No suitcases, no clothing in the closet. Also the two or three hundred in cash that he'd left behind in his wallet which she'd taken. According to the manager at the Plaza, Tess had come down with the suitcases that afternoon, then climbed into a taxi, and that was the last time anyone had seen her.

Upstairs the room was empty, save what he remembered had happened there. Webber felt sick and squatted on the floor. To know that Tess was alive somewhere and breathing the same air was maddening.

Fleeced, ensnared, and swindled. It happened all the time to Americans. Innocents abroad. For Tess, wasn't it degrading to be the one to have to do it? Apparently the men in her life were all swine. He remembered her mouth, tight and serious as the wound from an arrowhead.

"Grief isn't an event, it's a process." So said Dr. Deitch, his head as hairless and obtrusive as a thumb. "In order to get over things, sometimes it's necessary to interpose between the event itself and your future life . . . some other thing."

So then, was this some other thing?

WEBBER SPENT THE next few days in a solitude of sun and sea. Home was a one-room tourist cabin he'd moved to from the Plaza, at the end of a lane of crushed shells lined by frangipani trees, which filled the air with their sweet scent. There was a bed, a wicker table, and a rattan chair. He had wired the States for more money and kept it in an empty soda can. At night geckos crawled across the walls chirping, but he soon got used to them.

Days he spent at the beach or fishing. After a day of swimming the beach grew dull, and the next morning he rented a crude fifteen-foot *bangka*, a sort of canoe with pontoons to give it stability. With the help of a push pole he could skid the boat across the shallow lagoons at high tide. He investigated the small harbors, sticking close to shore. Each day dawned hot and clear, then in mid-afternoon there was a tropical shower. With a crude line and shrimp bait he caught small black fish, which he unhooked and threw back in. One hot, calm morning he hooked a marlin in shallow water and was profoundly shocked when it hurtled out of the water by the bow of his boat, twisting its powerful body as it threw his line. Afterwards he counted a hundred different shades of blue in the still water.

THAT AFTERNOON HE found a note stuck under his cabin door. It was a thin envelope and inside was a letter written in a looping childish hand. It was from Tess, and as he read on her matter-of-fact voice began to speak to him: "How are you, same here with me. I'm alone again with Ja-Ja in Lubao. Your new address I got from the Plaza. This is a hard letter for me to write. I'm so sorry to you if I wasn't always truthful. Still, if you can spare it I could use your help. I would like to see you. Just show my address and any taxi can take you where I live."

The nerve! Yet should any of this surprise him, in a country he didn't, and couldn't, know? Somehow he could not, and would not, refuse her.

Lubao was no more than a crossroads on the outskirts of town. It was a dismal district, all ditch and stagnant lagoon. There were shacks where children poked through piles of garbage along the roadside with sticks. The driver pulled up to Tess's place—a tin shack with two or three similar ones next door—and Webber climbed out of the taxi. A nondescript dog loped around the corner and barked, then stared good-naturedly. Feeling at the end of something, Webber took a deep breath and approached the building.

There was no proper door so he rapped on the plywood panel. From inside there was a rush and a shuffle, and then the panel opened.

Same height, wire-rimmed glasses. Same black, olive-tree hair. For some reason, her head looked smaller and oddly mis-shapen. She wore a chocolate-colored sleeveless dress and pink slippers with little pompoms that looked well chewed.

"My God," Tess said. "It's you, Webber. Come in." She flattened her back against the plywood panel and did her best to let him pass without touching her, then pulled the door closed, and followed Webber into the all-purpose room.

"My neighbor, he's working," she said, pointing, inviting Webber's gaze to follow out the open back of the room—it appeared to be her bedroom, kitchen, and laundry combined—to a primitive vista where a Filipino was caulking the hull of a boat with tar.

"Your husband?" Webber asked.

"No, the owner of this house. My neighbor. I'm tenant only."

Tess stood in the middle of the slanting, linoleum-floored room and made familiar Siamese gestures with her wrists and hands, offering Webber either a canvas chair or the couch, which at night must be her bed. Webber chose the chair, Tess the couch. How diminished, her circumstances! But then, hadn't their life together at the Plaza always been more his than hers? There was a makeshift cardboard closet over Tess's shoulder, and inside it Webber could see the dresses he had bought her, mocking him.

"You left quickly enough," he said.

Tess's eyebrows puckered. "I had to. I'm sorry."

"Where's your husband?"

"Gone again, that's our deal. He gets your money, and I get Ja-Ja."

"Where is she?" Webber asked.

"In the garden." Tess pointed outside again.

Webber looked out the back of the shabby room to where her neighbor was working on the boat. This was a garden? Indeed, there were some vegetables struggling in a rank corner of the yard. Ja-Ja, or what Webber took to be her, was sitting on the ground. Her hair was black and long.

"This was big trouble for you," said Tess. "Me, I have Ja-Ja back at least."

"Did they *make* you steal my money? I would have given it to you, you know."

Tess was stung. "I was too upset, and worried. Not thinking right. *They* got your money, not me. I have nothing."

Webber didn't know if he believed her—or if it mattered. She seemed a different person now, a little mother. Even her eyes, strangely spectacled, and her body hidden within the shapeless dress, seemed to suggest her complete removal from that girl he'd met back in Blue Hawaii, that girl who'd been so eager to please. Their tryst had been no more than a doomed extravagance.

"Webber." Tess said. "Edward. Alan. Webber." She had

always liked to roll all those vowels together along her tongue. She was still vigorously beautiful, of course—despite her surroundings. Webber watched her close her sooty eyes and open her mouth, leaning back on the couch with one naked foot on the floor.

"If you want, we can make love right here," she said.

"No," he said, shocked. "I'm leaving this afternoon."

"You're a nice man, Webber. Can you forgive this dumb girl her mistake?"

Webber rose from the chair and handed her the envelope. There was, inside, a little less than twenty-five hundred dollars—what he'd had wired to him from Washington, less his modest expenses for the week. All along, he'd planned on giving it to her—if he could only find her. It wasn't, after all, a question of the money; it was easier to give it to her now than worry later on about how he'd behaved. And wasn't that the important thing? He loved her, in a way, just for giving him a hint of life—or for showing him that such a thing was possible.

"My God," she said. "You giving me all of this?"

Outside, the muddy mutt barked. The taxi driver was still waiting by the road. Webber crossed the yard and climbed in, and as the driver started up he looked back and waved to Tess standing in the doorway of her house. Then she disappeared as she pulled back the plywood panel—which was, years later, how Webber remembered it. The third-world adventure he had paid for was over, and now other things lay ahead.

FROM something about a soldier

Charles Willeford

THE EAST INDIAN who had the concession to run a shop in the small room next to the bowling alley was a Sikh. He wore a braided beard, a white turban with his white linen suit, a white shirt, and a brocaded necktie. He slept in the back of the shop behind a curtain, and ate his meals at Charlie Corn's. According to Canavin, Sikhs were a warrior class in India, not shopkeepers, but this skinny Indian didn't look like he could fight off a sick Baluga. I don't know how he survived with his small exotic store. The stuff he carried in his shop was not the sort of merchandise that many white people would want, but he must have sold enough items to officers' wives to get by. He sold a few Filipino wood carvings and some wrinkled cotton dresses and blouses to those soldiers who had families in the States. But he never sold any of the expensive copper and ivory items he had on display. Incense was always burning in the shop, and it smelled like a mixture of charcoal and cheap perfume.

He always opened his store at six A.M., just as we came downstairs to stand on the front porch for roll call every morning.

He must have thought, in his strange Indian way, that someone would rush over after roll call to buy a hammered brass plate or a carved mahogany Moro head. I never saw anyone enter his shop before ten A.M., ever, but that's the way he operated. His margin of profit must have been very low, and he also gave jawbone. Jawbone is what soldiers call credit. The term dates back to the Indian wars in the West, when soldiers who could not pay had their names and the amount due at trading posts written on the jawbone of a buffalo. Those of us who had jawbone with him had our names on a private list, and if someone didn't pay him after a month or two, he told the first sergeant and the topkick would take the sum from the man's pay and give it to the Indian.

The first sergeant was married to a Filipino woman, and he had six children. He had been at Clark Field for more than ten years, and he could never go back to the States because of this mixed marriage. He came from Sacramento originally, and it is against the state law for a white man to be married to a non-white in California. Also, the Asian Exclusion Act doesn't allow Filipino women to emigrate to the U.S.A. Asian men can emigrate, but not Asian women. So as much as I disliked the first sergeant, a dour, unhappy man, I felt pity for him. He was doomed by his marriage to stay in the Philippines until he died. There were two retired soldiers married to Filipino women, who lived like natives in Sloppy Bottom, and the first sergeant would end up like them someday, scrounging cigarettes or a glass of gin from soldiers when they came over to the barrio. If I hadn't felt sorry for the first sergeant, knowing that, my heart would have been made of stone.

But thanks to the Indian and his little shop, I discovered Honeymoon Lotion.

Honeymoon Lotion came in a green one-liter bottle. There was a cork in the neck that had to be removed with a corkscrew. The label was red, yellow, and green, printed with runny garish ink, and there was a drawing of a naked Filipino couple hugging and kissing between two palm trees. In the background of this crude picture a yellow moon above a green sea drifted in a red sky. The predominant ingredient in Honeymoon Lotion was coconut oil, but when you opened the bottle not only could you smell coconuts, you were also overwhelmed with what seemed like a mixture of a half dozen sweet perfumes that could only be found in a Woolworth's back in the States.

Filipino women loved Honeymoon Lotion. When they had a bottle they would rub the oil all over their bodies after bathing (or instead of bathing), and their brown skins would glisten like highly polished coconut shells. Of course, they gave off a pungent odor of coconuts and a heady combination of cheap perfumes, and they were a little slippery to the touch, but a young man with a hard-on can get used to damned near anything. Once a man got used to the smell, it wasn't too bad; in fact, it probably covered up body odors that would have been much more unpleasant.

Best of all, Honeymoon Lotion only cost one peso—or fifty cents—and I had established jawbone with the Indian.

This was the beauty of being a fire truck driver. I was off every other day, and in the mornings when I was off duty, everyone else except for cooks and bakers or men who had been on guard duty the night before was working.

After the men marched down to the hangars, I would charge a bottle of Honeymoon Lotion to my account and head for the barrio and the Air Corps settlement, as it was called, which was a stretch of huts a couple of hundred yards away from Sloppy Bottom. There were nine, all in a single row, and this is where men with money in the squadron shacked up with their Filipino girlfriends. The men who had this kind of money were either sergeants or men with air mechanic ratings, because it was quite expensive to maintain a woman for your own personal use. The huts rented for fifteen pesos a month, and the average woman earned from twenty-five to thirty pesos a month in salary. In addition, there was an electricity bill and a rice allowance for each girl. Each woman had her own little house, completely free of relatives and children. The guys who shacked up didn't want any relatives around, naturally, and they saved some money by buying gin by the demijohn instead of getting it a grande at a time. The shack rats, as they were called, kept snacks around the hut, but they usually slept in the barracks from one to four P.M., during quiet hours, and then ate their supper in the mess hall before coming over to the settlement to spend the night. These guys became very fond of their women in time, and when they went back to the States they usually made an arrangement with another sergeant or rated A.M. to take over their woman and shack when they left. But this was only a short-term solution; none of these guys ever thought about what would become of these girls in another ten or fifteen years. Filipino women age quickly; a woman of thirty-five looks fifty-five, and very few of them live to become fifty-five.

If a woman got pregnant she was kicked out immediately, and the shack rat got another girl. The man who was paying her knew that he wasn't the father, because he mostly practiced anal intercourse to avoid becoming a father. Unlike white whores in the States, Filipino women were not inventive. They didn't give blow jobs, and the only sexual position they tolerated was the missionary position. They just sprawled on their backs, completely motionless, and waited patiently for it to be over. They were all Catholics, of course, and I think this had something to do with their attitude toward sex, but they didn't object to anal intercourse because they didn't consider it a sin. Perhaps when the priests gave them instructions as little girls, nothing about anal intercourse was mentioned. The professional whores in Angeles were all strictly missionary-position girls in the ordinary way, but not the women the shack rats kept in the Air Corps settlement.

At any rate, after I walked across the plains to the Air Corps settlement, about three miles, I would be dripping sweat. The shacks were all on stilts, with bamboo ladders leading up to split-bamboo porches. I would stroll casually down the dusty street, wiping my forehead with a handkerchief. The bottle of

Honeymoon Lotion, in a brown piece of wrapping paper, was in plain view. Either the girls would be sitting in the shade of their porches, or else two or three of them would be sitting on a neighbor's porch, giggling and talking. They all knew me, and finally one of them would say, "Hey, Wirrafold, come up and have some *lemonada*."

I would climb the ladder and accept a glass of *lemonada*, an acrid and overly sweet bottle of soda pop.

"Hasn't your old man got a demijohn of gin?" I would ask.

"You want too much, Wirrafold. I give you *lemonada*, you want gin in it. If I give you beer, you want egg in it."

They picked up this banter from their old men, I guessed, because I never saw a Filipino crack an egg into his beer, but the women almost always brought out the gin, unless the demijohn was too low or the label was marked with a pen. I would add two ounces of gin to my *lemonada* and finish my drink. After we talked a little, we would go inside the shack and I would get in some anal intercourse. I was seventeen, so the entire procedure, from the time I climbed the ladder until I left, rarely took more than fifteen minutes.

When I departed, I left the bottle of Honeymoon Lotion.

These women knew that I wouldn't say anything, and they were loyal to one another. The men who were paying the freight would have beaten me to a pulp if they ever found out that I was screwing their women while they were working on the line. But no one ever found out, and the only reason the system worked for me was because these guys hated the smell of Honeymoon Lotion. They wouldn't buy it for their women, and the women loved it.

The main problem I had was avoiding bamboo "chancres." The woven rush floor mats, or sometimes just plain split bamboo, could cause big blisters on your knees as you slid back and forth. So you had to learn how to screw without touching your knees to the floor. You got up on your toes and held your knees and legs straight. It was awkward. Sores of any kind take a long time to heal in the tropics and they have a tendency to get infected. So a man had to be very careful about scraping his knees on the floor. Also, because you had to accomplish this anal intercourse with the woman in a supine position, not in a prone position, it was not a particularly satisfying sex act. But it was better than nothing, and a bottle of Honeymoon Lotion was only one peso, whereas the whores in Angeles charged two. I used to wonder sometimes how these girls explained the Honeymoon Lotion on their bodies, and where they got it, when their men came home at night. That was their problem, not mine. But these shack rats were fools. No matter how much money a man pays a woman, he cannot expect her to remain faithful if he denies her the one thing she truly wants. And these women wanted Honeymoon Lotion. I learned a few things about women in the Philippines. Women are very simple creatures. If you want a woman, any woman, probe around until you find out the one thing in life she truly wants. Then, when you give it to her, she's yours.

It's that simple.

I WAS TRYING to save enough money to take a three-day pass to Manila, and that possibility seemed beyond my grasp. After paying my bills on payday, I rarely had more than eight pesos left.

In some respects eight pesos is a fairly good sum, although it didn't go as far as eight dollars would go back in the States. First, there was the cost of a taxi into Angeles, to the Iron Star and the Bullpen. The fare was four pesos. If you shared it with three other guys it could be cut down to one peso, but that still meant two pesos, because I had to come back from Angeles later that night.

Payday was a holiday, of course, but we didn't line up for our pay until about nine-thirty. It took that long for the major and the first sergeant to go up to Fort Stotsenburg, get the money, and count it out into small piles for each man in the squadron. The first sergeant also had to make sure he had deducted everything a man owed for P.X. checks, laundry, Charlie Corn chits, K.P.'s, the Indian, Old Soldiers' Home, bowling charges, and, if any, summary court-martial fines. Sometimes it was ten or ten-thirty before we got our money.

Hershey, or Padre as we called him, was the dayroom orderly, and he ran a crap game on the pool table in the dayroom and a ten-peso takeout game on the screened porch. The reason we called him Padre was because he had once been a Franciscan monk at a New England monastery. When he got angry at his cards he would mutter imprecations in Latin, and he got angry a lot—every time he lost a hand of poker. No one knew what his Latin phrases meant, but they sounded like terrible oaths when they rattled out of his phlegmy throat. It was common knowledge that Padre had paid the first sergeant for the dayroom orderly's job, because this was a standard practice throughout the Army. The dayroom orderly automatically owned the gambling concession. He also, or so it was believed, paid a percentage of his take each month to the first sergeant. But it was worth it, because Padre made a lot of money from the poker game, which he cut five percent. In the crap game he took ten percent from every seven or eleven that was thrown on the first cast. Padre didn't bankroll either game, and his overhead consisted of furnishing chips, cards, dice, and a midnight meal for the surviving gamblers. The midnight meal was always *pansit* and was prepared by the cook at Charlie Corn's. *Pansit* is the Filipino national dish, a combination of something like beef chop suey topped with soft noodles and drowned in a pungent soy sauce. There is nothing tastier than a large bowl of *pansit* at midnight.

I never had enough money to get into the ten-peso takeout poker game, but sometimes I would lose one or two pesos at the crap table. I invariably lost, because if I won the first throw I doubled up. My plan, if I ever got hot, was to double up for eight passes and then quit. But I never won eight passes, and I never knew anybody else who did, either.

Then I would go to the Iron Star in Angeles, a small bar that formed the hub of the Bullpen. The Army sanctioned the Iron Star and the four two-story whorehouses that surrounded the little plaza in Angeles. In the middle of the plaza there was an official Army prophylactic station with a Filipino Scout medic on duty. After getting a piece of ass, you had to go into the prophylactic station, fill your penis with ptargyrol, hold it in for five minutes, and let it out. The medic then gave you a tube of white ointment, and you had to smear this ointment over your genitals and rub it in well. You filled in a form, signed it as to date and time, and it was witnessed by the medic. He kept a copy and gave you one, which was proof that you had had a prophylactic. You also had to state, on the form, that you had used a condom during intercourse. If, later on, you developed a venereal disease, the fact that you had taken a prophylactic saved you from getting court-martialed. The whores, and there were eight of them, were inspected monthly by a doctor from the Fort Stotsenburg Hospital. He drove to Angeles, inspected each girl inside the little prophylactic station, and gave her a signed certificate for the month. They kept the certificates posted in their rooms. One girl, a Moro, had tarcolored skin and was so bow-legged she couldn't have caught a pig in a trench. Her flat face was incredibly ugly, but she was the most popular whore in the Bullpen because it was a well-known fact that Moros are immune from venereal diseases. I was a little skeptical about this "fact," but no one ever caught any V.D. from the Moro.

Despite the precautions, men still caught V.D. from time to time, although if a man did everything he was supposed to do it would be impossible. It would be almost impossible to enjoy a piece of ass, either, so that's why men often managed to get the clap or, more infrequently, chancres. There were about eight men in the squadron with syphilis and every Thursday morning they had to march up to the hospital and get shots— a Salvarsan shot one week and a mercury shot the next. It took more than a year of these shots to get rid of syphilis, so I never left the field without at least three condoms in my hip pocket.

The Iron Star, so called because there was an iron star nailed above the front double doors, which were never closed, was a bar and restaurant. You could sit at a table and drink beer and eat *sally goupons*, or order a bowl of *pansit*, or pancakes served with shredded coconut, powdered sugar, and goat butter.

Sally goupons were black bugs, about the size and shape of June bugs, that were fried in vegetable oil and then salted. They were a little crunchy, like Spanish peanuts, and once you got used to the exotic taste, they complemented San Miguel beer wonderfully. Some soldiers wouldn't eat them, but I became very fond of them and always asked for a small bowlful to go with my beer.

The girls drifted in and out of the Iron Star, between and looking for tricks, and sometimes they wheedled a ten-centavo *lemonada* from you. There was a flat single-time rate of two pesos, or six pesos for an all-night stand. There was no haggling or deviation from this set price. Filipino girls are not pretty, but they are not ugly either. They are different, that's all, and it takes a few months to get used to the fact that they look different from American white women. Because they have tiny noses, almost no noses at all, their faces seem flatter and rounder than they should be. They have short legs, slightly bowed, thick torsos, and small breasts. Their bare feet are much too large for their height and weight, and because their diet is so starchy—mostly rice—thin Filipino girls (at least those who ate as well as the whores in Angeles) are a rarity. In color they range from a deep chocolate brown, like the Moros, to a light-brown basketball color. *Mestizos*, who were half white and half Filipino, didn't work as whores. They usually went to Manila, where they could get good office jobs by passing themselves off as being of Spanish descent. *Mestizo* males were prized as houseboys by officers' wives, and after ingratiating themselves with an officer's family during a two- or three-year period were often taken back to the States by the family after the tour ended.

As you see, eight pesos didn't go very far on payday. One piece of ass, or sometimes two, a bowl of *pansit*, a couple of beers, and a taxi ride, and I would be broke until the seventh of the month when, once again, I could get jawbone at Charlie Corn's. There was no way, it seemed to me, that I could ever save enough money to go into Manila on a three-day pass.

I TOOK THE twenty-five pesos I cleared the first payday to Canavin and told him to hold it for me. I knew that if I kept it I would spend it.

"No matter what I say," I told Canavin, "don't give me any of that money back till I take my three-day pass."

Two days later I was after Canavin to give me just five pesos of it, but he told me to go fuck myself. He was unbudging, as I had suspected he would be, so I gave him another thirty pesos to hold for me the following payday. The next month I added my new winnings to all of my money held by Canavin and, wearing a new blue linen suit, took a three-day pass to Manila, riding down with Padre in his Ford phaeton.

In my starched tailor-made suit, wearing a white-on-white shirt and a navy blue silk tie with yellow polka dots and highly polished black wingtip shoes, I felt like a millionaire.

Padre dropped me off in the Plaza Goiti and left to go to the Estado Mayor poker game. His plans for returning to Clark Field were indefinite, but I told him I would take the train back to Angeles.

I checked into the New Washington Hotel, paying for two nights in advance. Then I walked to the Silver Dollar Bar.

The bar—with the words "SILVER DOLLAR" spelled out with silver dollars in the long mahogany bar top—was famous all over the Far East for its Singapore gin slings. These drinks were served in tall frosted glasses, and they were so strong that if you drank three of them, the house paid for the fourth. Padre had advised me not to drink more than two, and to take a long time between drinks. After all, each drink contained four and a half ounces of booze. I could feel the effects of the first one before I sipped even half of it, but I doubt if there is a better-tasting drink made anywhere else in the world.

In addition to the long polished mahogany bar with its brass rail, there were eight or ten white rattan tables with three or four peacock chairs to each table. There were slow-moving overhead fans, and the dark cool bar was an oasis after coming in from the steamy streets.

The first thing I saw when I pushed through the swinging doors from the street was a Filipino woman sitting on a table with her legs spread wide. Her pudenda were exposed to my startled view like a third unblinking eye. Three privates from Charlie Company, 31st Infantry, were down on their knees with their eyes at table level. They were staring and frowning at this woman's vagina with intense concentration. A Navy chief petty officer, in dress whites, was leaning back against the bar as he disinterestedly watched the scene, and he held a wad of pesos in his left hand. Two sailors were also in the bar, one sitting in a peacock chair and the other one down on his knees with the soldiers.

One of the sailors had claimed that any woman who wasn't a virgin would have at least one full inch of the bottom of her vagina overlap the flat surface of a table if she sat on it and spread her legs. The sailor had gotten an argument from the three soldiers, and bets had been made. The old chief, aloof from the argument, agreed to hold the money. One of the soldiers had gone out into the plaza and brought back a whore, paying her five pesos for her part in the experiment.

I was too late to get in on the bet because the woman was already in place on the table when I pushed through the swinging doors. But they let me take a look. Sure enough, the lips of that woman's vagina (or *pookie*, as the Filipinos call it) overlapped at least two inches on the table surface. If I hadn't seen it, I wouldn't have believed it, and I was certainly glad that I got there too late to place a bet. The other sailor and the three soldiers had bet against the sailor who had made the claim, and the chief had to hand him the money. The soldier who had paid the whore five pesos had lost another fifteen to the sailor, and now he was dead broke for the month. He wasn't a good loser, either.

After the sailor got his money from the chief, he bought a round of Singapore slings for everyone, so I got my first sling free. There was some discussion then, and we asked the sailor how he knew about the twat overlap. He said the rule applied to white women as well as Filipino women, and he had learned about it when he had pumped gas in a station in Toledo, Ohio, long before he joined the Navy. There was a little hole in the wall between the men's room and the ladies' room, and when a woman went in to use the bathroom he would go into the men's room and take a look. He was just a kid then, he said, and merely curious, but this low, upward view had provided him with a wealth of knowledge about vaginas. He had already won bets on the overlap in Honolulu and San Diego.

"But," he reminded us, "it won't work with a virgin. Only mature nonvirgins have the one-inch overlap."

The whore, hoping to get a little action, tried to sit at the table with us, but the gray-haired Chinese bartender ran her out. The Silver Dollar, he told her, was a decent place, frequented by important businessmen, and no soliciting was allowed.

I laughed when he said that, but I was the only one who did. The C.P.O. gave me a funny look and told me to take it easy on the slings. I nodded and said I would.

I didn't know any of these guys, and I kept quiet as they talked. My sense of humor had gotten me into trouble before. A few minutes later, the soldier who had paid the whore five pesos began to argue with the sailor who had won the money. He felt now that he had been tricked into a sucker bet, and he was getting ugly. I finished my second sling and sidled out as the voices began to get louder. I wasn't about to get mixed up in a fight during my first hour in town.

It was one P.M., and the sun blazed fiercely. I was feeling my drinks and perspiring through my jacket, not being used to wearing a jacket in hundred-degree heat. But I would have been just as euphoric if I hadn't had two Singapore slings.

I was in a city again, and a head taller than most of the natives. The streets teemed with people, and it was exciting just to be there, walking around and taking everything in. Here were department stores, music stores, bookstores (in the window of a bookstore there was a huge pyramid of Carl Crow's *400 Million Customers*), and the Ideal Theater (pronounced Id-de-all) was playing a new Laurel and Hardy movie. The Ideal Theater was air-conditioned, too, one of the few air-conditioned buildings in the city. As I passed by I felt the cold blast of air from the lobby, and I bought a white paper bag of *sally goupons* from a vendor in front of the theater.

There were more white businessmen downtown than I had expected to see, but the majority of the people were, of course, Filipinos. There were a good many beggars in rags, and those who weren't beggars didn't dress much better, but there were quite a few well-dressed Filipino men and women as well.

When I entered the walled city I knew to stay in the middle of the narrow streets and to look up every once in a while. Some balconies overlapped the narrow cobblestoned streets, and residents emptied pisspots and garbage or dumped a pail of dirty water into the street. This was an unsanitary area, all right, and there was an overpowering stench of urine, feces, and garbage in the moist air.

In addition to hole-in-the-wall shops in the walled city, there were guys with carts and wheelbarrows selling miscellaneous junk in the streets, and the crowded streets were like a thieves' market.

I found a small bar where a half dozen soldiers were drinking, ordered a beer, and asked one of the guys in the bar if he knew Henderson, my bunkie on the *Grant*.

"What outfit's he in?"

"I don't know. I just know he's in the Thirty-first."

"I don't know no Henderson, but you could probably check him out at battalion headquarters. You should've written him a letter, if you're from Clark Field, and he could've told you where to meet him."

"I didn't think of it."

I left the walled city, not wanting to walk around down there by myself when it got dark, and caught a Willys cab back to the New Washington Hotel. I took a shower and cooled off under the overhead fan, lying on top of the bed. I was used to afternoon naps. Walking around in the heat had made me sleepy, and yet I was much too excited to sleep. I wanted to get a girl, but couldn't summon the energy to go out and find one. I called down to the desk and asked them to send me up two bottles of cold San Miguel beer.

A few minutes later there was a knock on the door. The bellboy brought in the beer. There was a girl with him.

"You want a girl?" he said.

"How much?"

The girl was young, about nineteen or twenty I thought, but she looked younger because she was wearing a short pleated navy blue skirt and a white middy blouse. It was the same kind of uniform girls had to wear four days a week at John Adams Junior High School in Los Angeles. She had her hair cut in a Chinese bob, and the back of her neck had been shaved.

"Five pesos."

"Two."

"Five."

"I'll never pay five pesos for a short time. How much for all night?"

"Twelve pesos."

I thought about it for a moment. I had planned to take a cab later that evening to the Santa Ana Cabaret, and to dance a little before taking out one of the women for the night. The cab would cost three pesos; there was a one-peso admission charge to the cabaret; and I would have to pay the establishment another three pesos to take one of the dance-hall girls out of the place. Then I would have to give her six pesos for the night, plus buying some dance tickets and a few drinks at the bar. The evening would cost a lot more than the twelve pesos this bellboy was asking. Besides, here I was, already showered and naked on the bed.

"All right. Twelve it is."

I gave him twelve pesos and paid for the two beers. I told the girl to take a shower. While she showered, I slipped into my pants and undershirt, my shoes without socks, and left the hotel. I had seen the Chinaman's store across the street from my window. I bought six more bottles of beer, some *lemonadas*, and a bottle of Honeymoon Lotion. I was back in the room before the girl had finished her shower. I bought the *lemonada* for the girl and the beer for me. I wasn't too cheap to buy the girl beer, too, but Filipino women are notorious for their inability to tolerate alcohol. One or two beers and they go a little crazy. They throw things, tip over tables, and so on. In this respect, I guess Filipinos are like American Indians. The men can't tolerate much liquor either, but the women are more likely to throw drunken tantrums.

Naked, the girl looked like she was about fourteen, with adolescent chest bumps instead of fully developed breasts. Except for a four-inch scar on her left buttock (where her sister had slashed her with a bolo, she said), she didn't have a blemish on her body. She was delighted with the gift of Honeymoon Lotion, although she was disappointed when I told her not to open it. We talked and drank for a half hour before we did anything, and it was more like a date than a business deal. She told me her name was Elena Espineda. She was studying to become a barber and would have her license to cut hair within a year.

Elena wasn't a particularly satisfying lay, but I was used to that by now. At least while she was on her back the ugly scar didn't show, and she didn't keep asking "You through? You through?" like most of them did.

Afterward I drank two more beers and sent Elena out to buy two *pansit* dinners and a deck of playing cards. We ate dinner at the little table by the window, and I tossed the beer bottles, when I finished them, into the street, just to make the passersby jump. (Sometimes, when I drink, I do strange things myself.) She placed the dirty dishes and utensils in the hallway, wiped the table with a trick towel, and I taught her how to play "go fish." She was very serious about this game, and she had a good memory for cards.

"You will give me all your kings," she said solemnly, in an even flat voice, knowing I held three of them. And then, when I handed them over, and she made a book, she broke into squealing peals of delighted laughter.

After drinking so much beer, I had to take a leak. When I got up from the table to go to the bathroom, she said:

"I can pee farther than you."

I laughed and shook my head.

"You bet me five pesos?"

"Sure." I knew that I could piss farther than she could, and I didn't want to take her money. "Why not just see for fun. I don't want to take your money."

She went to her black patent-leather purse and took out a five-peso bill. She placed it on the table and weighted it with a beer bottle.

I took a five out of my wallet and put it under the bottle with hers. The floor was covered up by a tightly woven rush mat, not a rug, and I backed up against the wall and peed. My bladder was full, and the stream must have been at least four or five feet away as it splashed on the mat.

"You finished?" she said, widening her smile.

"Let me see you beat it."

She got down into the corner of the room, stretched her left leg up against the wall, and kept the other leg straight out on the floor. Then she reached down and pulled open the outer lips of her vagina with two fingers, and shot a stream of urine from that one corner all of the way across the room into the far corner by the opposite wall. If I hadn't seen it, I wouldn't have believed it. I could feel my jaw drop.

A man is supposed to learn from experience, and I should have learned from the bet in the Silver Dollar Bar that a man is foolish to bet on another person's game. I would have lost money on that one, too. And here, this little snip of a girl had beat me at what every man considers his own special province because of his built-in nozzle. But a woman, if she pulls back on her urethra, and practices, can always piss farther than a man. Of course, it was worth five pesos to learn this information about a woman's capabilities. Not many men know about it, and those who just hear about it won't believe it until they witness it. I doubt if very many women know they can do it, either. Most American women would probably consider it unladylike to practice pissing for distance.

Elena had won money on this trick before, she told me, and she had never had any trouble in getting a man to bet. As a rule, she said, she bet ten pesos, but she liked me because I had given her the present of the bottle of Honeymoon Lotion.

I thanked her for saving me five pesos, and laughed.

"You are happy? You not pissed off?"

"I'm pissed off, all right," I said, laughing again. "But *ako malagaya ini ibig gita!*"

Saying this in Tagalog pleased her, and when we went to bed the second time I got another surprise. Elena Espineda knew as much, or more, about making love as any American high school girl, and I got the best piece of ass I ever had in the Philippines.

THE BIGGEST ADVANTAGE in being at Nichols Field, compared with Clark Field, was that time passed faster. The biggest disadvantage was that more money was needed, and there was no way to make more. I had gotten used to living on very little at Clark Field, but there were a great many things to do in Manila, or even in Parañaque, right outside the main gate, and I was broke all the time. I was no longer the only gas truck driver selling a little gas on the side, either. All of the other gas truck drivers had customers, and I ran into competition. Luckily, the mess sergeant in the attack squadron owned a Model A Ford convertible, and he preferred to lend the car to me one night a month instead of paying for the gas. All I had to do was to keep his gas tank filled at all times, and on paydays he would give me the keys. With the car I got to know Manila very well, from Dewey Boulevard, where all the rich people lived, to the outskirts of town, where the cabarets were. With the car it was no trick to pick up a woman. Except for an occasional taxi ride, a good many Filipino women had never ridden in a car before, and they were happy to give you a free piece of *pookie* just for the chance to ride around the city with their hair blowing in the wind. It was exciting for them to ride in a car. There is something about a convertible that attracts young women. All you have to do is stop and ask the girl if she wants a ride, and in she hops. It's the uniform, too. Perhaps it's the combination of the uniform and the convertible that attracts them.

Outside the main gate in Parañaque there were dozens of small bars, and seven whorehouses, all within walking distance of the gate. Some of the freelance prostitutes who hung around outside the gate were only twelve and thirteen years old. I never took one of these young ones home because they invariably lived with their parents in one room. A man would have to screw them in the room while the father smoked a cigarette and the mother cooked something or other over a charcoal fire, both of them watching. There would also be two or three smaller children crawling around on the floor. Most of the guys in the Army claimed that there was no line, but I maintained that there had to be a line somewhere, and one of the lines I drew was in not screwing children. I also drew the line at accepting free blow jobs from binny-boys. There were literally thousands of homosexual Filipinos in Manila. At night when you walked around downtown, especially if you were in uniform, a binny-boy would proposition you in almost every block. Many of them were well-dressed, too, men you would never suspect of being homosexual. In Los Angeles you could always tell a homosexual because they all wore red neckties. But you couldn't tell with Filipinos because there's a touch of effeminacy in all Filipino men. It's a kind of gentleness, really, a reluctant passivity, but this quality makes them *seem* effeminate.

One weekend I looked up Henderson, and we got drunk together. We went to the Santa Ana Cabaret, and when we ran out of money we began to steal drinks when the owners left them on the bar to dance. We got caught at that, and the M.P. who was stationed there told the manager he was taking us to the guardhouse. But he just drove us downtown and let us go. He told us not to go back there, and that if he ever saw us out there again he would prefer charges against us.

HENDERSON HAD A ten-dollar bill and for two days before we got into Honolulu I tried to wheedle a loan of four dollars from him. I didn't want to go ashore without a cent in my pockets. He didn't want to go ashore alone, and he knew I would pay him back when I got my discharge money, so he finally agreed to a loan.

He changed the bill in the Black Cat Café in downtown Honolulu and handed me four dollars. At the same time I saw the headline in the *Honolulu Advertiser* reporting the death of Thomas Wolfe from tuberculosis of the brain.

I didn't buy the paper, but read the item on the top of the stack outside the café, and this news put a damper on my shore leave. Wolfe, who was only thirty-eight, was much too young to die, and although he wrote prose I identified with him as a fellow poet. A lot of his prose reads just like poetry, and there weren't all that many poets left in the United States. As if on cue, a black cloud came over, and a sudden rain pelted us for five minutes. The rain stopped abruptly and the sky cleared again, as it does in the tropics anyway, but I took the swift, angry rain as a bad omen.

Henderson, who only read Tiffany Thayer and Donald Henderson Clark, had never read anything by Thomas Wolfe, so I couldn't talk to him about the tragedy.

Henderson bought a pint of Gamecock bourbon, which tasted as if it was half fusel oil, but it was the cheapest whiskey in the drugstore. We drank half of the bottle in an alley before walking to the Dee Rooms. The Dee Rooms was purported to be the best whorehouse in town, although I doubt if there was that much difference among them. The prices were all standard, a straight two dollars, no matter what you wanted, with a ten-minute time limit. The women were all fairly young, recruited from the States, and most of them had signed a one- or a two-year contract with the madam. On paydays they could take on fifty or sixty guys apiece from Schofield Barracks. In two years these young women made a lot of money; then they went back to the States with a nice dowry and married some gullible businessman. When a transport like the *U.S. Grant* came in, or naval ships came back to Pearl Harbor after a month or two at sea, these women really cleaned up.

Henderson got laid and made the ten-minute time limit with no trouble (if you didn't make it in ten minutes you had to fork over another two dollars), but I told Henderson I didn't think I could do it that quickly. Actually, I was embarrassed about my lack of pubic hair. A little stubble had started to grow again, but I didn't want some white American girl to laugh at me or to kid me about having crabs. Also, I was reluctant to pay two dollars after having paid only one dollar—or two pesos—for the last two years in P.I. A piece of ass would have to be twice as good, and I didn't think that was the case—not with their American hurry-up policy. And these American girls, most of them from the Midwest, were large women, which meant bigger vaginas, not smaller, than the little Filipino girls had.

So while I waited for Henderson, looking these women over, I decided to save my money. The girls all wore rompers, with ribbons in their hair, and even though they were young, they weren't young enough to get away with dressing like little kids.

When Henderson came out, I asked him how he had managed to beat the time limit, and he told me he had gotten a blow job.

"Jesus," I said, kidding him, "you paid two bucks for a blow job? You could've got one of the sailors on the boat to give you one for nothing."

"That isn't the same, you bastard, and you know it. These girls are pros. Try the one I had, Pepper, she's really good."

"No. What I really want is a fried egg sandwich. I've been

thinking about a fried egg sandwich for the last three days. That, and a glass of milk."

Henderson didn't want to spend fifteen cents on a fried egg sandwich, but while I ate mine he grinned and said, "You bastard. You didn't want to get laid because you haven't got any pubic hair."

I had to laugh. "That's true. But I didn't want to spend two bucks either."

"Why don't you get a buzz job? It's only four bits, and the girls are all Japanese."

There were dozens of buzz joints in Honolulu, but they did their best business between paydays. On paydays the men from Wheeler Field and Schofield usually got laid, but during the month, when they were mostly broke, they could only afford the fifty-cent buzz jobs. A buzz job was a speedy release, because the girl tongued a man hard and then, with a hand massager, gripped his dick and turned on the switch. It was an incredibly fast jerk-off with the vibrating massager on the back of the woman's hand buzzing away. A Japanese girl who knew how to handle the massager could get a soldier in and out of the room in less than two minutes. These Japanese girls, wearing kimonos, were very formal, and you couldn't touch them because their fathers and brothers hung around to prevent any trouble with the clients.

But here I drew another line. A buzz job, I thought, was a demeaning mechanical procedure, for both the client and the girl. I wouldn't have accepted one if I could have gotten it free. But I didn't mention this to Henderson. In the Army, if a man has scruples of any kind, his only protection against ridicule is to keep them to himself. I had already noticed the line that I had drawn for myself was getting narrower and fainter as time passed. If a man wasn't careful the Army could coarsen him, and I knew I had to protect my sensitivity if I was ever going to write anything first-rate.

At that exact moment I decided to get out of the Army. I didn't tell Henderson about my decision. In another five days we would be docking in San Francisco. When I was discharged, the chances were that I would never see Henderson again. Besides, what I did or didn't do was none of his business.

through the fanlight
Isaac Babel

FROM *THE COLLECTED STORIES*
TRANSLATED BY Walter Morison

THERE'S A WOMAN I knew—a Madam Kebchik. In her day, Madam Kebchik will assure you, she would never accept less than five roubles—not for anything in the world. Now in her apartment she had a family setup, and in the apartment there were two girls—Marusya and Tamara. Marusya had more customers than Tamara.

One window of the girls' room looked on the street; the other—a fanlight just under the ceiling—had a view of the bathroom. I realized this, and said to Fanny Kebchik (her father's name was Joseph):

"Of an evening you'll put a ladder up to the little window in the bathroom. I'm going up the ladder to take a peek at Marusya when she's at home. Five roubles: is it a deal?"

Fanny said, What a spoilt fellow you are!, and we shook on it. Nowadays she didn't often get five roubles a time. When Marusya had guests I used to make the most of the little window. Everything was going along fine when one day I had a stupid accident.

There I was, standing on the ladder. As luck would have it,

Marusya hadn't switched the light off. This time the caller was an agreeable, easily pleased, cheerful sort of chap with a long mustache of the innocent variety. He took his things off just as though he was in his own bedroom. He undid his collar, took a look in the glass, found a pimple under his mustache, gave it a thorough examination and squeezed it out with his hanky. He pulled off a boot and gave it the once-over too: anything wrong with the soles?

They kissed, got undressed, and smoked a cigarette apiece. I was just going to climb down again. And at that moment I felt the ladder slipping and swaying beneath me. I clutched at the window frame, and my fist went through the glass. The ladder fell with a clatter. There I was, hanging right up at the ceiling. The apartment was in an uproar. In rushed Fanny, Tamara, and an official I'd never seen before in the uniform of the Finance Ministry. They helped me down; I was in a pitiful state. Into the bathroom came Marusya and her visitor—a lanky fellow he was. The girl looked at me closely, went all stiff, and said in quiet amazement:

"The beast! Oh, what a beast!"

She fell silent, looked around at us all with unseeing eyes, went over to the lanky individual, and for some reason or other kissed his hand, shedding a tear or two. Weeping, kissing his hand, she said:

"How sweet you are; goodness, how sweet!"

The lanky chap stood there looking a regular fool. My heart was pumping. I drove my nails into my palms and went off to Fanny's room.

A few minutes later Marusya knew all. All was known, and all forgotten. But what I was wondering is: Why was she kissing him?

"Madam Kebchik," I said, "put the ladder up for one last go. Ten roubles."

"Not merely up the ladder, but up the pole!" said Madam, and we struck a bargain.

And there I was standing once more at the fanlight looking

into the room, and what did I see? Marusya had wound her slim arms around her visitor. She was kissing him with long kisses, and tears were flowing from her eyes.

"Sweetheart," she whispered, "goodness, how sweet!" And gave herself with the passion of one in love. And her expression said that there was only one person to protect her in all the world: the lanky bloke.

And the lanky bloke wallowed in businesslike bliss.

naked man

Harold Norse

MERTON BRIGGS WAS a legend in my New York bohemian circle. A farm boy from Vermont, he became a composer and moved to Greenwich Village. His twelve-tone music was nominated for a major prize in 1945, the year World War II ended, but he didn't win. He left America and settled in Rome for the rest of his life. Rumor had it that he was a wino and lived in a whorehouse.

I first heard of him from a mutual friend in New York who gave me his address. I wrote to him, enclosing a photo, and said I was going to Rome. We met at the railway terminal built by Mussolini, the Fascist dictator. A lanky scarecrow with a blond moustache and a blotchy complexion, Briggs wore threadbare chino pants, a soiled cotton jacket, and a shirt and tie stained with spaghetti-sauce.

"I recognized you from your mug shot," he drawled in a dry New England voice. Clutching my portable Olivetti typewriter and nylon flight-bag, I followed him into the street where we boarded a bus.

"The hotel is the cheapest in the quarter," he said.

He eyed my faded dakron suit with a hole in the sleeve. I told him I lived in a cold-water flat in New York for $20 a month.

"That's luxury compared to its equivalent here," he said. "You won't find a bathtub, shower or hot water without paying extra. They live in post-war ruins."

We got out on the Via Nazionale and walked past a tenement on the Via dei Serpenti where he rented a room. Ragged children ran in and out of the building, yelling and laughing. It looked like an East Side slum. When I asked about employment he shook his head.

"Teaching English, eighty cents an hour," he said. "I get a dollar but I've been at it five years—ever since they hanged Mussolini upside down."

"As a high school English teacher could I earn more?" I asked hopefully.

"It's just basic English," he said. "Most Americans who teach here need lessons themselves. Only one job pays more—dubbing English for spaghetti-westerns in Cinecittà, the movies. That's Italian Hollywood. But it's hard to get."

We stopped before a delapidated stone building. "Your hotel," he said. "It's called The Piccolo Cavour."

The "hotel" looked like a ruin but I couldn't keep my eyes off the most ancient ruin of all, the Colosseum. It was across the street. I stared with awe at the most renowned theatre of death and savagery in the world.

"This is the ancient quarter, the cheapest in Rome," said Briggs. "It's all ruins. It has its drawbacks but I love it. It's like living in a Fellini film."

We entered the sleazy hotel and he muttered something in Italian to the fat lady at the desk. Then, after inviting me to join him for coffee in the morning, he left. The fat lady held up six fingers and extended a pudgy palm. I paid the six-hundred liras (less than a dollar) and an old charwoman led me up four flights of stairs. She kept turning and casting piercing looks at me. Finally she stopped before a door and inserted the biggest key I had ever seen in my life. It looked like a deadly weapon. She struggled with the lock and finally, creaking and groaning, the door opened.

I plunked down my luggage, wiped my face and neck with a sweat-soaked handkerchief and stared at the iron-barred window that opened onto the hall. It had shutters but no glass. The char poked a claw into my gut and I slipped her a fifty-lira note. She held it an inch from her eye and dug me in the belly again. She kept mumbling, "*Volere pompino?* Want a blowjob?" then groped me.

Briggs had warned that I'd find the Italians uninhibited but this was too much. Placing both hands firmly on her shoulders, I shoved her out the door. I could hear her swearing and grumbling all the way down the stairs.

The room was dark and dank with a foul stench. It had stone walls, a stone ceiling and a stone floor, like a prison cell. The lumpy straw mattress crackled when I sat on it. Briggs was right. Compared to this my coldwater flat in New York was luxurious. Suffocating in the heat, I passed out on the cot stark naked with the shutters open for air, though there wasn't any.

A loud bell shattered my sleep, reverberating in my ears after it stopped. Through the bars of the window without glass a woman peered at me. The dim hall light made it impossible to see her distinctly. This was indeed another world, I thought, an ancient world like Rome two-thousand years ago. The Rome of Catullus, Virgil and Cicero, the Rome of Petronius and Apuleius. My college Latin courses hadn't prepared me for this. But above all, we were across the street from the Colosseum.

The woman, who I now thought looked like Medusa, kept staring at me with a sinister glare. Would she turn me to stone? Her crimson dress exposed enormous breasts bursting from the thin material that barely contained them. Her eyes were immense black pools in a chalky face like a mime's, with no depth. Her raven hair, piled up in curls, looked like squirming vipers. I felt as if I'd been transported to ancient Rome and was confronting Medusa with serpents writhing on her head.

Then suddenly she vanished. I rose to my feet and tugged the light cord dangling from the ceiling. In the dim 20 Watts I saw tiny insects like silverfish swarming on the damp floor where the dripping wash-basin formed a slimy pool. With disgust I wiped my feet on a towel, doused the dim light bulb and crawled back to bed. Even the cot felt as hard as stone. All the same I dozed off until the shrill bell rang and I heard female voices.

"Nice boy."

"Nice legs."

"Nice face."

"Nize *cazzo!*"

"*Bellissimo!*"

"*Beeg* muscle."

"Beeg salami."

"Eet ees mine! I seen eet first!"

"Boolsheet! You geeve heem crabs!"

"Ha, you geev heem clap!"

She groped me and I slipped my hand under her skirt. This was met with gales of laughter.

THEN SUDDENLY AMERICAN voices caused another ripple of excitement. Yankee sailors in summer whites stumbled into my room and guffawed when they saw me naked on the cot being fondled by whores.

"God *damn!*" yelled a young blond gob to the girls. "Ain't ya seen a naked man before? Mine's bigger, ladies!"

He flipped out an enormous penis and waggled it at the whores. "How d'ya like *this* salami, gals?" he yelled. They threw their arms around him and the other sailors and staggered out in each other's arms. Alone again with bugs and the stench, I was sorry I missed a Roman orgy. Pagan Rome was alive and well. I was also aware that drunken Yankee sailors meant trouble.

I wondered why Briggs hadn't told me this was a whorehouse—the one he had lived in during his first years in Rome.

Then I realized that he might have thought it offensive. We hardly knew each other. For a moment I fantasized about running into the hall stark naked yelling "FIRE!" I was burning up. Unable to bear it any longer I got to my feet and, as I reached for my pants, a young girl appeared at the window and stared at me.

"Hallo, Joe," she said and ambled in. "You wake now?"

"Yeah," I said, wondering how they all seemed to know me.

"Uh keh," she said. "You too much sleep. You like love?"

"Sure, I like love," I said. "I *love* love."

"Three-thousand *lire*," she said.

Recalling Briggs' instructions on the folkways I hesitated.

"Too much, eh? Awright, two-t'ousan'. Don' make me mad, Joe."

"Okay," I said quickly. It was dirt cheap, about $2.35.

"*Va bene.* C'mon, Joe!" she snapped.

She disrobed and flung her dress on the cot and kept her black stockings on. She closed the shutters, a sexy touch. But it was pitch dark. I tugged the light-cord and almost gasped. She looked fifteen. What happened next was so fast that it almost didn't happen. I wrestled with a condom, pushed her onto the pallet, and—it was over. The tension had been too much. Premature orgasm.

"Money!" she said coldly with her hand out.

I was still trying to recover my breath.

"Wait! Don't go! I'll give you another two-thousand!"

Her eyes narrowed. "You gimme now. All!"

"Okay, but will you stay?"

A shrug. "You pay, I stay."

I fetched the money from my pants and handed it over. She counted four milles and stuck them carefully into her black nylons and got out of her spikes again. She sat on the cot and bent forward to remove the nylons.

"Don't take them off!" I whispered.

She flashed a childish smile. "You like?"

"Yes, very much."

She looked pleased but held up a hand. Was she shaking me down for more liras? "Wait!" she said. "One little minute!"

She lit a *Nazionale*, the cheapest brand, and blew smoke rings through her nose. One floated around my cock like a ring on a finger. She clapped her hands with a delightful girlish laugh.

"Uh keh," she said. "Good sign," She snuffed the cigarette.

Good sign? If that's how the Roman oracle worked in modern times I was all for it. Sheep guts were messy. Leave them to ancient Rome. She responded to my urgent thrusts with Latin intensity or a professional facsimile thereof. We copulated long enough for me to gain the release I sorely needed. When it was over we used the bug-plagued wash basin and cleaned up with soap and dried with towels I had brought. I wouldn't touch the infested rag on the sink.

"You speak English well," I fibbed to get the conversation going.

"I learn from sailors. GI's. But they talk funny. Stone in the mouth."

I laughed. "You understand *me*, don't you?"

"Ah, *si*, you talk Engleesh good. *Molto bene*. I unnerstan'."

"I teach English," I said. "Sailors speak a dialect from the South."

She seemed surprised. "You got dialect in America? In Italy we got much dialect—*molto dialetti*. In Rome we no unnerstan' Napolitan' or Milanes'."

Her business-like manner had vanished and I pressed my advantage by sticking to the subject, trying to reach her as a person, not a slut.

"We have dialects—Texas, Mississippi, the South. Mixed with French, Spanish and African."

"Oh, Tex-ahse!" She made a face. "Beeg boy, leetle brain."

I laughed. "My name is Harry. What's yours?"

"Gina."

"Nice name."

Her lips curled in a sullen, resentful expression. I wondered what was in that name to displease her so. Then suddenly I realized that the whole place was strangely quiet, like an empty theatre after the final performance is over. Probably, I thought, the sailors and whores passed out.

"Uh, do you live here, Gina, in this—hotel?" I almost said "hell-hole".

"Where else?"

"Tell me, why does the bell ring so loud?"

"Bell?" Her brow furrowed. "Ah, bell. It ring when girl come late in night. Is signal."

"Signal for what?"

"So everybody know who is coming. When police come is long bell, two, three times. For sailor, customer, not long. *Capito,* Joe *?*"

"My name is Harry," I said.

It was all the same to her. One trick is like another.

"Tell me, Gina. You know the old woman who showed me the room?" She nodded. "She put her hand on my ass."

"I know," she said.

My jaw dropped. "How do you know?"

"She wanna give you blowjob."

At my astonished look she tapped her forehead and, for the first time, she laughed. "Crazy old woman. Very beautiful when she is girl."

I told Gina she said *pompino* and I asked what it meant.

"Blowjob," said Gina.

"Who would pay that old turkey for a blowjob?"

"Oh, yes! Sailor. GI. They like. Feel good."

"BUT—SHE IS old! There are so many young girls here, like you."

"Ah, *sì.* But she geev better blowjob. No toothes. Italian boys, school boys, they like. Yes, Joe. *Sì.*"

"They *pay* her?" "

"*Sì, sì.* Boys like." She studied my perplexed expression. "In *Italia* boys and men don' worry if woman or man is old. We like love. We like *amore.* You are gentleman, Joe. You are young. You not understan'. Not like damn sailor. *Porca miseria!* Too much drunk, too—how you say?—*bestiale, animale.* Sometime they hit me."

"Bastards!" I said indignantly. "But some are nice, Gina."

"Oh, yes, some nice. Some *molto* bad."

I put my arm around her shoulder.

"Gina, why don't you stay?"

She held up three fingers. It was business as usual. Sex is money is love. But I couldn't face being alone again.

"Listen," I said. "I must change dollars to liras tomorrow. Can I pay later?"

"Oh, no, Joe." She shook her head firmly. "You pay dollar now very nice."

I told her I had travelers checks.

Her face lit up. "You give me?"

I hesitated. The smallest was twenty-dollars.

"Come on, Joe. I change *lire* for you. Downstair. *Subito.* Right away."

She looked at me sincerely. Too sincerely.

"Listen, Gina," I said, "are there any cold drinks downstairs? Cokes?" She nodded vigorously. "Well, why don't you get us some cold Cokes? I'm dying of thirst. I can't drink this water. It's dirty. We'll talk about checks later."

"Uh keh. Money." Her palm remained open. I signed the traveler's check. and gave it to her. She wriggled into the tight dress and slipped her feet into the stiletto spikes.

"How old are you, Gina?" I asked.

"Eighteen. You, Joe?"

"Twenty-five." I always lied about my age. I was 30.

"You look young, more young," she said and went downstairs.

I never saw her again.

SNAKE STREET—VIA dei Serpenti—was torn up and closed to traffic. Wooden railings divided the sidewalks from the gutters, now a series of gaping holes and ditches. Bystanders leaned over the railings and gawked at semi-nude laborers shoveling and pickaxing. Bare-chested in the sun, the muscular young workmen perspired and glistened like figures in Renaissance paintings by Da Vinci and Michelangelo. In Italy even the streets are art galleries.

Numero 26, a crumbling *palazzo* over a pizza parlor, looked like a tenement in New York's lower East Side. I had to pick my way past clusters of screaming kids and inquisitive women who stared as if I was a Martian. I was not yet used to the piercing stare among the plebes. The first sign of Americans, I would soon learn, was men's thick-soled shoes rounded at the toe. "Good for climbing mountains," sneered the Italians scornfully, shaking their heads at American baggy trousers and clodhoppers. Italians of the lower classes wore pointed leather shoes and tight pants. But they all loved American dollars.

I KNOCKED ON the heavy wooden door of Interno 8 on the 2nd floor.

"Good morning," said Briggs drily, extending a pale, delicate hand and motioning me to a chair. He sat on the edge of his neat double bed. "I hope you had a good night's sleep after the long ocean voyage and train trip."

He looked much frailer than at our first meeting.

"I had what can only be described as an infernal night," I said drily.

"It's a good base of operations until you get settled," he replied.

"Base operations describes it perfectly," I said. "Whores at my window, swearing, screaming, and roaring drunken sailors. Thanks, Briggs."

"Well, you're the first who ever thanked me for it," he said ironically.

"Not to mention creepy crawlies and medieval plumbing,"

I added. "Apparently the sink doubles as a toilet. I never bathed in a pissoir before."

"Which room were you in?" he asked coolly.

"Third floor. Cell-block 4 I call it. Iron bars for windowless windows and alarm bells. Like a prison. A toothless crone goosed me and offered a blowjob."

Briggs' lips twitched and curled in a wry smirk. "Oh, that's the room I lived in for a year," he said nostalgically, "when I first came to Rome."

"A year!" I exclaimed in astonishment. "One night was too much for me!"

"They were very nice to me," he said wistfully. "I composed on the beat-up piano downstairs. The whores sat and listened—a perfect audience. They love American torch songs. I wrote more music there than I've done since then."

As he reminisced I realized that he loved the place and that my critical stance, which he had anticipated, only heightened his nostalgia. The whores had treated him well. They even took care of him when he was too drunk or too sick to function. "Sex oils the machinery of art," Van Gogh said after his first whore. I didn't reveal what else occurred.

"Well, when push comes to shove," I said calmly, "maybe I could even write a book there." I grinned. "But not in that room. It begins in a whorehouse. This fantastic young floozie, only sixteen, comes into my room. I'm in bed naked as a new-born babe, horny and sweating. We have steamy sex while whores and sailors watch through a hole in the wall—the window, I mean. Then we all have a Roman orgy. Not a bad beginning for a novel, eh?"

I enjoyed his bewilderment at my complete change of tone and mood. Before he could speak I said, "Briggs, I really meant it when I thanked you. A young whore *did* come in last night and we got it on. I must say I like love. In fact I love love." He heaved a sigh of relief.

"I'm glad you're not stuffy like the other friends I've sent there," he said. "You might even get used to it."

"Never!" I said. "I'd have too little to complain about. Except the luxurious conditions, of course. Otherwise, it might be inspiring."

Two deep vertical creases between his eyebrows gave him the look of a worried hawk. Absently, he scratched some pink dry patches of flaking skin on his pale forehead—vitamin deficiency—and leaned forward.

"It's strange to be speaking English again," he said, sighing. "I haven't mingled with Americans for years."

Even the simplest sentence, drawled in his dry New England voice, had the fragile plaintiveness of a needy child.

HIS ROOM WAS neat and clean. Sunlight streamed through the French doors that opened onto a balcony with a wrought-iron railing and W.C. Visible through the glass doors were church domes and red-tiled roofs, over which loomed the famous gigantic pines of Rome. They were better than Respighi's musical rendition of them. Palm trees also rose from the courtyards. On top of his rented upright piano with worn ivories lay neatly-arranged heaps of old music manuscripts and scores. A few battered books were on the marble-topped dresser. The stained gray wallpaper depicted an 18th century hunting scene. Briggs said the room was cheap, paid monthly. Then there was a knock on the door and Gina walked in.

"Adriana, this is Harry," Briggs said in English.

Betraying no sign of recognition she nodded. I smiled and said, "Hi," wondering at the name change and extraordinary coincidence.

"Marcello is not here?" she asked in Italian, ignoring me coldly.

"I haven't seen him since yesterday," Briggs replied.

Gina—Adriana—pouted. She wore a plain black dress, loose and shopworn, and no makeup. There was nothing of the whore about her. She was just another pretty Italian girl.

"Excuse me," she said and went to the toilet on the balcony.

"She's beautiful," I said. "Who is she?"

Briggs lowered his voice. "The lover of my closest friend. They're very hard up and always fighting. He's jealous and possessive."

"With looks like hers who wouldn't be," I said. "But if he's so jealous, isn't she in the wrong business?" Beginning to enjoy the intrigue I also lowered my voice. "What does he do?" I asked.

"Nothing. He sleeps. He's her pimp." He cast a look at the balcony. "When he can't pay for a room I let him stay here. She sleeps here and there—no, not *here*, in my room, only there. I really don't know. They lie so much."

"*Signor Breeg!*" boomed a deep female voice from the balcony. "*Teléfono!*"

It was his landlady. "Excuse me a moment," said Briggs. "Telephone."

He started for the balcony, which led to the landlady's flat." Adriana speaks English," he said. "Get acquainted."

As soon as he left Adriana came in. I wondered if she had waited for this moment to return. She looked cold and hostile.

"It's good to see you again, Gina," I said, going over to her.

She hissed fiercely, "Sssss, for Chrissake! You dunno me! Never see me before! Unnerstan'? And don' call me Gina!"

"Okay, Adriana," I said, smiling. "Don't worry, I'm your friend."

"No! Goddam! I dunno you!"

Anger made her irresistible. I encircled her waist with my arm and tried to kiss her but she pulled violently away.

"You crazy? Fuck off!" Her eyes blazed.

"Now, listen, Gina, uh, Adriana, you still owe me something."

"I don' owe you nuttin," she growled, starting for the door. I blocked her. "Go away, you hear! I tear your eyes out!"

"Why are you mad at me?" I said soothingly. "I like you and want to see you again, tonight."

Her face contorted with rage. "Go away! I keel you!"

Her fury astonished me but I had to know what lay behind it. Her theft of my check and her bad luck at seeing that I was a friend of Briggs? It must have seemed obvious that our brief adventure would get back to Marcello, whom she feared. Still, since she was supporting him by whoring, it didn't make sense. But nothing did in those first days in Rome.

"Listen, Adriana, I'm going to American Express, to the Cambio. I'll give you three-thousand tonight," I whispered. "I want to be your friend."

Her manner underwent a startling change. She glanced at the balcony and came toward me with a cunning expression.

"You stay at the Piccolo Cavour?" she said in a hoarse whisper. "Yes."

"Uh keh. Don' say nothin' to Breeg, eh. Nothin' to nobody!"

I put a finger to my lips. "Nothing to nobody," I whispered, placing a hand on her ass. I kissed her but she pulled away and rushed out the door. Her exits were as precipitous as her entrances.

I realized that her shame at seeing me after ripping me off must have been the cause of her rage. But backing up my offer of "friendship" with more money and letting her keep the check was proof that my interest in her was genuine. Like music, money is international. Its notes, however, are sweeter than music.

"Where's Adriana?" Briggs asked as he entered from the balcony. I almost laughed. This was a sleazy Romeo and Juliet balcony scene and we were the character actors.

"She said something about trying to find Marcello. She was in a hurry."

"She's always in a hurry. And they're always looking for each other," he said. "Like Pyramis and Thisbe." Shakespeare, I thought, said it all.

"Why is she so nervous?" I asked. "She's awfully tense."

"She has good reason to be."

Briggs began changing his clothes, putting on a clean shirt and slipping his spindly legs into a more formal pair of blue serge pants.

"Her family was hunted by the Nazis when she was a kid," he said. "They raped her when she was ten. And after that when she was eleven."

I fell silent. Then I asked how old she was now.

"Sixteen."

Briggs chose a tie with no spaghetti sauce.

"The Nazis killed them all except Adriana. They gang-raped her in front of her family, who were stripped naked and forced to watch. They tortured and murdered her parents and brothers including two little ones in front of Adriana. Then they put her in a brothel for the SS. After the war it was the only way she knew how to stay alive. Italy was broke. It was only six years ago."

I was too stunned to reply. Finally I asked, "Was her family anti-Fascist or something?"

"Jews. Two-thousand years in Rome. But still Jews."

I decided not to see Adriana again. She didn't like love. She hated love. Love was murder. Love was hell. Mussolini killed love. Hitler killed love.

BRIGGS COLLECTED SOME English textbooks.

"Well, I've got to teach a student to say, *This is a man. This is a boy. This is a woman. This is a girl.* When they phone you stop everything and run. *Ciao.*" He rubbed his thumb and forefinger together.

"Why do you call her Adriana?" I asked. "Isn't her name Gina?"

Briggs looked at me curiously. "Was she—last night?" I nodded. "Gina is her professional name. That's what the Nazis called her. She loathes it, of course." He paused. Then, with a crooked little smile he said, "I wouldn't call her that around Marcello. He carries a knife. And he's hot-tempered."

"Thanks for the tip," I said, wondering why she used the name Gina if she hated it so much. And why Marcello would be upset if that's how she supports him. And again I realized that nothing made sense.

"Marcello's better than most of the youths in this quarter," said Briggs. "I've known him for years. I'm sure he'll like you."

"I've just decided to drop her for Marcello," I said with a grin.

"Bravo," said Briggs, smirking. "A safer choice. You'll have plenty of sex in Rome as long as you have money. The whole city is a whorehouse. And they love Americans." Again he rubbed his forefinger and thumb together.

the paper house
Norman Mailer

FROM *ADVERTISEMENTS FOR MYSELF*

F RIENDSHIP IN THE army is so often an accident. If Hayes and I were friends, it was due above all else to the fact that we were cooks on the same shift, and so saw more of one another than of anyone else. I suppose if I really consider it seriously, I did not even like him, but for months we went along on the tacit assumption that we were buddies, and we did a great many things together. We got drunk together, we visited the local geisha house together, and we even told each other some of our troubles.

It was not a bad time. The war was over, and we were stationed with an understrength company of men in a small Japanese city. We were the only American troops for perhaps fifty miles around, and therefore discipline was easy, and everyone could do pretty much what he wished. The kitchen was staffed by four cooks and a mess sergeant, and we had as many Japanese K.P.s to assist us. The work was seldom heavy, and duty hours passed quickly. I never liked the army so much as I did during those months.

Hayes saw to it that we had our recreation. He was more

aggressive than me, older and stronger, much more certain of his ideas. I had no illusions that I was anything other than the tail to his kite. He was one of those big gregarious men who need company and an uncritical ear, and I could furnish both. It also pleased him that I had finished two years of college before I entered the army, and yet he knew so much more than me, at least so far as the army was concerned. He would ride me often about that. "You're the one who's cracked the books," he would say as he slammed a pot around, "but it seems none of those books ever taught you how to boil water. What a cook!" His humor was heavy, small doubt about it. "Nicholson," he would yell at me, "I hear there's a correspondence course in short-arms inspections. Why don't you advance yourself? You too can earn seventy-eight bucks a month."

He was often in a savage mood. He had troubles at home, and he was bitter about them. It seems his wife had begun to live with another man a few months after he entered the army. He had now divorced her, but there were money settlements still to be arranged, and his vanity hurt him. He professed to hate women. "They're tramps, every one of them," he would announce. "They're tramps and I can tell you it's a goddam tramp's world, and don't forget that, sonny." He would shift a boiler from one stove to another with a quick jerk-and-lift of his powerful shoulders, and would call back to me, "The only honest ones are the honest-to-God pros."

I would argue with him, or at least attempt to. I used to write a letter every day to a girl I liked in my home town, and the more time went by and the more letters I wrote, the more I liked her. He used to scoff at me. "That's the kind I really go for," he would jeer. "The literary ones. How they love to keep a guy on the string by writing letters. That's the kind that always has ten men right in her own back yard."

"I know she dates other fellows," I would say, "but what is she supposed to do? And look at us, we're over at the geisha house almost every night."

"Yeah, that's a fine comparison. We're spending our money

at this end, and she's coining it at the other. Is that what you're trying to say?"

I would swear at him, and he would laugh. At such moments I disliked him intensely.

There was, however, quite another side to him. Many evenings after finishing work he would spend an hour washing and dressing, trimming his black mustache, and inspecting critically the press in his best uniform. We would have a drink or two, and then walk along the narrow muddy streets to the geisha house. He would usually be in a fine mood. As we turned in the lane which led to the house, and sat in the vestibule taking off our boots, or more exactly, waiting luxuriously while a geisha or a maid removed them for us, he would begin to hum. The moment we entered the clean pretty little room where the geishas greeted the soldiers, his good mood would begin to flood him. I heard him be even poetic once as he looked at the girls in their dress kimonos, all pretty, all petite, all chirping beneath the soft lights, all treading in dress slippers upon the bright woven straw mats. "I tell you, Nicholson," he said, "it looks like a goddam Christmas tree." He loved to sing at the geisha house, and since he had a pleasant baritone voice, the geishas would crowd about him, and clap their hands. Once or twice he would attempt to sing a Japanese song, and the errors he made in pitch and in language would be so amusing that the geishas would giggle with delight. He made, altogether, an attractive picture at such times, his blue eyes and healthy red face contrasting vigorously with his black mustache and his well-set body in its clean uniform. He seemed full of strength and merriment. He would clap two geishas to him, and call across the room with loud good cheer to another soldier. "Hey, Brown," he would shout, "ain't this a rug-cutter?" And to the answer, "You never had it so good," he would chuckle. "Say that again, Jack," he might roar. He was always charming the geishas. He spoke a burlesque Japanese to their great amusement, he fondled them, his admiration for them seemed to twinkle in his eyes. He was always hearty. Like many men who hate women, he knew how to give the impression that he adored them.

After several months he settled upon a particular girl. Her name was Yuriko, and she was easily the best of the geishas in that house. She was quite appealing with her tiny cat-face, and she carried herself with considerable charm, discernible even among the collective charm all geishas seemed to possess. She was clever, she was witty, and by the use of a few English words and the dramatic facility to express complex thoughts in pantomime, she was quite capable of carrying on extended conversations. It was hardly surprising that the other girls deferred to her, and she acted as their leader.

Since I always seemed to follow in Hayes's shadow, I also had a steady girl, and I suspect that Mimiko, whom I chose, had actually been selected for me by the artifice of Yuriko. Mimiko was Yuriko's best friend, and since Hayes and I were always together, it made things cosy. Those alternate Sundays when we were not on duty in the kitchen we would pay for the girls' time, and Hayes would use his influence, established by the judicious bribes of cans of food and pounds of butter to the motor pool sergeant, to borrow a jeep. We would take the girls out into the country, drive our jeep through back roads or mountain trails, and then descend to the sea where we would wander along the beach. The terrain was beautiful. Everything seemed to be manicured, and we would pass from a small pine forest into a tiny valley, go through little villages or little fishing towns nestled on the rocks, would picnic, would talk, and then toward evening would return the girls to the house. It was very pleasant.

They had other clients besides us, but they refused to spend the night with any other soldier if they knew we were coming, and the moment we entered the place, word was sent to Yuriko or Mimiko if they were occupied. Without a long wait, they would come to join us. Mimiko would slip her hand into mine and smile politely and sweetly, and Yuriko would throw her arms about Hayes and kiss him upon the mouth in the American style of greeting. We would all go together to one of the upper rooms and talk for an hour or two while sake was drunk. Then we would separate for the night, Yuriko with Hayes, and Mimiko with me.

Mimiko was not particularly attractive, and she had the placid disposition of a draft animal. I liked her mildly, but I would hardly have continued with her if it had not been for Yuriko. I really liked Yuriko. She seemed more bright and charming with every day, and I envied Hayes for his possession of her.

I used to love to listen to her speak. Yuriko would tell long stories about her childhood and her parents, and although the subject was hardly calculated to interest Hayes, he would listen to her with his mouth open, and hug her when she was done. "This baby ought to be on the stage," he would say to me. Once, I remember, I asked her how she had become a geisha, and she told about it in detail. "Papa-san, sick sick," she began, and with her hands, created her father for us, an old Japanese peasant whose back was bent and whose labor was long. "Mama-san sad." Her mother wept for us, wept prettily, like a Japanese geisha girl, with hands together in prayer and her nose touching the tip of her fingers. There was money owed on the land, the crops were bad, and Papa-san and Mama-san had talked together, and cried, and had known that they must sell Yuriko, now fourteen, as geisha. So she had been sold and so she had been trained, and in a few moments by the aid of a montage which came instinctively to her, she showed us herself in transition from a crude fourteen-year-old peasant to a charming geisha of sixteen trained in the tea ceremony, her diction improved, her limbs taught to dance, her voice to sing. "I, first-class geisha," she told us, and went on to convey the prestige of being a geisha of the first class. She had entertained only the wealthy men of the town, she had had no lovers unless she had felt the flutterings of weakness in her heart, her hands busy fluttering at her breast, her arms going out to an imaginary lover, her eyes darting from one of us to the other to see if we comprehended. In ten years she would have saved money enough to buy her freedom and to make an impressive marriage.

But, boom-boom, the war had ended, the Americans had come, and only they had money enough for geisha girls. And they did not want geisha girls. They wanted a *joro,* a common whore. And so first-class geishas became second-class geishas and third-class geishas, and here was Yuriko, a third-class geisha, humiliated and unhappy, or at least she would be if she did not love Hayes-san and he did not love her.

She was moody when she finished. "Hayes-san love Yuriko?" she asked, her legs folded beneath her, her small firm buttocks perched upon the straw mat while she handed him a sake cup, and extended her hand to the charcoal brazier.

"Sure, I love you, baby," Hayes said.

"I, first-class geisha," she repeated a little fiercely.

"Don't I know it," Hayes boomed.

Early the next morning as we walked back to the dormitory where the company was installed, Hayes was talking about it. "She jabbered at me all night," he said. "I got a hangover. That Jap sake."

"The story Yuriko told was sad," I murmured.

He stopped in the middle of the street, and put his hands on his hips. "Listen, Nicholson, wise up," he said angrily. "It's crap, it's all crap. They'd have you bleed your eyes out for them with those stories. Poor papa-san. They're all whores, you understand? A whore's a whore, and they're whores cause they want to be whores and don't know nothing better."

"It's not true," I protested. I felt sorry for the geishas. They seemed so unlike the few prostitutes I had known in the United States. There was one girl at the house who had been sold when she was thirteen, and had entered service a virgin. After her first night of work, she had wept for three days, and even now many of the soldiers selected her shame-facedly. "What about Susiko?" I said.

"I don't believe it, it's a gag," Hayes shouted. He gripped me by the shoulder and made a speech. "I'll wise you up. I don't say I'm Superman, but I know the score. Do you understand that? I know the score. I don't say I'm any better than anybody else, but I don't kid myself that I am. And it drives me nuts when people want to make me swallow bull." He released my shoulder as suddenly as he had gripped it. His red face was very red, and I sensed what rage he had felt.

"All right," I muttered.

"All right."

In time he came to treat Yuriko the way he treated anyone with whom he was familiar. He indulged his moods. If he were surly, he did not bother to hide it; if he were aggressive, he would swear at her; if he were happy, he would sing for her or become roisteringly drunk or kiss her many times before Mimiko and myself, telling her that he loved her in a loud voice which often seemed close to choler. Once he abused her drunkenly, and I had to pull him away. The next day he brought Yuriko a present, a model of a wooden shrine which he had purchased from a Japanese cabinet maker. All the while it was evident to me that Yuriko was in love with him.

I used to think of the rooms upstairs as paper rooms. They were made of straw and light wood and parchment glued to wooden frames, and when one lay on the pallet in the center of the floor, it seemed as if all the sounds in all the adjoining rooms flowed without hindrance through the sliding doors. Mimiko and I could often hear them talking in the next cubicle, and long after Mimiko would be asleep, I would lie beside her and listen to Yuriko's voice as it floated, breathlike and soft, through the frail partitions. She would be telling him about her day and the events which had passed in the house. She had had a fight with Mama-san, the wrinkled old lady who was her madame, and Tasawa had heard from her brother whose wife had just given him a child. There was a new girl coming in two days, and Katai who had left the day before had proven to be sick. Mama-san was limiting the charcoal for the braziers, she was stingy without a doubt. So it went, a pageant of domestic-ity. She had resewn the buttons on his battle jacket, he looked good, he was gaining weight, she would have to buy a new kimono for the number two kimono had become shabby, and the number three was hopeless. She was worried about Henderson-san who had become drunk two nights in a row and had struck Kukoma. What should she do about him?

And Hayes listened to her, his head in her lap no doubt, and mumbled gentle answers, relaxed and tender as she caressed the bitterness from his face, drawing it out with her finger tips while her childlike laugh echoed softly through the rooms. There were other sounds: of men snoring, girls giggling, two soldiers in a quarrel, and the soft muted whisper of a geisha crying somewhere in some one of the rooms. So it washed over me in this little house with its thirty paper cells in the middle of a small Japanese city while the Japanese night cast an artist's moon over the rice paddies and the pine forests where the trees grew in aisles. I envied Hayes, envied him with the touch of Mimiko's inert body against mine, envied him Yuriko's tenderness which she gave him so warmly.

He told her one night that he loved her. He loved her so much that he would re-enlist and remain in this Japanese city for at least another year. I overheard him through the parchment walls, and I would have asked him about it next morning if he had not mentioned it himself. "I told her that, and I was lying," he said.

"Well, why did you tell her?"

"You lie to a dame. That's my advice to you. You get them in closer and closer, you feed them whatever you want, and the only trick is never to believe it yourself. Do you understand, Nicholson?"

"No, I don't."

"It's the only way to handle them. I've got Yuriko around my finger." And he insisted on giving me a detailed account of how they made love until by the sheer energy of his account, I realized what he wished to destroy. He had been sincere when he spoke to Yuriko. With her hands on his face, and the night drifting in fog against the windows, he had wanted to re-enlist for another year, had wanted to suspend her fingers upon his face, and freeze time so it could be retained. It must have all seemed possible the night before, he must have believed it and wanted it, seen himself signing the papers in the morning. Instead, he had seen me, had seen the olive-drab color of my uniform, and had known it was not possible, was not at all possible within the gamut of his nature.

He was drunk the following night when he went to see her, moody and silent, and Yuriko was without diversion to him. I think she sensed that something was wrong. She sighed frequently, she chatted in Japanese with Mimiko, and threw quick looks at him to see whether his mood was changing. Then—it must have meant so much to her—she inquired timidly, "You re-enlist one year?"

He stared back at her, was about to nod, and then laughed shortly. "I'm going home, Yuriko. I'm due to go home in one month."

"You repeat, please?"

"I'm getting out of here. In one month. I'm not re-enlisting."

She turned away and looked at the wall. When she turned around, it was to pinch his arm.

"Hayes-san, you marry me, yes?" she said in a voice sharp with its hurt.

He shoved her away. "I don't marry you. Get away. You skibby with too many men."

She drew in her breath, and her eyes were bright for a moment. "Yes. You marry skibby-girl." Yuriko threw her arms about his neck. "American soldier marry skibby-girl."

This time he pushed her away forcefully enough to hurt her. "You just go blow," he shouted at her.

She was quite angry. "American soldier marry skibby-girl," she taunted.

I had never seen him quite as furious. What frightened me was that he contained it all and did not raise his voice. "Marry you?" he asked. I have an idea what enraged him was that the thought had already occurred to him, and it seemed outrageous to hear it repeated in what was, after all, the mouth of a prostitute. Hayes picked up his bottle and drank from it. "You and me are going to skibby, that's what," he said to Yuriko.

She held her ground. "No skibby tonight."

"What do you mean, 'no skibby tonight'? You'll skibby tonight. You're nothing but a *joro*."

Yuriko turned her back. Her little head was bent forward. "I, first-class geisha," she whispered in so low a voice we almost did not hear her.

He struck her. I tried to intervene, and with a blow he knocked me away. Yuriko fled the room. Like a bull, Hayes was after her. He caught her once, just long enough to rip away half her kimono, caught her again to rip away most of what was left. The poor girl was finally trapped, screaming, and more naked than not, in the room where the geishas met the soldiers. There must have been a dozen girls and at least as many soldiers for an audience. Hayes gripped her hairdress, he ripped it down, he threw her up in the air, he dropped her on the floor, he laughed drunkenly, and among the screams of the girls and the startled laughter of the soldiers, I got him out to the street. I could hear Yuriko wailing hysterically behind us.

I guided him home to his cot, and he dropped into a drunken sleep. In the morning, he was contrite. Through the dull headache of awakening, he certainly did not love her, and so he regretted his brutality. "She's a good girl, Nicholson," he said to me, "she's a good girl, and I shouldn't have treated her that way."

"You ripped her kimono," I told him.

"Yeah, I got to buy her another."

It turned out to be a bad day. At breakfast, everybody who passed on the chow line seemed to have heard what had happened, and Hayes was kidded endlessly. It developed that Yuriko had been put to bed with fever after we left, and all the girls were shocked. Almost everything had halted for the night at the geisha house.

"You dishonored her in public," said one of Hayes's buddies with a grin. "Man, how they carried on."

Hayes turned to me. "I'm going to buy her a good kimono." He spent the morning selecting articles of food to sell on the black market. He had to make enough to amass the price of a good kimono, and it worried him that the supplies might be too depleted. The afternoon was taken up with selling his goods, and at dinner we were two weary cooks.

Hayes changed in a hurry. "Come on, let's get over there." He hustled me along, did not even stop to buy a bottle. We were the first clients of the evening to appear at the geisha house. "Mama-san," he roared at the old madame, "where's Yuriko?"

Mama-san pointed upstairs. Her expression was wary. Hayes, however, did not bother to study it. He bounded up the stairs, knocked on Yuriko's door, and entered.

Yuriko was sweet and demure. She accepted his present with a deep bow, touching her forehead to the floor. She was friendly, she was polite, and she was quite distant. She poured us sake with even more ceremony than was her custom. Mimiko entered after a few minutes, and her face was troubled. Yet it was she who talked to us. Yuriko was quiet for a long time. It was only when Mimiko lapsed into silence that Yuriko began to speak.

She informed us in her mixture of English, Japanese and pantomime that in two weeks she was going to take a trip. She was very formal about it.

"A trip?" Hayes asked.

It was to be a long trip. Yuriko smiled sadly.

Hayes fingered his hat. She was leaving the geisha house?

Yes, she was leaving it forever.

She was going perhaps to get married?

No, she was not getting married. She was dishonored and no one would have her.

Hayes began to twist the hat. She had a *musume?* She was going away with a *musume?*

No, there was no *musume.* Hayes was the only *musume* in her life.

Well, where was she going?

Yuriko sighed. She could not tell him. She hoped, however, since she would be leaving before Hayes, that he would come to see her often in the next few weeks.

"Goddammit, where are you going?" Hayes shouted.

At this point, Mimiko began to weep. She wept loudly, her hand upon her face, her head averted. Yuriko leaped up to comfort her. Yuriko patted her head, and sighed in unison with Mimiko.

"Where are you going?" Hayes asked her again.

Yuriko shrugged her shoulders.

It continued like this for an hour. Hayes badgered her, and Yuriko smiled. Hayes pleaded and Yuriko looked sad. Finally, as we were about to leave, Yuriko told us. In two weeks, at two o'clock on Sunday afternoon, she was going to her little room, and there she would commit hari-kari. She was dishonored, and there was nothing else to be done about it. Hayes-san was very kind to apologize, and the jewels of her tears were the only fit present for his kindness, but apologies could never erase dishonor and so she would be obliged to commit hari-kari.

Mimiko began to weep again.

"You mean in two weeks you're going to kill yourself?" Hayes blurted.

"Yes, Hayes-san."

He threw up his arms. "It's crap, it's all crap, you understand?"

"Yes. Crap-crap," Yuriko said.

"You're throwing the bull, Yuriko."

"Yes, Hayes-san. Crap-crap."

"Let's get out of here, Nicholson." He turned in the doorway and laughed. "You almost had me for a minute, Yuriko."

She bowed her head.

Hayes went to see her three times in the week which followed. Yuriko remained the same. She was quiet, she was friendly, she was quite removed. And Mimiko wept every night on my pallet. Hayes forbore as long as was possible, and then at the end of the week, he spoke about it again. "You were kidding me, weren't you, Yuriko?"

Yuriko begged Hayes-san not to speak of it again. It was rude on her part. She did not wish to cause him unnecessary pain. If she had spoken, it was only because the dearer sentiments of her heart were in liege to him, and she wished to see him often in the week which remained.

He snorted with frustration. "Now, look, you . . . cut . . . this . . . out. Do you understand?"

"Yes, Hayes-san. No more talk-talk." She would not mention it again, she told us. She realized how it offended him. Death was an unpleasant topic of conversation in a geisha house. She would attempt to be entertaining, and she begged us to forgive her if the knowledge of her own fate might cause her to be sad at certain moments.

That morning, on the walk back to the schoolhouse, Hayes was quiet. He worked all day with great rapidity, and bawled me out several times for not following his cooking directions more accurately. That night we slept in our barrack, and in the early hours of the morning, he woke me up.

"Look, Nicholson, I can't sleep. Do you think that crazy honey is really serious?"

I was wide awake. I had not been sleeping well myself. "I don't know," I said. "I don't think she means it."

"I know she doesn't mean it." He swore.

"Yeah." I started to light a cigarette, and then I put it out. "Hayes, I was just thinking though. You know the Oriental mind is different."

"The Oriental mind! Goddammit, Nicholson, a whore is a whore. They're all the same I tell you. She's kidding."

"If you say so."

"I'm not even going to mention it to her."

All through the second week, Hayes kept his promise. More than once, he would be about to ask her again, and would force himself into silence. It was very difficult. As the days passed, Mimiko wept more and more openly, and Yuriko's eyes would fill with tears as she looked at Hayes. She would kiss him tenderly, sigh, and then by an effort of will, or so it seemed, would force herself to be gay. Once she surprised us with some flowers she had found, and wove them in our hair. The week passed day by day. I kept waiting for the other men in the company to hear the news, but Hayes said not a word and the geishas did not either. Still, one could sense that the atmosphere in the house was different. The geishas were extremely respectful to Yuriko, and quite frequently would touch her garments as she passed.

By Saturday Hayes could stand it no longer. He insisted that we leave the geisha house for the night, and he made Yuriko accompany us to the boot vestibule. While she was lacing our shoes, he raised her head and said to her, "I work tomorrow. I'll see you Monday."

She smiled vaguely, and continued tying the laces.

"Yuriko, I said I'd see you Monday."

"No, Hayes-san. Better tomorrow. No here, Monday. Gone, bye-bye. You come tomorrow before two o'clock."

"Yuriko, I'm on duty tomorrow. I said I'll see you Monday."

"Say good-by now. Never see me again." She kissed us on the cheek. "Good-by, Nick-san. Good-by, Hayes-san." A single tear rolled down each cheek. She fingered Hayes's jacket and fled upstairs.

That night Hayes and I did not sleep at all. He came over to my cot, and sat there in silence. "What do you think?" he asked after a long while.

"I don't know."

"I don't know either." He began to swear. He kept drinking from a bottle, but it had no effect. He was quite sober. "I'm damned if I'm going over there tomorrow," he said.

"Do what you think is best."

He swore loudly.

The morning went on and on. Hayes worked rapidly and was left with nothing to do. The meal was ready fifteen minutes early. He called chow at eleven-thirty. By one o'clock the K.P.s were almost finished with the pots.

"Hey, Koto," Hayes asked one of the K.P.s, a middle-aged man who had been an exporter and spoke English, "hey, Koto, what do you know about hari-kari?"

Koto grinned. He was always very polite and very colorless. "Oh, hari-kari. Japanese national custom," he said.

"Come on," Hayes said to me, "we've got till three o'clock before we put supper on." He was changing into his dress clothes by the time I followed him to the dormitory. He had neglected to hang them up the night before, and for once they were bedraggled. "What time is it?" he asked me.

"A quarter past one."

"Come on, hurry up."

He ran almost all the way to the geisha house, and I ran with him. As we approached, the house seemed quiet. There was nobody in the vestibule, and there was nobody in the receiving room. Hayes and I stood there in empty silence.

"*Yuriko!*" he bawled.

We heard her feet patter on the stairs. She was dressed in a white kimono, without ornament, and without makeup. "You do come," she whispered. She kissed him. "Bye-bye, Hayes-san. I go upstairs now."

He caught her arm. "Yuriko, you can't do it."

She attempted to free herself, and he held her with frenzy. "I won't let you go," he shouted. "Yuriko, you got to stop this. It's crap."

"Crap-crap," she said, and suddenly she began to giggle.

"Crap-crap," we heard all around. "Crap-crap, crap-crap, crap-crap."

Squealing with laughter, every geisha in the house entered the room. They encircled us, their voices going "crap-crap" like a flock of geese.

Yuriko was laughing at us, Mimiko was laughing at us, they were all laughing. Hayes shouldered his way to the door. "Let's get out of here." We pushed on to the street, but the geishas followed. As we retreated across the town, they flowed out from the geisha house and marched behind us, their kimonos brilliant with color, their black hair shining in the sunlight. While the townspeople looked and giggled, we walked home, and the geishas followed us, shouting insults in English, Japanese, and pantomime. Beneath their individual voices, with the regularity of marching feet, I could hear their cadence, "Crap-crap, crap-crap."

After a week, Hayes and I went back to the house for a last visit before we sailed for home. We were received politely, but neither Yuriko nor Mimiko would sleep with us. They suggested that we hire Susiko, the thirteen-year-old ex-virgin.

1951

FROM **the empty mirror**

Janwillem van de Wetering

O NE DAY A year the Zen authorities de-
clare a general amnesty for all Zen
monks. It is a day without rules. The master leaves the grounds
and the monks are free. Anything goes. The young monks had
often told me about the coming feast and walked about grinning when the day came closer.

'Ha,' Han-san said, 'it'll be marvellous again. Last year we
had a lot of fun, but you weren't here then. I would like to see
what you are going to do that day. We'll make sure there'll be
a good supply of *sake*, and lots to eat. We'll close the gate and
we won't let anyone in. If you feel like twisting the head monk's
nose, well, twist it. If you want to crash through your front wall
again, fine but perhaps you should restrain yourself a little this
time because I'll have to do the repairs, of course.'

I told myself to be very careful. I wasn't used to alcohol any
more, and whatever the monks intended to do would float on
liquor. And what can one do on a day without rules? I should
have preferred to retire to my room, with a book and a packet
of *shinsei*-cigarettes. To sit in the sun, perhaps, in a quiet cor-

ner of the temple garden, or play with the puppies which the monastery's mongrel had produced. They were charming puppies, tiny bundles of fluffy wool who had just learned to walk and performed tumbling games in the graveyard all day long. I knew they were going to be drowned and that there was nothing I could do to prevent their untimely death. What could I, a lay-brother, do with five small dogs? Their barking would disturb the monks during meditation and nobody in the neighbourhood wanted them.

The day came and everyone started it by sleeping late. At about 8 a.m. breakfast started and the monks wandered in and out of the kitchen without clearing the tables—normally the tables were cleared, scrubbed and stacked immediately after meals. I fried some bacon and eggs in the kitchen and made myself a large pot of coffee while the fat cook helped me curiously: bacon and coffee, in his way of thinking, were most exotic. In exchange I helped him to prepare the festive meal, fried noodles, vegetables and sizeable lumps of meat. We were going to have ice-cream as well and I promised to go and fetch it at the last moment as the monastery didn't have a refrigerator. At about eleven the *sake* bottle appeared and the young monks especially got drunk in no time at all. Nobody had any defence against alcohol and as *sake* is drunk quickly, although the cups are quite small, the effect is quickly noticeable. *Sake* is not wine, but a spirit, distilled from rice, and about as strong as whisky or gin.

Han-san sat next to me and dominated the conversation. When the others wanted to say something as well he lost his temper and demanded the right to finish his story. Another young monk, whose face had become as red as a sour plum and whose eyes swam about in blobs of pink jelly, took umbrage and the older monks had to separate the two fighters. Han-san stumped out of the kitchen and I found him, a couple of hours later, fast asleep in the shadow of a gravestone. I sat down near him and made myself comfortable with a thermos flask of coffee and a translation of the famous story of

Shanks' Mare, * the story of two Japanese good-for-nothings who leave Tokyo because the bill collectors become too active, and wander down to Kyoto along the highway. It's a good description of Japan in the early nineteenth century, and was an appropriate book to read on this day of freedom for the two heroes of the novel solve most of their problems by laughing and running away.

The sun went behind the clouds, it became chilly, and Han-san woke up, cramped on the cold stones.

'Give me some of that coffee,' Han-san said, 'a free day like this isn't much fun really. What can we do with it? I have a headache already and the evening hasn't even come yet. The others will probably be milling about in the temple and the head monk is watching them, of course. He hasn't had a drop himself, he is just pretending to join in the fun while he keeps things quiet so that there won't be too much of a mess to clear up tomorrow.'

'What would you like to do?' I asked. 'Put on your suit and cap and scale the wall?'

'No,' Han-san said. 'We shouldn't. It's tradition that we amuse ourselves within the walls of the monastery and the head monk will be counting heads all the time. It's a dull life in this monastery. If I had the courage I would become a disciple of Bobo-roshi—he runs a different show altogether.' Roshi means master. I also knew that Bobo is a four-letter word meaning copulation.

'Bobo-roshi?'

Han-san sat up and lit one of my cigarettes, something which he would normally never do without asking; but this time he just grabbed the packet.

'Yes,' he said, 'have you never heard about him? Peter knows him but it isn't like Peter to talk about Bobo-roshi. The head monk knows him quite well, I believe. Bobo-roshi is a Zen master, but different. If you like I'll tell you what I know, but I don't

---

* Ikku Jippensha, *Shank's Mare* (Tuttle, Tokyo, 1960).

know if it's all true; I only know about him by hearsay and I have only met him once. He seems to be an ordinary man but he laughs a lot and he has a very deep voice and he dresses strangely. He never wears the Zen robes but usually dresses in a simple kimono, like artists do, and sometimes he wears western clothes, jeans and a jersey, like you do. They say he has spent years in a Zen monastery, in the southern part of Kyoto. It's a severe monastery, the rules are applied very strictly, more strictly than here. For instance, I believe they get up at 2 a.m. every day. He is supposed to have been a very diligent monk, rather overdoing things even, making extra rules for himself and all that. But he didn't understand his *koan* and the master was hard on him; whenever he wanted to say something the master would pick up his bell and ring him out of the room. He was treated that way for years on end. He was doing extra meditation, sleeping in the lotus position, trying everything he could think of, but the *koan* remained as mysterious as ever. I don't know how long this situation lasted, six years, ten years maybe, but then he had enough. I don't think he even said goodbye, he just left, in ordinary clothes, with a little money he had saved, or which had been sent to him from home.

Now you must realise that he had been a monk a long time and didn't know anything about civilian life. He had never climbed the wall at night. He was a real monk, sober, quiet, always in command of himself. And there he was, in a sunny street, in a busy city, thousands of people about, all doing something, all going somewhere. He wandered about the city and found himself in the willow quarter, perhaps within an hour of leaving the monastery gate. In the willow quarter there are always women standing in their doors, or pretending to be busy in their gardens. One of the women called him, but he was so innocent that he didn't know what she wanted. He went to her and asked politely what he could do for her. She took him by the hand and led him into her little house. They say she was beautiful; who knows? Some of these women aren't beautiful at all but they are attractive in a way, or they wouldn't have any earnings.

She helped him undress—he must have understood then what was going on. She must have asked him for money and he must have given it to her. Then she took him to her bath, that's the custom here. Your shoulders are massaged and you are dried with a clean towel and they talk to you. Slowly you become very excited and when she feels you are ready she takes you to the bedroom. He must have been quite excited after so many years of abstaining. At the moment he went into her he solved his *koan*. He had an enormous *satori*, one of these very rare *satoris* which are described in our books, not a little understanding which can be deepened later but the lot at once, an explosion which tears you to pieces and you think the world has come to an end, that you can fill the emptiness of the universe in every possible sphere. When he left the woman he was a master. He never took the trouble to have his insight tested by other masters, but kept away from the Zen sect for many years. He wandered through the country and had many different jobs. He was a truckdriver, driving one of these huge long-distance monsters. He also worked as a waiter in a small restaurant, as a dock-worker, and sometimes he joined the beggars and the riffraff of the cities. They say he never forgot the link between his *satori* and sex, and he is supposed to have had many friends and girl-friends. Then he came back and rented a ramshackle house here in Kyoto. He has some disciples there now, odd birds who could never accept the monastic training as we have it here. They do as they please and observe no rules. He works with them in his own way, but he does use the Zen method, *koan* and meditation. The other masters recognise him, acknowledge his complete enlightenment, and never criticise him as far as I know. There are, of course, a lot of young monks who think that life in Bobo-roshi's house is one eternal party; perhaps it is really like that, but I rather think that it isn't.'

I had listened to Han-san with increasing surprise and it took me some time before I could think of an answer.

'So Zen training can be really free?'

Han-san looked at me sadly.

'Free. What is free? Those fellows have to work for their living, that is one discipline to start with. And they meditate, and I am sure it isn't just half an hour when they feel like it. Bobo-roshi may have fetched his *satori* from the whores' quarter but he had been through a long training before he went there. Water suddenly boils, but the kettle must have been on the fire for some time. There's always a preparation. And then he wandered about for many years before he started teaching; that must have been quite a discipline, too. I think that the training in Bobo-roshi's house is just as hard as ours, but it has a different form. You get nothing for nothing, I have learned that. Maybe they have a party there every now and then, but I climb the wall sometimes. And there are many things which our master can teach us.'

Han-san looked very disgruntled and I began to laugh.

'Ha ha. You haven't got the courage to go there, Han-san.'

'You come with me,' Han-san said. 'We have rested and we are sober again and now we can have some cups of *sake*. And when I have drunk enough I'll beat you up.'

And so it happened. Han-san got drunk again and became very troublesome. I think I took him to bed at least four times, and he came back every time and pushed everyone who strayed in his way.

Permissions

"Passable" from *Between Meals* by A.J. Liebling. Copyright © 1986 by A.J. Liebling. Reprinted by permission of Donadio & Olsen.

"Tammy" from *All-Night Visitors* by Clarence Major. Copyright © 1969, 1988 by Clarence Major. Reprinted by permission of the Author.

"Florangel" by Rachel Kushner. Copyright © 2002 by Rachel Kushner. Reprinted by permission of the author.

"Something Nice" from *Bad Behavior* by Mary Gaitskill. Copyright © 1988 by Mary Gaitskill. Reprinted by permission of Simon & Schuster Adult Publishing Group.

Excerpt from *The Sheltering Sky* by Paul Bowles. Copyright © 1949 by Paul Bowles, renewed © 1977 by Paul Bowles. Reprinted by permission of HarperCollins Publishers Inc.

"Glory Hole" from *Head of a Sad Angel* by Alfred Chester. Copyright © 1990 by Alfred Chester. Reprinted by permission of David R. Godine, Publisher. Originally published by Black Sparrow Press, 1990.

Excerpts from *The Orton Diaries* by Joe Orton, edited by John Lahr. Copyright © 1986 by the Administrator of the Estate of John Kingsley Orton (deceased), professionally known as Joe Orton. Introduction copyright © 1986 by John Lahr.

Excerpt from *Roman Nights and Other Stories* by Pier Paolo Pasolini, translated by John Shepley. Copyright © 1986 by John Shepley. Reprinted by permission of the Translator.

"For the Relief of Unbearable Urges" from *For the Relief of Unbearable Urges* by Nathan Englander. Copyright © 1999 by Nathan Englander. Used by permission of Alfred A. Knopf, a division of Random House, Inc.

"Good Night, My Dear" from *My Less Than Secret Life* by Jonathan Ames. Copyright © 2002 by Jonathan Ames. Reprinted with permission of Thunder's Mouth Press.

Excerpt from *You Shall Know Our Velocity* by Dave Eggers. Copyright © 2002 by Dave Eggers and McSweeney's Publishing. Reprinted with permission.

Excerpt from *Serenade* by James M. Cain. Copyright © 1937 and renewed © 1965 by James M. Cain. Used by permission of Alfred A. Knopf, a division of Random House, Inc.

"Part Four – 5" from *On the Road* by Jack Kerouac. Copyright © 1955, 1957 by Jack Kerouac, renewed © 1983 by Stella Kerouac, renewed © 1985 by Stella Kerouac and Jan Kerouac. Used by permission of Viking Penguin, a division of Penguin Group (USA) Inc.